Provincial Offences: Essential Tools for Law Enforcement

THIRD EDITION

Peter Maher
Dan Gilbert

payam
30-01-2017

2012
Emond Montgomery Publications
Toronto, Canada

Copyright © 2012 Emond Montgomery Publications Limited. All rights reserved. No part of this publication may be reproduced, stored in a retrieval system, or transmitted, in any form or by any means, photocopying, electronic, mechanical, recording, or otherwise, without the prior written permission of the copyright holder.

Emond Montgomery Publications Limited
60 Shaftesbury Avenue
Toronto ON M4T 1A3
http://www.emp.ca/college

Printed in Canada.

We acknowledge the financial support of the Government of Canada through the Canada Book Fund for our publishing activities.

Acquisitions editor: Bernard Sandler
Development editor: Sarah Gleadow
Marketing manager: Christine Davidson
Director, sales and marketing, higher education: Kevin Smulan
Supervising editor: Jim Lyons
Production editor: David Handelsman
Copy editor: Paula Kulig
Proofreader: Jamie Bush
Text designer and typesetter: Shani Sohn
Indexer: Paula Pike
Cover image: Bernard Sandler

Library and Archives Canada Cataloguing in Publication

Maher, Peter (N. Peter)
Provincial offences : essential tools for law enforcement / Peter Maher, Dan Gilbert. — 3rd ed.

Includes index.
ISBN 978-1-55239-389-5

1. Contraventions (Criminal law)—Ontario. 2. Summary proceedings—Ontario. 3. Contraventions (Criminal law)—Ontario—Textbooks. 4. Summary proceedings—Ontario—Textbooks. I. Gilbert, Dan (Dan Thomas) II. Title.

KEO1175.M34 2012 345.713'05 C2012-901312-9
KF9619.M34 2012

This third edition is dedicated to my daughter, an officer with the OPP, my students, and all future law enforcement officers. May you serve your citizens well by preserving the peace while utilizing knowledge and demonstrating professionalism. This conduct will reinforce the value of your role in the community you serve and maintain the respect your profession deserves.

I would also take opportunity to acknowledge my academic partner, now retired, Dan Gilbert. He is most successfully defining the role of grandfather and apparently enjoying retirement way too much. Carry on, Dan!

— Peter Maher

Contents

CHAPTER 6 Mental Health Act

CHAPTER 7 Coroners Act

CHAPTER 8 Child and Family Services Act

CHAPTER 9 Family Law Act

CHAPTER 10 Children's Law Reform Act

CHAPTER 11 Motorized Snow Vehicles Act

CHAPTER 12 Off-Road Vehicles Act

APPENDIX A

APPENDIX B

APPENDIX C

Preface

The third edition of *Provincial Offences: Essential Tools for Law Enforcement* is intended to guide students studying provincial laws commonly enforced in Ontario. Starting with the *Provincial Offences Act*, which governs the prosecution and execution of enforcement action for all pieces of legislation passed by the Ontario government, each chapter of the text covers a specific act commonly encountered by police officers and other public safety agencies in the province. Throughout the text, students are presented with scenarios like the ones they will encounter in their careers and are encouraged to apply their learning to these real-world situations.

HISTORY AND IMPORTANCE OF PROVINCIAL OFFENCES

Provincial offences have evolved over time to facilitate an orderly existence in our communities. Needless to say, if everyone were permitted to act without any restrictions, the result would be chaos. For example, the ability to park anywhere at any time would result in movement coming to a standstill, and the absence of rules of the road would result in highways too dangerous to travel.

Provincial law is shaped by the community, through pressure on lawmakers to place priority on certain issues. For example, the *Liquor Licence Act* controls the consumption and possession of alcohol in a way that the majority finds acceptable. This includes the strict prohibition against knowingly serving alcohol to minors. An understanding of the intent and application of provincial laws is essential, in part because provincial law is the basis of every new officer's career; depending on an officer's assignments and enforcement interest, this may remain the case throughout the officer's career.

However, provincial laws have a lower profile than criminal laws, and their enforcement is not viewed in the same way—at a glance, it appears less "glamourous." However, it must be remembered that the primary duty of police officers is always to keep the peace. When working under provincial statutes, therefore, officers' duties extend beyond simple "enforcement" into other areas that, while distinct from traditional "crime fighting," are equally important to an officer's ability to carry out his or her traditional peacekeeping function.

All officers should strive to perform their duties in a professional manner. For the most part, this will be accomplished largely by mastering and by applying the right tools, which are multifaceted. One set of "tools" in Ontario law enforcement are the provincial offences. Knowledge of these, combined with experience, is one of the defining features of a competent law enforcement professional.

WORKING WITH PROVINCIAL OFFENCES

Understanding the philosophy and intent of the various provincial acts is key to officers' ability to apply them. Provincial law attends to the majority and it changes with the majority. Unlike people who come into conflict with criminal laws, those who come into conflict with provincial laws are not criminals; a person convicted of a provincial offences violation will not have a criminal record or a fingerprint file. Thus, as mentioned, an important part of learning about and working with provincial offences is recognizing that they are not all enforcement-oriented—the role of an officer also includes intervening in certain situations and serving as a resource to help individuals understand the law in others.

Officers should therefore study provincial offences in the three tiers in which they will apply them:

- Enforcement
- Intervention
- Referral

The primary tier or tiers associated with a particular statute are set out at the beginning of each chapter.

Enforcement

Generally speaking, provincial laws are summary by design and fall within the application of "found committing." This means that an offence occurs by virtue of a particular act occurring and being observed. A related point is that in general, a guilty mind or *mens rea* is not a required element of most provincial offences; the mere commission of the act is a violation.

There are important exceptions both to the general rule of "found committing" and to the absence of a requirement for a guilty mind; once again, these reflect society's values and priorities. The first exception concerns the *Trespass to Property Act*, which in specific circumstances grants arrest authority to the landowner/agent and grants extended authorities to police officers similar to those applied in the *Criminal Code*. In a departure from "found committing," the TTPA authorizes arrest where an officer believes on reasonable and probable grounds that a person has trespassed and has made "fresh departure" from the premises, and the person refuses to provide his or her name or address or the officer has reasonable and probable grounds to believe that the name or address given is false. The extended arrest authority under the TTPA as compared to other provincial offences illustrates the importance our society places on protecting the rights of property owners.

The *mens rea* exception under the *Liquor Licence Act* requires a person who serves alcohol to someone under the age of 19 to do so *knowingly* in order to be charged with an offence. The act alone is not sufficient; for the act to be punishable, *intent* must exist.

The *Provincial Offences Act* provides for the most common action taken in the enforcement of various statutes: the issuance of a ticket, in various forms and under different parts of the Act. Further enforcement may be taken by effecting an arrest. Because there is no standard authority in the *Provincial Offences Act* covering arrest, officers must know what authority is provided by each statute. The application of an arrest outside of the parameters in the statute could result in a lawsuit for unlawful arrest and detention.

Intervention

Incidents that require intervention require a speedy response, and in our community this falls to the police, who are available 24 hours a day, 7 days a week. Some statutes create circumstances where officers do not have the power to enforce but where they are required to intervene in order to carry out their traditional role of keeping the peace and protecting various interests. It cannot be stressed enough that in intervention situations, the primary aim of police is to keep the peace. Because police presence has the potential to start something rather than simply solve something, officers' communication skills—in particular, negotiation and diplomacy—are key to effective intervention.

Example of intervention are found in the *Mental Health Act* and the *Child and Family Services Act*. The former outlines circumstances in which officers may resort to apprehension of an individual in the interests of both the individual and the community at large, while the latter authorizes officers to apprehend a child who is in need of protection without a warrant if certain criteria are met.

The distinction between "apprehension" and "arrest" may seem confusing. In both cases, an officer is taking physical control of a subject. However, the apprehension is being made to render assistance and address health and safety, whereas criminal arrest is applied for reasons including identification, safety, weapons, escape, and so on. The language describing the action is contained in the relevant statute. For example, a warrant to return an elopee under the *Mental Health Act* requires an officer to apprehend and return the subject to a psychiatric facility, whereas the *Liquor Licence Act* says an officer may arrest a subject for being drunk in a public place.

In extreme conflict situations, an officer may have to intervene according to a court order. For example, under the *Family Law Act*, a court may issue an order of apprehension that compels an officer to apprehend the child named in the warrant and surrender him or her to a specified parent; this is common in the case of a custody/access dispute, where one parent will not consent to the child visiting with the other parent.

Referral

In some cases, an officer will be called to attend at a situation involving conflict where no offence has been committed and the officer has no power under any statute to enforce or intervene. In such a situation, an officer may wonder: If there is no role for me to play or authority for me to act, then why am I here? Officers in such situations have other important roles to play: defusing the situation; providing accurate information that will help the individuals involved understand the laws that may be the subject of the conflict; and directing the individuals to the services they require to resolve the dispute. Again, the importance of communication skills in this type of situation must be emphasized.

For example, an officer may attend at a property where a dispute is unfolding between a tenant and landlord. The landlord may wish to have the tenant removed, and the tenant may be refusing to leave. This is not a police matter, however, and in this particular case, the officer has no authority to act. Instead, the officer's role is to quell the dispute and keep the peace—in this case, the landlord should be advised of the steps that he or she can take toward resolving the problem, beginning with contacting the Landlord and Tenant Board.

When acting in referral situations, officers must use their communication skills—particularly, diplomacy and negotiation—to de-escalate the situation. The act of the officer providing the necessary information in an appropriate manner will hopefully help to "keep the peace." The ability of an officer to provide responsible advice can come only from a clear understanding of the relevant laws and legal procedures, thus the importance of gaining as much knowledge and understanding with regard to the various acts as possible.

HOW THE TEXT IS ORGANIZED

Each chapter of the text follows a similar format. Chapters start with a basic introduction to the Act that is the subject of the chapter, followed by a list of common terminology that is crucial to interpreting and applying the provisions. Common offences and/or provisions are examined, and the arrest and search powers, if any, are described. A separate section indicates whether the Act authorizes use of force. The next section outlines the limitation periods, and the final section points out any non-police agencies involved in administering the provisions. Excerpts from the Act that are relevant to officers follow. At the end of each chapter, practical exercises challenge you to apply the various provisions, and review questions test your understanding of new information. You may have to research the Act as excerpted in the chapter in order to answer the questions.

Each chapter reviews—first in detail, then in summary—the information necessary to complete the provincial offences grid of the six important issues for each act located at the back of the book: (1) common offences and/or provisions, (2) arrest powers, (3) search powers, (4) use of force, (5) limitation period, and (6) non-police agencies involved. This grid will serve as a valuable study tool and a handy reference in the future. New to this edition are marginal notes, which highlight and explain key information in each chapter. Reviewing them will help you to gain a deeper understanding of certain sections of the various acts. Two new chapters provide coverage of the *Motorized Snow Vehicles Act* and the *Off-Road Vehicles Act*.

Some of the assignments in the text ask you to complete blank tickets. These are found at the back of the text, following the chapters. You may wish to work on copies of the tickets as you practise completing them correctly. Following the tickets, an appendix reproduces the forms commonly used to present a successful case to the courts in their entirety. You can use this appendix as a quick reference for future questions as to which form must be used when preparing a prosecution for court.

CHAPTER 1

Provincial Offences Act

INTRODUCTION

The *Provincial Offences Act* (POA) is the piece of legislation that governs all of the other provincial acts. The provincial government recognized a need to separate the adjudication of provincial offences, generally less serious offences involving the average citizen, from the criminal courts, where procedures tend to be much more complex and restrictive. Separating the two also made the provincial offences court more accessible and manageable for the charged person to challenge an alleged offence or simply to explain his or her side of the situation.

The POA sets out the process to follow in laying charges under the various provincial statutes, including the types of forms that must be used to present an allegation of a provincial offence before a court. The POA also sets standard limitation periods for those offences that do not prescribe their own, usually of six months. It details the procedure to follow for trials and any subsequent appeals of decisions of the provincial offences court. The Ontario Court of Justice maintains jurisdiction over the prosecution of provincial offences.

The POA separates offences into three streams of offences—part I, part II, and part III—and establishes different procedures for each. The remaining six parts of the legislation deal with procedures for all offences: part IV covers trials and sentencing; part V outlines general provisions; part VI outlines processes to follow when the defendant is a young person, aged 12 to 15, who finds himself or herself facing charges of breaching a provincial statute; part VII involves appeals and other forms of review; part VIII details procedures for arrest, bail, and search warrants; and part IX involves matters related to other statutes and the process of applications for judicial orders.

While the POA establishes the general guidelines for prosecution of provincial offences, it is imperative that the individual act containing the actual offence also be consulted, because it may well contain provisions that overrule the generalities of the POA. For example, the *Compulsory Automobile Insurance Act* extends the time limit for laying the charge of operating a motor vehicle without insurance to three years from the general time limit of six months contained in the POA. Individual acts also authorize arrest and search powers for specific offences, while the POA does not provide for arrest or search without warrant.

The POA simplifies and streamlines several procedures, but it is still imperative that officers, when involved in laying charges and then later testifying and presenting evidence in court, ensure that they properly prepare to assist the provincial prosecutor in successfully presenting the full case to the court.

Part I, II, and III Offences

PART I OFFENCES

The majority of provincial offences will be processed under the provisions of part I of the POA, which is the part that authorizes a "ticket," or an "offence notice" as it is called in the Act, to be issued, giving the defendant three options:

1. pay a fine,
2. plead guilty with an explanation, or
3. request a trial for the offence.

Because this part is used most frequently, and such a volume of offences is dealt with according to its procedures, it is more streamlined and simple than the processes under part III of the POA. Similarly, the fines under this process are capped at $500; there is no option of sentencing the defendant to jail; and the provincial offences officer must serve the defendant with a part I offence notice or summons within 30 days of the offence. If that time limit is not met, the part I provisions are not available to the officer, and proceedings must then follow part III procedures.

The defendant must select one of the three options within 15 days of the date of service of the offence notice or summons. The offence notice contains all three options, but the summons requires a person to attend court, thereby eliminating the option of paying a fine without appearing in court or pleading guilty with an explanation.

PART II OFFENCES

Part II of the POA deals with parking infractions. When a provincial offences officer believes that a vehicle has been parked in contravention of a parking bylaw, the officer has two options: (1) issue a certificate of parking infraction certifying that an infraction has taken place, or (2) issue a parking infraction notice indicating the set fine for the infraction.

Service of part II offence notices may be made by personal service, but part II also authorizes service by affixing the notice to the defendant's vehicle in a conspicuous place (such as the windshield). The provincial offences officer then files the certificate of parking infraction with the court office, along with evidence of the vehicle's ownership information if the charge is against the owner of the vehicle.

If a trial is held to contest the offence, the court may not impose a conviction unless three issues are presented at trial: (1) evidence of ownership of the vehicle if the charge is against the vehicle's owner; (2) a copy of the notice of trial, with the certificate of the person who issued the notice, indicating that the notice was served to the defendant and when it was served; and (3) the certificate of parking infraction.

A provincial offences officer may also use part III of the POA to process a charge for an infraction, but the procedures under part III are much more cumbersome than those under part II and are not used in most circumstances.

PART III OFFENCES

Part III of the POA is designed to handle the most serious provincial offences and those part I and part II offences that cannot be enforced within the restraints of those parts—for example, a *Highway Traffic Act* offence that could not be personally served on the defendant within 30 days.

Usually, the provincial offences officer starts part III proceedings by completing an information and summons and appearing before a justice of the peace. The officer must swear to the contents of the information, and the justice, if satisfied with the facts presented, may sign the information and summons. The summons must then be served on the defendant.

Section 22 of the POA authorizes a provincial offences officer to issue a summons on a defendant before an information is laid if the officer believes, on reasonable and probable grounds, that the defendant has committed an offence and he or she finds the defendant at or near the location of the offence. This section limits the use of part III tickets to those circumstances in which the defendant is found committing the offence.

As stated earlier, part III proceedings are much more time-consuming and usually are used for the situations when part I or part II procedures are not available. Common situations requiring part III proceedings are (1) the potential fine exceeds $500; (2) there is a possibility of a jail sentence upon conviction; and (3) more than 30 days have passed since the date of the offence and no service has been made.

TERMINOLOGY

Young Person

The term "young person," when used in the POA, refers to anyone who, at the time of the offence, (1) was between 12 and 15 years of age, or (2) appeared, in the absence of evidence to the contrary, to be between 12 and 15 years of age.

COMMON OFFENCES AND/OR PROVISIONS

The POA contains provisions for young persons similar to those found in the *Youth Criminal Justice Act* (which replaced the *Young Offenders Act*). When a young person is charged with an offence, a notice to the parent(s) is required and the use of a part I offence notice is prohibited, requiring instead the use of a part I or part III summons and essentially eliminating the out-of-court set fine option (ss. 95 and 96(1)).

In addition, the identity of a young person is not to be published (s. 99(1)). Accountability extends beyond the individual who publishes the young person's identity to every director, officer, and employee of a corporation who is involved in the publication (for example, by authorizing it) (s. 99(2)).

Finally, it is an offence for an individual to fail to attend or remain at a hearing without lawful excuse to do so, if that person is required by law to attend or remain in attendance, and to commit contempt in the Ontario Court of Justice in a proceeding under the POA (s. 42(1)).

ARREST POWERS

In general, provincial offences officers must rely upon the provisions of the individual acts for specific powers of arrest, if any—for example, the authority to arrest an individual for "drunk in a public place" under the *Liquor Licence Act.*

An exception is found in s. 145, which authorizes any person to arrest another person without a warrant whom he or she has reasonable and probable grounds to believe has committed an offence and is escaping from and freshly pursued by a police officer who has lawful authority to arrest the person. If the person who effects the arrest is not a police officer, that person must deliver the person arrested to a police officer immediately.

SEARCH POWERS

The POA does not authorize any powers of search without a warrant (all of those powers, if applicable, are found within the individual act itself). If a provincial offences officer requires a search warrant to obtain evidence of a provincial offence, provisions in the POA, beginning at s. 158, accommodate that procedure.

USE OF FORCE

Section 146(1) justifies a police officer, if that officer is acting on reasonable and probable grounds, to use as much force as is necessary to do what the officer is required or authorized to do by law. The purpose of this provision is to protect officers from civil suits that may otherwise arise as a result of officers performing duties authorized by provincial statutes.

The words "as much force as is necessary" in s. 146(1) are important because officers are accountable for the force they use. The greater the force an officer uses, the more difficult it will be to justify. Too much force could result in a civil suit against the officer and the service, or perhaps a charge of assault against the officer. In court process, the question of force may even cause a statement by the defendant to not be admitted. In practice, the words mean that officers should use as *little* force as is necessary to effect their legal purpose.

LIMITATION PERIOD

The POA provides for a general window of six months from the date of the offence for submitting an information or summons, unless specific references override this general limitation period within the individual act itself. For example, the *Liquor Licence Act* allows a window of two years from the date of the offence, thereby extending the general limitation of the POA. Other statutes may or may not extend this general six-month limit for any or all of their provisions.

NON-POLICE AGENCIES INVOLVED

1. Game wardens
2. Municipal law enforcement officers
3. Ontario Court of Justice
4. Other provincial offences officers

PROVINCIAL OFFENCES GRID COMPLETION

Common Offences and/or Provisions

No offences are contained in the POA; rather, the Act governs all of the other acts. There are several provisions for young persons, including restrictions on revealing their identity, requirements to notify parents, and prohibiting the use of a part I offence notice.

Arrest Powers

Under s. 145, a police officer may arrest without warrant an individual fleeing from pursuit, if the criteria outlined in the section are met. Other powers are found in the individual acts.

Search Powers

None given by the POA without a warrant. If a search warrant is required, refer to the Act starting at s. 158.

Use of Force

Under s. 146, a police officer is authorized to use as much force as is necessary to do what he or she is required or authorized to do by law.

Limitation Period

The POA provides a general window of six months from the date of the offence. See the individual acts for specific limitation periods.

Non-Police Agencies Involved

1. Game wardens
2. Municipal law enforcement officers
3. Ontario Court of Justice
4. Other provincial offences officers

Provincial Offences Act

RSO 1990, c. P.33

Interpretation

1(1) **Definitions**—In this Act,

"certificate" means a certificate of offence issued under Part I or a certificate of parking infraction issued under Part II;

"court" means the Ontario Court of Justice;

"judge" means a provincial judge;

"justice" means a provincial judge or a justice of the peace;

"offence" means an offence under an Act of the Legislature or under a regulation or by-law made under the authority of an Act of the Legislature;

"police officer" means a chief of police or other police officer but does not include a special constable or by-law enforcement officer;

"prescribed" means prescribed by the rules of court;

"prosecutor" means the Attorney General or, where the Attorney General does not intervene, means the person who issues a certificate or lays an information and includes an agent acting on behalf of either of them;

"provincial offences officer" means,

(a) a police officer,

(b) a constable appointed pursuant to any Act,

(c) a municipal law enforcement officer referred to in subsection 101(4) of the *Municipal Act, 2001* or in subsection 79(1) of the *City of Toronto Act, 2006*, while in the discharge of his or her duties,

(d) a by-law enforcement officer of any municipality or of any local board of any municipality, while in the discharge of his or her duties,

(e) an officer, employee or agent of any municipality or of any local board of any municipality whose responsibilities include the enforcement of a by-law, an Act or a regulation under an Act, while in the discharge of his or her duties, or

(f) a person designated under subsection (3);

"representative" means, in respect of a proceeding to which this Act applies, a person authorized under the *Law Society Act* to represent a person in that proceeding;

"set fine" means the amount of fine set by the Chief Justice of the Ontario Court of Justice for an offence for the purpose of proceedings commenced under Part I or II.

(2) Repealed.

(3) **Designation of provincial offences officers**—A minister of the Crown may designate in writing any person or class of persons as a provincial offences officer for the purposes of all or any class of offences.

General

2(1) **Purpose of Act**—The purpose of this Act is to replace the summary conviction procedure for the prosecution of provincial offences, including the provisions adopted by reference to the *Criminal Code* (Canada), with a procedure that reflects the distinction between provincial offences and criminal offences.

(2) **Interpretation**—Where, as an aid to the interpretation of provisions of this Act, recourse is had to the judicial interpretation of and practices under corresponding provisions of the *Criminal Code* (Canada), any variation in wording without change in substance shall not, in itself, be construed to intend a change of meaning.

PART I
COMMENCEMENT OF PROCEEDINGS BY CERTIFICATE OF OFFENCE

3(1) **Certificate of offence and offence notice**—In addition to the procedure set out in Part III for commencing a proceeding by laying an information, a proceeding in respect of an offence may be commenced by filing a certificate of offence alleging the offence in the office of the court.

(2) **Issuance and service**—A provincial offences officer who believes that one or more persons have committed an offence may issue, by completing and signing in the form prescribed under section 13,

(a) a certificate of offence certifying that an offence has been committed; and

(b) either an offence notice indicating the set fine for the offence or a summons.

(3) **Service**—The offence notice or summons shall be served personally upon the person charged within thirty days after the alleged offence occurred.

(4) Repealed.

(5) **Certificate of service**—Where service is made by the provincial offences officer who issued the certificate of offence, the officer shall certify on the certificate of offence that he or she personally served the offence notice or summons on the person charged and the date of service.

(6) **Affidavit of service**—Where service is made by a person other than the provincial offences officer who issued the certificate of offence, he or she shall complete an affidavit of service in the prescribed form.

(7) **Certificate as evidence**—A certificate of service of an offence notice or summons purporting to be signed by the provincial offences officer issuing it or an affidavit of service under subsection (6) shall be received in evidence and is proof of personal service in the absence of evidence to the contrary.

(8) **Officer not to act as agent**—The provincial offences officer who serves an offence notice or summons under this section shall not receive payment of any money in respect of a fine, or receive the offence notice for delivery to the court.

4. Filing of certificate of offence—A certificate of offence shall be filed in the office of the court as soon as is practicable, but no later than seven days after service of the offence notice or summons.

5(1) **Having a trial**—A defendant who is served with an offence notice may give notice of intention to appear in court for the purpose of entering a plea and having a trial of the matter.

(2) **Notice of intention to appear in offence notice**—If the offence notice includes a part with a notice of intention to appear, the defendant must give notice of intention to appear by,

(a) completing the notice of intention to appear part of the offence notice; and

(b) delivering the offence notice to the court office specified in it in the manner provided in the offence notice.

(3) **Notice of intention to appear to be filed in person**—If the offence notice requires the notice of intention to appear to be filed in person, the defendant must give the notice of intention to appear by,

(a) attending in person or by representative at the court office specified in the offence notice at the time or times specified in the offence notice; and

(b) filing a notice of intention to appear in the form prescribed under section 13 with the clerk of the court.

(4) **Specified court office**—A notice of intention to appear under subsection (3) is not valid if the defendant files the notice of intention to appear at a court office other than the one specified on the offence notice.

(5) **Notice of trial**—Where a notice of intention to appear is received under subsection (2) or (3), the clerk of the court shall, as soon as is practicable, give notice to the defendant and the prosecutor of the time and place of the trial.

(6) **Rescheduling time of trial**—The clerk of the court may, for administrative reasons, reschedule the time of the trial by giving a revised notice to the defendant and the prosecutor within 21 days of giving the notice referred to in subsection (5).

5.1(1) **Attendance to file notice, prescribed parts of Ontario**—This section applies in such parts of Ontario as are designated by regulation.

(2) **Section 5 inapplicable**—Section 5 does not apply where this section applies.

(3) **Filing**—A defendant who is served with an offence notice may give notice of intention to appear in court for the purpose of entering a plea and having a trial of the matter by attending in person or by representative at the court office specified in the offence notice at the time or times specified in the offence notice and filing a notice of intention to appear with the clerk of the court.

(4) **Form of notice**—A notice of intention to appear shall be in the form prescribed under section 13.

(5) **Trial**—If a defendant files a notice of intention to appear under subsection (3), the clerk of the court shall inform the defendant and the prosecutor of the time and place of the trial.

5.1(1) **Availability of meeting procedure**—This section applies where the offence notice requires the notice of intention to appear to be filed in person in the form prescribed under section 13.

(2) **Option for meeting with the prosecutor**—Instead of filing a notice of intention to appear under subsection 5 (3), a defendant may request a meeting with the prosecutor to discuss the resolution of the offence by,

(a) indicating that request on the offence notice; and

(b) delivering the offence notice to the court office specified on it within 15 days after the defendant was served with the offence notice.

(3) **Notice of meeting time**—Where a defendant requests a meeting with the prosecutor under subsection (2), the clerk of the court shall, as soon as is practicable, give notice to the defendant and the prosecutor of the time and place of their meeting.

(4) **Rescheduling the meeting time**—If the time for the meeting scheduled in the notice under subsection (3) is not suitable for the defendant, the defendant may, at least two days before the scheduled time of the meeting, deliver to the clerk of the court one written request to reschedule the time for the meeting and the clerk shall arrange a new meeting time to take place within 30 days of the time scheduled in the notice under subsection (3).

(5) **Notice of rescheduled meeting time**—Where a meeting time is rescheduled under subsection (4), the clerk of the court shall, as soon as is practicable, give notice to the defendant and the prosecutor of the rescheduled time and the place of their meeting.

(6) **Meeting by electronic method**—The defendant and the prosecutor may, if unable to attend in person because of remoteness, attend their meeting by electronic method in accordance with section 83.1.

(7) **Agreement on plea of guilty and submissions**—At their meeting, the defendant and the prosecutor may agree that,

(a) the defendant will enter a guilty plea to the offence or a substituted offence; and

(b) the defendant and the prosecutor will make submissions as to penalty, including an extension of time for payment.

(8) **Appearance before justice**—If an agreement is reached under subsection (7), the defendant shall, as directed by the prosecutor,

(a) appear with the prosecutor before a justice sitting in court and orally enter the plea and make submissions; or

(b) appear without the prosecutor before a justice sitting in court within 10 days, enter the plea orally and make the submissions in the form determined by the regulations.

(9) **Conviction**—Upon receiving the plea and submissions under subsection (8), the justice may,

(a) require the prosecutor to appear and speak to the submissions, if the submissions were submitted under clause (8)(b); and

(b) enter a conviction and impose the set fine or such other fine as is permitted by law in respect of the offence for which the plea was entered.

(10) **If no justice available**—If no justice is available after the meeting to conduct the proceeding under clause (8)(a), the clerk of the court shall, as soon as practicable, give notice to the defendant and the prosecutor of the time and place for their joint appearance before a justice.

(11) **Notice of trial**—The clerk of the court shall, as soon as is practicable, give notice to the defendant and the prosecutor of the time and place of the trial if,

(a) an agreement is not reached under subsection (7); or

(b) the justice does not accept the guilty plea and refers the matter to trial.

(12) **Rescheduling time of trial**—The clerk of the court may, for administrative reasons, reschedule the time of the trial by giving a revised notice to the defendant and the prosecutor within 21 days of giving the notice referred to subsection (11).

5.2(1) **Challenge to officer's evidence**—A defendant who gives notice of an intention to appear in court for the purpose of entering a plea and having a trial of the matter shall indicate on the notice of intention to appear or offence notice if the defendant intends to challenge the evidence of the provincial offences officer.

Section 1(9) of the *Good Government Act, 2009*, which amends s. 5.2 of the POA, is unproclaimed and no proclamation date has been set.

(2) **Notifying officer**—If the defendant indicates an intention to challenge the officer's evidence, the clerk of the court shall notify the officer.

Note: On a day to be named by proclamation of the Lieutenant Governor, section 5.2 is repealed.

6. Repealed.

7(1) **Plea of guilty with submissions**—A defendant who does not have the option of meeting with the prosecutor under section 5.1 and does not wish to dispute the charge in the offence notice, but wishes to make submissions as to penalty, including an extension of time for payment, may attend at the time and place specified in the notice and may appear before a justice sitting in court for the purpose of pleading guilty to the offence and making submissions as to penalty, and the justice may enter a conviction and impose the set fine or such lesser fine as is permitted by law.

Part I, s. 7 of the POA allows a defendant to plead guilty and receive a lesser monetary fine. However, in the matter of a driver's demerit points, the presiding justice cannot reduce or eliminate such a penalty. In order to avoid demerit points, the charge has to be amended to an offence level that does not impose points as a penalty.

(2) **Submissions under oath**—The justice may require submissions under subsection (1) to be made under oath, orally or by affidavit.

8(1) **Payment out of court**—A defendant who does not wish to dispute the charge in the offence notice may, in the manner indicated on the offence notice, pay the set fine and all applicable costs and surcharges fixed by the regulations.

(2) **Effect of payment**— Acceptance by the court office of payment under subsection (1) constitutes,

(a) a plea of guilty by the defendant;

(b) conviction of the defendant for the offence; and

(c) imposition of a fine in the amount of the set fine for the offence.

9(1) **Deemed not to dispute charge**—A defendant is deemed to not wish to dispute the charge where,

(a) at least 15 days have elapsed after the defendant was served with the offence notice and the defendant did not give notice of intention to appear under section 5, did not request a meeting with the prosecutor in accordance with section 5.1 and did not plead guilty under section 7 or 8;

(b) the defendant requested a meeting with the prosecutor in accordance with section 5.1 but did not attend the scheduled meeting with the prosecutor; or

(c) the defendant reached an agreement with the prosecutor under subsection 5.1(7) but did not appear at a sentencing hearing with a justice under subsection 5.1(8).

(2) **Action by justice**—Where a defendant is deemed to not wish to dispute the charge, a justice shall examine the certificate of offence and shall,

(a) where the certificate of offence is complete and regular on its face, enter a conviction in the defendant's absence and without a hearing and impose the set fine for the offence; or

(b) where the certificate of offence is not complete and regular on its face, quash the proceeding.

(3) **Conviction without proof of by-law**—Where the offence is in respect of an offence under a by-law of a municipality, the justice shall enter a conviction under clause (2)(a) without proof of the by-law that creates the offence if the certificate of offence is complete and regular on its face.

9.1(1) **Failure to appear at trial**—A defendant is deemed to not wish to dispute the charge where the defendant has been issued a notice of the time and place of trial and fails to appear at the time and place appointed for the trial.

(2) **Examination by justice**—If subsection (1) applies, section 54 does not apply, and a justice shall examine the certificate of offence and shall without a hearing enter a conviction in the defendant's absence and impose the set fine for the offence if the certificate is complete and regular on its face.

(3) **Quashing proceeding**—The justice shall quash the proceeding if he or she is not able to enter a conviction.

10. Signature on notice—A signature on an offence notice or notice of intention to appear purporting to be that of the defendant is proof, in the absence of evidence to the contrary, that it is the signature of the defendant.

Reopening

11(1) **Application to strike out conviction**—A defendant who was convicted without a hearing may, within 15 days of becoming aware of the conviction, apply to a justice to strike out the conviction.

(2) **Striking out the conviction**—Upon application under subsection (1), a justice shall strike out a conviction if satisfied by affidavit of the defendant that, through no fault of the defendant, the defendant was unable to appear for a hearing or for a meeting under section 5.1 or the defendant did not receive delivery of a notice or document relating to the offence.

(3) **If conviction struck out**—If the justice strikes out the conviction, the justice shall,

(a) proceed under section 7, if the offence notice does not require the notice of intention to appear to be filed in person and the defendant wishes to proceed under that section;

(b) direct the clerk of the court to give notice to the defendant and the prosecutor of the time and place of their meeting under subsection 5.1(3), if the offence notice requires the notice of intention to appear to be filed in person and the defendant wishes to proceed under that section; or

(c) direct the clerk of the court to give notice to the defendant and the prosecutor of the time and place of the trial.

(4) **Rescheduling time of trial**—The clerk of the court may, for administrative reasons, reschedule the time of the trial by giving a revised notice to the defendant and the prosecutor within 21 days of giving the notice referred to clause (3)(c).

(5) **Certificate**—A justice who strikes out a conviction under subsection (2) shall give the defendant a certificate of the fact in the prescribed form.

11.1(1) **Error by municipality**—A municipality or other body may apply to a justice requesting that a conviction be struck out if the defendant was convicted because of an error made by the municipality or other body.

(2) **Striking out conviction**—On an application by a municipality or other body, if a justice is satisfied that an error was made, the justice shall strike out the conviction.

(3) **Notice to defendant**—If the justice strikes out the conviction, the municipality or other body shall notify the defendant of that fact.

Consequences of conviction

12(1) **Penalty**—Where the penalty prescribed for an offence includes a fine of more than $1,000 or imprisonment and a proceeding is commenced under this Part, the provision for fine or imprisonment does not apply and in lieu thereof the offence is punishable by a fine of not more than the maximum fine prescribed for the offence or $1,000, whichever is the lesser.

(1.1) **Transitional**—Subsection (1) applies only to an offence committed on or after the day subsection 1(18) of Schedule 4 to the *Good Government Act, 2009* comes into force.

(2) **Other consequences of conviction**—Where a person is convicted of an offence in a proceeding initiated by an offence notice,

(a) a provision in or under any other Act that provides for an action or result following upon a conviction of an offence does not apply to the conviction, except,

(i) for the purpose of carrying out the sentence imposed,

(ii) for the purpose of recording and proving the conviction,

(iii) for the purposes of giving effect to any action or result provided for under the *Highway Traffic Act*, and

(iv) Repealed.

(v) for the purposes of section 16 of the *Smoke-Free Ontario Act*; and

(b) any thing seized in connection with the offence after the service of the offence notice is not liable to forfeiture.

13(1) **Regulations**—The Lieutenant Governor in Council may make regulations,

(a) Repealed.

(b) authorizing the use in a form prescribed under clause (1.1)(a) of any word or expression to designate an offence;

(c) Repealed.

(d) Repealed.

(1.1) **Same, Attorney General**—The Attorney General may make regulations,

(a) prescribing the form of certificates of offence, offence notices and summonses and such other forms as are considered necessary under this Part;

(b) respecting any matter that is considered necessary to provide for the use of the forms under this Part.

(2) **Sufficiency of abbreviated wording**—The use on a form prescribed under clause (1.1)(a) of any word or expression authorized by the regulations to designate an offence is sufficient for all purposes to describe the offence designated by such word or expression.

(3) **Idem**—Where the regulations do not authorize the use of a word or expression to describe an offence in a form prescribed under clause (1.1)(a), the offence may be described in accordance with section 25.

PART III
COMMENCEMENT OF PROCEEDING BY INFORMATION

21(1) **Commencement of proceeding by information**—In addition to the procedure set out in Parts I and II for commencing a proceeding by the filing of a certificate, a proceeding in respect of an offence may be commenced by laying an information.

(2) **Exception**—Where a summons or offence notice has been served under Part I, no proceeding shall be commenced under subsection (1) in respect of the same offence except with the consent of the Attorney General or his or her agent.

22. Summons before information laid—Where a provincial offences officer believes, on reasonable and probable grounds, that an offence has been committed by a person whom the officer finds at or near the place where the offence was committed, he or she may, before an information is laid, serve the person with a summons in the prescribed form.

In s. 23(1), "any person" may include a citizen, a police officer, and a bylaw officer, among others.

23(1) **Information**—Any person who, on reasonable and probable grounds, believes that one or more persons have committed an offence, may lay an information in the prescribed form and under oath before a justice alleging the offence and the justice shall receive the information.

(1.1) **Multiple defendants**—For greater certainty, an information laid under subsection (1) may include one or more persons.

(2) **Where information may be laid**—An information may be laid anywhere in Ontario.

24(1) **Procedure on laying of information**—A justice who receives an information laid under section 23 shall consider the information and, where he or she considers it desirable to do so, hear and consider in the absence of the defendant the allegations of the informant and the evidence of witnesses and,

(a) where he or she considers that a case for so doing is made out,

(i) confirm the summons served under section 22, if any,

(ii) issue a summons in the prescribed form, or

(iii) where the arrest is authorized by statute and where the allegations of the informant or the evidence satisfy the justice on reasonable and probable grounds that it is necessary in the public interest to do so, issue a warrant for the arrest of the defendant; or

(b) where he or she considers that a case for issuing process is not made out,

(i) so endorse the information, and

(ii) where a summons was served under section 22, cancel it and cause the defendant to be so notified.

(2) **Summons or warrants in blank**—A justice shall not sign a summons or warrant in blank.

25(1) **Counts**—Each offence charged in an information shall be set out in a separate count.

(2) **Allegation of offence**—Each count in an information shall in general apply to a single transaction and shall contain and is sufficient if it contains in substance a statement that the defendant committed an offence therein specified.

(3) **Reference to statutory provision**—Where in a count an offence is identified but the count fails to set out one or more of the essential elements of the offence, a reference to the provision creating or defining the offence shall be deemed to incorporate all the essential elements of the offence.

(4) **Idem**—The statement referred to in subsection (2) may be,

(a) in popular language without technical averments or allegations of matters that are not essential to be proved;

(b) in the words of the enactment that describes the offence; or

(c) in words that are sufficient to give to the defendant notice of the offence with which the defendant is charged.

(5) **More than one count**—Any number of counts for any number of offences may be joined in the same information.

(6) **Particulars of count**—A count shall contain sufficient detail of the circumstances of the alleged offence to give to the defendant reasonable information with respect to the act or omission to be proved against the defendant and to identify the transaction referred to.

Section 25(6) notes how important it is that defendants be able to understand what they are accused of. The certificate of offence or information must contain enough details to allow defendants to research the law and prepare a defence to the allegations. The information or certificate of offence should not contain short forms, since this could prevent the preparation of an adequate defence. For example, *Highway Traffic Act* should not be written as "HTA." Police and courts recognize this short form, but a citizen might not.

(7) **Sufficiency**—No count in an information is insufficient by reason of the absence of details where, in the opinion of the court, the count otherwise fulfils the requirements of this section and, without restricting the generality of the foregoing, no count in an information is insufficient by reason only that,

(a) it does not name the person affected by the offence or intended or attempted to be affected;

(b) it does not name the person who owns or has a special property or interest in property mentioned in the count;

(c) it charges an intent in relation to another person without naming or describing the other person;

(d) it does not set out any writing that is the subject of the charge;

(e) it does not set out the words used where words that are alleged to have been used are the subject of the charge;

(f) it does not specify the means by which the alleged offence was committed;

(g) it does not name or describe with precision any person, place, thing or time; or

(h) it does not, where the consent of a person, official or authority is required before proceedings may be instituted for an offence, state that the consent has been obtained.

(8) **Idem**—A count is not objectionable for the reason only that,

(a) it charges in the alternative several different matters, acts or omissions that are stated in the alternative in an enactment that describes as an offence the matters, acts or omissions charged in the count; or

(b) it is double or multifarious.

(9) **Need to negative exception, etc.**—No exception, exemption, proviso, excuse or qualification prescribed by law is required to be set out or negatived, as the case may be, in an information.

26(1) **Summons**—A summons issued under section 22 or 24 shall,

(a) be directed to the defendant;

(b) set out briefly the offence in respect of which the defendant is charged; and

(c) require the defendant to attend court at a time and place stated therein and to attend thereafter as required by the court in order to be dealt with according to law.

(2) **Service**—A summons shall be served by a provincial offences officer by delivering it personally to the person to whom it is directed or if that person cannot conveniently be found, by leaving it for the person at the person's last known or usual place of abode with an inmate thereof who appears to be at least sixteen years of age.

(3) **Service outside Ontario**—Despite subsection (2), where the person to whom a summons is directed does not reside in Ontario, the summons shall be deemed to have been duly served seven days after it has been sent by registered mail to the person's last known or usual place of abode.

(4) **Service on corporation**—Service of a summons on a corporation may be effected,

(a) in the case of a municipal corporation by,

(i) delivering the summons personally to the mayor, warden, reeve or other chief officer of the corporation or to the clerk of the corporation, or

(ii) mailing the summons by registered mail to the municipal corporation at an address held out by it to be its address;

(b) in the case of any corporation, other than a municipal corporation, incorporated or continued by or under an Act by,

(i) delivering the summons personally to the manager, secretary or other executive officer of the corporation or person apparently in charge of a branch office of the corporation, or

(ii) mailing the summons by registered mail to the corporation at an address held out by it to be its address;

(c) in the case of corporation not incorporated or continued by or under an Act by,

(i) a method provided under clause (b),

(ii) delivering the summons personally to the corporation's resident agent or agent for service or to any other representative of the corporation in Ontario, or

(iii) mailing the summons by registered mail to a person referred to in subclause (ii) or to an address outside Ontario, including outside Canada, held out by the corporation to be its address.

(4.1) **Date of mailed service**—A summons served by registered mail under subsection (4) is deemed to have been duly served seven days after the day of mailing.

(5) **Substitutional service**—A justice, upon motion and upon being satisfied that service cannot be made effectively on a corporation in accordance with subsection (4), may by order authorize another method of service that has a reasonable likelihood of coming to the attention of the corporation.

(6) **Proof of service**—Service of a summons may be proved by statement under oath or affirmation, written or oral, of the person who made the service.

27(1) **Contents of warrant**—A warrant issued under section 24 shall,

(a) name or describe the defendant;

(b) set out briefly the offence in respect of which the defendant is charged; and

(c) order that the defendant be forthwith arrested and brought before a justice to be dealt with according to law.

(2) **Idem**—A warrant issued under section 24 remains in force until it is executed and need not be made returnable at any particular time.

PART IV
TRIAL AND SENTENCING

Officers must understand the mechanics of court proceedings, as set out in part IV, whether they pertain to the prosecutor, the defence counsel or an agent, or a defendant appearing without a lawyer.

Trial

28. Application of Part—This Part applies to a proceeding commenced under this Act.

29(1) **Territorial jurisdiction**—Subject to subsection (2), a proceeding in respect of an offence shall be heard and determined by the Ontario Court of Justice sitting in the county or district in which the offence occurred or in the area specified in the transfer agreement made under Part X.

(2) **Idem**—A proceeding in respect of an offence may be heard and determined in a county or district that adjoins that in which the offence occurred if,

(a) the court holds sittings in a place reasonably proximate to the place where the offence occurred; and

(b) the place of sitting referred to in clause (a) is named in the summons or offence notice.

(3) **Transfer to proper county**—Where a proceeding is taken in a county or district other than one referred to in subsection (1) or (2), the court shall order that the proceed-

ing be transferred to the proper county or district and may where the defendant appears award costs under section 60.

(4) **Change of venue**—Where, on the motion of a defendant or prosecutor made to the court at the location named in the information or certificate, it appears to the court that,

(a) it would be appropriate in the interests of justice to do so; or

(b) both the defendant and prosecutor consent thereto,

the court may order that the proceeding be heard and determined at another location in Ontario.

(5) **Conditions**—The court may, in an order made on a motion by the prosecutor under subsection (3) or (4), prescribe conditions that it thinks proper with respect to the payment of additional expenses caused to the defendant as a result of the change of venue.

(6) **Time of order for change of venue**—An order under subsection (3) or (4) may be made even if a motion preliminary to trial has been disposed of or the plea has been taken and it may be made at any time before evidence has been heard.

(7) **Preliminary motions**—The court at a location to which a proceeding is transferred under this section may receive and determine any motion preliminary to trial although the same matter was determined by the court at the location from which the proceeding was transferred.

(8) **Delivery of papers**—Where an order is made under subsection (3) or (4), the clerk of the court at the location where the trial was to be held before the order was made shall deliver any material in his or her possession in connection with the proceeding forthwith to the clerk of the court at the location where the trial is ordered to be held. . . .

33(1) **Dividing counts**—A defendant may at any stage of the proceeding make a motion to the court to amend or to divide a count that,

(a) charges in the alternative different matters, acts or omissions that are stated in the alternative in the enactment that creates or describes the offence; or

(b) is double or multifarious,

on the ground that, as framed, it prejudices the defendant in the defendant's defence.

(2) **Idem**—Upon a motion under subsection (1), where the court is satisfied that the ends of justice so require, it may order that a count be amended or divided into two or more counts, and thereupon a formal commencement may be inserted before each of the counts into which it is divided.

34(1) **Amendment of information or certificate**—The court may, at any stage of the proceeding, amend the information or certificate as may be necessary if it appears that the information or certificate,

(a) fails to state or states defectively anything that is requisite to charge the offence;

(b) does not negative an exception that should be negatived; or

(c) is in any way defective in substance or in form.

(2) **Idem**—The court may, during the trial, amend the information or certificate as may be necessary if the matters to be alleged in the proposed amendment are disclosed by the evidence taken at the trial.

(3) **Variances between charge and evidence**—A variance between the information or certificate and the evidence taken on the trial is not material with respect to,

(a) the time when the offence is alleged to have been committed, if it is proved that the information was laid or certificate issued within the prescribed period of limitation; or

(b) the place where the subject-matter of the proceeding is alleged to have arisen, except in an issue as to the jurisdiction of the court.

(4) **Considerations on amendment**—The court shall, in considering whether or not an amendment should be made, consider,

Sections 34 and 36 address what can occur in court when an information or certificate is "defective," which may occur where, for example, the time is not noted, the wrong date is provided, or a location is referred to incorrectly (such a street corner being misnamed). In such a case, a court may (1) decide to amend either document, after considering such factors as the evidence at trial, whether the defendant has been misled or prejudiced by the defect, and whether an injustice would occur if an amendment were made; or (2) consider a motion to quash an information or certificate.

(a) the evidence taken on the trial, if any;

(b) the circumstances of the case;

(c) whether the defendant has been misled or prejudiced in the defendant's defence by a variance, error or omission; and

(d) whether, having regard to the merits of the case, the proposed amendment can be made without injustice being done.

(5) **Amendment, question of law**—The question whether an order to amend an information or certificate should be granted or refused is a question of law.

(6) **Endorsement of order to amend**—An order to amend an information or certificate shall be endorsed on the information or certificate as part of the record and the trial shall proceed as if the information or certificate had been originally laid as amended.

"Particulars" may include such things as an officer's notes or the identifying details of any instrument used to document the offence (for example, a radar unit).

35. Particulars—The court may, before or during trial, if it is satisfied that it is necessary for a fair trial, order that a particular, further describing any matter relevant to the proceeding, be furnished to the defendant.

36(1) **Motion to quash information or certificate**—An objection to an information or certificate for a defect apparent on its face shall be taken by motion to quash the information or certificate before the defendant has pleaded, and thereafter only by leave of the court.

(2) **Grounds for quashing**—The court shall not quash an information or certificate unless an amendment or particulars under section 33, 34 or 35 would fail to satisfy the ends of justice. . . .

39(1) **Issuance of summons**—Where a justice is satisfied that a person is able to give material evidence in a proceeding under this Act, the justice may issue a summons requiring the person to attend to give evidence and bring with him or her any writings or things referred to in the summons.

(2) **Service**—A summons shall be served and the service shall be proved in the same manner as a summons under section 26.

(2.1) **Exception**—Despite subsection (2), a summons served under this section may be served by a person other than a provincial offences officer.

(3) **Attendance**—A person who is served with a summons shall attend at the time and place stated in the summons to give evidence and, if required by the summons, shall bring with him or her any writing or other thing that the person has in his or her possession or under his or her control relating to the subject-matter of the proceeding.

(4) **Remaining in attendance**—A person who is served with a summons shall remain in attendance during the hearing and the hearing as resumed after adjournment from time to time unless the person is excused from attendance by the presiding justice.

40(1) **Arrest of witness**—Where a judge is satisfied upon evidence under oath or affirmation, that a person is able to give material evidence that is necessary in a proceeding under this Act and,

(a) will not attend if a summons is served; or

(b) attempts to serve a summons have been made and have failed because the person is evading service,

the judge may issue a warrant in the prescribed form for the arrest of the person.

(2) **Idem**—Where a person who has been served with a summons to attend to give evidence in a proceeding does not attend or remain in attendance, the court may, if it is established,

(a) that the summons has been served; and

(b) that the person is able to give material evidence that is necessary,

issue or cause to be issued a warrant in the prescribed form for the arrest of the person.

(3) **Bringing before justice**—The police officer who arrests a person under a warrant issued under subsection (1) or (2) shall immediately take the person before a justice. . . .

42(1) **Penalty for failure to attend**—Every person who, being required by law to attend or remain in attendance at a hearing, fails without lawful excuse to attend or remain in attendance accordingly is guilty of an offence and on conviction is liable to a fine of not more than $2,000, or to imprisonment for a term of not more than thirty days, or to both.

(2) **Proof of failure to attend**—In a proceeding under subsection (1), a certificate of the clerk of the court or a justice stating that the defendant failed to attend is admissible in evidence as proof, in the absence of evidence to the contrary, of the fact without proof of the signature or office of the person appearing to have signed the certificate. . . .

45(1) **Taking of plea**—After being informed of the substance of the information or certificate, the defendant shall be asked whether the defendant pleads guilty or not guilty of the offence charged in it.

(2) **Conviction on plea of guilty**—Where the defendant pleads guilty, the court may accept the plea and convict the defendant.

(3) **Conditions of accepting plea**—A court may accept a plea of guilty only if it is satisfied that the defendant,

(a) is making the plea voluntarily;

(b) understands that the plea is an admission of the essential elements of the offence;

(c) understands the nature and consequences of the plea; and

(d) understands that the court is not bound by any agreement made between the defendant and the prosecutor.

(4) **Validity of plea not affected**—The failure of a court to fully inquire into whether the conditions set out in subsection (3) are met does not affect the validity of the plea.

(5) **Refusal to plead** —Where the defendant refuses to plead or does not answer directly, the court shall enter a plea of not guilty.

(6) **Plea of guilty to another offence**—Where the defendant pleads guilty of an offence other than the offence charged, and whether or not it is an included offence and whether or not the defendant has pleaded not guilty to the offence charged, the court may, with the consent of the prosecutor, accept such plea of guilty and accordingly amend the certificate of offence, the certificate of parking infraction or the information, as the case may be, or substitute the offence to which the defendant pleads guilty.

Section 45(6) facilitates plea bargaining. This occurs when a defendant agrees to plead guilty to another—often less serious—offence as a way of receiving a lighter penalty. In return, the prosecution saves the time and expense of a trial. For example, a motorist who is charged with driving 20 kilometres over the speed limit, an offence that leads to demerit points if convicted, may want to plead guilty to a lesser charge of driving 15 kilometres over the speed limit, an offence that does not result in demerit points.

45.1(1) **Judicial pre-trial conferences**—On application by the prosecutor or the defendant or on his or her own motion, a justice may order that a pre-trial conference be held between the prosecutor and the defendant or a representative of the defendant.

(2) **Matters for consideration**—The court, or a justice of the court, shall preside over the pre-trial conference, the purpose of which is to,

(a) consider the matters that, to promote a fair and expeditious trial, would be better decided before the start of the proceedings and other similar matters; and

(b) make arrangements for decisions on those matters.

46(1) **Trial on plea of not guilty**—If the defendant pleads not guilty, the court shall hold the trial.

(2) **Right to defend**—The defendant is entitled to make full answer and defence.

(3) **Right to examine witnesses**—The prosecutor or defendant, as the case may be, may examine and cross-examine witnesses.

(4) **Agreed facts**—The court may receive and act upon any facts agreed upon by the defendant and prosecutor without proof or evidence.

(5) **Defendant not compellable**—Despite section 8 of the *Evidence Act*, the defendant is not a compellable witness for the prosecution.

As in criminal trials, the defendant cannot be forced by the Crown to testify in provincial offences court. If defence counsel allows the defendant to testify, the Crown then has the right to cross-examine, or question, the defendant as well.

Evidence and burden of proof

47(1) **Evidence taken on another charge**—The court may receive and consider evidence taken before the same justice on a different charge against the same defendant, with the consent of the parties.

(2) **Certificate as evidence**—Where a certificate as to the content of an official record is, by any Act, made admissible in evidence as proof, in the absence of evidence to the contrary, the court may, for the purpose of deciding whether the defendant is the person referred to in the certificate, receive and base its decision upon information it considers credible or trustworthy in the circumstances of each case.

(3) **Burden of proving exception, etc.**—The burden of proving that an authorization, exception, exemption or qualification prescribed by law operates in favour of the defendant is on the defendant, and the prosecutor is not required, except by way of rebuttal, to prove that the authorization, exception, exemption or qualification does not operate in favour of the defendant, whether or not it is set out in the information. . . .

50(1) **Appearance by defendant**—A defendant may appear and act personally or by representative.

(2) **Appearance by corporation**—A defendant that is a corporation shall appear and act by representative.

(3) **Exclusion of representatives**—The court may bar any person, other than a person who is licensed under the *Law Society Act*, from appearing as a representative if the court finds that the person is not competent properly to represent or advise the person for whom he or she appears, or does not understand and comply with the duties and responsibilities of a representative.

51. Compelling attendance of defendant—Although a defendant appears by representative, the court may order the defendant to attend personally, and, where it appears to be necessary to do so, may issue a summons in the prescribed form. . . .

53(1) **Failure of prosecutor to appear**—Where the defendant appears for a hearing and the prosecutor, having had due notice, does not appear, the court may dismiss the charge or may adjourn the hearing to another time upon such terms as it considers proper.

(2) **Idem**—Where the prosecutor does not appear at the time and place appointed for the resumption of an adjourned hearing under subsection (1), the court may dismiss the charge.

(3) **Costs**—Where a hearing is adjourned under subsection (1) or a charge is dismissed under subsection (2), the court may make an order under section 60 for the payment of costs.

(4) **Written order of dismissal**—Where a charge is dismissed under subsection (1) or (2), the court may, if requested by the defendant, draw up an order of dismissal stating the grounds therefor and shall give the defendant a certified copy of the order of dismissal which is, without further proof, a bar to any subsequent proceeding against the defendant in respect of the same cause. . . .

Like s. 45(6), s. 55 can encourage plea bargaining, where the Crown and defence counsel agree that a charge will be reduced in exchange for a guilty plea by the defendant. For example, a careless driving charge may be reduced to a speeding charge, which carries a lighter penalty.

55. Included offences—Where the offence as charged includes another offence, the defendant may be convicted of an offence so included that is proved, although the whole offence charged is not proved. . . .

Sentencing

Section 59 allows a court to fine a defendant less than the minimum amount specified for an offence, if the minimum is more than a defendant can afford to pay and doing so would create hardship. The fine is a penalty, whereas points are an administrative function tied directly to the offence and not related to the fine. As in s. 7, the court cannot interfere with demerit points associated with an offence, and the information would have to be amended to avoid such a penalty.

59(1) **Provision for minimum penalty**—No penalty prescribed for an offence is a minimum penalty unless it is specifically declared to be a minimum.

(2) **Relief against minimum fine**—Although the provision that creates the penalty for an offence prescribes a minimum fine, where in the opinion of the court exceptional circumstances exist so that to impose the minimum fine would be unduly oppressive or otherwise not in the interests of justice, the court may impose a fine that is less than the minimum or suspend the sentence.

(3) **Idem, re imprisonment**—Where a minimum penalty is prescribed for an offence and the minimum penalty includes imprisonment, the court may, despite the prescribed penalty, impose a fine of not more than $5,000 in lieu of imprisonment.

Costs

60(1) **Fixed costs on conviction**—Upon conviction, the defendant is liable to pay to the court an amount by way of costs that is fixed by the regulations.

(2) **Costs respecting witnesses**—The court may, in its discretion, order costs towards fees and expenses reasonably incurred by or on behalf of witnesses in amounts not exceeding the maximum fixed by the regulations, to be paid,

(a) to the court or prosecutor by the defendant; or

(b) to the defendant by the person who laid the information or issued the certificate, as the case may be,

but where the proceeding is commenced by means of a certificate, the total of such costs shall not exceed $100.

(3) **Costs collectable as a fine**—Costs payable under this section shall be deemed to be a fine for the purpose of enforcing payment.

60.1(1) **Surcharge**—If a person is convicted of an offence in a proceeding commenced under Part I or III and a fine is imposed in respect of that offence, a surcharge is payable by that person in the amount determined by regulations made under this Act.

(2) **Collection**—The surcharge shall be deemed to be a fine for the purpose of enforcing payment.

(3) **Priorities**—Any payments made by a defendant shall be credited towards payment of the fine until it is fully paid and then towards payment of the surcharge.

(3.1) **Part X agreements**—When an agreement made under Part X applies to a fine, payments made by the defendant shall first be credited towards payment of the surcharge, not as described in subsection (3).

(4) **Special purpose account**—Special purpose account Surcharges paid into the Consolidated Revenue Fund shall be credited to the victims' justice fund account and shall be deemed to be money received by the Crown for a special purpose.

(4.1) **Same**—Subsection (4) also applies to payments received under clause 165(5)(a).

(5), (6) Repealed.

(7) **Regulations**—The Lieutenant Governor in Council may make regulations,

(a) prescribing the amount of the surcharges or the method by which they are to be calculated;

(b) Repealed.

(c) exempting any offence or class of offence from the application of subsection (1).

(8) Repealed.

61. General penalty—Except where otherwise expressly provided by law, every person who is convicted of an offence is liable to a fine of not more than $5,000. . . .

PART V
GENERAL PROVISIONS

76(1) **Limitation**—A proceeding shall not be commenced after the expiration of any limitation period prescribed by or under any Act for the offence or, where no limitation period is prescribed, after six months after the date on which the offence was, or is alleged to have been, committed.

Section 1(47) of the *Good Government Act, 2009*, which amends s. 76.1(1), is unproclaimed, and no proclamation date has been set.

(2) **Extension**—A limitation period may be extended by a justice with the consent of the defendant.

76.1(1) **Electronic format and filing**—A document may be completed and signed by electronic means in an electronic format and may be filed by direct electronic transmission if the completion, signature and filing are in accordance with the regulations.

Note: On a day to be named by proclamation of the Lieutenant Governor, subsection (1) is repealed and the following substituted:

(1) **Electronic format and filing**—A document may, in accordance with the regulations, be completed, signed and filed by electronic means in an electronic format.

(1.1) **Electronic copy**—When a document is filed in paper form, an electronic copy may be retained instead of the paper original if there exists a reliable assurance as to the integrity of the information contained in the electronic copy.

(1.2) **Duty to ensure integrity**—A person who makes, stores or reproduces an electronic copy of a document for the purposes of subsection (1.1) shall take all reasonable steps to ensure the integrity of the information contained in the electronic copy.

(2) **Deemed original**—A printed copy of a document filed under subsection (1) or retained under subsection (1.1) shall be deemed to have been filed as the original document if it is printed in accordance with the regulations and for the purpose of disposing of a charge under this Act.

(3) **Interpretation**—In this section,

"document" includes a certificate of offence, certificate of parking infraction, a certificate requesting a conviction, an offence notice and a parking infraction notice.

(4) **Regulations**—The Lieutenant Governor in Council may make regulations respecting,

(a) the completion and signing of documents by electronic means;

(b) the filing of documents by direct electronic transmission;

(c) the printing of documents filed by direct electronic transmission.

77(1) **Parties to offence**—Every person is a party to an offence who,

(a) actually commits it;

(b) does or omits to do anything for the purpose of aiding any person to commit it; or

(c) abets any person in committing it.

(2) **Common purpose**—Where two or more persons form an intention in common to carry out an unlawful purpose and to assist each other therein and any one of them, in carrying out the common purpose, commits an offence, each of them who knew or ought to have known that the commission of the offence would be a probable consequence of carrying out the common purpose is a party to the offence.

78(1) **Counselling**—Where a person counsels or procures another person to be a party to an offence and that other person is afterwards a party to the offence, the person who counselled or procured is a party to the offence, even if the offence was committed in a way different from that which was counselled or procured.

(2) **Idem**—Every person who counsels or procures another person to be a party to an offence is a party to every offence that the other commits in consequence of the counselling or procuring that the person who counselled or procured knew or ought to have known was likely to be committed in consequence of the counselling or procuring.

79. Computation of age—In the absence of other evidence, or by way of corroboration of other evidence, a justice may infer the age of a person from his or her appearance.

80. Common law defences—Every rule and principle of the common law that renders any circumstance a justification or excuse for an act or a defence to a charge continues in force and applies in respect of offences, except in so far as they are altered by or inconsistent with this or any other Act.

81. Ignorance of the law—Ignorance of the law by a person who commits an offence is not an excuse for committing the offence.

Section 81 highlights the fact that, with respect to provincial offences, it is not necessary for an individual to know that an activity is illegal in order to be held accountable.

82. Representation—A defendant may act by representative. . . .

90(1) **Irregularities in form**—The validity of any proceeding is not affected by,

(a) any irregularity or defect in the substance or form of the summons, warrant, offence notice, parking infraction notice, undertaking to appear or recognizance; or

(b) any variance between the charge set out in the summons, warrant, parking infraction notice, offence notice, undertaking to appear or recognizance and the charge set out in the information or certificate.

(2) **Adjournment to meet irregularities**—Where it appears to the court that the defendant has been misled by any irregularity, defect or variance mentioned in subsection (1), the court may adjourn the hearing and may make such order as the court considers appropriate, including an order under section 60 for the payment of costs.

91(1) **Contempt**—Except as otherwise provided by an Act, every person who commits contempt in the face of a justice of the peace presiding over the Ontario Court of Justice in a proceeding under this Act is on conviction liable to a fine of not more than $1,000 or to imprisonment for a term of not more than thirty days, or to both.

(2) **Statement to offender**—Before a proceeding is taken for contempt under subsection (1), the justice of the peace shall inform the offender of the conduct complained of and the nature of the contempt and inform him or her of the right to show cause why he or she should not be punished.

(3) **Show cause**—A punishment for contempt in the face of the court shall not be imposed without giving the offender an opportunity to show cause why he or she should not be punished.

(4) **Adjournment for adjudication**—Except where, in the opinion of the justice of the peace, it is necessary to deal with the contempt immediately for the preservation of order and control in the courtroom, the justice of the peace shall adjourn the contempt proceeding to another day.

(5) **Adjudication by judge**—A contempt proceeding that is adjourned to another day under subsection (4) shall be heard and determined by the court presided over by a provincial judge.

(6) **Arrest for immediate adjudication**—Where the justice of the peace proceeds to deal with a contempt immediately and without adjournment under subsection (4), the justice of the peace may order the offender arrested and detained in the courtroom for the purpose of the hearing and determination. . . .

PART VI
YOUNG PERSONS

93. Definitions, Part VI—In this Part,

"parent," when used with reference to a young person, includes an adult with whom the young person ordinarily resides;

"young person" means a person who is or, in the absence of evidence to the contrary, appears to be,

(a) twelve years of age or more, but

(b) under sixteen years of age,

and includes a person sixteen years of age or more charged with having committed an offence while he or she was twelve years of age or more but under sixteen years of age.

94. Minimum age—No person shall be convicted of an offence committed while he or she was under twelve years of age.

Section 94 provides the same age threshold for liability as the *Criminal Code*.

The POA does not allow an offence notice to be issued to anyone under 16 years of age, as it would allow an "out of court" settlement. Instead, the officer must serve the young person's parents or guardian with a copy of the charge, since, by law, they are still accountable for children under 16 and should be made aware of the incident.

95. Offence notice not to be used—A proceeding commenced against a young person by certificate of offence shall not be initiated by an offence notice under clause 3(2)(a).

96(1) **Notice to parent**—Where a summons is served upon a young person or a young person is released on a recognizance under this Act, the provincial offences officer, in the case of a summons, or the officer in charge, in the case of a recognizance, shall as soon as practicable give notice to a parent of the young person by delivering a copy of the summons or recognizance to the parent.

(2) **Where no notice given**—Where notice has not been given under subsection (1) and no person to whom notice could have been given appears with the young person, the court may,

(a) adjourn the hearing to another time to permit notice to be given; or

(b) dispense with notice.

(3) **Saving**—Failure to give notice to a parent under subsection (1) does not in itself invalidate the proceeding against the young person. . . .

98(1) **Young person to be present at trial**—Subject to subsection 52(1) and subsection (2) of this section, a young person shall be present in court during the whole of his or her trial.

(2) **Court may permit absence**—The court may permit a young person to be absent during the whole or any part of his or her trial, on such conditions as the court considers proper.

(3) **Application of ss. 42, 54**—Sections 42 and 54 do not apply to a young person who is a defendant.

(4) **Failure of young person to appear**—Where a young person who is a defendant does not appear at the time and place appointed for a hearing and it is proved by the prosecutor, having been given a reasonable opportunity to do so, that a summons was served, an undertaking to appear was given or a recognizance to appear was entered into, as the case may be, or where the young person does not appear upon the resumption of a hearing that has been adjourned, the court may adjourn the hearing and issue a summons to appear or issue a warrant in the prescribed form for the arrest of the young person.

(5) **Compelling young person's attendance**—Where a young person does not attend personally in response to a summons issued under section 51 and it is proved by the prosecutor, having been given a reasonable opportunity to do so, that the summons was served, the court may adjourn the hearing and issue a further summons or issue a warrant in the prescribed form for the arrest of the young person.

99(1) **Identity of young person not to be published**—No person shall publish by any means a report,

(a) of an offence committed or alleged to have been committed by a young person; or

(b) of a hearing, adjudication, sentence or appeal concerning a young person who committed or is alleged to have committed an offence,

in which the name of or any information serving to identify the young person is disclosed.

(2) **Offence**—Every person who contravenes subsection (1) and every director, officer or employee of a corporation who authorizes, permits or acquiesces in a contravention of subsection (1) by the corporation is guilty of an offence and is liable on conviction to a fine of not more than $10,000.

(3) **Exceptions**—Subsection (1) does not prohibit the following:

1. The disclosure of information by the young person concerned.
2. The disclosure of information by the young person's parent or lawyer, for the purpose of protecting the young person's interests.
3. The disclosure of information by a police officer, for the purpose of investigating an offence which the young person is suspected of having committed.

4. The disclosure of information to an insurer, to enable the insurer to investigate a claim arising out of an offence committed or alleged to have been committed by the young person.
5. The disclosure of information in the course of the administration of justice, but not for the purpose of making the information known in the community.
6. The disclosure of information by a person or member of a class of persons prescribed by the regulations, for a purpose prescribed by the regulations. . . .

101(1) **Penalties limited**—Despite the provisions of this or any other Act, no young person shall be sentenced,

(a) to be imprisoned, except under clause 75(d); or

(b) to pay a fine exceeding $1,000.

(2) **Sentence where proceeding commenced by information**—Where a young person is found guilty of an offence in a proceeding commenced by information, the court may,

(a) convict the young person and,

(i) order the young person to pay a fine not exceeding the maximum prescribed for the offence or $1,000, whichever is less, or

(ii) suspend the passing of sentence and direct that the young person comply with the conditions prescribed in a probation order; or

(b) discharge the young person absolutely.

(3) **Term of probation order**—A probation order made under subclause (2)(a)(ii) shall not remain in force for more than one year from the date when it takes effect. . . .

104. Evidence of young person's age—In a proceeding under this Act, a parent's testimony as to a young person's age and any other evidence of a young person's age that the court considers credible or trustworthy in the circumstances are admissible. . . .

Release of young persons after arrest by officer

107(1) **Section 149 does not apply**—Section 149 does not apply to a young person who has been arrested.

(2) **Requirement to release**—Where a police officer acting under a warrant or other power of arrest arrests a young person, the police officer shall, as soon as is practicable, release the young person from custody unconditionally or after serving him or her with a summons unless the officer has reasonable and probable grounds to believe that it is necessary in the public interest for the young person to be detained in order to,

(a) establish the young person's identity; or

(b) prevent the continuation or repetition of an offence that constitutes a serious danger to the young person or the person or property of another.

(3) **Release by officer in charge**—Where a young person is not released from custody under subsection (2), the police officer shall deliver the young person to the officer in charge who shall, where in his or her opinion the conditions set out in clause (2)(a) or (b) do not or no longer exist, release the young person,

(a) unconditionally;

(b) upon serving the young person with a summons; or

(c) upon the young person entering into a recognizance in the prescribed form without sureties conditioned for his or her appearance in court.

(4) **Notice to parent**—Where the officer in charge does not release the young person under subsection (3), the officer in charge shall as soon as possible notify a parent of the young person by advising the parent, orally or in writing, of the young person's arrest, the reason for the arrest and the place of detention.

(5) **Release after young person brought before justice**—Sections 150 and 151 apply with necessary modifications to the release of a young person from custody under this section.

(6) **Place of custody**—No young person who is detained under section 150 shall be detained in any part of a place in which an adult who has been charged with or convicted of an offence is detained unless a justice so authorizes, on being satisfied that,

(a) the young person cannot, having regard to the young person's own safety or the safety of others, be detained in a place of temporary detention for young persons; or

(b) no place of temporary detention for young persons is available within a reasonable distance.

(7) **Idem**—Wherever practicable, a young person who is detained in custody shall be detained in a place of temporary detention designated under subsection 7(1) of the *Young Offenders Act* (Canada). . . .

PART VIII
ARREST, BAIL AND SEARCH WARRANTS

Arrest

> The arrest authority provided by s. 145 would extend to an officer who was responding to a call from another officer in pursuing a suspect. The responding officer is justified in arresting the suspect, because reasonable and probable grounds are satisfied by the call from the first officer.

> In s. 146(1), the words "as much force as is necessary" mean that officers should use as *little* force as is necessary to effect their legal purpose.

143. Officer in charge, Part VIII—In this Part,

"officer in charge" means the police officer who is in charge of the lock-up or other place to which a person is taken after his or her arrest.

144(1) **Execution of warrant**—A warrant for the arrest of a person shall be executed by a police officer by arresting the person against whom the warrant is directed wherever he or she is found in Ontario.

(2) **Idem**—A police officer may arrest without warrant a person for whose arrest he or she has reasonable and probable grounds to believe that a warrant is in force in Ontario.

145. Arrest without warrant—Any person may arrest without warrant a person who he or she has reasonable and probable grounds to believe has committed an offence and is escaping from and freshly pursued by a police officer who has lawful authority to arrest that person, and, where the person who makes the arrest is not a police officer, shall forthwith deliver the person arrested to a police officer.

146(1) **Use of force**—Every police officer is, if he or she acts on reasonable and probable grounds, justified in using as much force as is necessary to do what the officer is required or authorized by law to do.

(2) **Use of force by citizen**—Every person upon whom a police officer calls for assistance is justified in using as much force as he or she believes on reasonable and probable grounds is necessary to render such assistance.

147. Immunity from civil liability—Where a person is wrongfully arrested, whether with or without a warrant, no action for damages shall be brought,

(a) against the police officer making the arrest if he or she believed in good faith and on reasonable and probable grounds that the person arrested was the person named in the warrant or was subject to arrest without warrant under the authority of an Act;

(b) against any person called upon to assist the police officer if such person believed that the police officer had the right to effect the arrest; or

(c) against any person required to detain the prisoner in custody if such person believed the arrest was lawfully made.

148(1) **Production of process and giving of reasons**—It is the duty of every one who executes a process or warrant to have it with him or her, where it is feasible to do so, and to produce it when requested to do so.

(2) **Notice of reason for arrest**—It is the duty of every one who arrests a person, whether with or without warrant, to give notice to that person, where it is feasible to do so, of the reason for the arrest.

Bail

149(1) **Release after arrest by officer**—Where a police officer, acting under a warrant or other power of arrest, arrests a person, the police officer shall, as soon as is practicable, release the person from custody after serving him or her with a summons or offence notice unless the officer has reasonable and probable grounds to believe that,

(a) it is necessary in the public interest for the person to be detained, having regard to all the circumstances including the need to,

(i) establish the identity of the person,

(ii) secure or preserve evidence of or relating to the offence, or

(iii) prevent the continuation or repetition of the offence or the commission of another offence; or

(b) the person arrested is ordinarily resident outside Ontario and will not respond to a summons or offence notice.

(2) **Release by officer in charge**—Where a defendant is not released from custody under subsection (1), the police officer shall deliver him or her to the officer in charge who shall, where in his or her opinion the conditions set out in clauses (1)(a) and (b) do not or no longer exist, release the defendant,

(a) upon serving the defendant with a summons or offence notice;

(b) upon the defendant entering into a recognizance in the prescribed form without sureties conditioned for his or her appearance in court.

(3) **Cash bail by non-resident**—Where the defendant is held for the reason only that he or she is not ordinarily resident in Ontario and it is believed that the defendant will not respond to a summons or offence notice, the officer in charge may, in addition to anything required under subsection (2), require the defendant to deposit cash or other satisfactory negotiable security in an amount not to exceed,

(a) where the proceeding is commenced by certificate under Part I or II, the amount of the set fine for the offence or, if none, $300; or

(b) where the proceeding is commenced by information under Part III, $500.

150(1) **Person in custody to be brought before justice**—Where a defendant is not released from custody under section 149, the officer in charge shall, as soon as is practicable but in any event within twenty-four hours, bring the defendant before a justice and the justice shall, unless a plea of guilty is taken, order that the defendant be released upon giving his or her undertaking to appear unless the prosecutor having been given an opportunity to do so shows cause why the detention of the defendant is justified to ensure his or her appearance in court or why an order under subsection (2) is justified for the same purpose....

Search Warrants

158(1) **Search warrant**—A justice may at any time issue a warrant under his or her hand if the justice is satisfied by information upon oath that there are reasonable grounds to believe that there is in any place,

(a) anything on or in respect of which an offence has been or is suspected to have been committed; or

(b) anything that there are reasonable grounds to believe will afford evidence as to the commission of an offence.

(1.1) **Same**—The search warrant authorizes a police officer or person named in the warrant,

(a) to search the place named in the information for any thing described in clause (1)(a) or (b); and

(b) to seize the thing and deal with it in accordance with section 158.2.

(2) **Expiration**—Every search warrant shall name a date upon which it expires, which date shall be not later than fifteen days after its issue.

(3) **When to be executed**—Every search warrant shall be executed between 6 a.m. and 9 p.m. standard time, unless the justice by the warrant otherwise authorizes.

(4) **Definition**—In this section and in section 158.1,

"place" includes a building and a receptacle.

Telewarrants

158.1(1) **Submission of information**—Where a provincial offences officer believes that an offence has been committed and that it would be impracticable to appear personally before a justice to make application for a warrant in accordance with section 158, the provincial offences officer may submit an information on oath, by a means of telecommunication that produces a writing, to a justice designated for the purpose by the Chief Justice of the Ontario Court of Justice.

(2) **Filing of information**—The justice who receives an information submitted under subsection (1) shall, as soon as practicable, cause the information to be filed with the clerk of the court, certified by the justice as to time and date of receipt.

(3) **Same, alternative to oath**—A provincial offences officer who submits an information under subsection (1) may, instead of swearing an oath, make a statement in writing stating that all matters contained in the information are true to his or her knowledge and belief, and the statement is deemed to be made under oath.

(4) **Contents of information**—An information submitted under subsection (1) shall include,

(a) a statement of the circumstances that make it impracticable for the provincial offences officer to appear personally before a justice;

(b) a statement of the alleged offence, the place to be searched and the items alleged to be liable to seizure;

(c) a statement of the provincial offences officer's grounds for believing that items liable to seizure in respect of the alleged offence will be found in the place to be searched; and

(d) a statement as to any prior application for a warrant under this section or any other search warrant, in respect of the same matter, of which the provincial offences officer has knowledge.

(5) **Issuing warrant**—A justice to whom an information is submitted under subsection (1) may, if the conditions set out in subsection (6) are met,

(a) issue a warrant to a provincial offences officer conferring the same authority respecting search and seizure as may be conferred by a warrant issued by a justice before whom the provincial offences officer appears personally under section 158; and

(b) require that the warrant be executed within such time period as the justice may order.

(6) **Conditions**—The conditions referred to in subsection (5) are that the justice is satisfied that the information,

(a) is in respect of an offence and complies with subsection (4);

(b) discloses reasonable grounds for dispensing with an information presented personally; and

(c) discloses reasonable grounds, in accordance with section 158, for the issuance of a warrant in respect of an offence.

(7) **Application of s. 158(2) and (3)**—Subsections 158(2) and (3) apply to a warrant issued under this section.

(8) **Form, transmission and filing of warrant**—A justice who issues a warrant under this section shall,

(a) complete and sign the warrant, noting on its face the time, date and place of issuance;

(b) transmit the warrant by the means of telecommunication to the provincial offences officer who submitted the information; and

(c) as soon as practicable after the warrant has been issued, cause the warrant to be filed with the clerk of the court.

(9) **Copies**—The copy of the warrant that is transmitted to the provincial offences officer and any copies that are made from the transmitted copy have the same effect as the original for all purposes.

(10) **Providing or affixing copy when executing warrant**—When a provincial offences officer executes a warrant issued under this section,

(a) if the place to be searched is occupied, the provincial offences officer shall, before entering or as soon as practicable thereafter, give a copy of the warrant to any person present and ostensibly in control of the place; and

(b) if the place to be searched is unoccupied, the provincial offences officer shall, on entering or as soon as practicable thereafter, cause a copy of the warrant to be suitably and prominently affixed within the place.

(11) **Proof of authorization**—In any proceeding in which it is material for a court to be satisfied that a search or seizure was authorized by a warrant issued under this section, the warrant or the related information shall be produced and the court shall verify,

(a) in the case of the warrant, that it is signed by the justice and bears on its face a notation of the time, date and place of issuance;

(b) in the case of the related information, that it is certified by the justice as to time and date of receipt.

(12) **Presumption**—If the warrant or related information is not produced or if the matters set out in clause (11)(a) or (b) cannot be verified, it shall be presumed, in the absence of evidence to the contrary, that the search or seizure was not authorized by a warrant issued under this section.

158.2(1) **Duty of person who carries out seizure**—Subsection (2) applies when,

Section 158.2 imposes similar duties on officers carrying out seizures as the *Criminal Code.*

(a) a person has, under a warrant issued under this or any other Act or otherwise in the performance of his or her duties under an Act, seized any thing,

(i) upon or in respect of which an offence has been or is suspected to have been committed, or

(ii) that there are reasonable grounds to believe will afford evidence as to the commission of an offence; and

(b) no procedure for dealing with the thing is otherwise provided by law.

(2) **Same**—The person shall, as soon as is practicable, take the following steps:

1. The person shall determine whether the continued detention of the thing is required for the purposes of an investigation or proceeding.
2. If satisfied that continued detention is not required as mentioned in paragraph 1, the person shall,
   i. return the thing, on being given a receipt for it, to the person lawfully entitled to its possession, and
   ii. report to a justice about the seizure and return of the thing.
3. If paragraph 2 does not apply, the person shall,
   i. bring the thing before a justice, or
   ii. report to a justice about the seizure and detention of the thing.

159(1) **Order of justice re things seized**—When, under paragraph 3 of subsection 158.2(2), a thing that has been seized is brought before a justice or a report in respect of it is made to a justice, he or she shall, by order,

(a) detain the thing or direct it to be detained in the care of a person named in the order; or

(b) direct it to be returned.

(1.0.1) **Detention pending appeal, etc.**—A direction to return seized items does not take effect for 30 days and does not take effect during any application made or appeal taken in respect of the thing.

(1.1) **Same**—The justice may, in the order,

(a) authorize the examination, testing, inspection or reproduction of the thing seized, on the conditions that are reasonably necessary and are directed in the order; and

(b) make any other provision that, in his or her opinion, is necessary for the preservation of the thing.

(2) **Time limit for detention**—Nothing shall be detained under an order made under subsection (1) for a period of more than three months after the time of seizure unless, before the expiration of that period,

(a) upon motion, a justice is satisfied that having regard to the nature of the investigation, its further detention for a specified period is warranted and he or she so orders; or

(b) a proceeding is instituted in which the thing detained may be required. . . .

PROVINCIAL OFFENCES NOTICE AND SUMMONS

The most common form used in the enforcement of the POA is the provincial offence notice (PON) provided by part I. The sections below include instructions for completing and serving the PON, and are followed by reproductions—first unmarked and then annotated—of the pages of a PON and summons. The fronts and backs of pages in the snap set are shown side by side.

Instructions for Completing

It is important to understand what is required when filling out a PON. Responding to the five W's—who, what, why, where, and when—is the conventional approach, followed by the question, "Then what?"

"WHO?"

There are usually two people involved when a PON is being completed: the defendant and the officer. In addition to the names of the defendant and the officer, certain pieces of information are needed for identification purposes. For example, the defendant needs to provide a date of birth, while the officer is required to record his or her badge number.

"WHAT AND WHY?"

This question addresses the substance of the alleged offence. The offence must be clearly identified and specific information must be provided from the statute. For example, a PON given to someone allegedly driving over the speed limit could read: "Speeding: 85 kph in a 50 kph zone. Contrary to the *Highway Traffic Act*, s. 128." This gives the defendant a chance to research the charge and prepare a defence. (See s. 25(4)(c) of the POA.) Officers can find accepted short form wordings in the book, *Provincial Offences Wordings and Fines.*

"WHERE?"

It is important for the officer to provide the specifics of where an offence occurred so that there is no dispute about the location. If possible, include specific reference points, such as an address or where the offence occurred in relation to a cross street. Always include the name of the municipality.

"WHEN?"

The date and time recorded on the PON are specific to the incident. Note that the date is written in the following order: year, month, and day. For example, May 21, 2011 is written as 2011 05 21.

This is the standard format used in law enforcement for recording a date. Officers use this format in record-keeping and when conducting a CPIC (Canadian Police Information Centre) check.

"THEN WHAT?"

The defendant is given either a monetary fine or a notice to attend court. If the officer issues a fine, the defendant can do one of three things:

1. plead guilty and pay the fine by mail or in person,
2. plead guilty with an explanation, or
3. request a trial date.

Instructions for Service

The officer completes the certificate of offence, which is the top (white) copy of a ticket, except for the section requiring the officer's signature. The white copy is lifted and the yellow copy underneath, which is the offence notice, is pulled out. At this point, the officer signs the yellow offence notice and serves the defendant with the notice, which now has an original signature, not an imprint from the white copy. Once that is done, the officer signs the white copy under the words "And I further certify that I served an offence notice personally upon the person charged."

> If the officer had signed the white certificate of offence while the yellow offence notice was still attached, the defendant would have been served with a document that did not contain an original signature—an indication that the officer did not follow procedure in serving the defendant with the offence notice. This could raise questions about the officer's credibility and professionalism, and lead to a possible challenge in court from the defendant.

Officer Notes

The last page provides a space for the officer to record notes pertaining to the offence. They can be used to help refresh the officer's memory when the officer is giving evidence at a trial. As a general rule, it is important to be consistent and follow the same process when making notes. For example, it is recommended that a record always be kept of the weather at the time of the incident, since the conditions could be relevant in court, especially in the case of driving offences.

If the officer used any equipment in documenting the offence or aspects of the offence, particulars should also be noted (such as the model and serial number of a radar unit). In the event that the accuracy or quality of the unit is questioned in court, it will be possible to produce the exact piece of equipment for inspection.

A diagram of the scene is helpful to include in notes, especially if an officer is new or the scene is complex and may be difficult to remember at trial. When sketching a diagram, it is a good practice to place north at the top of the page.

The space provided for notes is limited, so it is important to make effective use of it. These tips may help:

1. Using the short forms of words saves space and is helpful if they make sense in the situation. Examples include: n/b for northbound; O/S for on scene; OBS for observed; and R/C for radio call. The short forms should be used in all of an officer's work, and the officer should be able to verify them so they are not given an alternative meaning.
2. The information on the front of a notice should not be repeated in an officer's notes. The space for notes should be saved for additional relevant information.

See Figure 15 for a sample of an officer's notes.

COMPOSITION OF THE TICKET AND SUMMONS

- **FIGURE 1** Form 1: Certificate of Offence
- **FIGURE 2** Form 3: Offence Notice
- **FIGURE 3** Computer Input
- **FIGURE 4** Enforcement Agency Record/Enforcement Agency Notes
- **FIGURE 5** Payment Notice
- **FIGURE 6** Summons

ENTITIES REPRESENTED IN THE TICKET

- **FIGURE 7** Annotated Form 3: Offence Notice—Original Signature
- **FIGURE 8** Annotated Form 1: Certificate of Offence—Officer Information
- **FIGURE 9** Annotated Form 1: Certificate of Offence—Offence Information
- **FIGURE 10** Annotated Form 1: Certificate of Offence—Defendant Information
- **FIGURE 11** Annotated Form 1: Certificate of Offence—Vehicle Information

STEPS IN COMPLETING THE TICKET FOR SETTLEMENT OR COURT APPEARANCE

- **FIGURE 12** Annotated Form 1: Certificate of Offence—Out-of-Court Settlement
- **FIGURE 13** Annotated Form 1: Certificate of Offence—Mandatory Court Appearance

OTHER INFORMATION ENTERED ON THE TICKET

- **FIGURE 14** Annotated Form 1: Certificate of Offence—Elements of a Driver's Licence Number
- **FIGURE 15** Annotated Form 1: Certificate of Offence—Sample Enforcement Agency Notes

FIGURE 1 Form 1: Certificate of Offence (white)

ICON Location Code / Code d'emplacement du RIII: 3860
Offence Number / N° d'infraction: 6571079A

Form 1 Reg. 950 *Provincial Offences Act* Ontario Court of Justice
Formule 1 Règl. 950 Loi sur les infractions provinciales *Cour de justice de l'Ontario*

Certificate of Offence / *Procès-verbal d'infraction*

I/Je soussigné(e) ____ (Print name/nom en lettres moulées)

Believe and certify that on the day of / *Crois et atteste que le* Y/A 2 0 __ M/M __ D/J __ Time/ *À (Heure)* __ M

Name / *Nom* ____ Family/*Nom de famille*

____ Given/*Prénom* ____ Initials/*Initiales*

Address / *Adresse* ____ Number and street/*Numéro et nom de la rue*

Municipality/*Municipalité* ____ P.O./*C.P.* ____ Province ____ Postal code/*Code postal*

Driver's licence No./*Numéro de permis de conduire* ____ Juris *Aut. lég.*

Birthdate/*Date de naissance* Y/A 1 9 __ M/M __ D/J __ | Sex *Sexe* | Motor Vehicle Involved *Véhicule impliqué* ☐ N/N | Collision Involved *Collision* ☐ Y/O | Witnesses *Témoins* ☐ Y/O

At/*À* ____

____ Municipality/*Municipalité*

Did commit the offence of: / *A commis l'infraction de :* ____

Contrary to: / *Contrairement à :* ____

Sect./*L'art.* ____

Plate number *N° de plaque d'immatriculation*	Juris *Aut. lég.*	Commercial *Utilitaire*	CVOR/*IUVU*	NSC/CNS	Code
		☐ Y/O	☐ Y/O	☐ Y/O	

CVOR No. - NSC No. / *N° de l'IUVU - N° du CNS* ____

And I further certify that I served an offence notice personally upon the person charged on the offence date. / *J'atteste également qu'à la date de l'infraction, j'ai signifié, en mains propres, un avis d'infraction à la personne accusée.*

☐ Or other service date of: / *Autre date de signification, le :*

Signature of issuing Provincial Offences Officer / *Signature de l'agent des infractions provinciales* | Officer No. *N° de l'agent* | Platoon *Peloton* | Unit *Unité*

Set fine of / *Amende fixée de* $ ____ | **Total payable** $ ____ **Montant total exigible** | Total payable includes set fine, applicable victim fine surcharge and costs. / *Le montant total exigible comprend l'amende fixée, la suramende compensatoire applicable et les frais.*

Summons issued. You are required to appear in court on / ***Assignation.*** *Vous êtes tenu(e) de comparaître devant le tribunal le* Y/A 2 0 __ M/M __ D/J __ Time / *À (Heure)* __ M

Ct. room/*Salle d'audience* ____ at the Ontario Court of Justice P.O.A. Office at / *à la Cour de justice de l'Ontario, Bureau des infractions provinciales au*
45 Cedar Pointe Drive, Barrie, Ontario
45, promenade Cedar Pointe, Barrie (Ontario)

Conviction entered pursuant to section 9 of the *Provincial Offences Act*. Set fine imposed.
Déclaration de culpabilité inscrite conformément à l'article 9 de la Loi sur les infractions provinciales. Amende fixée imposée.
Y/A 2 0 __ M/M __ D/J __

Justice/*Juge* ____ 03-680

POA 6000 v.1 rev. 01/09

The DATA Group of Companies S73059

Affidavit of service upon defendant

I, ____, make oath and say that on the ____ day of ____ yr 20 ____, I personally served the offence notice/summons* issued with the attached certificate of offence upon the defendant named in the attached certificate of offence.

**(strike out inapplicable term)*

The Corporate defendant named in the attached certificate of offence by leaving it with

____ Person Served

____ Position, at ____ Address

____ Signature of Provincial Offences Officer

____ Badge number ____ Unit

Sworn before me at ____

This ____ day of ____ yr 20 ____

____ A Justice of the Peace/Commissioner for Taking Affidavits

Court Record

Date	Adjourned to	Requested by	on Consent

Date ____

Pleads:
- ☐ Guilty
- ☐ Not Guilty
- ☐ Guilty to a substituted offence

- ☐ Failed to appear
- ☐ Charge Withdrawn

Finding of Court
- ☐ Guilty / Convicted
- ☐ Dismissed
- ☐ S.9.1 Conviction
- ☐ Quashed

- ☐ Suspended sentence
- ☐ Fine Imposed ____
- Costs [s.60(2)] ____
- Time to pay ____

Reasons: ____

The POA provides that the victim fine surcharge (s.60.1) and certain costs (s.60(1)) are added administratively upon conviction.

For Prosecutor	For Defendant
Reporter	Clerk

____ Justice

Defaulted fine enforcement

____ Justice

FIGURE 2 Form 3: Offence Notice (yellow)

ICON Location Code / Code d'emplacement du RIII **3860** Offence Number / Nº d'infraction **6571079A**

Form 3 Reg. 950 *Provincial Offences Act* Ontario Court of Justice
Formule 3 Règl. 950 Loi sur les infractions provinciales *Cour de justice de l'Ontario*

Offence Notice / *Avis d'infraction*

Believes and certifies that on the day of
Croit et atteste que le
(Print name/nom en lettres moulées)
Y/A 2 0 M/M D/J Time/ *À (Heure)* M

Name
Nom
Family/*Nom de famille*
Given/*Prénom* Initials/*Initiales*

Address
Adresse
Number and street/*Numéro et nom de la rue*
Municipality/*Municipalité* P.O./*C.P.* Province Postal code/*Code postal*

Driver's licence No./*Numéro de permis de conduire* Juris *Aut. lég.*

Birthdate/*Date de naissance* Y/A 1 9 M/M D/J
Sex *Sexe*
Motor Vehicle Involved *Véhicule impliqué* ☐ N/N
Collision Involved *Collision* ☐ Y/O
Witnesses *Témoins* ☐ Y/O

At/*À*

Municipality/*Municipalité*

Did commit the offence of:
A commis l'infraction de :

Contrary to:
Contrairement à :

Sect./*L'art.*

Plate number *Nº de plaque d'immatriculation*	Juris *Aut. lég.*	Commercial *Utilitaire*	CVOR/*IUVU*	NSC/CNS	Code
		☐ Y/O	☐ Y/O	☐ Y/O	

CVOR No. - NSC No. / *Nº de l'IUVU - Nº du CNS*

And I further certify that I served an offence notice personally upon the person charged on the offence date.
J'atteste également qu'à la date de l'infraction, j'ai signifié, en mains propres, un avis d'infraction à la personne accusée.

☐ Or other service date of:
Autre date de signification, le :

Signature of issuing Provincial Offences Officer *Signature de l'agent des infractions provinciales*	Officer No. *Nº de l'agent*	Platoon *Peloton*	Unit *Unité*

Set fine of *Amende fixée de*	Total payable	Total payable includes set fine, applicable victim fine surcharge and costs.
$	$	$ *Le montant total exigible comprend l'amende fixée, la suramende compensatoire applicable et les frais.*
	Montant total exigible	

Important:
You have 15 days from the day you receive this notice to choose one of the options on the back of the notice.

Important :
À compter de la réception du présent avis, vous avez 15 jours pour choisir une des options décrites au verso de l'avis.

Date of service if other than offence date
Date de la signification de l'avis si elle diffère de celle de l'infraction
Y/A M/M D/J

Important – If you do not exercise one of the following options within 15 days of receiving this notice, you will be deemed not to dispute the charge and a justice may enter a conviction against you. Upon conviction, additional costs will be added to the total payable. If the fine goes into default, an administrative fee will be added and steps will be taken to enforce your defaulted fine. For example, information may be provided to a consumer reporting agency and for certain offences, including speeding, your driver's licence may be suspended.

***Important** – Si vous n'exercez pas l'une des options suivantes dans un délai de 15 jours à compter de la réception du présent avis, vous serez réputé(e) ne pas contester l'accusation et un juge pourra inscrire une déclaration de culpabilité contre vous. En cas de déclaration de culpabilité, des frais additionnels s'ajouteront au montant total exigible. En cas de défaut de paiement de l'amende, des frais d'administration s'ajouteront et des mesures seront prises pour exécuter le paiement de votre amende. Par exemple, l'information peut être transmise à une agence de renseignements sur le consommateur et dans le cas de certaines infractions, dont l'excès de vitesse, votre permis de conduire pourra être suspendu.*

OPTION 1

Plea of Guilty – Voluntary Payment of Total Payable: I plead guilty and payment of the **total payable** is enclosed (follow the instructions on the "payment notice.")

***Plaidoyer de culpabilité – Paiement volontaire du montant total exigible** : Je plaide coupable et le montant total exigible est joint à la présente (suivre les instructions figurant sur « l'avis de paiement »).*

Signature Signature

OPTION 2

Plea of Guilty – Submissions as to Penalty: I want to appear before a justice to enter a plea of guilty and make submissions as to penalty (amount of fine or time to pay). **Note: You must attend** the court office shown below within the times and days shown. Bring this notice with you.

***Plaidoyer de culpabilité – Observations au sujet de la peine** : Je désire comparaître devant un juge pour inscrire un plaidoyer de culpabilité et présenter des observations au sujet de la peine (montant de l'amende ou délai de paiement). **Remarque : Vous devez vous présenter** au greffe du tribunal ci-après aux dates et heures indiquées. Apportez le présent avis.*

Ontario Court of Justice, Provincial Offences Office
45 Cedar Pointe Drive, Barrie, Ontario
Monday, Tuesday, Wednesday and Thursday 9 a.m. to 12 noon - Telephone (705) 739-4291
Cour de justice de l'Ontario, Bureau des infractions provinciales
45, promenade Cedar Pointe, Barrie (Ontario)
Lundi, Mardis, Mercredi et Jeudi de 9 H à 12 H - Téléphone (705) 739-4291

OPTION 3

Trial Option, Ontario Court of Justice, Provincial Offences Office / *Procès, Cour de justice de l'Ontario, Bureau des infractions provinciales*

The City of Barrie
45 Cedar Pointe Drive
Barrie ON L4N 5R7

Ville de Barrie
45, promenade Cedar Pointe
Barrie ON L4N 5R7

Notice of intention to appear in court:
☐ I intend to appear in court to enter a plea of not guilty **at the time and place set for the trial** and I wish to have the trial conducted in the English language.

I request a ________ language interpreter for the trial. (Leave blank if inapplicable).

☐ I intend to challenge the evidence of the Provincial Offences Officer. I request that the officer attend the trial.

If you fail to notify the **court office** of address changes, you may not receive important notices (e.g., your Notice of Trial). You may be convicted in your absence if you do not attend the trial.

Signature ________

Avis d'intention de comparaître devant le tribunal :
*☐ J'ai l'intention de comparaître devant le tribunal pour inscrire un plaidoyer de non-culpabilité à **l'heure et au lieu prévus pour le procès** et je désire que le procès se déroule en français.*

Je demande l'aide d'un interprète de langue ________ pour le procès. (À remplir s'il y a lieu.)

☐ J'ai l'intention de contester la preuve de l'agent des infractions provinciales. Je demande que l'agent assiste au procès.

*Si vous omettez de prévenir le **greffe du tribunal** de tout changement d'adresse, vous pourriez ne pas recevoir d'importants avis (par ex., votre avis de procès). Si vous n'assistez pas au procès, vous pourriez être déclaré(e) coupable en votre absence.*

Signature ________

Changes to your address (if applicable). Address / ***Changement d'adresse (le cas échéant).*** *Adresse*

Representative's name and address (if applicable) / ***Nom et adresse du représentant** (le cas échéant)*

FIGURE 3 Computer Input

ICON Location Code
Code d'emplacement du RIII
3860

Offence Number
N° d'infraction
6571079A

Computer Input/Record Document
Entrées informatiques/Registre des documents

Believes and certifies that on the day of
Croit et atteste que le

(Print name/*nom en lettres moulées*)

Y/A 2 0 M/M D/J Time/ *À (Heure)* M

Name
Nom

Family/*Nom de famille*

Given/*Prénom* Initials/*Initiales*

Address
Adresse

Number and street/*Numéro et nom de la rue*

Municipality/*Municipalité* P.O./*C.P.* Province Postal code/*Code postal*

Driver's licence No./*Numéro de permis de conduire* Juris *Aut. lég.*

Birthdate/*Date de naissance* Y/A 1 9 M/M D/J

Sex *Sexe*

Motor Vehicle Involved *Véhicule impliqué* ☐ N/N

Collision Involved *Collision* ☐ Y/O

Witnesses *Témoins* ☐ Y/O

At/À

Municipality/*Municipalité*

Did commit the offence of:
A commis l'infraction de :

Contrary to:
Contrairement à :

Sect./*L'art.*

Plate number *N° de plaque d'immatriculation*	Juris *Aut. lég.*	Commercial *Utilitaire* ☐ Y/O	CVOR/*IUVU* ☐ Y/O	NSC/CNS ☐ Y/O	Code

CVOR No. - NSC No. / *N° de l'IUVU - N° du CNS*

And I further certify that I served an offence notice personally upon the person charged on the offence date.
J'atteste également qu'à la date de l'infraction, j'ai signifié, en mains propres, un avis d'infraction à la personne accusée.

☐ Or other service date of:
Autre date de signification, le :

Signature of issuing Provincial Offences Officer *Signature de l'agent des infractions provinciales*	Officer No. *N° de l'agent*	Platoon *Peloton*	Unit *Unité*

Set fine of *Amende fixée de* $ $	**Total payable** $ $ ***Montant total exigible***	Total payable includes set fine, applicable victim fine surcharge and costs. *Le montant total exigible comprend l'amende fixée, la suramende compensatoire applicable et les frais.*

Summons issued. You are required to appear in court on
Assignation. *Vous êtes tenu(e) de comparaître devant le tribunal le*

Y/A 2 0 M/M D/J Time / *À (Heure)* M

Ct. room/*Salle d'audience*

FIGURE 4 Enforcement Agency Record/Enforcement Agency Notes

ICON Location Code / Code d'emplacement du RIII 3860
Offence Number / N° d'infraction 6571079A

Provincial Offences Act Ontario Court of Justice
Loi sur les infractions provinciales *Cour de justice de l'Ontario*

Enforcement Agency Record/ ***Registre des documents de l'agence d'exécution***

Believes and certifies that on the day of / *Croit et atteste que le* (Print name/*nom en lettres moulées*)
Y/A 2 0 M/M D/J Time/ *À (Heure)* M

Name / *Nom*
Family/*Nom de famille*
Given/*Prénom* Initials/*Initiales*

Address / *Adresse*
Number and street/*Numéro et nom de la rue*
Municipality/*Municipalité* P.O./*C.P.* Province Postal code/*Code postal*

Driver's licence No./*Numéro de permis de conduire* Juris / *Aut. lég.*

Birthdate/*Date de naissance* Y/A 1 9 M/M D/J
Sex / *Sexe*
Motor Vehicle Involved / *Véhicule impliqué* N/N
Collision Involved / *Collision* Y/O
Witnesses / *Témoins* Y/O

At/*À*
Municipality/*Municipalité*

Did commit the offence of:
A commis l'infraction de :

Contrary to:
Contrairement à :

Sect./*L'art.*

Plate number / *N° de plaque d'immatriculation*	Juris / *Aut. lég.*	Commercial / *Utilitaire*	CVOR/*IUVU*	NSC/CNS	Code
		Y/O	Y/O	Y/O	

CVOR No. - NSC No. / *N° de l'IUVU - N° du CNS*

And I further certify that I served an offence notice personally upon the person charged on the offence date.
J'atteste également qu'à la date de l'infraction, j'ai signifié, en mains propres, un avis d'infraction à la personne accusée.

Or other service date of:
Autre date de signification, le :

Signature of issuing Provincial Offences Officer / *Signature de l'agent des infractions provinciales*	Officer No. / *N° de l'agent*	Platoon / *Peloton*	Unit / *Unité*

Set fine of / *Amende fixée de* $ ¢
Total payable $ ¢ ***Montant total exigible***
Total payable includes set fine, applicable victim fine surcharge and costs.
Le montant total exigible comprend l'amende fixée, la suramende compensatoire applicable et les frais.

Summons issued. You are required to appear in court on
Assignation. *Vous êtes tenu(e) de comparaître devant le tribunal le*
Y/A 2 0 M/M D/J Time / *À (Heure)* M
Ct. room/*Salle d'audience* at the Ontario Court of Justice P.O.A. Office at
à la Cour de justice de l'Ontario, Bureau des infractions provinciales au

Enforcement Agency notes/*Notes de l'agence d'exécution*

FIGURE 5 Payment Notice

Remember to keep a record of this payment.
N'oubliez pas de conserver un reçu de paiement.

Sign the plea of guilty on the offence notice (Option 1) and mail the offence notice with this payment notice to

Veuillez signer le plaidoyer de culpabilité sur l'avis d'infraction (Option 1) et adresser l'avis d'infraction accompagné de l'avis de paiement à l'adresse suivante

Pay to:

ONTARIO COURT OF JUSTICE
PROVINCIAL OFFENCES OFFICE
THE CITY OF BARRIE
45 CEDAR POINTE DRIVE
BARRIE ON L4N 5R7

Payez À:

COUR DE JUSTICE DE L'ONTARIO
BUREAU DES INFRACTIONS PROVINCIALES
VILLE DE BARRIE
45, PROMENADE CEDAR POINTE
BARRIE ON L4N 5R7

6571079A

OFFENCE NUMBER
No D'INFRACTION

Provincial Offences Act, Ontario Court of Justice
Loi sur les infractions provinciales Cour de justice de l'Ontario

Payment Notice/Avis de Paiement

To pay the total payable shown, forward your payment of the total payable with this notice and the offence notice to the address shown on this notice. Sign the plea of guilty on the offence notice (Option 1).

Pour acquitter le montant total exigible, faites parvenir votre paiement, accompagné de cet avis et de l'avis d'infraction, à l'adresse qui figure sur le présent avis. N'oubliez pas de signer le plaidoyer de culpabilité sur l'avis d'infraction (Option 1).

Complete the following information / ***Veuillez donner les renseignements suivants***

Name/*Nom* ______

Address/*Adresse* ______

______

Telephone/*Téléphone* ______

☐ Cheque/money order enclosed *Chèque/mandat joint* ☐ Visa ☐ Master Card

Card number *Nº de carte* ______

Card expiry date *Date d'expiration* (month) *(mois)* ______ (year) *(année)* ______

3860

See back for mailing address and instructions / *Pour connaître l'adresse postale et les instructions, prière de voir au verso.*

Make cheque or money order payable to
The City of Barrie
and write the number of the offence notice on the front of the cheque/money order. Do not send cash or post-dated cheques with your payment. If you have any questions, call **705-739-4291**.

Dishonoured cheques will be subject to an administrative charge and the amount may be referred to collection services.

Faire un chèque ou mandat à l'ordre du
La Ville de Barrie
et écrire le numéro d'avis d'infraction au recto du chèque/mandat. Ne pas envoyer d'espèces ou de chèques postdatés avec votre paiement. Pour plus de renseignements, composez le ***705-739-4291.***

Les chèques impayés sont assujettis à des frais administratifs et les renseignements concernant le montant impayé peuvent être transmis au service de recouvrement.

Cardholder's name
Nom du détenteur de la carte ______

Cardholder's signature
Signature du détenteur de la carte ______

Total Payable
Montant total exigible $ ______ $

Date of Offence:
Date de l'infraction : ______

Online Payment Option
www.paytickets.ca

Option de paiement en ligne
www.paietickets.ca

FIGURE 6 Summons (pink)

ICON Location Code
Code d'emplacement du RIII 3860

Form 6 Reg. 950 *Provincial Offences Act* Ontario Court of Justice
Formule 6 Règl. 950 Loi sur les infractions provinciales Cour de justice de l'Ontario

Summons / *Assignation*

Believes and certifies that on the day of
Croit et atteste que le

(Print name/*nom en lettres moulées*)

Y/A M/M D/J Time/ *À (Heure)*

2 0 M

Name
Nom

Family/*Nom de famille*

Given/*Prénom* Initials/*Initiales*

Address
Adresse

Number and street/*Numéro et nom de la rue*

Municipality/*Municipalité* P.O./*C.P.* Province Postal code/*Code postal*

Driver's licence No./*Numéro de permis de conduire*

Birthdate/*Date de naissance*
Y/A M/M D/J
1 9

Sex / *Sexe*

Motor Vehicle Involved / *Véhicule impliqué* ☐ N/N

Collision Involved / *Collision* ☐ Y/O

Witnesses / *Témoins* ☐ Y/O

At/*À*

Municipality/*Municipalité*

Did commit the offence of:
A commis l'infraction de :

Contrary to:
Contrairement à :

Sect./*L'art.*

Plate number *N° de plaque d'immatriculation*	Juris *Aut. lég.*	Commercial *Utilitaire*	CVOR/*IUVU*	NSC/CNS	Code
		☐ Y/O	☐ Y/O	☐ Y/O	

CVOR No. - NSC No. / *N° de l'IUVU - N° du CNS*

This is therefore to command you in Her Majesty's name to appear before the Ontario Court of Justice.
Pour ces motifs, il vous est enjoint, au nom de Sa Majesté, de comparaître devant la Cour de justice de l'Ontario.

Officer No. *N° de l'agent*	Platoon *Peloton*	Unit *Unité*

Y/A M/M D/J Time / *À (Heure)*

2 0 M

Ct. room/*Salle d'audience* at the Ontario Court of Justice P.O.A. Office at
à la Cour de justice de l'Ontario, Bureau des infractions provinciales au
45 Cedar Pointe Drive, Barrie, Ontario
45, promenade Cedar Pointe, Barrie (Ontario)

And to attend thereafter as required by the court in order to be dealt with according to law. this summons is served under Part I of the *Provincial Offences Act*.
Et d'être présent(e) par la suite selon les exigences du tribunal, afin d'être traité(e) selon la loi. La presente assignation vous est signifiée conformément à la partie I de la Loi sur les infractions provinciales.

Signature of Provincial Offences Officer
Signature de l'agent des infractions provinciales

Note to defendant

You are required to appear in court. You may appear personally or by representative.

When you appear you may:

(A) Plead guilty to the offence
or
(B) Set a date for trial
or
(C) The trial may proceed.

If you do not appear:

(A) The court may issue a warrant for your arrest
or
(B) The trial may proceed in your absence.

Remarque à l'intention du défendeur/de la défenderesse

Vous êtes tenu(e) de comparaître devant le tribunal. Vous pouvez comparaître en personne ou par représentant.

Lors de votre comparution :

(A) soit vous pouvez plaider coupable à l'infraction;
(B) soit vous pouvez fixer une date de procès;
(C) soit le procès peut avoir lieu.

Si vous ne comparaissez pas :

(A) soit le tribunal peut décerner un mandat d'arrestation contre vous;
(B) soit le procès peut avoir lieu en votre absence.

For information on access to Ontario Courts
for persons with disabilities, call **705-739-4291**

Pour plus de renseignements sur l'accès des personnes handicapées aux tribunaux de l'Ontario, composez le ***705-739-4291***

FIGURE 7 Annotated Form 3: Offence Notice—Original Signature

ICON Location Code
Code d'emplacement du RIII 3860
Offence Number
N° d'infraction 6571079A

Form 3 Reg. 950 *Provincial Offences Act* Ontario Court of Justice
Formule 3 Règl. 950 Loi sur les infractions provinciales *Cour de justice de l'Ontario*

Offence Notice / *Avis d'infraction*

Believes and certifies that on the day of
Croit et atteste que le
(Print name/nom en lettres moulées)
Y/A 2 0 M/M D/J Time/ *À (Heure)* M

Name
Nom
Family/*Nom de famille*
Given/*Prénom* Initials/*Initiales*

Address
Adresse
Number and street/*Numéro et nom de la rue*
Municipality/*Municipalité* P.O./C.P. Province Postal code/*Code postal*

Driver's licence No./*Numéro de permis de conduire*

Birthdate/*Date de naissance* Y/A 1 9 M/M D/J
Sex *Sexe*
Motor Vehicle Involved *Véhicule impliqué* ☐ N/N
Collision Involved *Collision* ☐ Y/O
Witnesses *Témoins* ☐ Y/O

At/*À*

Municipality/*Municipalité*

Did commit the offence of:
A commis l'infraction de :

Contrary to:
Contrairement à :

Sect./*L'art.*

Plate number *N° de plaque d'immatriculation* | Juris *Aut. lég.* | Commercial *Utilitaire* ☐ Y/O | CVOR/*IUVU* ☐ Y/O | NSC/CNS ☐ Y/O | Code

CVOR No. - NSC No. / *N° de l'IUVU - N° du CNS*

And I further certify that I served an offence notice personally upon the person charged on the offence date.
J'atteste également qu'à la date de l'infraction, j'ai signifié, en mains propres, un avis d'infraction à la personne accusée.

☐ Or other service date of:
Autre date de signification, le :

Signature of issuing Provincial Offences Officer
Signature de l'agent des infractions provinciales
Officer No. *N° de l'agent* | Platoon *Peloton* | Unit *Unité*

Set fine of *Amende fixée de* $
Total payable $ **Montant total exigible** $
Total payable includes set fine, applicable victim fine surcharge and costs.
Le montant total exigible comprend l'amende fixée, la suramende compensatoire applicable et les frais.

Important:
You have 15 days from the day you receive this notice to choose one of the options on the back of the notice.

Important :
À compter de la réception du présent avis, vous avez 15 jours pour choisir une des options décrites au verso de l'avis.

Date of service if other than offence date
Date de la signification de l'avis si elle diffère de celle de l'infraction
Y/A M/M D/J

This section does not need to be original.

When all the forms are still together, the officer fills out everything except the signature. This offence notice (Form 3, the yellow copy) is removed from the snap set, signed (the signature must be original), and served to the defendant before the face of the ticket (Form 1, Certificate of Offence) is signed.

FIGURE 8 Annotated Form 1: Certificate of Offence—Officer Information

ICON Location Code / Code d'emplacement du RIII **3860**

Offence Number / N° d'infraction **6571079A**

Form 1 Reg. 950 *Provincial Offences Act* Ontario Court of Justice
Formule 1 Règl. 950 Loi sur les infractions provinciales *Cour de justice de l'Ontario*

Certificate of Offence / *Procès-verbal d'infraction*

I/Je soussigné(e) ← Officer's name.

(Print name/nom en lettres moulées)

Believe and certify that on the day of / *Crois et atteste que le* — Y/A 2 0 — M/M — D/J — Time/ *À (Heure)* — M

Name / *Nom* — Family/*Nom de famille* — Given/*Prénom* — Initials/*Initiales*

Address / *Adresse* — Number and street/*Numéro et nom de la rue*

Municipality/*Municipalité* — P.O./C.P. — Province — Postal code/*Code postal*

Driver's licence No./*Numéro de permis de conduire* — Juris / *Aut. lég.*

Birthdate/*Date de naissance* Y/A 1 9 — M/M — D/J — Sex / *Sexe* — Motor Vehicle Involved / *Véhicule impliqué* ☐ N/N — Collision Involved / *Collision* ☐ Y/O — Witnesses / *Témoins* ☐ Y/O

At/*À*

Municipality/*Municipalité*

Did commit the offence of:
A commis l'infraction de :

Contrary to:
Contrairement à :

Sect./*L'art.*

Plate number / *N° de plaque d'immatriculation*	Juris / *Aut. lég.*	Commercial / *Utilitaire*	CVOR/*IUVU*	NSC/CNS	Code
		☐ Y/O	☐ Y/O	☐ Y/O	

CVOR No. - NSC No. / *N° de l'IUVU - N° du CNS*

And I further certify that I served an offence notice personally upon the person charged on the offence date.
J'atteste également qu'à la date de l'infraction, j'ai signifié, en mains propres, un avis d'infraction à la personne accusée.

☐ Or other service date of:
Autre date de signification, le :

Signature of issuing Provincial Offences Officer / *Signature de l'agent des infractions provinciales*	Officer No. / *N° de l'agent*	Platoon / *Peloton*	Unit / *Unité*

← Officer's badge number, platoon, and unit.

← NOTE: Officer signs Certificate of Offence (Form 1) *after* the Offence Notice (Form 3, the yellow copy) has been signed and served on the defendant.

Set fine of / *Amende fixée de*	**Total payable**	Total payable includes set fine, applicable victim fine surcharge and costs.
$ $	$ $ **Montant total exigible**	*Le montant total exigible comprend l'amende fixée, la suramende compensatoire applicable et les frais.*

Summons Issued. You are required to appear in court on — Y/A 2 0 — M/M — D/J — Time / *À (Heure)* — M
Assignation. *Vous êtes tenu(e) de comparaître devant le tribunal le*

Ct. room/*Salle d'audience* — at the Ontario Court of Justice P.O.A. Office at
à la Cour de justice de l'Ontario, Bureau des infractions provinciales au
45 Cedar Pointe Drive, Barrie, Ontario
45, promenade Cedar Pointe, Barrie (Ontario)

Conviction entered pursuant to section 9 of the *Provincial Offences Act*. Set fine imposed.
Déclaration de culpabilité inscrite conformément à l'article 9 de la Loi sur les infractions provinciales. Amende fixée imposée.
Y/A 2 0 — M/M — D/J

03-568

Justice/*Juge*

POA 6000 v.1 rev. 01/09

The DATA Group of Companies S73059

FIGURE 9 Annotated Form 1: Certificate of Offence—Offence Information

ICON Location Code / Code d'emplacement du RIII 3860

Offence Number / Nº d'infraction 6571079A

Form 1 Reg. 950 *Provincial Offences Act* Ontario Court of Justice
Formule 1 Règl. 950 Loi sur les infractions provinciales *Cour de justice de l'Ontario*

Certificate of Offence / *Procès-verbal d'infraction*

I/Je soussigné(e)

(Print name/nom en lettres moulées)

Believe and certify that on the day of / *Crois et atteste que le* — Y/A 2 0 — M/M — D/J — Time/ *À (Heure)* M ← Date and time of offence.

Name / *Nom* — Family/*Nom de famille* — Given/*Prénom* — Initials/*Initiales*

Address / *Adresse* — Number and street/*Numéro et nom de la rue*

Municipality/*Municipalité* — P.O./C.P. — Province — Postal code/*Code postal*

Driver's licence No./*Numéro de permis de conduire* — Juris. *Aut. lég.*

Birthdate/*Date de naissance* Y/A 1 9 M/M D/J — Sex *Sexe* — Motor Vehicle Involved *Véhicule impliqué* N/N — Collision Involved *Collision* Y/O — Witnesses *Témoins* Y/O

At/*À* — Municipality/*Municipalité* ← Location of offence.

Did commit the offence of: / *A commis l'infraction de :* ← Short-form wording of the offence (consult a wording and fines book).

Contrary to: / *Contrairement à :* — Sect./*L'art.* ← Statute and the section for the offence.

Plate number *Nº de plaque d'immatriculation*	Juris *Aut. lég.*	Commercial *Utilitaire*	CVOR/*IUVU*	NSC/CNS	Code
		Y/O	Y/O	Y/O	

CVOR No. - NSC No. / *Nº de l'IUVU - Nº du CNS*

And I further certify that I served an offence notice personally upon the person charged on the offence date.
J'atteste également qu'à la date de l'infraction, j'ai signifié, en mains propres, un avis d'infraction à la personne accusée.

Or other service date of: / *Autre date de signification, le :*

Signature of issuing Provincial Offences Officer *Signature de l'agent des infractions provinciales*	Officer No. *Nº de l'agent*	Platoon *Peloton*	Unit *Unité*

Set fine of *Amende fixée de*	Total payable *Montant total exigible*	
$ $	$ $	Total payable includes set fine, applicable victim fine surcharge and costs. *Le montant total exigible comprend l'amende fixée, la suramende compensatoire applicable et les frais.*

Summons issued. You are required to appear in court on — Y/A 2 0 — M/M — D/J — Time / *À (Heure)* M
Assignation. *Vous êtes tenu(e) de comparaître devant le tribunal le*

Ct. room/*Salle d'audience* — at the Ontario Court of Justice P.O.A. Office at *à la Cour de justice de l'Ontario, Bureau des infractions provinciales au*
45 Cedar Pointe Drive, Barrie, Ontario
45, promenade Cedar Pointe, Barrie (Ontario)

Conviction entered pursuant to section 9 of the *Provincial Offences Act*. Set fine imposed.
Déclaration de culpabilité inscrite conformément à l'article 9 de la Loi sur les infractions provinciales. Amende fixée imposée.

Y/A 2 0 — M/M — D/J

03-588

Justice/*Juge*

POA 6000 v.1 rev. 01/09

The DATA Group of Companies S73059

FIGURE 10 Annotated Form 1: Certificate of Offence—Defendant Information

ICON Location Code / Code d'emplacement du RIII 3860
Offence Number / N° d'infraction 6571079A

Form 1 Reg. 950 *Provincial Offences Act* Ontario Court of Justice
Formule 1 Règl. 950 Loi sur les infractions provinciales *Cour de justice de l'Ontario*

Certificate of Offence / *Procès-verbal d'infraction*

I/Je soussigné(e)

(Print name/nom en lettres moulées)

Believe and certify that on the day of / *Crois et atteste que le* — Y/A 2 0 — M/M — D/J — Time/ *À (Heure)* M

Name / *Nom* — Family/*Nom de famille* — Given/*Prénom* — Initials/*Initiales*

Defendant's name.

Address / *Adresse* — Number and street/*Numéro et nom de la rue* — Municipality/*Municipalité* — P.O./*C.P.* — Province — Postal code/*Code postal*

Defendant's address.

Driver's licence No./*Numéro de permis de conduire* — Juris / *Aut. lég.*

Jurisdiction where driver's licence was issued (e.g., for Ontario write "ON").

Birthdate/*Date de naissance* Y/A 1 9 — M/M — D/J — Sex / *Sexe* — Motor Vehicle Involved / *Véhicule impliqué* N/N — Collision Involved / *Collision* Y/O — Witnesses / *Témoins* Y/O

Defendant's driver's licence number.

Defendant's date of birth.

At/*À*

Municipality/*Municipalité*

Did commit the offence of:
A commis l'infraction de :

Contrary to:
Contrairement à :

Sect./*L'art.*

Plate number / *N° de plaque d'immatriculation*	Juris / *Aut. lég.*	Commercial / *Utilitaire*	CVOR/*IUVU*	NSC/CNS	Code
		Y/O	Y/O	Y/O	

CVOR No. - NSC No. / *N° de l'IUVU - N° du CNS*

And I further certify that I served an offence notice personally upon the person charged on the offence date.
J'atteste également qu'à la date de l'infraction, j'ai signifié, en mains propres, un avis d'infraction à la personne accusée.

Or other service date of:
Autre date de signification, le :

Signature of issuing Provincial Offences Officer / *Signature de l'agent des infractions provinciales*	Officer No. / *N° de l'agent*	Platoon / *Peloton*	Unit / *Unité*

Set fine of / *Amende fixée de*	**Total payable** / ***Montant total exigible***	
$ $	$ $	Total payable includes set fine, applicable victim fine surcharge and costs. *Le montant total exigible comprend l'amende fixée, la suramende compensatoire applicable et les frais.*

Summons Issued. You are required to appear in court on
Assignation. *Vous êtes tenu(e) de comparaître devant le tribunal le*
Y/A 2 0 — M/M — D/J — Time / *À (Heure)* M

Ct. room/*Salle d'audience* — at the Ontario Court of Justice P.O.A. Office at
à la Cour de justice de l'Ontario, Bureau des infractions provinciales au
45 Cedar Pointe Drive, Barrie, Ontario
45, promenade Cedar Pointe, Barrie (Ontario)

Conviction entered pursuant to section 9 of the *Provincial Offences Act*. Set fine imposed.
Déclaration de culpabilité inscrite conformément à l'article 9 de la Loi sur les infractions provinciales. Amende fixée imposée.
Y/A 2 0 — M/M — D/J

03-588

Justice/*Juge*

POA 6000 v.1 rev. 01/09

The DATA Group of Companies S73059

FIGURE 11 Annotated Form 1: Certificate of Offence—Vehicle Information

ICON Location Code
Code d'emplacement du RIII
3860

Offence Number
N° d'infraction
6571079A

Form 1 Reg. 950 *Provincial Offences Act* Ontario Court of Justice
Formule 1 Règl. 950 Loi sur les infractions provinciales *Cour de justice de l'Ontario*

Certificate of Offence / *Procès-verbal d'infraction*

I/Je soussigné(e)
(Print name/nom en lettres moulées)

Believe and certify that on the day of
Crois et atteste que le
Y/A 2 0 M/M D/J Time/ *À (Heure)* M

Name
Nom
Family/*Nom de famille*
Given/*Prénom* Initials/*Initiales*

Address
Adresse
Number and street/*Numéro et nom de la rue*
Municipality/*Municipalité* P.O./C.P. Province Postal code/*Code postal*

Driver's licence No./*Numéro de permis de conduire*
Juris *Aut. lég.*

Birthdate/*Date de naissance* Y/A 1 9 M/M D/J
Sex *Sexe*
Motor Vehicle Involved *Véhicule impliqué* ☐ N/N
Collision Involved *Collision* ☐ Y/O
Witnesses *Témoins* ☐ Y/O

If a vehicle was not involved in the offence, indicate here.

At/*À*
Municipality/*Municipalité*

Did commit the offence of:
A commis l'infraction de :

Contrary to:
Contrairement à :

Sect./*L'art.*

Plate number
N° de plaque d'immatriculation
Juris *Aut. lég.*
Commercial *Utilitaire* ☐ Y/O
CVOR/*IUVU* ☐ Y/O
NSC/CNS ☐ Y/O
Code

Vehicle's plate number.

Jurisdiction where driver's licence was issued (e.g., for Ontario write "ON").

CVOR No. - NSC No. / *N° de l'IUVU - N° du CNS*

And I further certify that I served an offence notice personally upon the person charged on the offence date.
J'atteste également qu'à la date de l'infraction, j'ai signifié, en mains propres, un avis d'infraction à la personne accusée.

☐ Or other service date of:
Autre date de signification, le :

Signature of issuing Provincial Offences Officer
Signature de l'agent des infractions provinciales
Officer No. *N° de l'agent*
Platoon *Peloton*
Unit *Unité*

Set fine of
Amende fixée de
$ $

Total payable
$ $
Montant total exigible

Total payable includes set fine, applicable victim fine surcharge and costs.
Le montant total exigible comprend l'amende fixée, la suramende compensatoire applicable et les frais.

Summons issued.
You are required to appear in court on
Assignation.
Vous êtes tenu(e) de comparaître devant le tribunal le
Y/A 2 0 M/M D/J Time / *À (Heure)* M

Ct. room/*Salle d'audience*
at the Ontario Court of Justice P.O.A. Office at
à la Cour de justice de l'Ontario, Bureau des infractions provinciales au
45 Cedar Pointe Drive, Barrie, Ontario
45, promenade Cedar Pointe, Barrie (Ontario)

Conviction entered pursuant to section 9 of the *Provincial Offences Act*. Set fine imposed.
Déclaration de culpabilité inscrite conformément à l'article 9 de la Loi sur les infractions provinciales. Amende fixée imposée.
Y/A 2 0 M/M D/J

03-588

Justice/*Juge*

POA 6000 v.1 rev. 01/09

The DATA Group of Companies S73059

FIGURE 12 Annotated Form 1: Certificate of Offence—Out-of-Court Settlement

ICON Location Code
Code d'emplacement du RIII 3860
Offence Number
N° d'infraction 6571079A

Form 1 Reg. 950 *Provincial Offences Act* Ontario Court of Justice
Formule 1 Règl. 950 Loi sur les infractions provinciales *Cour de justice de l'Ontario*

Certificate of Offence / *Procès-verbal d'infraction*

I/Je soussigné(e)

(Print name/nom en lettres moulées)

Believe and certify that on the day of
Crois et atteste que le
Y/A 2 0 M/M D/J Time/ *À (Heure)* M

Name
Nom
Family/*Nom de famille*
Given/*Prénom* Initials/*Initiales*

Address
Adresse
Number and street/*Numéro et nom de la rue*

Municipality/*Municipalité* P.O./C.P. Province Postal code/*Code postal*

Driver's licence No./*Numéro de permis de conduire* Juris *Aut. lég.*

Birthdate/*Date de naissance* Y/A 1 9 M/M D/J
Sex *Sexe*
Motor Vehicle Involved *Véhicule impliqué* N/N
Collision Involved *Collision* Y/O
Witnesses *Témoins* Y/O

At/À

Municipality/*Municipalité*

Did commit the offence of:
A commis l'infraction de :

Contrary to:
Contrairement à :

Sect./*L'art.*

Plate number *N° de plaque d'immatriculation*	Juris *Aut. lég.*	Commercial *Utilitaire*	CVOR/*IUVU*	NSC/CNS	Code
		Y/O	Y/O	Y/O	

CVOR No. - NSC No. / *N° de l'IUVU - N° du CNS*

And I further certify that I served an offence notice personally upon the person charged on the offence date.
J'atteste également qu'à la date de l'infraction, j'ai signifié, en mains propres, un avis d'infraction à la personne accusée.

Or other service date of:
Autre date de signification, le :

Signature of issuing Provincial Offences Officer
Signature de l'agent des infractions provinciales
Officer No. *N° de l'agent* Platoon *Peloton* Unit *Unité*

Set fine of
Amende fixée de
$

Total payable
$
Montant total exigible

Total payable includes set fine, applicable victim fine surcharge and costs.
Le montant total exigible comprend l'amende fixée, la suramende compensatoire applicable et les frais.

Summons issued. You are required to appear in court on
Assignation. *Vous êtes tenu(e) de comparaître devant le tribunal le*
Y/A 2 0 M/M D/J Time / *À (Heure)* M

Ct. room/*Salle d'audience* at the Ontario Court of Justice P.O.A. Office at
à la Cour de justice de l'Ontario, Bureau des infractions provinciales au
45 Cedar Pointe Drive, Barrie, Ontario
45, promenade Cedar Pointe, Barrie (Ontario)

Conviction entered pursuant to section 9 of the Provincial Offences Act. Set fine imposed.
Déclaration de culpabilité inscrite conformément à l'article 9 de la Loi sur les infractions provinciales. Amende fixe imposée.
Y/A 2 0 M/M D/J

03-588

Justice/*Juge*

POA 6000 v.1 rev. 01/09

The DATA Group of Companies 573050

This value is the fine amount assigned to the offence (consult a wordings and fines book).

The total fine consists of the set fine for the offence, the victim surcharge amount according to the sliding scale in the workings and fines book, and court charges.

If the offence involves a community safety zone speedng offence, the total fine represents the set fine from the community safety zone fine chart (higher than regular speeding fines), the victim surcharge amount, and court charges.

FIGURE 13 Annotated Form 1: Certificate of Offence—Mandatory Court Appearance

ICON Location Code
Code d'emplacement du RIII 3860

Offence Number
N° d'infraction 6571079A

Form 1 Reg. 950 *Provincial Offences Act* Ontario Court of Justice
Formule 1 Règl. 950 Loi sur les infractions provinciales Cour de justice de l'Ontario

Certificate of Offence / *Procès-verbal d'infraction*

I/Je soussigné(e)
(Print name/*nom en lettres moulées*)

Believe and certify that on the day of
Crois et atteste que le
Y/A 2 0 M/M D/J Time/ *À (Heure)* M

Name
Nom
Family/*Nom de famille*
Given/*Prénom* Initials/*Initiales*

Address
Adresse
Number and street/*Numéro et nom de la rue*
Municipality/*Municipalité* P.O./C.P. Province Postal code/*Code postal*

Driver's licence No./*Numéro de permis de conduire*
Juris *Aut. lég.*

Birthdate/*Date de naissance* Y/A 1 9 M/M D/J
Sex *Sexe*
Motor Vehicle Involved *Véhicule impliqué* ☐ N/N
Collision Involved *Collision* ☐ Y/O
Witnesses *Témoins* ☐ Y/O

At/*À*
Municipality/*Municipalité*

Did commit the offence of:
A commis l'infraction de :

Contrary to:
Contrairement à :

Sect./*L'art.*

Plate number *N° de plaque d'immatriculation*
Juris *Aut. lég.*
Commercial *Utilitaire* ☐ Y/O
CVOR/*IUVU* ☐ Y/O
NSC/CNS ☐ Y/O
Code

CVOR No. - NSC No. / *N° de l'IUVU - N° du CNS*

And I further certify that I served an offence notice personally upon the person charged on the offence date.
J'atteste également qu'à la date de l'infraction, j'ai signifié, en mains propres, un avis d'infraction à la personne accusée.
☐ Or other service date of:
Autre date de signification, le :

Signature of issuing Provincial Offences Officer
Signature de l'agent des infractions provinciales
Officer No. *N° de l'agent*
Platoon *Peloton*
Unit *Unité*

Set fine of
Amende fixée de
$ $
Total payable
$ $
Montant total exigible
Total payable includes set fine, applicable victim fine surcharge and costs.
Le montant total exigible comprend l'amende fixée, la suramende compensatoire applicable et les frais.

Summons issued.
You are required to appear in court on
Y/A 2 0 M/M D/J Time / *À (Heure)* M
Assignation.
Vous êtes tenu(e) de comparaître devant le tribunal le
Ct. room/*Salle d'audience*
at the Ontario Court of Justice ~~P.O.A. Office~~ at
à la Cour de justice de l'Ontario, ~~*Bureau des infractions provinciales*~~ *au*
45 Cedar Pointe Drive, Barrie, Ontario
45, promenade Cedar Pointe, Barrie (Ontario)

Conviction entered pursuant to section 9 of the *Provincial Offences Act.* Set fine imposed.
Déclaration de culpabilité inscrite conformément à l'article 9 de la Loi sur les infractions provinciales. Amende fixée imposée.
Y/A 2 0 M/M D/J

Justice/*Juge*

03-588

POA 6000 v.1 rev. 01/09

The DATA Group of Companies S73059

When the court appearance information is entered, the fine boxes should be crossed out.

These notations indicate court appearance information.

FIGURE 14 Annotated Form 1: Certificate of Offence—Elements of a Driver's Licence Number

ICON Location Code / Code d'emplacement du RIII 3860
Offence Number / N° d'infraction 6571079A

Form 1 Reg. 950 *Provincial Offences Act* Ontario Court of Justice
Formule 1 Règl. 950 Loi sur les infractions provinciales *Cour de justice de l'Ontario*

Certificate of Offence / *Procès-verbal d'infraction*

I/Je soussigné(e)
(Print name/nom en lettres moulées)

Believe and certify that on the day of / *Crois et atteste que le* Y/A 2 0 M/M D/J Time/ *À (Heure)* M

Name / *Nom*
Family/*Nom de famille*
Given/*Prénom* Initials/*Initiales*

Address / *Adresse*
Number and street/*Numéro et nom de la rue*
Municipality/*Municipalité* P.O./C.P. Province Postal code/*Code postal*

Driver's licence No./*Numéro de permis de conduire* Juris *Aut. lég.*

M0162 37655 10512

Birthdate/*Date de naissance* Y/A 1 9 M/M D/J | Sex *Sexe* | Motor Vehicle Involved *Véhicule impliqué* N/N | Collision Involved *Collision* Y/O | Witnesses *Témoins* Y/O

At/*À*
Municipality/*Municipalité*

Did commit the offence of:
A commis l'infraction de :

Contrary to:
Contrairement à :

Sect./*L'art.*

Plate number *N° de plaque d'immatriculation*	Juris *Aut. lég.*	Commercial *Utilitaire*	CVOR/*IUVU*	NSC/CNS	Code
		Y/O	Y/O	Y/O	

CVOR No. - NSC No. / *N° de l'IUVU - N° du CNS*

And I further certify that I served an offence notice personally upon the person charged on the offence date.
J'atteste également qu'à la date de l'infraction, j'ai signifié, en mains propres, un avis d'infraction à la personne accusée.
Or other service date of:
Autre date de signification, le :

Signature of issuing Provincial Offences Officer *Signature de l'agent des infractions provinciales*	Officer No. *N° de l'agent*	Platoon *Peloton*	Unit *Unité*

Set fine of *Amende fixée de* $	Total payable $ *Montant total exigible*	Total payable includes set fine, applicable victim fine surcharge and costs. *Le montant total exigible comprend l'amende fixée, la suramende compensatoire applicable et les frais.*

Summons issued. You are required to appear in court on Y/A 2 0 M/M D/J Time / *À (Heure)* M
Assignation. Vous êtes tenu(e) de comparaître devant le tribunal le
Ct. room/*Salle d'audience* at the Ontario Court of Justice P.O.A. Office at
à la Cour de justice de l'Ontario, Bureau des infractions provinciales au
45 Cedar Pointe Drive, Barrie, Ontario
45, promenade Cedar Pointe, Barrie (Ontario)

Conviction entered pursuant to section 9 of the Provincial Offences Act. Set fine imposed.
Déclaration de culpabilité inscrite conformément à l'article 9 de la Loi sur les infractions provinciales. Amende fixée imposée.
Y/A 2 0 M/M D/J

Justice/*Juge* 03-588

POA 6000 v.1 rev. 01/09

The DATA Group of Companies 573059

Owner's initial

The letter ("M" in this case) is the first letter of the owner's surname.

Owner's date of birth (DOB)

The owner's DOB is shown in the last six digits of the driver's licence number. The first two of these digits are the year, the next two are the month, and the last two are the day. For example, the last six digits here (510512) represent the 51st year, the 5th month, and the 12th day—or May 12, 1951.

Owner's sex

The owner's sex is also encoded within these last six digits. A male's DOB is represented as in the example above. For a female's DOB, 50 is added to the digits that represent the month.

Example

Sex: **Male**
DOB: May 12, 1951
Driver's licence number:
M0162 37655 10512

Sex: **Female**
DOB: May 12, 1951
Driver's licence number:
M0162 37655 15512

Because a female's DOB is encoded by adding 50 to the month, it is deciphered by subtracting 50 from the month, as follows:

51 – 50 = 01 = January
52 – 50 = 02 = February
53 – 50 = 03 = March
54 – 50 = 04 = April
55 – 50 = 05 = May
56 – 50 = 06 = June
57 – 50 = 07 = July
58 – 50 = 08 = August
59 – 50 = 09 = September
60 – 50 = 10 = October
61 – 50 = 11 = November
62 – 50 = 12 = December

FIGURE 15 Annotated Certificate of Offence: Sample Enforcement Agency Notes

Enforcement Agency notes/*Notes de l'agence d'exécution*

Notes	Annotation
Wea: warm/dry	Weather notes (always enter).
Rds: good	Road conditions.
Traffic: medium to light	Traffic conditions.
Radar: mobile #3427	Record unit if using radar.
- conduct traffic obs while on patrol	Short-form notes to describe events, purpose of patrol, location, etc.
in a marked unit	
- was travelling s/b on Yonge	
N/O Price - posted 70 kph zone	
- lone on-coming vehicle	
- enter radar at 113 kph	
- pull to right - as vehicle pass	
- U-turn and overtake	
- red lights on	
- driver pulls to right - stop	
- advise driver re: speed on radar	Advise driver of reason and note reply.
- reply: thought perhaps it was	
100 kph zone	
- offer to view radar: declined	Good practice, not mandatory.
- check signs south of location:	Check signs to ensure that all is in order.
in order and postd at 70 kph	
- radar checked at set up and	Note test of radar.
take down: OK	

ASSIGNMENT: PROVINCIAL OFFENCES ACT

From the situations described in the following questions, gather the necessary data required to complete the blank PONs or summons found in the back of the text (it is recommended that you work on copies of these materials, as you will require more for assignments later in the text). To help you visualize the incidents and practise creating diagrams, it is recommended that you create a sketch to illustrate the scenarios described.

You are the officer in these three situations, and your basic information is as follows:

- Badge #3345
- Platoon #2
- Uniform Branch of your police service
- Court date: 2nd Tuesday of every month
- Court time: 0900 hours (9 a.m.)
- Courtroom: #7

Consult a wordings and fines book, such as *Provincial Offences: Wordings and Fines*, for short-form notations.

1. You are conducting traffic observations on an intersection on the 20th of the month in the present year at 1400 hours (2 p.m.). The intersection is that of Pine Street and Grove Street in the city of Barrie. You are parked south of Grove Street, on Pine Street facing north. The intersection is a four-way stop controlled by stop signs. You observe a vehicle approach the intersection. It is travelling eastbound at approximately 45 kph. While approaching the stop sign, the vehicle does not slow and proceeds straight through the intersection. You follow and stop the vehicle after a short distance. When you advise the driver of the violation, he replies that he didn't see the sign and apologizes. He produces the required documents and you prepare a PON for him for the offence of "disobey stop sign—fail to stop." Use his information and the proper wording, section number, and amount(s) of the fine(s). Also complete the officer's notes for this violation:

Driver:	James Robert McCarthy
Home address:	114 Black Oak Rd. Barrie, ON L3M 3T2
Driver's Licence Number:	M0162 37655 10512
Vehicle:	1998 Pontiac Trans Am
Current year val tag for plate:	AAF 175

2. While travelling east on Cundles Road West, you stop at a red light at its intersection with Bayfield Street North. There is a vehicle to your right, in the curb lane, also stopped at the light. As the north and south traffic stops, a green arrow lights for left turns only. The female driver to the right of you attempts to drive through the intersection but almost collides with a vehicle travelling east and turning left onto southbound Bayfield

Street North. She stops suddenly and allows the other vehicle to turn. When the light changes to solid green, she proceeds through the intersection and pulls over. You pull in behind her, get out, and approach the vehicle. She is upset and apologizes; she didn't see the green arrow, and she thought it would turn to a solid green light, which would allow her to proceed. She produces her licence, but she doesn't have anything else. Prepare a PON for her and complete the officer's notes using the following scenario information:

Driver:	Ruth Martin
Home address:	127 4th Street Collingwood, ON L2T 3M5
Driver's licence number:	M0173 61435 45710
Vehicle:	1999 Oldsmobile
Current year val tag for plate:	872 FRR

3. While on foot patrol, you perform a bar check at Nick's Bar and Grill, located at 45 Dunlop Street East in the city of Bradford. At 2130 (9:30 p.m.) the owner approaches you and says that there is a man at the bar who is using profane language and upsetting customers. The owner has told the man twice to finish his drink and leave, but he refuses. The owner asks you to speak to the man and get him to leave. You tell the owner that he must ask the man to leave a third time, but this time you will accompany him. You follow the owner to the bar, and he again tells the man to leave. The patron refuses, saying he is not doing anything wrong and the cops can't make him move, either. At this point, you tell the man he is under arrest for trespassing and take him by the arm. As you escort him out the door, he apologizes and says he didn't want to anger you but the owner was really irritating him. You search him and locate his identification. After running a check on him through the dispatcher, you prepare a summons for him and complete the officer's notes concerning his refusing to leave the bar when directed under the *Liquor Licence Act* using the following information:

Defendant:	James William Knight
Home address:	244 Innisfil Street Barrie, ON L3M 3T2
Date of birth:	May 22, 1972

CHAPTER 2

Liquor Licence Act

INTRODUCTION

The primary tier associated with the *Liquor Licence Act* is enforcement through the issuance of a part I or part III offence notice. Officers also have the power to arrest if an excessive amount of alcohol is consumed in a public setting and safety concerns arise.

An officer enforces laws that regulate people's behaviour. The *Liquor Licence Act* (LLA) controls the possession and consumption of alcohol in Ontario, thereby contributing to the general safety of the province's citizens.

The law has changed over the years, to the satisfaction *and* dissatisfaction of Ontario's citizens. Past laws may be examined in order to appreciate those of the present. At points of interest in these lessons, the history or modification of a particular section is addressed. For example, the legal drinking age at one time was 21 years. It was reduced to 18, then increased to 19 when it was found that high school students abused the law. However, liquor-licensed establishments had already hired a significant number of 18-year-old servers and did not want to relinquish the cheap labour, which is why, today, a person only needs to be 18 in order to work in a bar.

Because LLA laws are regulatory in nature, it stands to reason that not everyone will look upon them positively; moreover, people are not likely to be receptive to officer intervention when they are in apparent contravention of these laws. All officers must be mindful of the fact that liquor alters a person's normal behaviour. Unfortunately, some of these alterations are negative and can result in conflict.

Inspection of the LLA reveals that it does not establish a definition for the terms "intoxicated" or "drunk." Yet some of the powers of arrest clearly include the designation of drunk. In order to keep a reasonable picture of what drunkenness is or may be, one might consider the following general statement: "drunkenness is the state that results when the consumption of alcohol negatively affects a person's motor and mental skills."

The consumption of alcohol may place a person in a position where they may not be able to care for their own safety or that of others, at which point an officer may assume that responsibility. The so-called happy drunk is generally not considered a hazard by officers; however, the abusive and aggressive drunk is a problem and force may have to be used to control that person, which may result in a complaint. People who are under the influence may suffer a memory loss after a night of heavy drinking. It is not uncommon for an officer to be accused of theft by an arrested person who started an evening of drinking with several hundred dollars in their wallet and who finds only a few left the next day.

A number of officers can attest to their shock at being attacked by a drunk who started out as a reasonable person but, when faced with a night in jail, exploded and became a formidable opponent. They have felt resentment at having their integrity challenged by someone who accuses them of stealing a sum of money entrusted to them in the course of an arrest.

Officers must also be aware of a few other concerns relating to this legislation. A licensed premises, such as a hotel or nightclub, is in business to make money predominantly from the sale of liquor. If a licensed premises contravenes the law concerning its licence to operate, it may face charges. These charges may result in the suspension of operation, which in turn means a loss of revenue. When substantial losses are involved, an in-depth court battle may ensue. The officer in charge of such a case may find him- or herself preparing as if it were a serious criminal trial, where every point is likely to be challenged. Therefore, an officer must be conversant with the law and conduct a thorough investigation, which often involves undercover operations over an extended period of time. The other and often more serious concern is for people's safety, whether individuals heavily under the influence of liquor and unable to care for themselves, or innocent citizens whose safety may be compromised by the reckless actions of drunks.

When consumed in large amounts, liquor can place a person at risk of "alcohol poisoning." An officer's recognition of such poisoning may result in medical intervention that could save the person's life. Clearly, the drunk who cannot stand to walk, let alone stay out of traffic, is a danger to him- or herself and to others. An officer encountering this person needs to know the legal alternatives to incarceration, such as detox units. These facilities may be free-standing or part of a hospital and are designed to provide a person an opportunity to recover from problems associated with liquor in a safe environment. An officer must know that detox units are provided for by law, how they operate, and who qualifies to use them.

The traditional remedy for drunk persons has been incarceration in a cell until sober, which has been disastrous. The prisoner has violated a regulatory law by being drunk and posing a danger to someone, including him- or herself. He or she is not a criminal but is being treated as such. Consider the following compounding factors and the subsequent result. Alcohol is a known depressant. Its abuse can have terrible effects, especially when combined with the trauma of being arrested. A usually law-abiding citizen who wakes up in a cell may be depressed and embarrassed. In some instances, these persons hang themselves. The result is devastating not only for the deceased's family but also for the officers involved in the subsequent inquest. Officers who are well trained to deal with such situations stand a better chance of finding a resolution that benefits everyone involved.

Officers must know the law and exercise professional judgment when dealing with situations where liquor is involved. The following words capture the truth with humour: "Very many people drink, very few drink very well." The LLA deals with regulations and offences with which police officers will frequently be confronted. The *Highway Traffic Act* is the only provincial statute cited more often than the LLA.

In terms of practical "street work," situations an officer encounters when dealing with this legislation are known to generate more complaints than other legislation. To avoid complaints, officers must be conversant with the LLA's legislative powers and be knowledgeable of other authorities that suggest alternative action when a situation demands it.

The LLA outlines rules that govern obtaining, possessing, consuming, and delivering liquor. These rules are based on a number of variables:

1. the age of the person (is the person a minor, under 19 years of age?);
2. the location in which the person possesses or consumes or is under the influence of liquor (private place, residence, licensed premises, or public place);
3. the condition of the container (is it sealed, closed, or open?) and what constitutes the actual container; and
4. the type of the liquor and its percentage of alcohol.

TERMINOLOGY

> As mentioned, the LLA does not contain a definition of "drunk." The following is offered here as a guide: "Drunkenness is the state that results when the consumption of alcohol negatively affects a person's motor and mental skills."

To properly understand the legislation contained in the LLA, first spend some time learning the definitions of certain terms. Most of these definitions are found in s. 1, including those for alcohol, beer, permit, sell, spirits, and wine.

Alcohol, Beer, Liquor, Spirits, and Wine

These terms seem interchangeable to some, but, when testifying in court, an officer should have a firm understanding of the differences and similarities among them. Figure 16 shows the relationship among the various terms.

From an examination of the figure, it is apparent that beer, spirits, and wine are particular types of liquor. The simplified differentiation between liquor and alcohol depends on whether the substance is suitable for human consumption. Not all alcohol is designed for human consumption (for example, antifreeze or alcohol in aftershave lotions). A point to remember: all liquor is alcohol, but not all alcohol is liquor.

The definition of liquor is further clarified by examining the alcoholic content of a beverage. For a substance to be subject to the LLA, it must contain in excess of 0.5% alcohol. An example of a beverage containing less than 0.5% alcohol is "Near Beer."

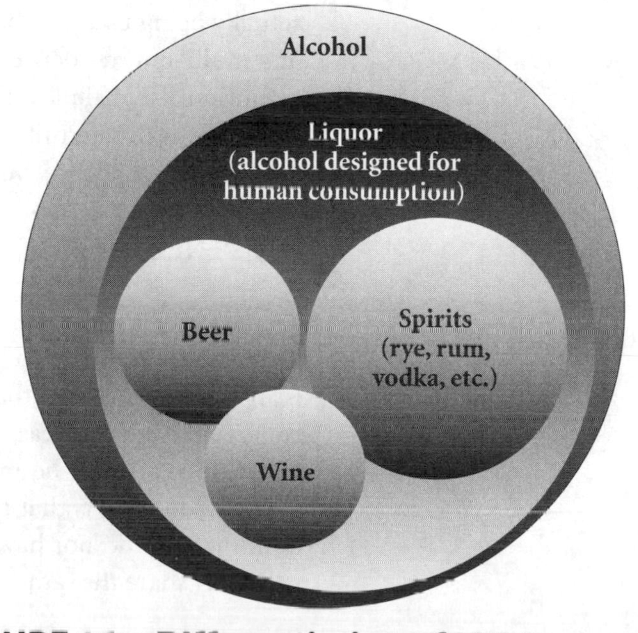

FIGURE 16 Differentiation of LLA Terms

Possession

"Possession" has been defined by the courts and includes the following three essential elements, each of which must be proven to establish that a defendant has, in fact, been in possession of a prohibited substance. The defendant must have

1. *knowledge* of the existence of the substance,
2. *consented* to the possession of the substance, and
3. some level of *control* over the substance.

Private Place

"Private place" is defined in s. 3 of Ontario Regulation 718. This section deals with indoor places, motor vehicles, and boats, which are all considered private places if they meet the regulation's requirements.

Indoor places to which the public is not ordinarily invited or permitted are private places, unless a public invitation is extended. One exception is facilities available for rent by members of the public for occasional use. These facilities are not private places for the purposes of the LLA.

Motor vehicles can be private places if they meet four conditions. First, they must be equipped with sleeping accommodation; second, they must also be equipped with cooking facilities; third, they must be parked off the highway (which is defined in the *Highway Traffic Act* as including the roadway, shoulder, boulevard, and everything between the property lines on either side of it); and fourth, they must actually be used as a residence.

Public Place

"Public place" is not specifically defined in the LLA or the regulations, but we can deduce that any place that does not have the characteristics of a private place is a public place. In addition, a premises or place of business that extends an express or implied invitation to the public to enter or attend is a public place. Examples of an express invitation are signs saying "Come on In," "Exotic Dancers Featured Here," and "Licensed under the LLA," which specifically invite the public to enter Danny's Table Bar, watch exotic dancers, and buy liquor. An example of an implied invitation is Joe's Bar and Grill, which is in business to serve customers; therefore, it can be inferred that the public is invited to spend money there.

Residence

The definition of "residence" is found in s. 31(1) of the LLA and refers to a place actually being used as a bona fide residence, whether it is a single-family residence or a multi-unit residence, such as a rooming house or an apartment building. The definition also includes all facilities provided for the use of residents, provided that the public is not permitted access. This provision would make a tenant parking lot a part of the residence, but a visitors' lot would be a public place.

RESIDENCE EXCEPTIONS

Common Area

As anyone who has tried to learn a second language will attest, for every rule there is an exception. One of the exceptions to multi-occupancy dwellings under the LLA concerns common areas, such as hallways, laundry rooms, or lobbies. A resident is allowed to consume liquor in a common area but cannot be intoxicated there; the rationale for this is that these areas are designated for the use of everyone in the building. You do not have the right to impose your habits or lifestyles on others who may share the same common areas but not the same habits.

Campsite

Other situations where a person of legal age may have liquor are commonsensical. Camping is a very popular pastime. If a tent is set up and intended for use as a residence by the occupant for that night, then it is deemed to be his or her residence. Furthermore, the land around the tent is deemed to be part of the residence. This example addresses the land on which the tent or trailer is set up—one's yard—but not the soccer field down the road. Likewise, people stopped on the shoulder of a highway are not intending to stay there for the night and use that facility as their residence.

Boats

Another popular pastime is boating. Persons travelling in their boat may claim the privileges of a residence concerning liquor under certain circumstances. The vessel can be considered their residence if: (1) it is anchored or moored (that is, not moving), (2) it is equipped with permanent cooking, sleeping, and washroom facilities, and (3) it is the intention of the operators to use the vessel for their residence at this time. A 16-foot fishing boat carrying two fishermen trolling for trout on Georgian Bay is not a residence; therefore, the fishermen may not legally consume alcohol on board.

Sell (and Sale)

The definition of "sell" includes a provision that the seller must recover the cost of the liquor before the definition applies. Therefore, it is imperative to prove this fact if a charge such as bootlegging is levied.

COMMON OFFENCES AND/OR PROVISIONS

Intoxicated in Public Place or Common Area

Probably the most common offence in the LLA is the one laid when a police officer comes across a person who is drunk, or intoxicated by the consumption of liquor. The offence must occur in either a public place or a common area (there is no offence if the person is in a private place). The charge of drunk is simple enough to determine, because most people have experienced or observed those under the influence of alcohol enough to ascertain whether they are drunk. However, the qualifications of a charge of drunk and an arrest for drunk must be examined carefully. For a drunk arrest, the person must (1) display negative symptoms caused by intoxication resulting from the consumption of alcohol (*not* drugs), and (2) be a danger to anyone as a result of these symptoms.

Consider an officer who encounters a person in an intoxicated state on the street and simply issues them an offence notice and sends them on their way. A short distance down the street the person falls off the curb into traffic, where injury or death results. The important questions here are obvious: Did the officer have a duty to safeguard the person, and in not doing so was the officer negligent? What about sending someone home in a cab, or dropping them off at the door of their residence, not knowing whether someone is there who can assume responsibility for the person? The same questions arise when a person is arrested and incarcerated for drunk, and before the subject is sober, an officer releases him and tragedy follows. Was the officer liable for the tragedy and therefore negligent?

Consider further, the same officer arrests the person for drunk. Meanwhile, a number of the person's friends show up and volunteer to take their buddy home. The officer relinquishes the responsibility for the drunk person to his friends. The group is then involved in an altercation, in which the original drunk is injured. It would seem that the officer acted responsibly and is not at risk, except that all the friends were drunk as well. How can one drunk person safely assist another?

It is always wise to arrange for the release of a person who has been arrested for drunk. If he or she is manageable and not violent, and a sober adult known to the subject offers to take responsibility for him or her, an officer should consider this option and have the adult sign his or her memo book or prisoner release form, thereby accepting responsibility for the intoxicated person. Of course, this action is dependent on the policy of the particular police service and the officer in charge.

Alternative to Arrest

An additional provision exists in the legislation for situations involving intoxicated persons. Section 36(1) permits an officer to take an intoxicated person to a hospital designated by the regulations, also known as a detox unit. Generally, the subject must need some supervision and not be violent. The detox staff will ensure that the person sobers up in a safe environment and will then send them on their way. An officer must realize that this action is an alternative to charging an offender with drunk and placing him or her in a cell. A person placed in detox cannot, by law, be charged with drunk or with being intoxicated in a public place or common area.

Unlawful Sale of Liquor

Section 5(1) is clear in stating that the legal sale of liquor may take place only under the authority of a liquor licence or permit issued under a manufacturer's licence. All other sales are illegal.

The unlawful sale of liquor is commonly called "bootlegging." Years ago (and sometimes still in remote areas), bootleggers were well-known entities. The absence of an authorized liquor outlet or restricted hours of operation for an outlet, coupled with a high demand and a ready client base, often led to the success of such entrepreneurs. These two complaints have been mostly remedied by recent changes to the LLA. Franchise liquor outlets may be found in service stations and food stores, and their hours of operation are often the same as those of regular retail outlets.

It is interesting to note the origin of the term "bootlegger." In the past, men at sea and on horse wore high leather boots, often folded down at the top. Small flasks and containers of liquor were carried within these boots and eventually sold, hence the descriptive term.

One problem that still exists despite more lenient laws is the regulation of after-hours clubs. These clubs are found in larger urban areas, where they cater to a subculture that parties well into the next day. Despite the increased legal hours of operation of liquor outlets, such clubs continue to be popular.

After-hours clubs generally are located in industrial or low residential occupancy areas. Their hours of operation usually do not conflict with industry, and the absence of residents allows for an undetected and unreported operation. Considerable profits have been realized by such clubs. Liquor is sold at dramatically increased prices, and membership fees are common. Under the guise of an entertainment operation, the operator makes large profits and, unlike a regularly licensed premises, is untaxed. Unfortunately, these clubs do not offer the safety precautions that other public places do. Fire prevention measures are meagre or non-existent, and crimes often go unreported because of the operation's clandestine nature.

These premises can be difficult to detect and infiltrate. A good undercover officer and periods of observation are required to determine who operates the various functions of the club and who makes the money. The operation's refuse may have to be examined. Wine, liquor, and beer bottles can be counted to estimate the amount of business and, therefore, profit. Once unpaid sales taxes can be determined, a fine can be established.

Unlawful Purchase of Liquor

Section 27 provides that liquor may be legally purchased only from either a government store or a person authorized by a licence or permit to sell liquor. Any other purchase is an offence against the person making the purchase. (See also Offences Relating to Minors.) In the 1950s, a person wishing to purchase liquor had to go to a government store to do so. The purchaser had to fill out a purchase form stating the brand and quantity of liquor to be purchased. The destination of the liquor, such as a residence or cottage, had to be specified. The buyer had to produce a government-issued card to complete the sale and transport the liquor directly to that address.

Unlawful Possession of Liquor

The LLA sets out the circumstances in which it is lawful to possess liquor. Regulations have progressed significantly from the 1960s, when a person was not permitted to "display liquor to the public view," but there are still restrictions on how and where a person may lawfully possess liquor.

Section 31(2) stipulates that possession of liquor is lawful in only three areas: (1) a residence, (2) a licensed premise, or (3) a private place. We have already explored the definitions of private place and residence, and a "premises in respect of which a licence or permit is issued" simply refers to bars, lounges, and other places that have received a liquor licence or, at least, a special occasion permit, with respect to the possession and distribution of liquor. Section 31(3) establishes an exception to these rules: anyone of legal age lawfully can walk into a public place or move from one place to another with liquor as long as the packaging in which it is contained (such as a bottle) is closed. For example, a person may go to a house party carrying a sealed container of rum and may walk home with the remaining part bottle of rum, provided that the bottle is closed, with the cap on the mouth of the bottle.

Legal Possession Exceptions

In light of the problem of impaired operation of motor vehicles, the province has imposed additional regulations on liquor possessed in motor vehicles or on boats. In these conveyances, it is insufficient that the liquor simply be in a closed container; extra steps are required to legally possess it in those circumstances. The rules for legally conveying liquor in a motor vehicle or a motorized snow vehicle (as defined in the *Highway Traffic Act*) are found in ss. 32(1) and 32(2). Sealed liquor is permitted in all circumstances, but once the seal is broken (by an initial opening that breaks the cap seal or, in the case of beer, when the cap is opened and the carbonation seal is broken), the liquor package must then be closed *and* packed either in baggage that is fastened shut or in some manner in which the liquor is not readily available to *any* person in the vehicle. In a boat, the closed container of liquor must be placed in a closed compartment of the boat (not just in baggage or a cooler, but in a compartment that is structurally part of the boat).

The rules can be summarized as follows. Any person who is 19 years of age or older may possess sealed liquor anywhere at any time. Once the seal is broken, possession of liquor is permitted if its container is closed, the person is 19 or older, and the liquor is not in a boat or other motorized vehicle. If the liquor is in a motorized vehicle and it is not sealed, then the container must be closed and placed in closed baggage or anywhere not accessible to any person in the vehicle; in a boat, the container must be closed and placed in a closed compartment of the boat.

Unlawful Consumption of Liquor

Ontario permits consumption of liquor by persons over the age of 19 in the same three areas where possession is permitted. Any consumption in areas other than those permitted is illegal and subject to a charge under s. 31(2) of the LLA. (See Offences Relating to Minors Exceptions.)

Unlawful Consumption or Sale of Alcohol That Is Not Liquor

In some circumstances, police officers may encounter persons consuming alcohol that is not liquor (remember the definition of liquor, which includes any alcohol in a form appropriate for human consumption). Some people have been known to drink aftershave, mouthwash, antifreeze, or other liquids that contain alcohol, even though most people would not consider those substances suitable for human consumption. The LLA addresses these situations in s. 33, creating offences of (1) drinking alcohol in a form that is not liquor; or (2) supplying alcohol in a form that is not liquor to another person, if the person supplying the alcohol knows or ought to have known that the other person intends to drink it. The second offence is sometimes used to discipline a disreputable merchant who sells those types of alcoholic liquids repeatedly to the same person(s), in such a quantity that it unreasonable to expect that the product will be used for the intended purpose.

In urban areas it is not uncommon to encounter persons who are habitually drunk. Sometimes the apparent odour of sweet breath resembling aftershave—a lotion with a high concentration of alcohol—is detectable. Cooking sherry and vanilla extract are other common substitutes. These liquids were not designed to be consumed as alcoholic beverages, but they are an inexpensive source that may be obtained outside of a licensed store. Many persons suffering from alcohol addiction wear multiple and heavy coats, and is not uncommon to find bottles of alcohol in the many pockets and linings.

Offences Relating to Minors

Police officers frequently must investigate offences relating to minors (persons under 19 years of age), and s. 30 of the LLA sets out several types of these offences. The section also outlines exceptions to those offences and establishes certain conditions under which minors may legally possess and/or consume liquor; but those situations are limited.

An acronym commonly used by students studying offences relating to minors is POACH. Each letter of this word refers to one of the activities prohibited by persons under the age of 19 with respect to liquor:

Purchase liquor,
Obtain liquor (in any manner other than purchasing),
Attempt to purchase liquor,
Consume liquor, or
Have liquor in possession.

OFFENCES RELATING TO MINORS EXCEPTIONS

The two situations in which minors may legally possess liquor are found in ss. 30(9) and 30(13). The first situation is if the person is 18 years old and in possession of liquor in the course of employment on premises in which the sale of liquor is authorized (such as a bar or dining lounge). It is of interest here to note why this age is different. Until the late 1960s, the legal age to drink was 21. However, this age was in conflict with other apparent responsibilities. One could go to war at a younger age, and through changes to the voting age, one could vote at 18. Being old enough to vote and go to war seemed inconsistent with being refused a drink. The legal drinking age was then changed to 18. Some consequences immediately became apparent. A number of young people were now able to gain employment in liquor-licensed establishments. Also, a large number of final-year high school students were able to buy liquor. The ensuing protest resulted in the legal drinking age being increased to 19, but in order to maintain the labour force one could still be 18 and work in a licensed premises.

The second situation is if the young person is supplied with liquor by a parent or a person having lawful custody of the young person, in a residence or private place. Section 30(13) permits a parent or legal guardian to give a glass of wine or other alcoholic beverage to a young person in a residence or private place; it does not permit the young person to become intoxicated or permit the parent or guardian to supply liquor to an intoxicated youth. In many cultures, wine and beer are consumed at meals, regardless of age. In some cases, religious traditions contradict alcohol age restrictions. To accommodate tradition, the s. 30(13) exception was enacted. As detailed above, it applies to the child and that child's parent(s), not the neighbour's child and not the child in the parents' home while the parents are on vacation.

The LLA establishes a list of identification that a person who sells or supplies liquor may refer to for proof of a customer's age, unless there is reason to doubt either the authenticity of the document or that it was issued to the person presenting it. Although a licensee may accept any identification with a photo, date of birth, and that reasonably appears to have been issued by a government, a licensee is *not* obligated to honour any identification not stipulated in the LLA.

The following forms of identification are set out in s. 41(5) of Regulation 719 to the LLA:

1. an Ontario driver's licence with a photo;
2. a Canadian passport;
3. a Canadian citizenship card with a photo;
4. a Canadian armed forces identification card;
5. a secure certificate of Indian status issued by the Government of Canada;
6. a photo card issued by the Liquor Control Board of Ontario (LCBO);
7. a permanent resident card issued by the Government of Canada; and
8. any photo card issued under the *Photo Card Act, 2008*.

The Ontario Health Card is not one of the forms of identification prescribed by regulation, and this is often a source of disagreement between bouncers and patrons who do not have other documentation. The website of the Alcohol and Gaming Commission of Ontario advises the following regarding accepting the Ontario Health Card as proof of legal age:

- By law, no one can be required to produce the Ontario Health Card, nor can the health number be collected. You should not ask for the Ontario Health Card as identification, but if offered voluntarily you may accept it at your discretion.
- While the health card meets the criteria for validating a patron's age in that it has a photo and date of birth, and is issued by the government, a licensee may not ask for the card for identification.

ARREST POWERS

In the LLA, two situations authorize a peace officer to arrest without a warrant.

1. Intoxicated in a Public Place or Common Area (LLA s. 31(5))

Three factors must exist for an arrest under s. 31(5) to be lawful:

1. the intoxication of the individual resulted from liquor consumption,
2. the intoxicated individual is in a public place or in a common area within a residence that consists of multiple dwellings, and
3. in the opinion of the officer, the arrest is necessary to ensure the safety of any person (including the officer).

Officers must not forget to make notes on each of these factors and be prepared to articulate their grounds regarding each in court.

2. Refusal to Identify (LLA s. 48)

Under s. 48, an officer may arrest a person without a warrant if:

1. the person is committing an offence against the LLA or its regulations, and
2. the person refuses to give his or her name and address, or the officer has reasonable grounds to believe that the name and address given are false.

Three other authorities appear to give arrest powers, but they are actually situations that give rise to the application of the *Trespass to Property Act*. Section 34(2) authorizes the holder of a liquor licence to remove a person from the premises in three situations:

1. the person is unlawfully on the premises (for example, the person is under 19 years of age);
2. the person is on the premises for an unlawful purpose (for example, drug dealing); or
3. the person is contravening the law on the premises (for example, carrying liquor in a backpack).

The LLA requires that the licence holder not permit such a person to remain on the premises, and authorizes the licence holder to request that the person leave; if he or she refuses to leave, the LLA authorizes the use of no more force than is necessary to remove the person. Section 34(5) permits the licensee or its employee to request that any undesirable person leave the premises, and such person is prohibited from re-entering the premises on the same day as the request.

All three of these provisions can result in persons being required to leave a premises. If they refuse to comply, then they are engaging in prohibited activity. The most effective remedy to that situation appears to be to apply the *Trespass to Property Act* provision detailing the offence of failing to leave a premises when directed to do so. The offence under the trespass legislation also includes the power of arrest without warrant by the police officer or any person in charge of the premises, or by any person authorized by the person in charge of the premises.

In the event that a patron refuses to leave when directed and the police are called, a simple process is often followed by many police agencies. The attending officer(s) should speak to the management of the premises and confirm the nature of the call. They will want to be sure that the patron has already refused a management request or demand to leave. Management will be directed to attend to the patron again, this time in the officer's presence. The demand to leave is to be repeated. If the patron again refuses, he or she is trespassing and "found committing" the offence in the officer's presence. The officer may now make a lawful arrest and remove the person from the premises. The person can be charged under the LLA or the *Trespass to Property Act*. Following these steps also avoids the impression that the officer is a bouncer for the premises.

Vacate Order by Police Officer

> Remember that a police officer does not have the authority to arrest for refusal to leave a premises under the LLA; this authority comes from the *Trespass to Property Act*.

SECTION 34(3): ORDER TO VACATE PREMISES

Section 34(3) empowers an officer to vacate a licensed premises despite any wishes of the operator or owner. If the officer believes that

- a breach or
- a disturbance
- is being committed on the premises and, as a result,
- there is a threat to public safety,

the officer may order the evacuation of the premise and order the operator and staff to assist as necessary. See also LLA s. 34(4).

SECTION 34.1(1): REMOVING PERSONS FROM PREMISES WHERE CONTRAVENTION SUSPECTED

Section 34.1(1) confers a wide-reaching power on police officers that should be used only in extreme circumstances. The use of the word "premises" includes a residence. Once an officer is lawfully on or in a premises and observes evidence of a contravention, such as minor consumption within the premises, the officer may apply this authority. Note that this section does not provide the officer with authority to enter the premises without cause.

Section 34.1(1) permits a police officer to order the evacuation of *any* premises if the officer has reasonable grounds to believe that any provision of the LLA or its regulations is being contravened on the premises. For example, a small house party hosted by a 19-year-old whose parents are away turns into an uncontrollable disaster involving hundreds of uninvited guests, where the potential for injury to persons or damage to the premises and neighbouring premises is high. Individuals who are required to leave a premises under this section may not remain on the premises and may not re-enter the premises on the same day unless authorized by police. This provision does not apply to individuals who actually reside in the premises (in this case, the 19-year-old).

SEARCH POWERS

The LLA grants two kinds of search powers to police officers. The first are granted exclusively to police and authorize police officers to carry out searches of vehicles and boats. The second are designated primarily to inspectors under the Act but, with a few exceptions, are shared by police officers. These pertain to inspections of licensed establishments and events.

Under s. 32(5), any police officer who has reasonable grounds to believe that liquor is being kept unlawfully in a vehicle or boat (as defined in s. 32) may, at any time and without a warrant, enter and search both the vehicle or boat and any persons found within. For example:

1. A car is pulled over and while talking to the driver the officer detects the odour of alcohol from within and sees a beer cap on the floor. The officer is allowed to search the vehicle and occupant(s) legally because these observations have given rise to the necessary belief.
2. A truck is parked in a lot by a school dance. Two people sit inside the vehicle and two stand outside. Approaching, the officer sees an empty bottle of beer on the floor. The officer is authorized to search the truck and its occupants, but not the two people standing outside.

Section 44 outlines the powers granted to liquor inspectors. Such inspectors, who are designated by the Registrar and employed by the Alcohol and Gaming Commission, may enter a licensed premises without a warrant at any reasonable time, inspect it, and remove any relevant items to ensure compliance with the LLA and its regulations. These powers are generally used with respect to licensed premises. Under s. 44(13), they are transferred to police officers.

Seizure

In addition to search powers, the LLA also authorizes police officers to seize items in two circumstances. First, s. 47(1) authorizes seizure of anything, including liquor, that may provide evidence of an offence under the LLA or that the officer reasonably believes

1. was used or is being used in connection with the commission of an LLA offence; and

2. unless seized, could continue to be used or would be used again in the commission of an LLA offence; or
3. resulted from the commission of an LLA offence.

Second, and similar to the first, is a provision in s. 47(1.1) that authorizes the seizure of liquor and the packages in which the liquor is kept if an LLA offence appears to have been committed and the officer reasonably believes that a further offence will be committed if the liquor is not seized.

The following two examples illustrate seizure under the LLA:

1. *Seizure of evidence of the offence.* An officer observes a young person walking down the street on a Friday evening in July. He is carrying a gym bag that appears to be heavily laden. Water drips on the sidewalk in line with his travel and apparently is coming from the bag. He tries to ignore the officer's gaze. On investigation the officer finds that the bag contains 12 beers on ice (which is melting, causing the trail), the youth is 17 years old, and he is on his way to a bush party. The officer charges him with underage possession, seizes the bag and beer as evidence of the offence, and drops him off at home to his parents.
2. *Seizure of evidence in situation likely to continue the offence.* On a Friday evening, a van pulls off the highway and into a service centre. The side door slides open and two persons inside are observed drinking what appears to be beer. Investigation reveals that they are on their way to a cottage for a long weekend. They are of legal age and have two cases of beer with them. They are charged with drinking in a public place or one of the many other appropriate charges and all the beer is seized. A package is defined as an individual bottle, so other factors must be taken into account. They have already been drinking in a vehicle. They are halfway to their cottage. It is after store hours. It is reasonable to believe that when they resume their trip they will resume drinking and the offences will continue, so both cases of beer are seized.

Both powers provide opportunities for the person(s) from whom items are seized to apply to the courts within 30 days for return of their property. If the court decides the application has merit, it may order the return of the items, vest the applicant with interest in the items, or order the Crown to make compensation to the applicant. If no application is made within the 30-day period, or if the court does not order the return of the items, the items are forfeited to the Crown.

Search with Warrant

An officer who encounters a situation requiring entry and search of a premises or dwelling is required to implement the search warrant provisions outlined in s. 158 of the POA. To obtain a warrant to search, an officer must be able to support an allegation of a contravention against the LLA by way of a sworn information before a judge or justice of the peace. The application for the warrant is made according to the provisions of the POA, and will contain the officer's grounds and reasons in order to validate the need for the warrant.

> An officer with a warrant who is obstructed or prevented from entering a premises and carrying out a search may rely on s. 129 of the *Criminal Code*. Section 129 makes it an offence to obstruct an officer in the lawful execution of his or her duties. Most often, an explanation of the fact that such an act is an arrestable offence will resolve the problem.

The warrant will grant a police officer the authority to enter and search in situations where a licence under the LLA is non-existent and where a search is required, such as a raid on an after-hours club or a bootlegger working out of a dwelling or premises that is secure, and to which entry is not provided to the police.

USE OF FORCE

It must be emphasized that police are accountable for the force they use, and the greater the force an officer uses, the more difficult it will be to justify. Excessive force could result in a civil suit against the officer and the service, or even in a charge of assault. Officers should therefore use as *little* force as necessary to effect their legal purpose.

There is no specific provision for the use of force in the application of arrest or search in the LLA specifically for officers. If force is required in order to enforce the provisions of the Act, s. 25 of the *Criminal Code* or s. 146(1) of the POA applies.

Section 34 of the LLA authorizes a permit or licence holder to use as much force as is necessary to remove or cause to be removed a person who is unlawfully on the premises, who is on the premises for an unlawful purpose, or who is contravening the law on the premises. Clearly, this authority is dedicated to the licence holder, not the police. Allegations of excessive force by ejected patrons are common and are investigated where the evidence suggests they are valid.

Under s. 34.1, any police officer who has reasonable grounds to believe that the Act or a provision of the regulations made pursuant to the Act is being contravened on any premises may order the evacuation of those premises, except for the persons who actually reside on the premises. Evacuation is a very powerful tool, and officers should use it only when absolutely necessary.

LIMITATION PERIOD

This statute of limitations is extreme. It is important to remember, however, that a part III summons must be used to commence proceedings any time that a charge is laid more than 30 days from the date of the offence.

While the POA provides a general limitation period of six months from the date of the offence, the LLA provides its own limitation period of two years. This provision is found in s. 61(8) of the LLA, and it allows investigators of offences against the Act or its regulations up to two years to lay charges.

NON-POLICE AGENCIES INVOLVED

Liquor Inspectors

Liquor inspectors are employed by the Alcohol and Gaming Commission and make compliance inspections of premises licensed under the LLA. The inspectors work closely with the police agencies having jurisdiction in the area, which helps everyone to fulfill their duties.

Alcohol and Gaming Commission

The Alcohol and Gaming Commission (the board) is responsible for issuing licences to establishments that sell or serve liquor. They also are entrusted with inspecting and monitoring those establishments to ensure compliance with the LLA and its regulations. That task is carried out largely by the liquor inspectors referred to above. The board is the adjudication body that conducts hearings on disciplinary actions that may be taken under the LLA.

PROVINCIAL OFFENCES GRID COMPLETION

Common Offences and/or Provisions

1. Offences relating to minors, or those under 19 years of age (POACH)
2. Intoxicated in public place or common area
3. Unlawful sale/purchase
4. Unlawful possession
5. Unlawful consumption

Arrest Powers

1. Intoxicated in public place or common area, and danger to anyone
2. LLA offence committed and person fails to identify him- or herself (until the arresting officer is satisfied by the proven identification)

Search Powers

1. Vehicle or vessel and any person found in it
2. Police officer carrying out powers of an inspector of licensed premises under the LLA

Use of Force

1. No specific use of force for arrest or search (refer to *Criminal Code* s. 25 or POA s. 146).
2. A permit or licence holder is authorized to use as much force as is necessary to remove or cause to be removed a person who is unlawfully on the premises or who is contravening the law on the premises.
3. Police officer who reasonably believes the LLA or its regulations are being contravened on any premises may order everyone, except those who actually reside there, to vacate the premises.

Limitation Period

Two years from date of offence; not limited to six months general provision.

Non-Police Agencies Involved

1. Liquor inspector
2. Alcohol and Gaming Commission

Liquor Licence Act

RSO 1990, c. L.19

1(1) **Definitions**—In this Act,

"alcohol" means a product of fermentation or distillation of grains, fruits or other agricultural products, and includes synthetic ethyl alcohol;

"beer" means any beverage containing alcohol in excess of the prescribed amount obtained by the fermentation of an infusion or decoction of barley, malt and hops or of any similar products in drinkable water;

"Board" means the board of the Alcohol and Gaming Commission of Ontario established under the *Alcohol and Gaming Regulation and Public Protection Act, 1996*;

"conservation officer" means a conservation officer appointed under subsection 87(1) of the *Fish and Wildlife Conservation Act, 1997* who is engaged in carrying out his or her duties;

"ferment on premise facility" means premises where equipment for the making of beer or wine on the premises is provided to individuals;

"government store" means a government store established under the *Liquor Control Act*;

"licence" means a licence issued under this Act;

"liquor" means spirits, wine and beer or any combination thereof and includes any alcohol in a form appropriate for human consumption as a beverage, alone or in combination with any other matter;

"manufacturer" means a person who produces liquor for sale;

"municipality" means a local municipality;

"Ontario wine" means,

(a) wine produced in Ontario from grapes, cherries, apples or other fruits grown in Ontario, the concentrated juice of those fruits or other agricultural products containing sugar or starch and includes Ontario wine to which is added herbs, water, honey, sugar or the distillate of Ontario wine or cereal grains grown in Ontario,

(b) wine produced by the alcoholic fermentation of Ontario honey, with or without the addition of caramel, natural botanical flavours or the distillate of Ontario honey wine, or

(c) wine produced from a combination of,

(i) apples grown in Ontario or the concentrated juice thereof to which is added herbs, water, honey, sugar or the distillate of Ontario wine or cereal grains grown in Ontario, and

(ii) the concentrated juice of apples grown outside of Ontario,

in such proportion as is prescribed;

"permit" means a permit issued under this Act;

"prescribed" means prescribed by the regulations;

"Registrar" means the Registrar of Alcohol and Gaming within the meaning of the *Alcohol and Gaming Regulation and Public Protection Act, 1996*;

"regulations" means the regulations made under this Act;

"sell" means to supply for remuneration, directly or indirectly, in any manner by which the cost is recovered from the person supplied, alone or in combination with others, and "sale" has a corresponding meaning;

"spirits" means any beverage containing alcohol obtained by distillation;

"supply" includes a licensee's permitting the consumption on licensed premises of wine that a patron has brought onto the premises, in accordance with the regulations, for the patron's consumption, alone or in the company of others;

"Tribunal" means the Licence Appeal Tribunal established under the *Licence Appeal Tribunal Act, 1999* or whatever other tribunal is prescribed by the regulations;

"wine" means any beverage containing alcohol in excess of the prescribed amount obtained by the fermentation of the natural sugar contents of fruits, including grapes, apples and other agricultural products containing sugar, and including honey and milk.

(2) **Interpretation of "interested person"**—For the purposes of this Act, a person is deemed to be interested in another person if,

(a) the first person has, or may have in the opinion of the Registrar based on reasonable grounds, a beneficial interest of any kind, either directly or indirectly, in the other person's business, including but not limited to a holder, directly or indirectly, of shares or other securities;

(b) the first person exercises, or may exercise in the opinion of the Registrar based on reasonable grounds, direct or indirect control over the other person's business; or

(c) the first person has provided, or may have provided in the opinion of the Registrar based on reasonable grounds, direct or indirect financing to the other person's business. . . .

Licences and Permits

5(1) **Licence or permit required**—No person shall keep for sale, offer for sale or sell liquor except under the authority of a licence or permit to sell liquor or under the authority of a manufacturer's licence.

(2) **Soliciting orders**—No person shall canvass for, receive or solicit orders for the sale of liquor unless the person is the holder of a licence or permit to sell liquor or unless the person is the holder of a licence to represent a manufacturer.

(3) **Delivery for fee**—No person shall deliver liquor for a fee except under the authority of a licence to deliver liquor.

(4) **Exception**—Subsections (1), (2) and (3) do not apply to the sale or delivery of liquor by or under the authority of the Liquor Control Board of Ontario under the *Liquor Control Act*.

5.1 Licence required, ferment on premise facility—No person shall operate a ferment on premise facility except under the authority of a licence to operate such a facility.
. . .

10(1) **Licence to deliver**—A person may apply to the Registrar for a licence to deliver liquor. . . .

19(1) **Special occasion permit**—A person may apply to the Registrar for a permit authorizing the holder thereof to sell or serve liquor on a prescribed special occasion.

(2) **Requirements**—An applicant for a permit for a special occasion is entitled to be issued the permit except if,

(a) the applicant would not be entitled to the issuance of a licence to sell liquor for any ground under clauses 6(2)(d) to (g) or subsection 6(4) or (4.1); or

(b) the premises for which the permit is applied are disqualified under section 20. . . .

Liquor Licence Act

O. Reg. 389/91, as amended by O. Reg. 282/02

SPECIAL OCCASION PERMITS

General

2. The following classes of special occasion permits are established:

1. A sales permit authorizing the sale and service of liquor.
2. A no-sale permit authorizing the service of liquor without charge.
3. An auction permit authorizing the sale of liquor by way of auction.

3. For the purpose of subsection 19(1) of the Act, the following are the prescribed special occasions:

1. A reception for invited guests only that is conducted without the intention of gain or profit.

Note: On July 1, 2012, paragraph 1 is revoked and the following substituted:

1. A private event for invited guests only that is conducted without the intention of gain or profit.

2. A public event that is,
   i. conducted by a charitable organization registered under the *Income Tax Act* (Canada) or by a non-profit association or organization for the advancement of charitable, educational, religious or community objects,
   ii. an event of provincial, national or international significance, or
   iii. an event designated by a municipal council as an event of municipal significance.
3. Revoked.
4. A trade show or consumer show at which the major themes, exhibits and demonstrations are directly related to an aspect of the hospitality industry and conducted without the intention of gain or profit and to which,
   i. in the case of a trade show, only persons involved in the hospitality industry and their guests are permitted, and
   ii. in the case of a consumer show, the general public is admitted.

Note: On July 1, 2012, paragraph 4 is revoked and the following substituted:

4. An industry promotional event,
   i. at which a manufacturer, a licensed representative of a manufacturer or the event organizer acting on behalf of a manufacturer or a licensed representative of a manufacturer may provide samples of liquor and take orders for liquor purchases, and
   ii. that is conducted without the intention of gain or profit from the sale of liquor and is for the purpose of promoting a manufacturer's products.

5. An event at which market research on a liquor product will be carried out by or on behalf of the manufacturer of the product.

Note: On July 1, 2012, paragraph 5 is revoked.

6. Revoked.

7. An auction conducted by or on behalf of,
   i. a charitable organization that is registered under the *Income Tax Act* (Canada),
   ii. an administrator or executor of an estate acting within the scope of his, her or its duties, or
   iii. a Sheriff acting within the scope of his or her duties.

Note: On July 1, 2012, paragraph 7 is revoked.

3.1(1) An application for a special occasion permit shall be made on a form provided by the Registrar.

(2) The application shall be made to a store manager employed by the Liquor Control Board of Ontario or to an employee of that Board whose responsibilities include the considering of applications for such permits,

(a) at a government store in the municipality where the event is to take place; or

(b) if there is no government store in the municipality where the event is to take place, at the government store that is closest to the premises where the event is to take place.

Note: On July 1, 2012, subsection (2) is revoked and the following substituted:

(2) The application shall be made to the Liquor Control Board of Ontario or to the Registrar.

(3) At the request of a person referred to in subsection (2), the applicant shall,

(a) attend at the government store in person to make the application; and

(b) produce one of the types of identification referred to in paragraphs 1 to 4 of subsection 29(5) or a passport issued by a government of another country.

(4) An applicant for a permit shall ensure that the premises at which the event is to take place are not disqualified premises under section 20 of the Act.

Responsible Use

27. Unlawful purchase—No person shall purchase liquor except from a government store or from a person authorized by licence or permit to sell liquor.

28. Unlawful gift—No manufacturer or employee, agent or licensed representative of a manufacturer shall give any liquor to any person, except as permitted by the regulations.

29. Sale to intoxicated person—No person shall sell or supply liquor or permit liquor to be sold or supplied to any person who is or appears to be intoxicated.

30(1) **Rules, persons under 19**—No person shall knowingly sell or supply liquor to a person under nineteen years of age.

(2) **Idem**—No person shall sell or supply liquor to a person who appears to be under nineteen years of age.

(3) **Permitting possession or consumption**—No licensee or employee or agent of a licensee shall knowingly permit a person under nineteen years of age to have or consume liquor in the licensee's licensed premises.

(4) **Idem**—No licensee or employee or agent of a licensee shall permit a person who appears to be under nineteen years of age to have or consume liquor in the licensee's licensed premises.

(4.1) **Person under 19, use of ferment on premise facility**—No licensee of a ferment on premise facility or employee or agent of such a licensee shall,

(a) knowingly permit a person under 19 years of age to use the facility for the making of beer or wine;

(b) permit a person who appears to be under 19 years of age to use the facility for the making of beer or wine.

(5) **Exception to subss. (3) and (4)**—Subsections (3) and (4) do not prohibit a licensee or employee or agent of a licensee from permitting a person eighteen years of age to be in possession of liquor during the course of the person's employment on the licensee's licensed premises.

(6) **Reliance on documentation**—A person who sells or supplies liquor to another person, permits another person to have or consume liquor in licensed premises or permits a person to use a ferment on premise facility to make beer or wine on the basis of documentation of a prescribed type is not in contravention of subsection (2), (4) or (4.1) if there is no apparent reason to doubt the authenticity of the documentation or that it was issued to the person producing it.

(7) **Court may determine apparent age**—In a prosecution for a contravention of subsection (2), (4) or (4.1), the court may determine, from the appearance of the person and from other relevant circumstances, whether a person to whom liquor was served or supplied, a person who was permitted to have or consume liquor or a person who was permitted to use a ferment on premise facility to make beer or wine appears to be under 19 years of age.

(8) **Possession or consumption**—No person under nineteen years of age shall have, consume, attempt to purchase, purchase or otherwise obtain liquor.

(9) **Exception to subs. (8)**—Subsection (8) does not prohibit a person eighteen years of age from being in possession of liquor during the course of the person's employment on premises in which the sale or service of liquor is authorized.

(10) **Entering premises**—No person under nineteen years of age shall enter or remain on premises in which the sale of liquor is authorized if the person knows that a condition of the licence or permit for the premises prohibits the entry of persons under nineteen years of age.

(11) **Exception to subs. (10)**—Subsection (10) does not apply to a person eighteen years of age who is employed on premises in which the sale or service of liquor is authorized while the person is on the premises during the course of his or her employment.

(12) **Improper documentation**—No person shall present as evidence of his or her age any documentation other than documentation that was lawfully issued to him or her.

Liquor Licence Act

RRO 1990, Reg. 718, as amended by O. Reg. 159/03

GENERAL

3(1) For the purposes of clauses 30(13)(a) and 31(2)(c) of the Act, "private place" means a place, vehicle or boat described in this section.

(2) An indoor place to which the public is not ordinarily invited or permitted is considered to be a private place except at the times when the public is invited or permitted access to it.

(3) Despite subsection (2), an indoor place that is available for rental by members of the public for occasional use is not a private place.

(4) A motor vehicle equipped with sleeping accommodation and cooking facilities is considered to be a private place while it is parked and being used as a residence.

(5) Despite subsection (4), a motor vehicle is not considered to be a private place while it is on a highway or a King's Highway within the meaning of the *Highway Traffic Act*.

(6) A boat that is used exclusively to carry freight and is under the command of a person certified under the *Canada Shipping Act* is considered to be a private place.

(7) A boat with permanent sleeping accommodations and permanent cooking and sanitary facilities, other than a boat used to carry passengers for hire is considered to be a private place while the boat is at anchor or is secured to the dock or land.

(8) If a boat is considered under subsection (7) to be a private place and is secured to a dock or land to which the public is not ordinarily invited or permitted then the dock or land is considered to be a private place except at the times when the public is invited or permitted access to it.

(9) A boat that is used exclusively to carry passengers for hire and has sleeping accommodation for all passengers is considered to be a private place if it is under the command of a person certified under the *Canada Shipping Act*.

(10) A boat that is owned or operated by the Canadian Coast Guard is considered to be a private place. . . .

17(4) The following types of identification are prescribed for the purposes of subsection 30(6) of the Act in relation to the delivery of liquor:

1. A driver's licence issued by the province of Ontario with a photograph of the person to whom the licence was issued.
2. A Canadian passport.
3. A Canadian citizenship card with a photograph of the person to whom the card was issued.
4. A Canadian armed forces identification card with a photograph of the person to whom the card was issued.
5. A secure certificate of Indian status issued by the Government of Canada.
6. A photo-identification card issued by the Liquor Control Board of Ontario.
7. A permanent resident card issued by the Government of Canada.
8. A photo card issued under the *Photo Card Act, 2008*.

(13) **Supply by parent**—This section does not apply,

(a) to the supplying of liquor to a person under nineteen years of age in a residence as defined in section 31 or in a private place as defined in the regulations by a parent of the person or a person having lawful custody of the person; or

(b) to the consumption of liquor by a person who is supplied liquor in a manner described in clause (a), if the liquor is consumed at the place where it is supplied.

. . .

Unlawful possession or consumption

31(1) **Definition**—In this section,

"residence" means a place that is actually occupied and used as a dwelling, whether or not in common with other persons, including all premises used in conjunction with the place to which the general public is not invited or permitted access, and, if the place occupied and used as a dwelling is a tent, includes the land immediately adjacent to and used in conjunction with the tent.

(2) **Unlawful possession or consumption**—No person shall have or consume liquor in any place other than,

(a) a residence;

(b) premises in respect of which a licence or permit is issued; or

(c) a private place as defined in the regulations.

(3) **Exception**—Subsection (2) does not apply to the possession of liquor that is in a closed container.

(3.1) **Same**—Despite clause (2)(b), no person shall consume beer or wine in a licensed ferment on premise facility except as permitted by the regulations.

(4) **Intoxication**—No person shall be in an intoxicated condition,

(a) in a place to which the general public is invited or permitted access; or

(b) in any part of a residence that is used in common by persons occupying more than one dwelling in the residence.

(5) **Arrest without warrant**—A police officer may arrest without warrant any person whom he or she finds contravening subsection (4) if, in the opinion of the police officer, to do so is necessary for the safety of any person.

(6) **Interpretation**—In this section, a reference to a police officer includes a conservation officer.

32(1) **Conveying liquor in vehicle, boat**—No person shall drive or have the care or control of a motor vehicle as defined in the *Highway Traffic Act* or a motorized snow vehicle, whether it is in motion or not, while there is contained in the vehicle any liquor, except under the authority of a licence or permit.

(2) **Exception**—Subsection (1) does not apply if the liquor in the vehicle,

(a) is in a container that is unopened and the seal unbroken; or

(b) is packed in baggage that is fastened closed or is not otherwise readily available to any person in the vehicle.

(3) **Conveying liquor in boat**—No person shall operate or have the care or control of a boat that is underway while there is contained in the boat any liquor, except under the authority of a licence or permit.

(4) **Exception**—Subsection (3) does not apply if the liquor in the boat,

(a) is in a container that is unopened and the seal unbroken; or

(b) is stored in a closed compartment.

(5) **Search of vehicle or boat**—A police officer who has reasonable grounds to believe that liquor is being unlawfully kept in a vehicle or boat may at any time, without a warrant, enter and search the vehicle or boat and search any person found in it.

(6) **Definitions**—In this section,

"boat" includes any ship or boat or any other description of vessel used or designed to be used in the navigation of water;

"police officer" includes a conservation officer.

33. Unlawful consumption or supply of alcohol—No person shall,

(a) drink alcohol in a form that is not a liquor; or

(b) supply alcohol in a form that is not a liquor to another person, if the person supplying the alcohol knows or ought to know that the other person intends it to be used as a drink.

33.1(1) **Prohibition, possession of liquor**—No person shall possess liquor in excess of the prescribed quantity unless,

(a) the liquor was purchased by an individual from a government store for his or her personal use;

(b) the liquor was manufactured by an individual in accordance with the law for his or her personal use or for service at an event at which liquor may be served under the authority of a permit;

(c) the liquor was legally imported into Ontario;

(d) the liquor is possessed by or under the authority of the Liquor Control Board of Ontario under the *Liquor Control Act*; or

(e) the liquor is possessed by or under the authority of a licence or permit issued by the Registrar under this Act.

(2) **Personal use**—In this section, references to an individual's personal use of liquor refer to,

(a) consuming the liquor;

(b) serving the liquor to other individuals at a residence as defined in section 31 or at a private place as defined in the regulations;

(c) giving the liquor to another individual as a gift.

34(1) **Removing person from premises**—The holder of a licence or permit issued in respect of premises shall ensure that a person does not remain on the premises if the holder has reasonable grounds to believe that the person,

(a) is unlawfully on the premises;

(b) is on the premises for an unlawful purpose; or

(c) is contravening the law on the premises.

(2) **Idem**—The holder of a licence or permit may request a person referred to in subsection (1) to leave the premises immediately and if the request is not forthwith complied with may remove the person or cause the person to be removed by the use of no more force than is necessary.

(3) **Order to vacate premises**—If there are reasonable grounds to believe that a disturbance or breach of the peace sufficient to constitute a threat to the public safety is being caused on premises for which a licence or permit is issued, a police officer may require that all persons vacate the premises.

(4) **Idem**—The holder of the licence or permit for premises that are required to be vacated under subsection (3) shall take all reasonable steps to ensure that the premises are vacated.

(5) **Right to refuse entry**—A licensee or employee of a licensee who has reason to believe that the presence of a person on the licensee's licensed premises is undesirable may,

(a) request the person to leave; or

(b) forbid the person to enter the licensed premises.

(6) **Not to remain after request to leave**—No person shall,

(a) remain on licensed premises after he or she is requested to leave by the licensee or an employee of the licensee; or

(b) re-enter the licensed premises on the same day he or she is requested to leave.

34.1(1) **Removing persons from premises where contravention suspected**—If there are reasonable grounds to believe that this Act or a prescribed provision of the regulations is being contravened on any premises, a police officer may require that all persons vacate the premises.

(2) **Same**—Subsection (1) does not apply in respect of persons actually residing in the premises.

35(1) **By-law designating recreational area**—The council of a municipality may by by-law designate a recreational area within the municipality that is owned or controlled by the municipality as a place where the possession of liquor is prohibited.

(2) **Non-application of subs. (1)**—A designation under subsection (1) does not prevent the Registrar from issuing any licence or permit under this Act.

(3) **Unlawful possession**—No person shall have liquor in a place designated under subsection (1).

(4) **Exception to subs. (3)**—Subsection (3) does not apply to a person in possession of liquor under the authority of a licence or permit or in possession of liquor purchased on premises in respect of which a licence or permit is issued.

(5) **Definition**—In this section,

"municipality" includes an upper-tier municipality.

36(1) **Taking to hospital in lieu of charge**—A police officer who finds a person apparently in contravention of subsection 31(4) may take the person into custody and, in lieu of laying an information in respect of the contravention, may escort the person to a hospital designated by the regulations.

(2) **Protection from liability**—No action or other proceeding for damages shall be instituted against any physician or any hospital or officer or employee of a hospital on the grounds only that the person examines or treats without consent a person who is brought to the hospital under subsection (1).

(3) **Exception**—Subsection (2) does not apply if consent to the examination or treatment is required under the *Health Care Consent Act, 1996.*

37(1) **Detention in institution**—If it appears that a person in contravention of subsection 31(4) may benefit therefrom, the court making the conviction may order the person to be detained for treatment for a period of ninety days or such lesser period as the court thinks advisable in an institution designated by the regulations.

(2) **Idem**—If, at any time during a person's period of detention ordered under subsection (1), the superintendent of the institution is of the opinion that further detention in the institution will not benefit the person, the superintendent may release the person.

(3) **Consent to treatment**—An order under subsection (1) does not authorize the administration of a treatment without consent, if consent to the treatment is required under the *Health Care Consent Act, 1996*. . . .

39. Civil liability—The following rules apply if a person or an agent or employee of a person sells liquor to or for a person whose condition is such that the consumption of liquor would apparently intoxicate the person or increase the person's intoxication so that he or she would be in danger of causing injury to himself or herself or injury or damage to another person or the property of another person:

1. If the person to or for whom the liquor is sold commits suicide or meets death by accident while so intoxicated, an action under Part V of the *Family Law Act* lies against the person who or whose employee or agent sold the liquor.
2. If the person to or for whom the liquor is sold causes injury or damage to another person or the property of another person while so intoxicated, the other person is entitled to recover an amount as compensation for the injury or damage from the person who or whose employee or agent sold the liquor. . . .

42. Intoxicating liquor—Liquor shall be deemed to be an intoxicating liquor for purposes of the *Importation of Intoxicating Liquors Act* (Canada).

Compliance

43(1) **Persons designated by Registrar**—The Registrar may designate persons employed by the Alcohol and Gaming Commission of Ontario as persons who may carry out inspections for the purpose of determining whether there is compliance with this Act and the regulations.

(2) **Certificate of designation**—A person designated under subsection (1) who is exercising a power under this Act shall, on request, produce his or her certificate of designation.

44(1) **Inspections**—For the purpose of ensuring compliance with this Act and the regulations, a person designated under subsection 43(1) may,

(a) enter any place at any reasonable time;

(b) request the production for inspection of documents or things that may be relevant to the inspection;

(c) inspect and, upon giving a receipt therefor, remove, for the purpose of making copies or extracts, documents or things relevant to the inspection;

(d) inquire into negotiations, transactions, loans or borrowings of a licensee or permit holder and into assets owned, held in trust, acquired or disposed of by a licensee or permit holder that are relevant to an inspection;

(e) conduct such tests as are reasonably necessary; and

(f) remove materials or substances for examination or test purposes subject to the licensee, permit holder or other occupant of the premises being notified thereof.

(2) **Entry to dwellings**—Subsection (1) does not apply to confer a power of entry to a room actually used as a dwelling without the consent of the occupier.

(3) **Warrant**—A justice of the peace may issue a warrant authorizing the person named in the warrant,

(a) to do anything set out in clause (1)(a), (c), (e) or (f);

(b) to search for and seize any document or thing relevant to the inspection; or

(c) to enter and search a room actually used as a dwelling.

(4) **Requirements for warrant to issue**—A warrant may be issued under subsection (3) if the justice of the peace is satisfied on information under oath that,

(a) in the case of a warrant to be issued under clause (3)(a),

(i) a person designated under subsection 43(1) has been prevented from doing anything permitted under clause (1)(a), (c), (e) or (f),

(ii) there are reasonable grounds to believe that such a person may be prevented from doing any of those things, or

(iii) there are reasonable grounds to believe that there has been or is likely to be a contravention of this Act or the regulations;

(b) in the case of a warrant to be issued under clause (3)(b), it is necessary to search for and seize a document or thing that there are reasonable grounds to believe will afford evidence relevant to a contravention of this Act or the regulations; or

(c) in the case of a warrant to be issued under clause (3)(c), it is necessary that a room actually used as a dwelling be entered for the purposes of carrying out an inspection or there is, in such a room, a document or thing that there are reasonable grounds to believe is relevant to an inspection under this Act.

(5) **Execution of warrant**—A warrant issued under this section shall specify the hours and days during which it may be executed.

(6) **Expiry**—Unless renewed, a warrant under this section expires not later than thirty days after the date on which it is made.

(7) **Notice not required**—A warrant under this section may be issued or renewed before or after expiry upon application without notice.

(8) **Renewal of warrant**—A warrant under this section may be renewed for any reason for which it may be issued.

(9) **Experts**—A person carrying out an inspection under this Act is entitled to call upon such experts as are necessary to assist the person in carrying out the inspection.

(10) **Assistance**—A person doing anything under the authority of a warrant issued under this section is authorized to call on such police officers to assist and to use such force as is necessary in the execution of the warrant.

(11) **Copies**—A person carrying out an inspection under this Act who takes material in order to copy it shall make the copy with reasonable dispatch and shall promptly return the material taken.

(12) **Admissibility of copies**—Copies of, or extracts from, documents and things removed under this section and certified as being true copies of, or extracts from, the originals by the person who made them are admissible in evidence to the same extent as, and

have the same evidentiary value as, the documents or things of which they are copies or extracts.

(13) **Police officers**—Every police officer has the powers set out in clauses (1)(a), (b) and (c) and subsections (2) to (12) apply with necessary modifications to police officers as if they were persons designated under subsection 43(1).

45(1) **Obstruction**—No person shall obstruct a person carrying out an inspection under this Act or withhold, destroy, conceal or refuse to provide any relevant information or thing required for the purpose of the inspection.

(2) **Facilitating inspection**—It is a condition of each licence and permit issued under this Act that the licensee or permit holder facilitate an inspection relevant to the licence or permit.

46. Forfeiture of liquor—Liquor kept for sale or offered for sale in contravention of subsection 5(1) and liquor purchased in contravention of section 27 is forfeited to the Crown.

Possession of proceeds

46.1(1) **Definition**—In this section and in section 47,

"proceeds," in relation to an offence under this Act, means,

(a) personal property, other than money, derived in whole or in part, directly or indirectly, from the commission of the offence, and

(b) money derived directly or indirectly from the commission of the offence.

(2) **Possession of proceeds**—No person shall knowingly possess the proceeds of an offence under this Act.

Seizure

47(0.1) **Definition**—In this section and in section 48,

"police officer" includes a conservation officer.

(1) **Seizure**—A police officer may seize any thing, including liquor, if,

(a) he or she reasonably believes that the thing will afford evidence of an offence under this Act;

(b) he or she reasonably believes that,

(i) the thing was used or is being used in connection with the commission of an offence under this Act, and

(ii) unless the thing is seized it is likely that it would continue to be used or would be used again in the commission of an offence under this Act; or

(c) he or she reasonably believes that the thing is proceeds from the commission of an offence under this Act.

(1.1) **Same**—If an offence appears to have been committed under this Act and a police officer reasonably believes, in view of the offence apparently committed and the presence of liquor, that a further offence is likely to be committed, the police officer may seize the liquor and the packages in which it is kept.

(2) **Order of restoration**—The Ontario Court of Justice may, upon the application of any person made within thirty days of a seizure under subsection (1) or (1.1), order that the things seized be restored forthwith to the applicant if the court is satisfied that,

(a) the applicant is entitled to possession of the things seized;

(b) the things seized are not required as evidence in any proceeding;

(c) continued detention of the things seized is not necessary to prevent the commission of an offence; and

(d) it is unlikely that the things will be forfeited on conviction under subsection (5).

(3) **Idem**—If the court is satisfied that an applicant under subsection (2) is entitled to possession of the things seized but is not satisfied as to all of the matters mentioned in clauses (2)(b), (c) and (d), it shall order that the things seized be restored to the applicant,

(a) upon the expiration of three months from the date of the seizure, if no proceeding in respect of an offence has been commenced; or

(b) upon the final conclusion of any such proceeding.

(4) **Forfeiture**—If no application has been made for the return of a thing seized under subsection (1) or (1.1) or an application has been made but upon the hearing of the application no order of restoration has been made, the thing seized is forfeited to the Crown.

(5) **Same**—If a person is convicted of an offence under this Act, the court shall order that any thing seized under subsection (1) or (1.1) in connection with the offence be forfeited to the Crown, unless the court considers that the forfeiture would be unjust in the circumstances.

(6) **Relief against forfeiture**—Any person with an interest in a thing forfeited under this section may apply to the Superior Court of Justice for relief against the forfeiture and the court may make an order providing for any relief that it considers just, including, but not limited to, one or more of the following orders:

1. An order directing that the thing or any part of the thing be returned to the applicant.
2. An order directing that any interest in the thing be vested in the applicant.
3. An order directing that an amount be paid by the Crown to the applicant by way of compensation for the forfeiture.

(7) **Same**—The court shall not order any relief under subsection (6) unless the court is satisfied that the applicant did not, directly or indirectly, participate in, or benefit from, any offence in connection with which the thing was seized.

48. Arrest without warrant—If a police officer finds a person apparently in contravention of this Act or apparently in contravention of a prescribed provision of the regulations and the person refuses to give his or her name and address or there are reasonable grounds to believe that the name or address given is false, the police officer may arrest the person without warrant. . . .

An arrest under s. 48 is valid and in force only until the officer is reasonably satisfied as to the identity of the subject. At that point, the person must be released and served an appropriate part I or part III offence notice for the violation that precipitated the encounter resulting in an arrest.

51. Analyst's certificate or report—A certificate or report purporting to be signed by a federal or provincial analyst as to the composition of any liquor or any other substance is admissible in evidence in any proceeding under this Act, and in the absence of evidence to the contrary, is proof of the information set out in the certificate or report and of the authority of the person giving it or making it, without proof of the appointment or signature of the person. . . .

Offences

61(1) **Offences**—A person is guilty of an offence if the person,

(a) knowingly furnishes false information in any application under this Act or in any statement or return required to be furnished under this Act;

(b) knowingly fails to comply with an order under subsection 38 (2); or

(c) contravenes any provision of this Act or the regulations.

(2) **Derivative**—A director or officer of a corporation who caused, authorized, permitted or participated in an offence under this Act by the corporation is guilty of an offence.

(3) **Penalties**—Upon conviction for an offence under this Act, other than a contravention of subsection 30(1), (2), (3), (4) or (4.1),

(a) a corporation is liable to a fine of not more than $250,000; and

(b) an individual is liable to a fine of not more than $100,000 or to imprisonment for a term of not more than one year or both.

(3.0.1) **Same, sale, etc., to a minor**—Upon conviction for contravening subsection 30(1), (2), (3), (4) or (4.1),

(a) a corporation is liable to a fine of not more than $500,000; and

(b) an individual is liable to a fine of not more than $200,000 or to imprisonment for a term of not more than one year or both.

(3.1) **Exception**—An individual who is convicted of an offence under subsection 31(2) or (4) is not liable to imprisonment.

(4) Repealed.

(4.1) **Forfeiture upon conviction**—Where a person is convicted of a contravention of section 33.1, all liquor found in the person's possession and seized under the search warrant is forfeited to the Crown.

(5) **Additional penalty**—In addition to any other penalty or action under this Act, the licence of a licensee who contravenes subsection 30(1) or (2) shall be suspended for a period of not less than seven days.

(6) **Minimum fine**—If a licensee contravenes subsection 30(1), (2), (3), (4) or (4.1), the fine imposed under this section shall be not less than $500.

(7) **Idem**—If a person who is not a licensee contravenes subsection 30(1), (2), (3), (4) or (4.1), the fine imposed under this section shall be not less than $100.

(8) **Limitation**—Subject to subsection (9), no proceeding under this section shall be commenced more than two years after the offence was committed.

(9) **Idem**—No proceeding under clause (1)(a) and no proceeding under subsection (2) that relates to a matter referred to in clause (1)(a) shall be commenced more than one year after the facts upon which the proceeding is based first came to the knowledge of the Registrar.

(10) **Additional penalty**—In addition to any other penalty, where a person is convicted of a contravention of section 33.1, the court shall impose a penalty, payable to the Board, of not more than $100 for each litre of liquor that was forfeited under subsection (4.1).

Regulations

62(1) **Regulations**—The Lieutenant Governor in Council may make regulations,

1. prescribing anything that is referred to in this Act as being prescribed;
2. governing the issuance, renewal, transfer and expiry of licences;
3. governing the issuance and expiry of permits;
4. prescribing conditions that attach to licences and permits;
5. prescribing the special occasions for which permits may be issued;
6. Repealed.
7. Repealed.
8. exempting any person, product or premises from any provision of this Act or the regulations;
9. requiring licensees and permit holders to provide the Registrar with such information and returns respecting the sale of liquor and the premises, methods and practices connected therewith as is prescribed and requiring any information provided to be verified by oath;

9.1 requiring licensees operating a ferment on premise facility to provide the Registrar with such information and returns respecting the operation of the facility as is prescribed and requiring any information provided to be verified on oath;

10. controlling the advertising of liquor or its availability for sale and requiring that advertisements be subject to the approval of the Registrar;

10.1 controlling the advertising of goods and services provided in connection with the making of beer and wine at a ferment on premise facility and requiring that advertisements be subject to the approval of the Registrar;

10.2 governing the information that may or must appear on labels and containers of liquor sold or kept for sale at a government store;

11. prescribing standards for licensed premises and premises used by permit holders for the sale and service of liquor;
11.1 prescribing standards for ferment on premise facilities;
12. prescribing or prohibiting methods and practices in connection with the serving of liquor;
12.1 prescribing or prohibiting methods and practices in connection with the making of beer or wine at ferment on premise facilities;
13. prohibiting licensees and permit holders from permitting any person to engage in prescribed activities on their premises;
14. governing the sale and service of liquor by a holder of a licence to sell liquor in a place other than licensed premises;
15. prescribing classes of premises on which a person under the age of nineteen years may not enter;
16. Repealed.
17. governing the issuance of documentation for proof of age;
18. prescribing hours of sale of liquor;
19. authorizing the Registrar to extend the hours of sale of liquor during events of municipal, provincial, national or international significance;
20. prohibiting manufacturers and employees, agents and licensed representatives of manufacturers from offering or giving inducements or engaging in prescribed practices with respect to the sale or promotion of liquor;
20.1 prohibiting operators of ferment on premise facilities and their employees and agents from offering or giving inducements or engaging in prescribed practices with respect to the provision of any service provided at such a facility;
21. prescribing the circumstances in which a manufacturer or employee, agent or licensed representative of a manufacturer may give liquor as a gift;
22. prescribing the circumstances in which a manufacturer may obtain a licence to sell liquor despite subsection 6(4);
23. regulating and controlling the possession and delivery of liquor sold under a licence or permit;
23.1 regulating and controlling the possession, storage, removal and consumption of beer and wine at a ferment on premise facility;
24. authorizing the Board to approve training courses for the service or delivery of liquor;
25. authorizing the Registrar to approve a temporary physical extension of licensed premises;
26. authorizing the Registrar to exempt any person from the requirement to provide information in respect of an application for a licence or permit;
27. governing the approval by the Registrar of the possession, service or consumption of liquor for research or educational purposes;
28. prescribing the circumstances in which, following a prescribed change of ownership in respect of a licence, liquor may be kept for sale, offered for sale or sold or delivered for a fee under the authority of the licence despite subsection 16(1) or (2);
29. designating classes of persons for the purpose of section 19;
30. defining "private place" for purposes of sections 30 and 31;
30.1 prescribing quantities of spirits, wine and beer for the purposes of section 33.1;
31. designating hospitals for purposes of section 36;

32. designating institutions for purposes of section 37, governing the transfer and admission of persons to and detention of persons in such institutions and providing for the management of such institutions;
33. prescribing licences that may be issued in a municipality despite section 52;
34. prohibiting or regulating and controlling the possession of liquor in provincial parks, in a park managed or controlled by The Niagara Parks Commission, The St. Lawrence Parks Commission, The St. Clair Parkway Commission or on lands owned or controlled by a conservation authority established or continued under the *Conservation Authorities Act*.

(2) **Scope of regulations**—A regulation may be general or particular in its application.

(3) **Conditions, qualifications, requirements**—Any provision of a regulation may be subject to such conditions, qualifications or requirements as are specified in the regulation.

(4) **Incorporation by reference**—A regulation under this Act that incorporates another document by reference may provide that the reference to the document includes amendments made to the document from time to time after the regulation is made.

Liquor Licence Act

RRO 1990, Reg. 718, as amended by O. Reg. 159/03

GENERAL

9(1) **Exemptions from Provisions of the Act**—The Act does not apply with respect to a product capable of human consumption that contains 0.5 of 1 per cent or less of alcohol by volume or 0.4 of 1 per cent or less of alcohol by weight.

(2) The Act does not apply with respect to concentrated food and beverage flavouring extracts that are not palatable when consumed alone.

(3) The Act does not apply with respect to denatured cooking wine that contains 20 per cent or less alcohol by volume and 1.5 per cent or more salt by volume.

ASSIGNMENT 1: LIQUOR LICENCE ACT

1. The LLA exists to control people's behaviour concerning liquor. Which two physical actions are the focus of this legislation?

2. Define drunkenness.

3. Give at least two examples of a drunk person posing problems for an officer.

4. Explain why the court preparation for a charge under the LLA against an establishment has to be carefully prepared.

5. In enforcing the LLA, what is one of an officer's main concerns?

6. Give an example of a safety hazard that someone under the influence may face.

7. What is a legal alternative to incarceration for a person under the influence?

8. What primary effect does alcohol have on a person?

9. An incarcerated drunk is sometimes at risk. Describe the risk and what may give rise to it.

10. In enforcing the LLA (and other laws), what should be an officer's two main concerns regarding his or her performance?

ASSIGNMENT 2: LIQUOR LICENCE ACT

1. In terms of frequency, what other provincial legislation may be encountered more than the LLA?

2. What is a negative spinoff an officer may encounter when enforcing the LLA?

3. Define liquor.

4. What factor determines whether or not a substance containing alcohol is deemed to be liquor?

5. Give two examples of substances that contain alcohol but that are not considered to be liquor.

6. Alcohol must be in a specific concentration to be governed by the LLA. What is that percentage?

7. What are the three essential elements that are considered in an investigation of "possession"?

8. If a person has a bottle of liquor in his or her pocket, would he or she be deemed to have control of it?

9. If a person hides a case of beer in nearby bushes, does he or she still have control, and therefore possession, of the liquor?

10. Why is all liquor deemed to be alcohol but not all alcohol deemed to be liquor?

ASSIGNMENT 3: PRIVATE PLACE AND PUBLIC PLACE UNDER THE LIQUOR LICENCE ACT

1. What is the main difference between private and public places?

2. Why is a residence considered to be a private place?

3. A boat, a motorhome, and a tent are not considered private places under the LLA unless certain conditions exist. What are those conditions?

4. If a tent qualifies as a residence, what land is also considered to be part of the residence?

5. In multiple-residence facilities, such as an apartment building, what are the exceptions to a private place? Give two examples.

6. What is the limitation period for any charge under the LLA?

7. What is the most common charge under the LLA?

8. To make a legal arrest for drunk, is the only requirement that the person under arrest be drunk?

9. In a single-dwelling home, can a person be arrested in their residence on a charge of drunk?

10. What legal alternative is available to making a drunk arrest?

ASSIGNMENT 4: POSSESSION UNDER THE LIQUOR LICENCE ACT

1. If you wish to hold an event involving liquor, whether it is for sale or not, how do you legally do it in a place that is not your residence?

2. What age do you have to be to legally consume liquor in a public place?

3. What is the minimum age allowed for persons involved in the hospitality industry handling liquor?

4. How may an open bottle of liquor legally be transported in a motor vehicle?

5. What two main conditions must exist for a minor to consume liquor legally?

6. Give four examples of personal identification accepted under the LLA.

7. What are the two arrest authorities under the LLA?

8. Under an arrest for "fail to identify," how long may the arrest be continued?

9. A patron of a licensed premises is asked to leave by hotel staff and refuses. Officers arrive and the person still refuses to leave. Under what authority is the arrest made?

10. An officer has the authority to order the evacuation of a licensed premises. This power can be exercised when a breach or a disturbance is occurring. What must the officer also believe for the authority to exist?

ASSIGNMENT 5: SEARCH, SEIZURE, AND CHARGE UNDER THE LIQUOR LICENCE ACT

1. If an officer suspects that liquor is being kept illegally in a vehicle or vessel, what may he or she search?

2. As an officer, you are authorized to inspect licensed premises under the authority of the LLA. If someone, such as an employee of the premises, obstructs your entry for this purpose, do you have an arrest authority? If so, what legislation provides the authority?

3. With respect to the commission of an offence under the LLA, what may an officer seize under normal circumstances?

4. If there is other alcohol present during an offence but that alcohol is not involved in the offence, under what conditions may that other alcohol be seized?

5. A case of beer is open in a vehicle and the driver is drinking from an open bottle of the same beer. What may be seized from the driver?

6. What is a reasonable definition of a package or a container suitable for transporting liquor?

7. What legislation allows an officer to obtain a warrant to search a premises operating without a permit issued under the LLA?

8. A person may apply for the return of liquor that has been seized from them. This application must be made within what time period?

9. How long after an offence under the LLA does an officer have to lay a charge?

10. An officer charges a minor with a liquor infraction, such as minor consume. Can this minor be given an out-of-court settlement option through a provincial offences ticket? (Hint: refer to the section on POA provincial offence notices.)

ASSIGNMENT 6: PROVINCIAL OFFENCE NOTICE (PON) (USING THE POA AND LLA)

In the section "Blank Tickets for Assignments and Practice" on page 301, you will find the documentation needed to complete this assignment:

- a copy of a PON;
- a copy of a summons insert; and
- a separate copy of a PON's Enforcement Agency Notes page (for question 2).

You will assume the role of the officer in this assignment and investigate the described occurrence.

1. There are situations in this scenario that offer a few opportunities for arrest. Select one and prepare a short synopsis of it, highlighting the following points:
   a. Who was arrested?
   b. By what authority were they arrested?
   c. Why was the application of arrest resorted to and how did you follow through with it?
2. Select one infraction, not related to the situation you chose for question 1, concerning one of the male patrons, and prepare the paperwork for it in the form of a PON using the appropriate inserts, if necessary. The information you may require for courts and dates is noted under the "Your Information" section. The PON must have sufficient officer notes to support the elements of the offence you charge.

Your Information

- Minor Traffic Court dates: Every Thursday at 1300 hours (1 p.m.) in courtroom 3 (this court is called Minor Traffic when in fact it handles all provincial offences)
- Young Offenders Court dates: Second Wednesday of every month at 1400 hours (2 p.m.) in courtroom 7

Scenario

It is Friday, February 14. This year you were approved by the Barrie Regional Police Service as a uniformed constable. On this date you are on foot patrol with Constable John Stevens working the nightshift (1600 hours [4 p.m.] to 0400 hours [4 a.m.]).

At 2030 hours (8:30 p.m.) you enter a licensed premises known as the Pit, located at 354 Dunlop Street West in the city of Barrie, on a " routine check." It is a popular gathering place for young people. When checking the men's washroom you discover a young male passed out on the floor. After waking him, you notice that he reeks of booze, his speech is slurred, and he has vomit on his shirt.

You pat him down but are unable to find any identification. He verbally identifies himself as Derrick Wildman, 19 years old, of 123 Home Street in Barrie, where he lives with his mom, Debbie, and his twin brother, John, who is at the bar with him. Derrick states that his red leather jacket is over the back of the chair on which he sat. His brother John is still in the bar with two other friends.

Your partner stays with Derrick and you enter the bar spotting a table with three males seated. A fourth chair has a red leather jacket hanging on the back of it. Two of the males appear to be under 19 years of age, and every chair has a half-empty bottle of beer in front of it.

You approach and ask them for ID. They demand to know what right you have to ask and why you are bothering them. After advising them of your function, two of the males supply photo ID validating them as legal. The third patron looks like the male in the washroom and offers a health card identifying himself as Jeremy James. He states he is 19 years old and lives at 117 Brown Street in a nearby town. You request photo ID; he says he doesn't have any, because his driver's licence and wallet were stolen two weeks ago. He says he filed a police report of the theft.

As you move around the table you reach the chair with the jacket over it. You ask who owns it because they are all wearing jackets. They reply that it belongs to another guy who just left to go down the street and get a pack of cigars. You check the jacket's pockets and discover a photo ID for Derrick Wildman, born June 25, 1985. In the inside pocket there is a half bottle of liquor, or mickey, labelled Captain Morgan Rum.

While recording names and addresses, you request that dispatch check files for stolen property and reports relating to a driver's licence for Jeremy James. Dispatch advises there is neither a file of a report nor any entry of a stolen licence in the Canadian Police Information Centre (CPIC).

As the party who identifies himself as Jeremy James reaches for his beer, you tell him that he will not be consuming his beverage any further. You are not satisfied that he is of legal age to consume, and you will charge him for that. You demand further ID, but he cannot produce any.

This concludes the scenario. Review the particulars of the assignment and complete it accordingly.

CHAPTER 3

Trespass to Property Act

INTRODUCTION

The primary tier associated with the *Trespass to Property Act* is enforcement through the issuance of a part I or part III offence notice. Referral is a secondary tier.

The *Trespass to Property Act* (TTPA) is another law commonly enforced by Ontario police. It provides a powerful tool in protecting property owners' rights and in resolving disputes in certain circumstances. The TTPA creates three offences and provides a variety of methods to notify people that they cannot trespass, or engage in certain activities on a particular property. The Act also establishes arrest authorities for both the police and the property owner, or a person authorized by the owner to act on their behalf. The arrest authorities for police are extended to those situations in which a trespasser has recently departed from the premises. There are also provisions in the Act for compensation to victims for damages incurred in trespassing occurrences to a maximum value of $1,000.

TERMINOLOGY

Occupier

"Occupier" refers to anyone with control over the premises or with authorization to exercise control over the premises.

The provision to have someone designated to act on the owner's behalf clearly provides for an agent's role. In some cases an agent may be obvious, such as a uniformed employee of a company. In other situations, the owner may be well advised to provide written authority to the specific person. This authority would authorize that person to act on his or her behalf with regard to a specific property for the purposes of the TTPA. Such written authority may be produced by the agent to validate his or her role, or it may be filed with the local police agency.

Premises

The definition of "premises" is broad enough to include almost any kind of property or land and includes vehicles, trailers, and portable structures.

Trains, rail cars, and aircraft are also covered by the TTPA, except while in motion. The reason for the exception is that these conveyances when in motion are covered by their own specific legislation such as the *Railways Act*. In addition, an owner or agent may be hard-pressed to order a trespasser off the property while it is moving (for example, a plane at 5,000 feet).

COMMON OFFENCES AND/OR PROVISIONS

There are only three offences under the TTPA.

1. *Enter the premises when entry is prohibited.* This offence involves someone entering a premises when one of the four methods for providing notice outlined below is in place. Most often, a sign clearly posted at the entrance is the method. This is the most commonly used section of the TTPA.
2. *Engage in prohibited activity on the premises.* To commit this offence, a person engages in some type of activity clearly forbidden by sign or by verbal instruction. One of the more common types of prohibition signs is one that says "No Hunting." This sign prohibits hunting but does not forbid entry onto the premises for other purposes.
3. *Fail to leave the premises when directed to do so.* Even in the absence of signs or notices, a person is required to leave a premises when directed to do so by its owner or person in charge. This offence commonly occurs in bars when someone has caused some problem but then refuses to leave until they have finished their drink. The person must leave immediately upon being asked to do so (although some persuasion is often a wise course of action in an effort to gain compliance).

Liability and Defences

1. *Absolute liability.* The offence of trespassing is an "absolute liability" offence, which means the onus is on the offender to prove his or her innocence. If the landowner has property that meets the criteria of lands that do not need to be posted or has used proper signs, then it is very difficult for an offender to prove they are not at fault.
2. *Colour of right.* A possible defence for an offender may be found in "colour of right." This means that the person had an honest belief that they had an interest in or title to the land in question that would establish their right to do as they wished on the land. For example, one neighbour erects a fence in a remote boundary area. The other neighbour challenges the action and is able to prove that the fence is to be erected on his land. However, the original neighbour honestly believed that he had located a property stake that identified the land as his. Even though the original neighbour was wrong in locating the boundaries, he had an honest belief that he was right. There will not be a trespassing conviction against the original neighbour in this matter.

3. *Implied permission.* In Canada it is customary to receive people at the front door of a residence. Generally, the front door faces or is the closest door to a public travelway such as a sidewalk. A person who wants to speak to the occupant of the premises is expected to approach the front door. A person who acts in this fashion is not trespassing unless such entry or access is clearly posted as being prohibited at the obvious point of entry. (However, a person who is found near one's back door at 4 a.m. is not given the same consideration. This person's activities and motives are certainly suspect and are not given any "implied permission." This kind of activity is more in line with "prowling by night" or "break and enter." See *Criminal Code* ss. 177 and 348.)

A person who has committed the offence of trespass where damage has occurred may be found liable for that damage as well. On application, the court may make a finding holding the accused liable for damages not to exceed $1,000. If a complainant had to take the matter to court on their own and if they had to hire a prosecutor (lawyer) to act on their behalf, the complainant may seek restitution to cover those costs. If the damages exceed $1,000 and the court awards the maximum of $1,000, the complainant may not pursue the matter further in small claims court. For example, if a motorcyclist trespasses onto a golf course and damages four or five greens, it will most likely cost a lot more than $1,000 to repair them. The charge of trespass should be prosecuted in this situation, but the owner should seek damages in civil court, where the $1,000 ceiling does not apply.

Methods of Providing Notice of Trespass

The TTPA provides four methods of prohibiting entry onto a premises.

1. *No notice required.* No notice of trespass is required if the premises is a garden, field, or other land that is under cultivation. Such premises may be a lawn; an orchard; a vineyard; a premises on which trees have been planted and have not attained an average height of more than two metres; woodlots on land used primarily for agricultural purposes; or land enclosed in such a manner that indicates the occupier's intention to keep persons and/or animals off the property.
2. *Orally or in writing.* An occupier may give oral or written notice to a person that their presence is not welcome on the property. Either of these methods will be deemed sufficient under the Act. The standard practice is to advise occupiers to send a registered letter to the person being given notice; usually, a copy is sent to the police service having jurisdiction over the premises. Oral notice is sufficient; however, a witness would strengthen the occupier's testimony for those situations where the person charged with an offence disputes having received notice. Another method of verification is to send written notice to back up the oral notice.
3. *By means of signs posted on the premises.* An occupier may erect a sign clearly visible from the approach to each ordinary entrance to the premises. The sign need only be visible in daylight, under normal circumstances, in order to meet the requirements of the TTPA. The sign may either name the prohibited activity or portray the activity in graphic

form. The sign must demonstrate that the activity is prohibited by drawing an oblique line drawn through the word or graphic. If only one purpose is indicated as prohibited in the sign, then s. 4(2) states that all other activities are permitted.

Signs may also give notice, by words or graphic representation, that an activity is permitted on a premises. Section 4 of the TTPA stipulates that when notice is given that one or more activities are permitted, all other activities are prohibited without further notice. Therefore, if a farmer posts signs on the property indicating that mountain biking is permitted, entry to or presence on the premises for any other purpose would be prohibited and constitute an offence under the TTPA. See figures 17 and 18.

4. *By coloured markings.* An occupier may post red or yellow circular signs, at least 10 cm in diameter, at the approach to each ordinary entrance to the premises. Posting red signs indicates that entry to the premises is prohibited. Yellow signs used in conjunction with an activity or list of activities signifies that entry on the premises is prohibited except for the activities listed. Green signs used in conjunction with an activity indicate that the activity is permitted.

FIGURE 17 Permitted Activity Sign

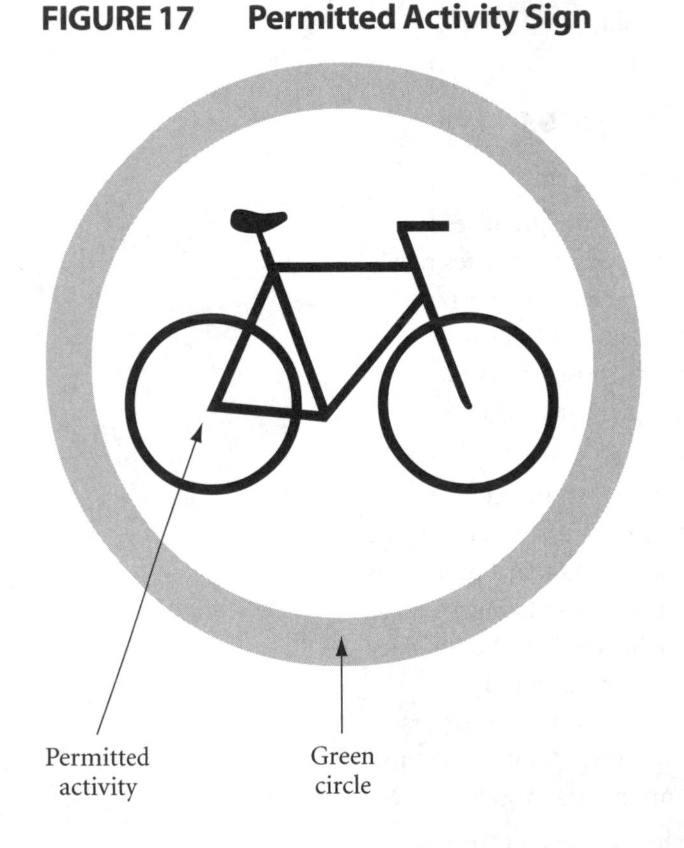

FIGURE 18 Prohibited Activity Sign

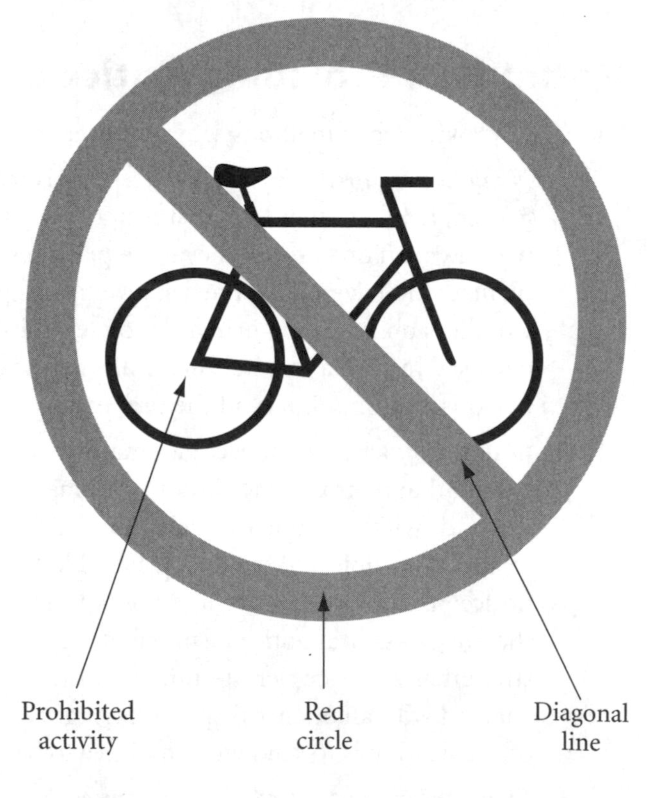

Trespass While Using a Motor Vehicle

An additional investigative power is provided if an offence is committed under the TTPA by means of a motor vehicle. In these cases, the owner of the motor vehicle, even when the owner is not the driver committing the offence, is liable for the offence and the resulting fine. This provision does not apply if the driver is actually convicted of the offence; therefore, the driver should be charged if he or she can be identified. If the investigating officer cannot identify the driver but can provide the identity of the motor vehicle's owner, then the owner may be charged. Pointing out this fact during an investigation frequently helps an owner overcome any reluctance to identify an acquaintance who borrowed the vehicle. This provision does not apply if the motor vehicle was in the driver's possession without the owner's consent.

ARREST POWERS

There are two powers of arrest without warrant given by the TTPA:

1. when the suspect is located on the premises (s. 9); and
2. when the suspect has just left the premises (s. 10).

With regard to the first situation, a person found committing an offence on the premises may be arrested by a police officer, the occupier, or a person authorized by the occupier. If any person other than a police officer makes the arrest, that person must promptly notify the police and turn the arrested person over to a police officer.

The arrest power with regard to the second situation, in which a suspect has left the premises, is limited in certain ways. The only person authorized to make such an arrest is a police officer. The officer must have reasonable and probable grounds to believe that the person has trespassed and has made a "fresh" departure from the premises, and the person must refuse to give his or her name or address. Alternatively, the person may provide a name or address that the officer believes on reasonable and probable grounds to be false.

An occupier may request police attendance to enforce the provisions of the TTPA if a trespasser will not leave a property. In order for the police to be able to exercise their authority lawfully, the occupier must demand, in the officer's presence, that the trespasser leave the premises. If the trespasser fails to comply with the demand, the officer has the legal authority to effect the arrest, as the person as been "found committing."

Under the *Liquor Licence Act*, the owner/agent of the licensed establishment may cause the removal of any unwanted persons. Where the owner/agent calls the police to assist in removing a non-compliant patron, the police do not have any authority to arrest under the LLA. However, under the TTPA, the police *do* have the authority if the above steps are followed, as the licensed property qualifies as a "premises" under the TTPA.

SEARCH POWERS

There are no specific search powers contained in the TTPA. If an arrest is made, then a search can be conducted under the common law powers of searching incident to an arrest, to protect the officer or the suspect, to preserve any evidence in the possession of the person being arrested, and/or to establish identification.

USE OF FORCE

There is no specific use of force authority in relation to police officers' arrest and search powers under the TPPA. Section 146(1) of the POA applies (an officer who is acting on reasonable and probably grounds may use as much force as is necessary to carry out his or her lawful purpose).

LIMITATION PERIOD

The TTPA has the general limit of six months from the date of the offence, as defined in the POA.

NON-POLICE AGENCIES INVOLVED

In a property dispute between adjacent property owners, a municipal "fence viewer" may be involved in the dispute with a view to resolving it. Fence viewing is a service performed by citizens appointed by a local governing authority, such as a township council. Viewers are selected because they are knowledgeable in fence construction and livestock, and are reputed to be reasonable people. When there is a dispute, usually over fence boundaries and responsibilities (outside of survey conflicts), one of the parties may apply to have the "viewing committee" visit the property and examine the problem. The committee "views" the physical situation, hears representations from all sides, and makes a finding. Generally, the finding is implemented and provides a remedy to the dispute. Compliance by the parties is the norm.

PROVINCIAL OFFENCES GRID COMPLETION

Common Offences and/or Provisions

Three equally common offences:

1. enter premises when entry is prohibited,
2. engage in a prohibited activity on the premises, and
3. fail to leave the premises when directed to do so.

Arrest Powers

On the premises, a police officer, an occupier, or a person authorized by the occupier may arrest any person found committing an offence against the Act. Off the premises, only police officers may arrest a person who has "freshly departed" and who also refuses to identify him- or herself or who gives a name and address that the police officer has reasonable and probable grounds to believe are false.

Search Powers

No powers of search without warrant under the TTPA.

Use of Force

No specific use of force authority under the TTPA (refer to *Criminal Code* s. 25 or POA s. 146(1)).

Limitation Period

Six months from the date of the offence.

Non-Police Agencies Involved

Fence viewers of the municipality.

Trespass to Property Act

RSO 1990, c. T.21

1(1) **Definitions**—In this Act,

"occupier" includes,

(a) a person who is in physical possession of premises, or

(b) a person who has responsibility for and control over the condition of premises or the activities there carried on, or control over persons allowed to enter the premises, even if there is more than one occupier of the same premises;

"premises" means lands and structures, or either of them, and includes,

(a) water,

(b) ships and vessels,

(c) trailers and portable structures designed or used for residence, business or shelter,

(d) trains, railway cars, vehicles and aircraft, except while in operation.

(2) **School boards**—A school board has all the rights and duties of an occupier in respect of its school sites as defined in the *Education Act*.

2(1) **Trespass an offence**—Every person who is not acting under a right or authority conferred by law and who,

(a) without the express permission of the occupier, the proof of which rests on the defendant,

(i) enters on premises when entry is prohibited under this Act, or

(ii) engages in an activity on premises when the activity is prohibited under this Act; or

(b) does not leave the premises immediately after he or she is directed to do so by the occupier of the premises or a person authorized by the occupier,

is guilty of an offence and on conviction is liable to a fine of not more than $2,000.

(2) **Colour of right as a defence**—It is a defence to a charge under subsection (1) in respect of premises that is land that the person charged reasonably believed that he or she had title to or an interest in the land that entitled him or her to do the act complained of.

3(1) **Prohibition of entry**—Entry on premises may be prohibited by notice to that effect and entry is prohibited without any notice on premises,

(a) that is a garden, field or other land that is under cultivation, including a lawn, orchard, vineyard and premises on which trees have been planted and have not attained an average height of more than two metres and woodlots on land used primarily for agricultural purposes; or

(b) that is enclosed in a manner that indicates the occupier's intention to keep persons off the premises or to keep animals on the premises.

(2) **Implied permission to use approach to door**—There is a presumption that access for lawful purposes to the door of a building on premises by a means apparently provided and used for the purpose of access is not prohibited.

4(1) **Limited permission**—Where notice is given that one or more particular activities are permitted, all other activities and entry for the purpose are prohibited and any additional notice that entry is prohibited or a particular activity is prohibited on the same premises shall be construed to be for greater certainty only.

(2) **Limited prohibition**—Where entry on premises is not prohibited under section 3 or by notice that one or more particular activities are permitted under subsection (1), and notice is given that a particular activity is prohibited, that activity and entry for the purpose is prohibited and all other activities and entry for the purpose are not prohibited.

5(1) **Method of giving notice**—A notice under this Act may be given,

(a) orally or in writing;

(b) by means of signs posted so that a sign is clearly visible in daylight under normal conditions from the approach to each ordinary point of access to the premises to which it applies; or

(c) by means of the marking system set out in section 7.

(2) **Substantial compliance**—Substantial compliance with clause (1)(b) or (c) is sufficient notice.

6(1) **Form of sign**—A sign naming an activity or showing a graphic representation of an activity is sufficient for the purpose of giving notice that the activity is permitted.

(2) **Idem**—A sign naming an activity with an oblique line drawn through the name or showing a graphic representation of an activity with an oblique line drawn through the representation is sufficient for the purpose of giving notice that the activity is prohibited.

7(1) **Red markings**—Red markings made and posted in accordance with subsections (3) and (4) are sufficient for the purpose of giving notice that entry on the premises is prohibited.

(2) **Yellow markings**—Yellow markings made and posted in accordance with subsections (3) and (4) are sufficient for the purpose of giving notice that entry is prohibited except for the purpose of certain activities and shall be deemed to be notice of the activities permitted.

(3) **Size**—A marking under this section shall be of such a size that a circle ten centimetres in diameter can be contained wholly within it.

(4) **Posting**—Markings under this section shall be so placed that a marking is clearly visible in daylight under normal conditions from the approach to each ordinary point of access to the premises to which it applies.

8. Notice applicable to part of premises—A notice or permission under this Act may be given in respect of any part of the premises of an occupier.

9(1) **Arrest without warrant on premises**—A police officer, or the occupier of premises, or a person authorized by the occupier may arrest without warrant any person he or she believes on reasonable and probable grounds to be on the premises in contravention of section 2.

(2) **Delivery to police officer**—Where the person who makes an arrest under subsection (1) is not a police officer, he or she shall promptly call for the assistance of a police officer and give the person arrested into the custody of the police officer.

(3) **Deemed arrest**—A police officer to whom the custody of a person is given under subsection (2) shall be deemed to have arrested the person for the purposes of the provisions of the *Provincial Offences Act* applying to his or her release or continued detention and bail.

10. Arrest without warrant off premises—Where a police officer believes on reasonable and probable grounds that a person has been in contravention of section 2 and has made fresh departure from the premises, and the person refuses to give his or her name and address, or there are reasonable and probable grounds to believe that the name or address given is false, the police officer may arrest the person without warrant.

The arrest authority under s. 10 is necessary in order for the law to be enforced, as a suspect whose identity is not known cannot be held accountable for his or her actions. An arrest in such cases remains in effect until the officer is satisfied with the identification provided by the suspect.

11. Motor vehicles and motorized snow vehicles—Where an offence under this Act is committed by means of a motor vehicle, as defined in the *Highway Traffic Act*, or by means of a motorized snow vehicle, as defined in the *Motorized Snow Vehicles Act*, the driver of the motor vehicle or motorized snow vehicle is liable to the fine provided under this Act and, where the driver is not the owner, the owner of the motor vehicle or motorized snow vehicle is liable to the fine provided under this Act unless the driver is convicted of the offence or, at the time the offence was committed, the motor vehicle or motorized snow vehicle was in the possession of a person other than the owner without the owner's consent.

12(1) **Damage award**—Where a person is convicted of an offence under section 2, and a person has suffered damage caused by the person convicted during the commission of the offence, the court shall, on the request of the prosecutor and with the consent of the person who suffered the damage, determine the damages and shall make a judgment for damages against the person convicted in favour of the person who suffered the damage, but no judgment shall be for an amount in excess of $1,000.

(2) **Costs of prosecution**—Where a prosecution under section 2 is conducted by a private prosecutor, and the defendant is convicted, unless the court is of the opinion that the prosecution was not necessary for the protection of the occupier or the occupier's interests, the court shall determine the actual costs reasonably incurred in conducting the prosecution and, despite section 60 of the *Provincial Offences Act*, shall order those costs to be paid by the defendant to the prosecutor.

(3) **Damages and costs in addition to fine**—A judgment for damages under subsection (1), or an award of costs under subsection (2), shall be in addition to any fine that is imposed under this Act.

(4) **Civil action**—A judgment for damages under subsection (1) extinguishes the right of the person in whose favour the judgment is made to bring a civil action for damages against the person convicted arising out of the same facts.

(5) **Idem**—The failure to request or refusal to grant a judgment for damages under subsection (1) does not affect a right to bring a civil action for damages arising out of the same facts.

(6) **Enforcement**—The judgment for damages under subsection (1), and the award for costs under subsection (2), may be filed in the Small Claims Court and shall be deemed to be a judgment or order of that court for the purposes of enforcement.

ASSIGNMENT: TRESPASS TO PROPERTY ACT

Scenario

A landowner sees some ATVs in his field. With the aid of binoculars, he observes the vehicles and drivers and gathers fairly accurate descriptions of them. He then walks down the road to the field, but before he arrives, the trespassers flee down a concession road. At this point the owner's rights to protect his property are limited; he no longer has the right to arrest. But that does not mean he cannot talk to them.

The owner finds some damage to his crop, so he calls the police. The responding officer speaks to the owner and receives his complaint and descriptions. In checking the area he comes across what appears to be the same group of ATVs. The riders and vehicles fit the owner's descriptions. The officer now has reasonable and probable grounds to believe these people have committed the offence of trespass. However, one ATV driver is missing from the group, and it appears that this driver has something to do with an ATV capsized in a creek.

QUESTIONS

1. Can the officer charge the drivers with trespass?

2. The other drivers do not offer any information concerning the absent driver to the officer. Can the owner of this vehicle be charged with trespass?

3. One of the drivers refuses to produce any documentation for the officer or identify himself. The officer arrests the driver to investigate his identity. Under what circumstances can the driver continue to be held in custody?

4. Another driver offers verbal identification only, and the officer has doubts as to the validity of this information. What can the officer do in this situation?

5. Does the farmer have any recourse under this legislation to be compensated for his crop damage? If so, what is the allowable limit of compensation?

6. At a subsequent trial, one of the drivers states that the farmer's land wasn't posted with any signs prohibiting their entry. Is this a real defence in this situation?

7. Could the farmer have pursued and arrested the drivers of the ATVs?

8. A subsequent investigation by the officer leads to the identity of the driver of the capsized ATV. This driver is also charged with trespass. Can the owner of the ATV continue to be charged or convicted of the same offence?

9. Because there is damage to the farmer's crop and he wants compensation, should the officer give the offenders a court date or an out-of-court settlement?

GROUP ASSIGNMENTS: LIQUOR LICENCE ACT AND TRESPASS TO PROPERTY ACT

The following assignments are designed to be completed in groups in class. They cover material from both the LLA and TTPA.

It is recommended that as you read the scenarios, you highlight or note the key players and their roles, as well as the descriptions and facts. This will allow you to address the charges in the questions.

Scenario: Bacardi Skateboarders

You are police constable #181 with the Barrie Regional Police Service. You are working the nightshift on March 28 from 7 p.m. to 7 a.m. in uniform and operating marked police cruiser #407. At 21:15 hours, you receive a radio call to attend the Bayfield Mall at 320 Bayfield Street, Barrie, Ontario, regarding disorderlies. You are directed to see the security officer, Jessica Evans, outside Bowlerama. You are aware that there have been persistent problems at this mall with regard to disorderly youths, illegal consumption of liquor, and disruptive behaviour toward other mall patrons.

Since Bowlerama has a rear entrance, you approach the mall using this entrance. Upon your approach, you observe a group of youths leaving that exit and heading onto Cundles Road West. One youth is carrying an orange skateboard, and another a blue hockey bag. None of the other members of the group stand out.

At 21:26 hours, you meet Officer Evans outside the mall door, and she advises that the group of disorderly youths left the mall just prior to your arrival. She states that one youth in particular is known to the mall security as Jimmy Brant, DOB 31 March 1992, of 49 Coulter Street, Barrie. He was carrying an orange Excalibur skateboard. This male has been served a trespass notice from March 11, prohibiting him from entry to the mall property. This was as a result of his being caught skateboarding through the mall halls, in spite of signs clearly prohibiting this activity.

Another male youth in his company was carrying a blue duffle bag, which contained two bottles of Bacardi white rum. All of the youths had been drinking from these bottles and, upon the approach of the mall security, ran from the mall.

Because of the increasing problems with disorderlies in this mall, the management has recently requested that charges be laid whenever appropriate in trespass situations. The officer advises that all of the youths who had been drinking appeared to be under the age of 19.

Recalling the group of youths that you noticed on your arrival, you advise Officer Evans that you will investigate them and advise her of the results.

A short time later, at approximately 21:37 hours, you find the same group of youths approaching the gully area just behind the mall on Cundles Road West.

As you round the corner, you see the youth with the blue hockey bag throw it over the guardrail and into the gully. You leave your cruiser and approach them. You ask them what they are doing, explaining that you are investigating an occurrence at the mall concerning trespassers. The first person you speak to is the youth with the orange skateboard; he denies being in the mall. You ask for identification and he says that he has none, but verbally identifies himself as Fred Hamelink. You then speak to the youth whom you saw throw the hockey bag, and he produces a valid Ontario driver's licence in the name of Robin Laking, of 14 Springhome Road, Barrie. The class G driver's licence number is L3526 39678 90228.

In speaking to these two youths, you detect a strong odour of an alcoholic beverage from both of their breaths. You ask them to sit in the back of the cruiser while you check their identifications, and they agree. You lean over the guardrail and retrieve the blue bag. It is open and you can see two partly empty bottles of Bacardi white rum.

QUESTIONS

1. Based on the information above and your knowledge of the relevant statutes, respond to the following questions. For each, circle "Yes" or "No" in response to the question, and explain your reasoning in the space provided using details from the scenario and from the appropriate statutes.

   Is there a power of arrest in the trespass situation? (Yes / No)

   Is there a power of arrest in the liquor situation? (Yes / No)

   Is there any power of search in the trespass situation? (Yes / No)

   Is there any power of search in the liquor situation? (Yes / No)

   Is there any power of seizure in the liquor situation? (Yes / No)

2. Prepare the following PONs: a trespass charge for Brant and a possession of liquor by minor for Laking. In the officer's notes section, record appropriate notes to support each charge.

Scenario: School Dance

You are police constable #181 with the Barrie Regional Police Service. You are working a "paid duty" shift, to earn extra money during your time off, on the night of March 7. You are at a local high school, East Lake Collegiate, located at 37 Johnson Street, Barrie, Ontario.

For this type of detail, you are present for a high school dance. In speaking to the principal, you are advised that although the Students' Council is paying for your service, you have full authority to act as an agent for the owner, the Barrie District School Board, with respect to school property.

You are instructed that the rules for the dance are:

- no drinking or attending the dance under the influence of alcohol;
- students who leave the dance after 9 p.m. will not be permitted to return;
- any person not a student wishing to enter and attend the dance must be signed in as a guest of a current student; and
- any persons suspended from class are prohibited from being on school property, this event included.

These rules are also posted on a sign attached to the glass door that serves as the entry door.

Traditionally, problems at dances are minor. They usually consist of students who have been drinking, and who are generally underage, and students who are not allowed on school property attempting to get inside. Of course, you can also expect emotional rescue events with couples breaking up; students hiding liquor in washroom garbage cans; and students attempting to smuggle liquor into the dance, using the traditional statement, "I have to get something in my locker." This usually prompts the response, "That wouldn't be booze, would it?"

The dance is starting to get busy, and everyone seems to be having fun. During your observations in the lobby, your attention is drawn to a male who has gone in and out a few times and doesn't seem to be part of any particular group. In speaking to a faculty member on duty, you are advised that the male was a student at the school until this fall, when he dropped out. The teacher is not sure of his age. He is John Stevens, a boyfriend of a female student currently attending the school, and she signs him in for these events.

Just before 9 p.m., while checking the parking lot, you observe Stevens coming out again, and you decide to investigate his activities. You observe him travel to a parked car at the end of a row of cars in the lot. As he enters the vehicle, the dome light allows you to observe three persons already in the car. There are a male and female in the back seat, and a female in the front passenger's seat who appears to be drinking a beer.

As you reach the driver's door, Stevens takes a drink from a bottle that appears to be beer as well. Upon tapping the roof with your flashlight and shining it into the car, Stevens drops his beer into his lap with the expected results. In response to your instruction, he rolls the window down. While speaking, you observe the front seat passenger trying to discreetly hide a beer under her jacket.

You ask the time-honoured question, "What are you guys doing here?" In response, you get the traditional answer: "Nothing, officer." You inform the occupants that you observed them drinking and demand that they surrender any alcohol in their possession. Stevens hands you a dripping bottle of a beer labelled Molson Golden, and the girlfriend reaches into her coat and hands over her beer, labelled Molson Canadian.

A teacher appears and states that he was advised by another student that there seemed to be a problem in the parking lot. He remains as you conduct your investigation.

The girlfriend produces a student card identifying herself as Susan Evans, DOB 28 March 1991. Stevens confirms his identity with a valid Ontario driver's licence. All four tell you that they are attending the dance and were just getting some "fresh air." The two in the back seat, both 17 years old, produce valid student cards. The teacher advises you that he is going back into the school.

A visual check of the car reveals that the only real places to hide more alcohol are in the console and glovebox. In response to your instructions, both are opened and reveal nothing. As there are no keys in the ignition, you request them from Stevens. Upon opening the trunk, you discover an open Molson's Pleasure Pack with eight bottles missing.

Turning back to the occupants, you have each one exit the auto upon your command. The males are not wearing jackets, and their clothes are such that they couldn't hide any more beer on their persons. The girls have jackets and purses. You have them remove their jackets and hand them over to you, along with their purses. Both jackets are checked, with negative results. In the purse belonging to Evans, you discover a 12-ounce bottle of Seagram's rye.

The teacher returns and advises that he checked the sign-in list and discovered that Stevens's name does not appear as a guest. Evans's name is not there either as having signed anyone in.

QUESTIONS

1. Based on the information above and your knowledge of the relevant statutes, respond to the following questions. For each, circle "Yes" or "No" in response to the question, and explain your reasoning in the space provided using details from the scenario and from the appropriate statutes. You are limited to 25 words for each explanation.

   Is there authority for a charge of trespassing against Stevens? (Yes / No)

   Is there authority for the search of the vehicle's occupants? (Yes / No)

Is there authority for the search of the car? (Yes / No)

Can you seize the case of beer? (Yes / No)

Is there any power of seizure for the liquor found in Evans's purse? (Yes / No)

2. Prepare a PON for Stevens under the TTPA and for Evans under the LLA. Supplementary information is provided below to help you complete the forms. Submit the forms to your instructor with your answer sheet, including appropriate notes on the reverse to support each charge. You are limited to 75 words for the evidence on the back of each ticket. Use them wisely!

SUPPLEMENTARY DATA

Stevens's driver's licence number:	S1345 68878 90512
Stevens's home address:	123 Anne Street Barrie, ON L4M 4T2
Evans's home address:	47 Fall Lane Barrie, ON L2M 1T5
Your court date:	21st of the month, 2 p.m., courtroom 7

CHAPTER 4

Residential Tenancies Act, 2006

INTRODUCTION

The primary tier associated with the *Residential Tenancies Act* is referral, and the main duty of officers is to refer landlords and tenants to the Landlord and Tenant Board. Officers may also assist the Ministry of Municipal Affairs and Housing's Investigation and Enforcement Unit with enforcing the Act.

The *Residential Tenancies Act, 2006* (RTA), which replaced the *Tenant Protection Act, 1997*, provides the rules that govern the interactions between landlords and tenants. It deals with tenancy agreements and outlines the duties and responsibilities of both the landlord and the tenant during a tenancy agreement. For example, there are provisions for rights of entry for the landlord under certain circumstances, rights of access and seizure during abandonment of the tenancy, and procedures for recovery of the tenant's possessions within certain timeframes.

There are several offences enacted under the Act, but they are used only in those situations that cannot be resolved through negotiation between the parties with the assistance of a mediator.

The Act is an important piece of legislation because its proper enforcement can prevent landlord and tenant disputes from escalating into criminal assaults, or worse.

Law enforcement officers who are called to landlord and tenant disputes perform two steps: the first step is to referee and the second is to refer.

As referees, officers fulfill an important part of their primary mandate: "to preserve the peace." The officer must first determine whether the RTA applies to the dispute, or whether the dispute falls under one of the many exemptions described in the Act. For example, the Act does not apply to a living accommodation that is a member unit of a non-profit housing co-operative. Officers therefore need to be familiar with the exemptions so that they can determine whether the Act applies to the dispute at hand.

If an officer concludes that the dispute is governed by the Act, he or she advises the parties of their rights as well as their obligations. Officers do not usually perform enforcement under this Act. They usually refer the parties to other government agencies that oversee it.

Usually, it is the Investigation and Enforcement Unit (IEU) of the Ministry of Municipal Affairs and Housing that lays charges under this Act, although there is nothing precluding officers from laying a charge by way of part III of the *Provincial Offences Act*. However, for a number of reasons, it is more logical for the IEU to lay the charges. For example, the relevant histories of the parties may not be available to the officer at the time of the dispute. As well, expert advice may be needed if the circumstances of the dispute are complex and the relevant sections of the Act are convoluted. Further, if charges are laid by the IEU, the ministry provides prosecutors for the legal proceedings that follow.

Landlord and tenant disputes often occur after hours, on holidays, and on long weekends when there is usually no immediate assistance from outside agencies available. It is here that a knowledgeable officer with good communication skills can solve problems by giving sound advice and negotiating a reasonable interim truce until the parties can contact the necessary government agencies for further assistance.

The province has also provided two agencies to assist the police in enforcing this Act. The Landlord and Tenant Board mediates disputes between parties involved. This can be a powerful tool for the officer, who can often diffuse the situation by referring the people involved in the dispute to the Board. If enforcement is to be considered, the Ministry of Municipal Affairs and Housing's Investigation and Enforcement Unit can assist or take over the investigation.

Although the two provincial agencies do provide valuable assistance in resolving these types of disputes, police officers or private security officers working for a landlord should keep in mind the volatility of these disputes and handle them accordingly, with a view to minimizing the risks of further offences. Accordingly, it would be wise to be aware of some of the commonly used provisions of the Act.

This chapter refers only to the sections and definitions in the Act that are routinely encountered by law-enforcement and security officers. For additional sections, refer to the complete statute.

TERMINOLOGY

Landlord

A "landlord" can be

1. the owner of a rental unit, or any other person who permits occupancy of a rental unit, other than a tenant who occupies a rental unit in a residential complex and who permits another person to also occupy the unit or any part of the unit;
2. the heirs, assigns, personal representatives, and successors in title of a person referred to in (1), above; or
3. a person, other than a tenant occupying a rental unit in a residential complex, who is entitled to possession of the residential complex and who attempts to enforce any of the rights of a landlord under a tenancy agreement or the Act, including the right to collect rent.

Rent

"Rent" includes the amount of any consideration paid or given or required to be paid or given by or on behalf of a tenant to a landlord or the landlord's agent for the right to occupy a rental unit and for any services and facilities and any privilege, accommodation, or thing that the landlord provides for the tenant in respect of the occupancy of the rental unit, whether or not a separate charge is made for services and facilities or for the privilege, accommodation, or thing. Rent does not include an amount paid by a tenant to a landlord to reimburse the landlord for property taxes paid by the landlord with respect to a mobile home or a land lease home owned by a tenant.

Rental Unit

A "rental unit" is any living accommodation used or intended for use as rented residential premises. It includes

1. a site for a mobile home or site on which there is a land lease home used or intended for use as rented residential premises; and
2. a room in a boarding house, rooming house, or lodging house and a unit in a care home.

Residential Complex

A "residential complex" is

1. a building or related group of buildings in which one or more rental units are located;
2. a mobile home park or land lease community; or
3. a site that is a rental unit.

Residential Unit

A "residential unit" is any living accommodation used or intended for use as residential premises. It includes

1. a site for a mobile home or on which there is a land lease home used or intended for use as a residential premises; and
2. a room in a boarding house, rooming house, or lodging house and a unit in a care home.

Tenancy Agreement

A "tenancy agreement" is a written, oral, or implied agreement between a tenant and a landlord for occupancy of a rental unit and includes a licence to occupy a rental unit.

Tenant

A "tenant" is a person who pays rent in return for the right to occupy a rental unit and includes the tenant's heirs, assigns, and personal representatives, but does not include a person who has the right to occupy a rental unit by virtue of being

1. a co-owner of the residential complex in which the rental unit is located; or
2. a shareholder of a corporation that owns the resident complex.

Utilities

"Utilities" are heat, electricity, and water.

Vital Service

A "vital service" is hot or cold water, fuel, electricity, gas, or, during the part of each year prescribed by the regulations, heat.

Accommodation Not Included

Temporary housing provided for farm workers—for example, those who pick seasonal fruit—is not covered by the RTA. Similarly, accommodation provided to the travelling public—for example, a lodge, a bed and breakfast, or a hotel or motel—is not included in the RTA. Such accommodation is covered by the *Innkeepers Act*. Correctional facilities are also not included in the RTA.

Further exceptions are noted in the following situations.

- The Act does not generally apply to a roommate of a tenant unless the roommate has also entered into a tenancy agreement with the landlord.
- A tenant who shares a washroom or kitchen with the owner or owner's spouse, as well as each party's immediate family, is not addressed by this Act. This situation is generally governed by common law. The tenant can be asked to leave without reason, provided that appropriate notice is given. This notice is usually the same time period as the rental payment period (that is, if rent is paid monthly, the required notice is one month). If the tenant in this type of shared situation has failed to pay rent, he or she must leave when asked to do so by the owner. This provision is not to be confused with the types of rental arrangements and units covered by this Act.

COMMON OFFENCES

Sections 233, 234, and 235 of the Act outline a number of offences, but they are seldom used because the Landlord and Tenant Board attempts to mediate disputes and charges are not required in most circumstances.

If enforcement is required, there is a second government agency available—the Ministry of Municipal Affairs and Housing's Investigation and Enforcement Unit.

Here is a selected list of offences that an officer may consider in various situations:

- Landlord knowingly changes locks and does not give the tenant a replacement key (s. 233(b))
- Tenant knowingly changes locks without the landlord's permission (s. 233(b))
- Landlord knowingly withholds or interferes with a vital service (fuel, electricity, gas, hot or cold water, or heat) during prescribed times (s. 233(a))
- Landlord knowingly harasses or threatens in a manner which induces the tenant to move (s. 233(i))
- Tenant knowingly harasses, obstructs, or interferes with a landlord enforcing a right (s. 233(j))
- Landlord knowingly seizes a tenant's property without lawful authority (s. 233(d))
- Landlord enters a rental unit without proper notice (s. 234(a))
- Landlord unlawfully recovers possession of a rental unit (unlawful eviction) (s. 234(w))
- Landlord fails to make an evicted tenant's property available for retrieval (s. 234(b))
- Person attempts to commit any of the offences in ss. 233, 234, or 235 (s. 236).

For more information, see "Non-Police Agencies Involved," below.

COMMONLY ENCOUNTERED PROVISIONS

Tenant's Belongings

The tenant has 72 hours following eviction by the sheriff to retrieve his or her belongings (s. 41(3)), during reasonable hours (defined by O. Reg. 516/06 as 8:00 a.m. until 8:00 p.m.). The landlord is not permitted to hold the tenant's belongings to secure payment of rent arrears. If there are rents owing, the landlord must take the appropriate legal steps to retrieve those monies. If the landlord fails to make the tenant's belongings available for retrieval during this period, there is an offence under the Act that might be laid under part III of the *Provincial Offences Act.*

Death of a Tenant: Tenancy Termination and Disposal of Property of the Deceased (ss. 91-92)

The death of a tenant is more common than many people realize.

If the deceased was the sole occupant of a rental unit, the tenancy is deemed to be terminated 30 days after the death of the tenant. This period allows time for locating family, securing property, and collecting any unpaid rent.

The landlord is responsible for the safekeeping of the deceased tenant's property during this period. Dangerous or unhygienic concerns, such as rotting food that may attract infestation, may be addressed immediately. After 30 days, the landlord may dispose of the balance of the property, and this disposal is often done by sale. A claimant may come forward to establish a real interest or right to the property for a period of up to six months after the death. The landlord must pay the claimant the proceeds of any sale of such property minus a reasonable handling fee.

NOTE: If an officer is unable to locate any next of kin of the deceased, the city clerk's office will act as public executor of the estate and arrange for a funeral. This function falls under the Social Services office. In organized areas such as counties, the county's Administrator of Public Works performs this role.

Notice of Termination of Tenancy Agreements

Notice of termination is probably the most frequently asked-about provision of the RTA. The tenant's ability to terminate the agreement is covered in s. 47, which permits the tenant to terminate a tenancy at the end of that tenancy period or at the end of the term of a tenancy for a fixed term by giving notice of that termination to the landlord in accordance with s. 44.

The landlord must have a valid reason for termination of the tenancy. The Act permits a landlord to give a tenant notice to end the tenancy early and the reason for the termination must fall into one of two categories of permitted reasons—"for cause" or "no fault," as explained in the following paragraphs.

"For cause" reasons for termination are used when the tenant does something that he or she should not do, or does not do something that he or she should do. Some examples of "for cause" reasons for terminating a tenancy are:

- not paying the rent in full;
- causing damage to the rental unit;
- disturbing other tenants or the landlord; and
- illegal activity in the rental unit or residential complex.

"No fault" reasons for termination are not related to what the tenant has done or not done. Some examples of those reasons are:

- the landlord plans to do major repairs or renovations that require a building permit and the work cannot be done until the unit is empty;
- the landlord requires the rental unit because the landlord, a member of the landlord's immediate family, or their caregiver wishes to move into the unit; and
- the landlord has agreed to sell the property and the purchaser requires all or part of the property because the purchaser, a member of the purchaser's immediate family, or their caregiver wishes to move into the unit. (This reason for eviction applies only in rental buildings with three or fewer units and in condominiums.)

Abandonment

A landlord cannot recover possession of a rental unit as being abandoned if arrears of rent are not owing or if there is no strong evidence that the tenant has vacated the unit.

A landlord may apply to the Landlord and Tenant Board for an order terminating the tenancy if the landlord believes that the tenant has abandoned the rental unit (s. 79).

The landlord cannot dispose of property in the abandoned unit unless he or she gets an order from the Board terminating the tenancy and 30 days have passed after obtaining the order, or the landlord gives 30 days' notice to both the tenant and the Board of the landlord's intention to dispose of the property.

The landlord, if notified by the tenant that the tenant wishes to remove his or her property within the 30-day notice period, shall make the property available to the tenant at a reasonable time, and place the property in a location within reasonable distance of the rental unit (s. 42(5)).

The Eviction Process

A tenant can be evicted only if a landlord obtains an order terminating a tenancy from the Board, and only the sheriff can enforce that order.

In order to properly evict a tenant, a landlord must complete the following steps:

1. Serve the tenant with a valid Notice of Termination.
2. Apply to the Board for a hearing, and serve the tenant with the Application and Notice of Hearing.
3. Obtain an order terminating a tenancy from the Board.
4. Deliver the order terminating a tenancy to the sheriff for enforcement.

A landlord who has completed the property eviction process and was successful will also be given a Writ of Possession which directs the possession of the unit back to the lawful owner/landlord.

If the sheriff is concerned that the public peace may be at risk during an eviction, he or she may ask to be accompanied to the residence by the police. As well, the police are usually called if the tenant refuses to leave after being served with an eviction notice by the sheriff. Attending officers should keep in mind that a refusal to vacate could very well constitute a violation of the *Trespass to Property Act*, where provisions of arrest and subsequent prosecution may exist.

Vital Services

A landlord is not permitted to withhold or interfere with a vital service. Vital services are defined as fuel, gas, electricity, hot or cold water, and heat (between September 1 and June 15). O. Reg. 517/06 provides details on requirements for various services, including plumbing, electrical, heating, lighting, and ventilation.

Rights of Entry

There are provisions for the rights of landlords to enter the tenant's premises, but those rights are significantly curtailed in an effort to preserve the privacy of the tenant. A landlord may enter a tenant's premises between the hours of 8:00 a.m. and 8:00 p.m. only if 24 hours' written notice has been given to the tenant. The notice must set out the reason for the entry and the date and time of the entry. Entry can only be for specific reasons:

1. to carry out a repair or replacement or do work in the rental unit;
2. to allow a potential mortgagee or insurer of the residential complex to view the rental unit;
3. to allow a person who holds a certificate of authorization within the meaning of the *Professional Engineers Act* or another qualified person to make a physical inspection of the rental unit to satisfy a requirement imposed under s. 9(4) of the *Condominium Act, 1998*; or
4. to carry out an inspection of the rental unit, if
   - the inspection is for the purpose of determining whether or not the rental unit is in a good state of repair and fit for habitation and complies with health, safety, housing, and maintenance standards, consistent with the landlord's obligations under s. 20(1) or s. 161, and
   - it is reasonable to carry out the inspection; or
5. for any other reasonable reason for entry specified in the tenancy agreement.

A landlord can enter a unit without written notice at any time where

- there is an emergency (such as a fire or flooding); or
- the tenant consents to the entry at the time of entry.

A landlord can enter a unit without written notice between 8:00 a.m. and 8:00 p.m. if

- the rental agreement requires the landlord to clean the unit, unless the agreement provides for different hours for cleaning; and
- the landlord enters the unit to show the unit to prospective tenants after notice of termination has been given by the landlord, or the tenant, and the landlord has made reasonable efforts in advance to advise the tenant of the entry.

ARREST POWERS

There are no arrest powers conferred by this Act.

SEARCH POWERS

There are no search without warrant powers conferred by this Act.

USE OF FORCE

There is no specific use of force for arrest or search in the Act. If force is required in order to enforce the provisions of the Act, use *Criminal Code* s. 25 or *Provincial Offences Act* s. 146 as your authority.

LIMITATION PERIOD

No charges may be laid under this Act unless proceedings are commenced within two years of the date of the alleged offence. In the case of an offence alleging the furnishing of false information as required by the Act, the time limit is two years from the date that the facts came to the attention of the minister. These limits are contained in s. 239(1).

NON-POLICE AGENCIES INVOLVED

Landlord and Tenant Board

This agency resolves disputes between landlords and tenants regarding rights and responsibilities of both sides. Parties in dispute can be referred to the Board for mediation. The Board can be reached within the Toronto calling area at 416-645-8080 and outside Toronto at 1-888-332-3234.

Ministry of Municipal Affairs and Housing, Investigation and Enforcement Unit

This section of the ministry deals with issues of compliance investigations and enforcement of violations of the Act. If charges are contemplated, the IEU should be contacted. The IEU can be reached within the Toronto calling area at 416-585-7214 and outside Toronto at 1-888-772-9277. For a mailing address and fax number, go to www.mah.gov.on.ca/page1177.aspx.

Citizens' Inquiry Bureau

This bureau provides a bilingual information and referral service. It provides an access point to information on government programs and services, locations, and staff, including legal clinic telephone numbers. 1-800-267-8097.

Landlord's Self-Help Centre

The Centre is a non-profit legal clinic that provides information, advice, and referrals to small-scale landlords. The Centre can be reached within the Toronto calling area at 416-504-5190 and outside Toronto at 1-800-730-3218. For more information, go to www.landlordselfhelp.com.

PROVINCIAL OFFENCES GRID COMPLETION

Common Offences and/or Provisions

Not commonly used, as mediation is the main focus of the provincial government's approach to this Act. Police officers and security professionals involved in these types of disputes should keep the peace and attempt to prevent additional offences from occurring.

Arrest Powers

None

Search Powers

None

Use of Force

No specific use of force authority contained in the RTA. Use *Criminal Code* s. 25 or *Provincial Offences Act* s. 146.

Limitation Period

Applications for tribunal hearing must be commenced within two years of the alleged infraction of the provisions.

Non-Police Agencies Involved

1. Landlord and Tenant Board
2. Ministry of Municipal Affairs and Housing, Investigation and Enforcement Unit
3. Citizens' Inquiry Bureau
4. Landlord's Self-Help Centre

Residential Tenancies Act, 2006

SO 2006, c. 17

PART I
INTRODUCTION

1. Purposes of Act—The purposes of this Act are to provide protection for residential tenants from unlawful rent increases and unlawful evictions, to establish a framework for the regulation of residential rents, to balance the rights and responsibilities of residential landlords and tenants and to provide for the adjudication of disputes and for other processes to informally resolve disputes.

2(1) Interpretation—In this Act,

"Board" means the Landlord and Tenant Board; . . .

"landlord" includes,

(a) the owner of a rental unit or any other person who permits occupancy of a rental unit, other than a tenant who occupies a rental unit in a residential complex and who permits another person to also occupy the unit or any part of the unit, . . .

"rent" includes the amount of any consideration paid or given or required to be paid or given by or on behalf of a tenant to a landlord or the landlord's agent for the right to occupy a rental unit and for any services and facilities and any privilege, accommodation or thing that the landlord provides for the tenant in respect of the occupancy of the rental unit, whether or not a separate charge is made for services and facilities or for the privilege, accommodation or thing, but "rent" does not include,

(a) an amount paid by a tenant to a landlord to reimburse the landlord for property taxes paid by the landlord with respect to a mobile home or a land lease home owned by a tenant;

"residential unit" means any living accommodation used or intended for use as residential premises, and "residential unit" includes,

(a) a site for a mobile home or on which there is a land lease home used or intended for use as a residential premises, and

(b) a room in a boarding house, rooming house or lodging house and a unit in a care home; . . .

"tenancy agreement" means a written, oral or implied agreement between a tenant and a landlord for occupancy of a rental unit and includes a licence to occupy a rental unit;

"tenant" includes a person who pays rent in return for the right to occupy a rental unit and includes the tenant's heirs, assigns and personal representatives, but "tenant" does not include a person who has the right to occupy a rental unit by virtue of being,

(a) a co-owner of the residential complex in which the rental unit is located, or

(b) a shareholder of a corporation that owns the residential complex;

"utilities" means heat, electricity and water;

"vital service" means hot or cold water, fuel, electricity, gas or, during the part of each year prescribed by the regulations, heat. . . .

(3) **Interpretation, abandoned**—For the purposes of this Act, a tenant has not abandoned a rental unit if the tenant is not in arrears of rent. . . .

5. Exemptions from Act—This Act does not apply with respect to,

(a) living accommodation intended to be provided to the travelling or vacationing public or occupied for a seasonal or temporary period in a hotel, motel or motor hotel, resort, lodge, tourist camp, cottage or cabin establishment, inn, campground, trailer park, tourist home, bed and breakfast vacation establishment or vacation home;

(b) living accommodation whose occupancy is conditional upon the occupant continuing to be employed on a farm, whether or not the accommodation is located on that farm;

(c) living accommodation that is a member unit of a non-profit housing co-operative;

(d) living accommodation occupied by a person for penal or correctional purposes;

(e) living accommodation that is subject to the *Public Hospitals Act*, the *Private Hospitals Act*, the *Long-Term Care Homes Act, 2007*, the *Ministry of Correctional Services Act* or the *Child and Family Services Act*;

(f) short-term living accommodation provided as emergency shelter;

(g) living accommodation provided by an educational institution to its students or staff where,

(i) the living accommodation is provided primarily to persons under the age of majority, or all major questions related to the living accommodation are decided after consultation with a council or association representing the residents, and

(ii) the living accommodation does not have its own self-contained bathroom and kitchen facilities or is not intended for year-round occupancy by full-time students or staff and members of their households;

(h) living accommodation located in a building or project used in whole or in part for non-residential purposes if the occupancy of the living accommodation is conditional upon the occupant continuing to be an employee of or perform services related to a business or enterprise carried out in the building or project;

(i) living accommodation whose occupant or occupants are required to share a bathroom or kitchen facility with the owner, the owner's spouse, child or parent or the spouse's child or parent, and where the owner, spouse, child or parent lives in the building in which the living accommodation is located;

(j) premises occupied for business or agricultural purposes with living accommodation attached if the occupancy for both purposes is under a single lease and the same person occupies the premises and the living accommodation; . . .

PART III
RESPONSIBILITIES OF LANDLORDS

20(1) **Landlord's responsibility to repair**—A landlord is responsible for providing and maintaining a residential complex, including the rental units in it, in a good state of repair and fit for habitation and for complying with health, safety, housing and maintenance standards.

(2) **Same**—Subsection (1) applies even if the tenant was aware of a state of non-repair or a contravention of a standard before entering into the tenancy agreement.

21(1) **Landlord's responsibility re services**—A landlord shall not at any time during a tenant's occupancy of a rental unit and before the day on which an order evicting the tenant is executed, withhold the reasonable supply of any vital service, care service or food that it is the landlord's obligation to supply under the tenancy agreement or deliberately interfere with the reasonable supply of any vital service, care service or food.

(2) **Non-payment**—For the purposes of subsection (1), a landlord shall be deemed to have withheld the reasonable supply of a vital service, care service or food if the land-

lord is obligated to pay another person for the vital service, care service or food, the landlord fails to pay the required amount and, as a result of the non-payment, the other person withholds the reasonable supply of the vital service, care service or food.

22. Landlord not to interfere with reasonable enjoyment—A landlord shall not at any time during a tenant's occupancy of a rental unit and before the day on which an order evicting the tenant is executed substantially interfere with the reasonable enjoyment of the rental unit or the residential complex in which it is located for all usual purposes by a tenant or members of his or her household.

23. Landlord not to harass, etc.—A landlord shall not harass, obstruct, coerce, threaten or interfere with a tenant.

24. Changing locks—A landlord shall not alter the locking system on a door giving entry to a rental unit or residential complex or cause the locking system to be altered during the tenant's occupancy of the rental unit without giving the tenant replacement keys.

25. Privacy—A landlord may enter a rental unit only in accordance with section 26 or 27.

Entry Without Notice

26(1) **Entry without notice, emergency, consent**—A landlord may enter a rental unit at any time without written notice,

(a) in cases of emergency; or

(b) if the tenant consents to the entry at the time of entry.

(2) **Same, housekeeping**—A landlord may enter a rental unit without written notice to clean it if the tenancy agreement requires the landlord to clean the rental unit at regular intervals and,

(a) the landlord enters the unit at the times specified in the tenancy agreement; or

(b) if no times are specified, the landlord enters the unit between the hours of 8 a.m. and 8 p.m.

(3) **Entry to show rental unit to prospective tenants**—A landlord may enter the rental unit without written notice to show the unit to prospective tenants if,

(a) the landlord and tenant have agreed that the tenancy will be terminated or one of them has given notice of termination to the other;

(b) the landlord enters the unit between the hours of 8 a.m. and 8 p.m.; and

(c) before entering, the landlord informs or makes a reasonable effort to inform the tenant of the intention to do so.

27(1) **Entry with notice**—A landlord may enter a rental unit in accordance with written notice given to the tenant at least 24 hours before the time of entry under the following circumstances:

1. To carry out a repair or replacement or do work in the rental unit.
2. To allow a potential mortgagee or insurer of the residential complex to view the rental unit.
3. To allow a person who holds a certificate of authorization within the meaning of the *Professional Engineers Act* or a certificate of practice within the meaning of the *Architects Act* or another qualified person to make a physical inspection of the rental unit to satisfy a requirement imposed under subsection 9(4) of the *Condominium Act, 1998*.
4. To carry out an inspection of the rental unit, if,
   i. the inspection is for the purpose of determining whether or not the rental unit is in a good state of repair and fit for habitation and complies with health, safety, housing and maintenance standards, consistent with the landlord's obligations under subsection 20(1) or section 161, and
   ii. it is reasonable to carry out the inspection.
5. For any other reasonable reason for entry specified in the tenancy agreement.

(2) **Same**—A landlord or, with the written authorization of a landlord, a broker or salesperson registered under the *Real Estate and Business Brokers Act, 2002*, may enter a rental unit in accordance with written notice given to the tenant at least 24 hours before the time of entry to allow a potential purchaser to view the rental unit.

(3) **Contents of notice**—The written notice under subsection (1) or (2) shall specify the reason for entry, the day of entry and a time of entry between the hours of 8 a.m. and 8 p.m.

28. Entry by canvassers—No landlord shall restrict reasonable access to a residential complex by candidates for election to any office at the federal, provincial or municipal level, or their authorized representatives, if they are seeking access for the purpose of canvassing or distributing election material. . . .

PART IV
RESPONSIBILITIES OF TENANTS

33. Tenant's responsibility for cleanliness—The tenant is responsible for ordinary cleanliness of the rental unit, except to the extent that the tenancy agreement requires the landlord to clean it.

34. Tenant's responsibility for repair of damage—The tenant is responsible for the repair of undue damage to the rental unit or residential complex caused by the wilful or negligent conduct of the tenant, another occupant of the rental unit or a person permitted in the residential complex by the tenant.

35(1) **Changing locks**—A tenant shall not alter the locking system on a door giving entry to a rental unit or residential complex or cause the locking system to be altered during the tenant's occupancy of the rental unit without the consent of the landlord.

(2) **Landlord application**—If a tenant alters a locking system, contrary to subsection (1), the landlord may apply to the Board for an order determining that the tenant has altered the locking system on a door giving entry to the rental unit or the residential complex or caused the locking system to be altered during the tenant's occupancy of the rental unit without the consent of the landlord.

(3) **Order**—If the Board in an application under subsection (2) determines that a tenant has altered the locking system or caused it to be altered, the Board may order that the tenant provide the landlord with keys or pay the landlord the reasonable out-of-pocket expenses necessary to change the locking system.

36. Tenant not to harass, etc.—A tenant shall not harass, obstruct, coerce, threaten or interfere with a landlord. . . .

PART V
SECURITY OF TENURE AND TERMINATION OF TENNANCIES

. . .

41(1) **Disposal of abandoned property if unit vacated**—A landlord may sell, retain for the landlord's own use or otherwise dispose of property in a rental unit or the residential complex if the rental unit has been vacated in accordance with,

(a) a notice of termination of the landlord or the tenant;

(b) an agreement between the landlord and the tenant to terminate the tenancy;

(c) subsection 93(2); or

(d) an order of the Board terminating the tenancy or evicting the tenant.

(2) **Where eviction order enforced**—Despite subsection (1), where an order is made to evict a tenant, the landlord shall not sell, retain or otherwise dispose of the tenant's property before 72 hours have elapsed after the enforcement of the eviction order.

(3) **Same**—A landlord shall make an evicted tenant's property available to be retrieved at a location close to the rental unit during the prescribed hours within the 72 hours after the enforcement of an eviction order.

(4) **Liability of landlord**—A landlord is not liable to any person for selling, retaining or otherwise disposing of a tenant's property in accordance with this section.

(5) **Agreement**—A landlord and a tenant may agree to terms other than those set out in this section with regard to the disposal of the tenant's property.

(6) **Enforcement of landlord obligations**—If, on application by a former tenant, the Board determines that a landlord has breached an obligation under subsection (2) or (3), the Board may do one or more of the following:

1. Order that the landlord not breach the obligation again.
2. Order that the landlord return to the former tenant property of the former tenant that is in the possession or control of the landlord.
3. Order that the landlord pay a specified sum to the former tenant for,
   i. the reasonable costs that the former tenant has incurred or will incur in repairing or, where repairing is not reasonable, replacing property of the former tenant that was damaged, destroyed or disposed of as a result of the landlord's breach, and
   ii. other reasonable out-of-pocket expenses that the former tenant has incurred or will incur as a result of the landlord's breach.
4. Order that the landlord pay to the Board an administrative fine not exceeding the greater of $10,000 and the monetary jurisdiction of the Small Claims Court.
5. Make any other order that it considers appropriate.

42(1) **Disposal of property, unit abandoned**—A landlord may dispose of property in a rental unit that a tenant has abandoned and property of persons occupying the rental unit that is in the residential complex in which the rental unit is located in accordance with subsections (2) and (3) if,

(a) the landlord obtains an order terminating the tenancy under section 79; or

(b) the landlord gives notice to the tenant of the rental unit and to the Board of the landlord's intention to dispose of the property.

(2) **Same**—If the tenant has abandoned the rental unit, the landlord may dispose of any unsafe or unhygienic items immediately.

(3) **Same**—The landlord may sell, retain for the landlord's own use or otherwise dispose of any other items if 30 days have passed after obtaining the order referred to in clause (1)(a) or giving the notice referred to in clause (1)(b) to the tenant and the Board.

(4) **Tenant's claim to property**—If, before the 30 days have passed, the tenant notifies the landlord that he or she intends to remove property referred to in subsection (3), the tenant may remove the property within that 30-day period.

(5) **Same**—If the tenant notifies the landlord in accordance with subsection (4) that he or she intends to remove the property, the landlord shall make the property available to the tenant at a reasonable time and at a location close to the rental unit.

(6) **Same**—The landlord may require the tenant to pay the landlord for arrears of rent and any reasonable out-of-pocket expenses incurred by the landlord in moving, storing or securing the tenant's property before allowing the tenant to remove the property.

(7) **Same**—If, within six months after the date the notice referred to in clause (1)(b) is given to the tenant and the Board or the order terminating the tenancy is issued, the tenant claims any of his or her property that the landlord has sold, the landlord shall pay to the tenant the amount by which the proceeds of sale exceed the sum of,

(a) the landlord's reasonable out-of-pocket expenses for moving, storing, securing or selling the property; and

(b) any arrears of rent.

(8) **No liability**—Subject to subsections (5) and (7), a landlord is not liable to any person for selling, retaining or otherwise disposing of the property of a tenant in accordance with this section.

Notice of Termination—General

43(1) **Notice of termination**—Where this Act permits a landlord or tenant to give a notice of termination, the notice shall be in a form approved by the Board and shall,

(a) identify the rental unit for which the notice is given;

(b) state the date on which the tenancy is to terminate; and

(c) be signed by the person giving the notice, or the person's agent.

(2) **Same**—If the notice is given by a landlord, it shall also set out the reasons and details respecting the termination and inform the tenant that,

(a) if the tenant vacates the rental unit in accordance with the notice, the tenancy terminates on the date set out in clause (1)(b);

(b) if the tenant does not vacate the rental unit, the landlord may apply to the Board for an order terminating the tenancy and evicting the tenant; and

(c) if the landlord applies for an order, the tenant is entitled to dispute the application.

Period of Notice

44(1) **Period of notice, daily or weekly tenancy**—A notice under section 47, 58 or 144 to terminate a daily or weekly tenancy shall be given at least 28 days before the date the termination is specified to be effective and that date shall be on the last day of a rental period.

(2) **Period of notice, monthly tenancy**—A notice under section 47, 58 or 144 to terminate a monthly tenancy shall be given at least 60 days before the date the termination is specified to be effective and that date shall be on the last day of a rental period.

(3) **Period of notice, yearly tenancy**—A notice under section 47, 58 or 144 to terminate a yearly tenancy shall be given at least 60 days before the date the termination is specified to be effective and that date shall be on the last day of a yearly period on which the tenancy is based.

(4) **Period of notice, tenancy for fixed term**—A notice under section 47, 58 or 144 to terminate a tenancy for a fixed term shall be given at least 60 days before the expiration date specified in the tenancy agreement, to be effective on that expiration date.

(5) **Period of notice, February notices**—A tenant who gives notice under subsection (2), (3) or (4) which specifies that the termination is to be effective on the last day of February or the last day of March in any year shall be deemed to have given at least 60 days notice of termination if the notice is given not later than January 1 of that year in respect of a termination which is to be effective on the last day of February, or February 1 of that year in respect of a termination which is to be effective on the last day of March....

Notice by Tenant

47. Tenant's notice to terminate, end of period or term—A tenant may terminate a tenancy at the end of a period of the tenancy or at the end of the term of a tenancy for a fixed term by giving notice of termination to the landlord in accordance with section 44.

Notice by Landlord at End of Period or Term

48(1) **Notice, landlord personally, etc., requires unit**—A landlord may, by notice, terminate a tenancy if the landlord in good faith requires possession of the rental unit for the purpose of residential occupation by,

(a) the landlord;

(b) the landlord's spouse;

(c) a child or parent of the landlord or the landlord's spouse; or

(d) a person who provides or will provide care services to the landlord, the landlord's spouse, or a child or parent of the landlord or the landlord's spouse, if the person receiving the care services resides or will reside in the building, related group of buildings, mobile home park or land lease community in which the rental unit is located.

(2) **Same**—The date for termination specified in the notice shall be at least 60 days after the notice is given and shall be the day a period of the tenancy ends or, where the tenancy is for a fixed term, the end of the term.

(3) **Earlier termination by tenant**—A tenant who receives notice of termination under subsection (1) may, at any time before the date specified in the notice, terminate the tenancy, effective on a specified date earlier than the date set out in the landlord's notice.

(4) **Same**—The date for termination specified in the tenant's notice shall be at least 10 days after the date the tenant's notice is given.

49(1) **Notice, purchaser personally requires unit**—A landlord of a residential complex that contains no more than three residential units who has entered into an agreement of purchase and sale of the residential complex may, on behalf of the purchaser, give the tenant of a unit in the residential complex a notice terminating the tenancy, if the purchaser in good faith requires possession of the residential complex or the unit for the purpose of residential occupation by,

(a) the purchaser;

(b) the purchaser's spouse;

(c) a child or parent of the purchaser or the purchaser's spouse; or

(d) a person who provides or will provide care services to the purchaser, the purchaser's spouse, or a child or parent of the purchaser or the purchaser's spouse, if the person receiving the care services resides or will reside in the building, related group of buildings, mobile home park or land lease community in which the rental unit is located. . . .

Notice by Landlord Before End of Period or Term

59(1) **Non-payment of rent**—If a tenant fails to pay rent lawfully owing under a tenancy agreement, the landlord may give the tenant notice of termination of the tenancy effective not earlier than,

(a) the 7th day after the notice is given, in the case of a daily or weekly tenancy; and

(b) the 14th day after the notice is given, in all other cases. . . .

(3) **Notice void if rent paid**—The notice of termination is void if, before the day the landlord applies to the Board for an order terminating the tenancy and evicting the tenant based on the notice, the tenant pays,

(a) the rent that is in arrears under the tenancy agreement; and

(b) the additional rent that would have been due under the tenancy agreement as at the date of payment by the tenant had notice of termination not been given. . . .

61(1) **Termination for cause, illegal act**—A landlord may give a tenant notice of termination of the tenancy if the tenant or another occupant of the rental unit commits an illegal act or carries on an illegal trade, business or occupation or permits a person to do so in the rental unit or the residential complex.

(2) **Notice**—A notice of termination under this section shall set out the grounds for termination and shall provide a termination date not earlier than,

(a) the 10th day after the notice is given, in the case of a notice grounded on an illegal act, trade, business or occupation involving,

(i) the production of an illegal drug,

(ii) the trafficking in an illegal drug, or

(iii) the possession of an illegal drug for the purposes of trafficking; or

(b) the 20th day after the notice is given, in all other cases.

(3) **Definitions**—In this section,

"illegal drug" means a controlled substance or precursor as those terms are defined in the *Controlled Drugs and Substances Act* (Canada);

"possession" has the same meaning as in the *Controlled Drugs and Substances Act* (Canada);

"production" means, with respect to an illegal drug, to produce the drug within the meaning of the *Controlled Drugs and Substances Act* (Canada);

"trafficking" means, with respect to an illegal drug, to traffic in the drug within the meaning of the *Controlled Drugs and Substances Act* (Canada).

62(1) **Termination for cause, damage**—A landlord may give a tenant notice of termination of the tenancy if the tenant, another occupant of the rental unit or a person whom the tenant permits in the residential complex wilfully or negligently causes undue damage to the rental unit or the residential complex.

(2) **Notice**—A notice of termination under this section shall,

(a) provide a termination date not earlier than the 20th day after the notice is given;

(b) set out the grounds for termination; and

(c) require the tenant, within seven days,

(i) to repair the damaged property or pay to the landlord the reasonable costs of repairing the damaged property, or

(ii) to replace the damaged property or pay to the landlord the reasonable costs of replacing the damaged property, if it is not reasonable to repair the damaged property.

(3) **Notice void if tenant complies**—The notice of termination under this section is void if the tenant, within seven days after receiving the notice, complies with the requirement referred to in clause (2)(c) or makes arrangements satisfactory to the landlord to comply with that requirement.

63(1) **Termination for cause, damage, shorter notice period**—Despite section 62, a landlord may give a tenant notice of termination of the tenancy that provides a termination date not earlier than the 10th day after the notice is given if the tenant, another occupant of the rental unit or a person whom the tenant permits in the residential complex,

(a) wilfully causes undue damage to the rental unit or the residential complex; or

(b) uses the rental unit or the residential complex in a manner that is inconsistent with use as residential premises and that causes or can reasonably be expected to cause damage that is significantly greater than the damage that is required in order to give a notice of termination under clause (a) or subsection 62(1). . . .

64(1) **Termination for cause, reasonable enjoyment**—A landlord may give a tenant notice of termination of the tenancy if the conduct of the tenant, another occupant of the rental unit or a person permitted in the residential complex by the tenant is such that it substantially interferes with the reasonable enjoyment of the residential complex for all usual purposes by the landlord or another tenant or substantially interferes with another lawful right, privilege or interest of the landlord or another tenant....

66(1) **Termination for cause, act impairs safety**—A landlord may give a tenant notice of termination of the tenancy if,

(a) an act or omission of the tenant, another occupant of the rental unit or a person permitted in the residential complex by the tenant seriously impairs or has seriously impaired the safety of any person....

Death of Tenant

91(1) **Death of tenant**—If a tenant of a rental unit dies and there are no other tenants of the rental unit, the tenancy shall be deemed to be terminated 30 days after the death of the tenant.

(2) **Reasonable access**—The landlord shall, until the tenancy is terminated under subsection (1),

(a) preserve any property of a tenant who has died that is in the rental unit or the residential complex other than property that is unsafe or unhygienic; and

(b) afford the executor or administrator of the tenant's estate, or if there is no executor or administrator, a member of the tenant's family reasonable access to the rental unit and the residential complex for the purpose of removing the tenant's property....

PART VII
RULES RELATING TO RENT

General Rules

105(1) **Security deposits, limitation**—The only security deposit that a landlord may collect is a rent deposit collected in accordance with section 106.

(2) **Definition**—In this section and in section 106,

"security deposit" means money, property or a right paid or given by, or on behalf of, a tenant of a rental unit to a landlord or to anyone on the landlord's behalf to be held by or for the account of the landlord as security for the performance of an obligation or the payment of a liability of the tenant or to be returned to the tenant upon the happening of a condition.

106(1) **Rent deposit may be required**—A landlord may require a tenant to pay a rent deposit with respect to a tenancy if the landlord does so on or before entering into the tenancy agreement.

(2) **Amount of rent deposit**—The amount of a rent deposit shall not be more than the lesser of the amount of rent for one rent period and the amount of rent for one month.

(3) **Same**—If the lawful rent increases after a tenant has paid a rent deposit, the landlord may require the tenant to pay an additional amount to increase the rent deposit up to the amount permitted by subsection (2).

(4) **Qualification**—A new landlord of a rental unit or a person who is deemed to be a landlord under subsection 47(1) of the *Mortgages Act* shall not require a tenant to pay a rent deposit if the tenant has already paid a rent deposit to the prior landlord of the rental unit.

(5) **Exception**—Despite subsection (4), if a person becomes a new landlord in a sale from a person deemed to be a landlord under subsection 47(1) of the *Mortgages Act*, the new landlord may require the tenant to pay a rent deposit in an amount equal to the amount with respect to the former rent deposit that the tenant received from the proceeds of sale. . . .

(7) **Deduction applied to rent deposit**—The landlord may deduct from the amount payable under subsection (6) the amount, if any, by which the maximum amount of the rent deposit permitted under subsection (2) exceeds the amount of the rent deposit paid by the tenant and the deducted amount shall be deemed to form part of the rent deposit paid by the tenant. . . .

PART XVI
OFFENCES

. . .

235(1) **Harassment, interference with reasonable enjoyment**—Any landlord or superintendent, agent or employee of the landlord who knowingly harasses a tenant or interferes with a tenant's reasonable enjoyment of a rental unit or the residential complex in which it is located is guilty of an offence.

(2) **Exception**—For the purposes of subsection (1), the carrying out of repairs, maintenance and capital improvements does not constitute harassment or interference with a tenant's reasonable enjoyment of a rental unit or the residential complex in which it is located unless it is reasonable to believe,

(a) that the date or time when the work is done or the manner in which it is carried out is intended to harass the tenant or interfere with the tenant's reasonable enjoyment; or

(b) that the repairs, maintenance or capital improvements were carried out without reasonable regard for the tenant's right to reasonable enjoyment. . . .

238(1) **Penalties**—A person, other than a corporation, who is guilty of an offence under this Act is liable on conviction to a fine of not more than $25,000. . . .

239(1) **Limitation**—No proceeding shall be commenced respecting an offence under clause 234(v) more than two years after the date on which the facts giving rise to the offence came to the attention of the Minister.

(2) **Same**—No proceeding shall be commenced respecting any other offence under this Act more than two years after the date on which the offence was, or is alleged to have been, committed.

Ontario Regulation 516/06
General

PART I
INTERPRETATION AND EXEMPTIONS

...

4(1) **Definition of "vital service"**—For the purpose of the definition of "vital service" in subsection 2(1) of the Act, September 1 to June 15 is prescribed as the part of the year during which heat is a vital service.

(2) For the purposes of subsection (1), heat shall be provided so that the room temperature at 1.5 metres above floor level and one metre from exterior walls in all habitable space and in any area intended for normal use by tenants, including recreation rooms and laundry rooms but excluding locker rooms and garages, is at least 20 degrees Celsius.

(3) Subsection (2) does not apply to a rental unit in which the tenant can regulate the temperature and a minimum temperature of 20 degrees Celsius can be maintained by the primary source of heat. . . .

PART II
MATTERS RELATING TO RENT

Reasonable Enjoyment During Repairs

...

9. Receipt—A document constitutes a receipt for the purposes of section 109 of the Act if it includes, at a minimum,

(a) the address of the rental unit to which the receipt applies;

(b) the name of the tenants to whom the receipt applies;

(c) the amount and date for each payment received for any rent, rent deposit, arrears of rent, or any other amount paid to the landlord and shall specify what the payment was for;

(d) the name of the landlord of the rental unit; and

(e) the signature of the landlord or the landlord's authorized agent. . . .

> Section 109 of the RTA requires a landlord to provide any tenant or former tenant with a receipt upon request, free of charge, for any payment made to the landlord. Section 9 of this regulation sets out the information that a valid receipt must include. It is always advisable to issue and obtain a receipt because, in the event of a dispute, an oral agreement is more difficult to enforce.

PART VI
GENERAL

46. Hours for retrieval of property—For the purposes of subsection 41(3) of the Act, a landlord shall make an evicted tenant's property available between the hours of 8 a.m. and 8 p.m.

Ontario Regulation 517/06
Maintenance Standards

PART III
UTILITIES AND SERVICES

Plumbing

9(1) **Maintenance**—Plumbing and drainage systems in a residential complex, and their appurtenances, shall be maintained free from leaks, defects and obstructions and adequately protected from freezing.

(2) A residential complex shall be provided with a means of sewage disposal.

(3) The means of sewage disposal shall be maintained in a good state of repair.

10(1) **Required fixtures**—Subject to subsections (2), (3) and (4), every rental unit shall contain the following fixtures:

1. A toilet.
2. A kitchen sink.
3. A washbasin.
4. A bathtub or shower.

(2) Subsection (1) does not apply to rental units that share a fixture described in paragraph 1, 2 or 4 of subsection (1) if no more than two rental units share the fixture and access to the fixture from each rental unit is possible without,

(a) passing through another rental unit;

(b) travelling along an unheated corridor; or

(c) travelling outside the building containing the rental units.

(3) Subsection (1) does not apply to a boarding house or lodging house if,

(a) there is at least one toilet, one washbasin and one bathtub or shower for every five rental units;

(b) all tenants have access to a kitchen sink; and

(c) all fixtures mentioned in clauses (a) and (b) are available in each building containing rental units.

(4) Subsection (1) does not apply to a residential complex or rental unit that has never been provided with piped water.

(5) The fixtures required by this section shall be maintained in a good state of repair and in a safely operable condition and shall be supplied with a supply of potable water sufficient for normal household use at a flow and pressure sufficient for the intended use of the fixtures.

11(1) **Hot and cold running water**—Every kitchen sink, washbasin, bathtub and shower shall be provided, by safe equipment, with hot and cold running water.

(2) The ordinary temperature of the hot water provided must be at least 43 degrees Celsius.

12(1) **Washroom requirements**—Every washroom shall be enclosed and shall have,

(a) a water-resistant floor; and

(b) a door that can be,

(i) secured from the inside, and

(ii) opened from the outside in an emergency.

(2) The walls and ceiling around a bathtub or shower shall be water-resistant.

(3) In subsection (1),

"washroom" means an area containing a toilet, urinal, bathtub, shower or washbasin.

13. Toilets and urinals—No toilet or urinal shall be located in a room used for or intended to be used for sleeping or preparing, consuming or storing food.

Electrical

14(1) **Supply of electrical power**—A supply of electrical power shall be provided to all habitable space in a residential complex.

(2) The wiring and receptacles necessary to provide electrical power shall be maintained free of conditions dangerous to persons or property.

(3) Every kitchen shall have outlets suitable for a refrigerator and a cooking appliance.

(4) If a rental unit has a meter for electricity for the purpose of billing the tenants of that rental unit, the meter shall be properly maintained and kept accessible to the tenants.

(5) This section does not apply to a residential complex that has never been connected to an electrical power system.

Heating

15(1) **Maintenance of room temperature**—Heat shall be provided and maintained so that the room temperature at 1.5 metres above floor level and one metre from exterior walls in all habitable space and in any area intended for normal use by tenants, including recreation rooms and laundry rooms but excluding locker rooms and garages, is at least 20 degrees Celsius.

(2) Subsection (1) does not apply to a rental unit in which the tenant can regulate the temperature and a minimum temperature of 20 degrees Celsius can be maintained by the primary source of heat.

(3) Every residential complex shall have heating equipment capable of maintaining the temperature levels required by subsection (1).

(4) No rental unit shall be equipped with portable heating equipment as the primary source of heat.

(5) Only heating equipment approved for use by a recognized standards testing authority shall be provided in a room used or intended for use for sleeping purposes.

16(1) **Fuel and utilities**—Fuel supplied to a residential complex or rental unit shall be supplied continuously in adequate quantities.

(2) Utilities supplied to a residential complex or rental unit shall be supplied continuously.

(3) The supply of fuel and utilities may be interrupted for such reasonable period of time as may be required for the purpose of repair or replacement.

(4) Subsections (1) and (2) do not apply if the tenancy agreement makes the tenant responsible for the supply of fuel or utilities and the supply has been discontinued because of arrears in payment.

17. Maintenance of heating systems—Heating systems, including stoves, heating appliances, fireplaces intended for use, chimneys, fans, pumps and filtration equipment, shall be maintained in a good state of repair and in a safely operable condition.

18(1) **Air supply and fuel storage**—A space that contains heating equipment that burns fuel shall have a natural or mechanical means of supplying the air required for combustion.

(2) If heating equipment burns solid or liquid fuel, a storage place or receptacle for the fuel shall be provided in a safe place and maintained in a safe condition.

Lighting and Ventilation

19(1) **Artificial lighting**—Adequate artificial lighting shall be available at all times in all rooms, stairways, halls, corridors, garages, and basements of a residential complex that are accessible to tenants.

(2) Artificial lighting shall be provided in exterior common areas to permit these areas to be used or passed through safely, and to provide security.

(3) Subsections (1) and (2) do not apply to a residential complex that has never been connected to an electrical power system.

(4) Artificial lighting that has been installed in outbuildings normally used by tenants, including garages, shall be kept in operable condition.

(5) Artificial lighting shall be maintained in a good state of repair.

20. Ventilation—All habitable space shall be provided with natural or mechanical means of ventilation that is adequate for the use of the space.

21(1) **Smoke, gases and toxic fumes**—Chimneys, smoke-pipes, flues and gas vents shall be kept clear of obstructions and maintained so as to prevent the escape of smoke and gases into a building containing one or more rental units.

(2) Parking garages shall be maintained so as to prevent the accumulation of toxic fumes and the escape of toxic fumes into a building containing one or more rental units.

22(1) **Rooms that require windows**—Subject to subsections (2) and (3), every bedroom, living room and dining room shall have a window (which may be part of a door) to the outside of the building.

(2) A window is not required in a dining room if it has artificial lighting.

(3) A window is not required in a living room or dining room if,

(a) there is an opening in a dividing wall to an adjoining room;

(b) the adjoining room has a window to the outside; and

(c) the total window area of the adjoining room is at least 5 per cent of the combined floor areas of the living room or dining room and the adjoining room.

23(1) **Doors, windows and skylights**—Every existing opening in the exterior surface of a building designed for a door or window shall be equipped with a door or window capable of performing the intended function.

(2) Doors, windows and skylights shall be maintained so that,

(a) they are weathertight; and

(b) any damaged or missing parts are repaired or replaced.

ASSIGNMENT: RESIDENTIAL TENANCIES ACT, 2006

1. In responding to a landlord and tenant complaint, the officer must bear in mind that his or her purpose is to preserve the peace and refer people to the appropriate agency. What agencies are involved in settling this type of dispute?

2. If the landlord has turned off the heat, can the officer arrest the landlord and force the heat to be turned on?

3. A landlord has seized a tenant's guitar and refuses to return it until two months of back rent is paid. Is he or she allowed to hold the property until the arrears are paid?

4. Where a tenant pays rent by the month, how much notice is the landlord required to give if he or she wishes the property to be vacated?

5. A landlord wonders if there is any damage to his or her property after hearing some noises in a young tenant's apartment the night before. Is the landlord allowed to enter the premises to inspect it while the tenant is at school?

6. A tenant with rent in arrears moves out during the night. The landlord wants the premises cleaned and rented out to a new tenant as soon as possible. The tenant has left a fridge, a stove, and some personal possessions. The landlord wants to know if the fridge and stove can be sold or rented out with the apartment. What is your advice?

7. The same landlord wants to throw out the personal property left behind by the tenant. Can he or she do this?

8. The landlord looks at the ceiling of a basement apartment and sees a water stain forming. It is obviously water from the apartment above, and that tenant is away on holiday. What can the landlord do?

9. A tenant has had a dispute with the landlord in the past and has changed the locks of the apartment door. The landlord has heard about the lock change from another tenant and challenged the occupant. What advice are you going to give the landlord and tenant?

10. You respond to a dispute between a landlord and tenant concerning the use of hydro. You find out that the tenant occupies the top floor of a house but shares the kitchen with the owner. Do the provisions of the RTA apply to either the landlord or the tenant?

CHAPTER 5
Blind Persons' Rights Act

INTRODUCTION

The tiers associated with the *Blind Persons' Rights Act* are intervention and referral.

Many blind persons in our society today enjoy a relatively high degree of independence through the aid of guide dogs, white canes, audible traffic light signals, and other measures that have been introduced to increase their mobility. Unfortunately, blind persons occasionally encounter some barriers to their use of guide dogs. The *Blind Persons' Rights Act* (BPRA) confirms the right of persons with this specific disability to have their guide dogs accompany them in public facilities and live with them in a self-contained dwelling unit. Accordingly, this statute permits guide dogs to enter premises even where dogs are prohibited, because of their important role in increasing the mobility of the blind persons they serve.

Enforcement of the BPRA usually consists of the responding officer confirming the provisions of the law to whoever denies a guide dog entrance, and the subsequent admission of the blind person and his or her guide dog to the public facility or dwelling unit. Occasionally, it may be necessary to prosecute offenders with one of the three offences outlined in the BPRA. A provision exists in the BPRA whereby blind persons and their properly trained guide dogs may receive identification cards from the government. The possession of such cards is a convenience and not mandatory. When dealing with a denial of entry, subjects should be asked if they have one of these identification cards. The possession and production of the card certainly lends credibility to a claim and may resolve a dispute in short order. The BPRA also contains a section outlining the requirements to return identification cards issued under the legislation at the request of the attorney general.

An officer's duties under the BPRA involve intervention and referral. With intervention, an officer responding to a complaint involving guide dogs will explain the rights contained in the Act to promote understanding and help to settle the matter. With referral, the blind person may need to be advised of the identification card issued by the government. Presenting such a card may allow them to establish their entitlements and avoid conflict.

TERMINOLOGY

Blind Person

A "blind person" is a person who, because of blindness, is dependent on a guide dog or white cane.

Guide Dog

A "guide dog" is a dog trained for the specific purpose of being a guide dog for a blind person and having the qualifications prescribed by the regulations.

COMMON OFFENCES AND/OR PROVISIONS

There are four offences contained within the BPRA.

Most companies who provide transportation services are aware of their obligations under the BPRA. However, there may be times when contract or part-time employees will object to having a dog in their vehicle and will refuse to drive a blind person. The same situation can occur in restaurants. In those cases, an officer may be called to settle a dispute. By law, the business must serve the blind person and the guide dog must be allowed entry to accompany its owner.

DISCRIMINATION OF ACCOMMODATION, SERVICE, OR FACILITY, DUE TO A GUIDE DOG'S PRESENCE (S. 2(1))

This subsection prohibits a person from denying access to any accommodation, service, or facility to which the public is permitted, or discriminating against the person with respect to the accommodation, service, or facility, for the reason that the person denied access, or discriminated against, is a blind person with a guide dog.

The law states that a blind person with a guide dog cannot be discriminated against when seeking accommodation. However, this only applies to self-contained properties, not shared facilities, as some tenants in the latter may not want to be exposed to a dog due to allergies or a fear of dogs.

DENYING OCCUPANCY OF SELF-CONTAINED ACCOMMODATION DUE TO A GUIDE DOG'S PRESENCE (S. 2(2))

This subsection provides that no person, directly or indirectly, alone or with another, shall deny any person occupancy of any self-contained accommodation, or shall discriminate against the person with respect to any term or condition of occupancy of a self-contained dwelling unit, for the reason that the person denied occupancy, or discriminated against, is a blind person keeping or customarily accompanied by a guide dog.

USE OF A WHITE CANE BY SOMEONE OTHER THAN A BLIND PERSON (S. 3)

This section prohibits a person, other than a blind person, from using a cane or walking stick, the major part of which is white, in any public place, public thoroughfare, or public conveyance. This provision ensures that the public recognizes the white cane as a sign that the person carrying it is a blind person.

This section is also in force to address another factor: the fraud artist. There are those who present themselves to the public as being unfortunate and disadvantaged. One could pretend to be blind and by using a white cane try to appeal to people's sympathies in panhandling for money. In order to preserve the identification and consideration for actual blind persons by society, this section protects the specific right to use the cane.

FAILING TO RETURN IDENTIFICATION ISSUED UNDER THIS ACT (S. 4(3))

This section requires a person to return identification issued under the BPRA when the attorney general of the province issues a request for its return.

The first two offences, the main provisions of the BPRA, carry a penalty of a fine of up to $5,000. If a person is convicted of either of the latter two offences, that person is subject to a fine of up to $500.

ARREST POWERS

There are no arrest powers under the BPRA.

SEARCH POWERS

There are no search powers under the BPRA.

USE OF FORCE

The BPRA contains no provisions for the use of force. Refer to *Criminal Code* s. 25 or POA s. 146 for general provisions on the use of force.

LIMITATION PERIOD

The BPRA does not extend the general limitation period contained in the POA, so the limitation period of six months applies.

NON-POLICE AGENCIES INVOLVED

There are no agencies involved in the enforcement of the BPRA, although the Canadian National Institute for the Blind (CNIB) could become involved as a resource for such things as giving testimony in court as expert witnesses to the benefits of guide dogs or white canes, or providing speakers to help inform the public of these rights. Any complaint would likely be handled by the office of the Ontario Ombudsman.

PROVINCIAL OFFENCES GRID COMPLETION

Common Offences and/or Provisions

1. Discrimination of accommodation, service, or facility due to a guide dog's presence (s. 2(1))
2. Denying occupancy of self-contained accommodation due to a guide dog's presence (s. 2(2))
3. Use of a white cane by someone other than a blind person (s. 3)
4. Failing to return identification issued under the BPRA (s. 4(3))

Arrest Powers

None.

Search Powers

None.

Use of Force

No specific use of force authority under the BPRA (refer to *Criminal Code* s. 25 or POA s. 146).

Limitation Period

Six months from the date of the offence.

Non-Police Agencies Involved

CNIB

Blind Persons' Rights Act

RSO 1990, c. B.7

1(1) **Definitions**—In this Act,

"blind person" means a person who because of blindness is dependent on a guide dog or white cane;

"guide dog" means a dog trained as a guide for a blind person and having the qualifications prescribed by the regulations.

(2) **Application**—This Act applies despite any other Act or any regulation, by-law or rule made thereunder.

(3) **Act binds Crown**—This Act binds the Crown.

2(1) **Guide dogs permitted in places to which public admitted**—No person, directly or indirectly, alone or with another, by himself, herself or itself or by the interposition of another, shall,

(a) deny to any person the accommodation, services or facilities available in any place to which the public is customarily admitted; or

(b) discriminate against any person with respect to the accommodation, services or facilities available in any place to which the public is customarily admitted, or the charges for the use thereof,

for the reason that he or she is a blind person accompanied by a guide dog.

(2) **Guide dogs permitted in self-contained dwelling unit**—No person, directly or indirectly, alone or with another, by himself, herself or itself or by the interposition of another, shall,

(a) deny to any person occupancy of any self-contained dwelling unit; or

(b) discriminate against any person with respect to any term or condition of occupancy of any self-contained dwelling unit,

for the reason that he or she is a blind person keeping or customarily accompanied by a guide dog.

(3) **Other facilities**—Nothing in this section shall be construed to entitle a blind person to require any service, facility or accommodation in respect of a guide dog other than the right to be accompanied by the guide dog.

3. Restriction on use of white cane—No person, other than a blind person, shall carry or use a cane or walking stick, the major part of which is white, in any public place, public thoroughfare or public conveyance.

4(1) **Identification cards**—The Attorney General or an officer of his or her Ministry designated by the Attorney General in writing may, upon application therefor, issue to a blind person an identification card identifying the blind person and his or her guide dog.

(2) **Cards as proof of qualification**—An identification card issued under subsection (1) is proof, in the absence of evidence to the contrary, that the blind person and the guide dog identified therein are qualified for the purposes of this Act.

(3) **Surrender of cards**—Any person to whom an identification card is issued under subsection (1) shall, upon the request of the Attorney General or an officer designated under subsection (1), surrender the identification card for amendment or cancellation.

5. Regulations—The Lieutenant Governor in Council may make regulations prescribing qualifications for guide dogs.

6(1) **Penalty**—Every person who is in contravention of section 2 is guilty of an offence and on conviction is liable to a fine not exceeding $5,000.

(2) **Idem**—Every person who is in contravention of section 3 or of subsection 4(3) or who, not being a blind person, purports to be a blind person for the purpose of claiming the benefit of this Act is guilty of an offence and on conviction is liable to a fine not exceeding $500.

ASSIGNMENT: BLIND PERSONS' RIGHTS ACT

1. A person accompanied by a dog enters a restaurant and identifies himself as being blind. He requests service and a seating location where the dog may sit at his feet. The restaurant declines to provide these accommodations. You become involved in the conversation. What advice do you offer?

2. While on foot patrol, you observe a male pedestrian in the company of what appears to be a guide dog. The man is having a heated discussion with a cab driver. As you approach, the cab driver invites you to remove the man and his dog from his cab, because he refuses to transport an animal. What advice do you give in this situation?

3. Regarding question 2, the cab driver disputes that the man is blind because he seems to move along quite well. Is there any further information that can be offered at this time to validate the man's claim of blindness?

4. On your beat you observe a man standing at a street corner. He has on a pair of dark glasses and is moving a white cane about in front of him. He stops passersby, handing them cards designed to solicit money. Later in the day you see the same male without dark glasses and the white cane is folded up in his hand. He is definitely walking about without difficulty. Since begging or panhandling is not illegal, what possible action(s) can you take?

5. You are called to a landlord and tenant dispute. The landlord operates a building that rents out separate rooms, with shared baths on each floor and a common kitchen on the ground level. The landlord does not want to rent to a person because of his dog. The prospective tenant is blind and uses the dog to function. This person is adamant that the landlord cannot refuse him tenancy, as it is his right under the BPRA. What position do you take here?

CHAPTER 6

Mental Health Act

INTRODUCTION

> **The tiers associated with the *Mental Health Act* are enforcement, intervention, and referral.**

The *Mental Health Act* (MHA) is a powerful piece of legislation that permits a physician, justice of the peace, police officer, or judge to order the apprehension and psychological examination of a person without the person's consent. These powers should not to be taken lightly, because they authorize apprehension without the usual safeguard of a court hearing, which accompanies any other form of apprehension without consent. Although the apprehension is not technically an arrest, it is a suspension of a person's liberty without the person's consent and should therefore be treated with the same care as a power of arrest.

Mental illness is a generic term for a variety of disorders marked by disturbances in thinking, feeling, and relating, and characterized by changes in thinking, mood, or behaviour (or some combination thereof). Symptoms similar to those caused by mental illness can also be caused by other factors, including head injury, medical conditions such as diabetes and epilepsy, and substance abuse. Mental illnesses range from mild to severe, with severe illnesses including schizophrenia, mood disorders, and paranoia. Mental disturbances can be non-psychotic or psychotic. In a psychotic mental disturbance—such as a hallucination or a delusion—an individual loses touch with reality.

Mental illness is more common than many people think, and police have frequent contact with individuals with mental disorders. With new psychiatric and psychological treatment approaches, many individuals with mental illnesses have been deinstitutionalized and reintegrated into the community, and this has resulted in increased contact between the police and individuals with mental illness.

Interacting with a person who is experiencing a manifestation of a mental disorder requires a significant application of tact and diplomacy by the person intervening in the situation. Honesty is also a prerequisite, because any deceit may ease the present situation but permanently complicate future interactions with the individual.

In some situations, a person suffering from a mental disorder may have committed a provincial or even a criminal offence. These cases demand a delicate balancing act to deal with the suspect, the victim, and the justice system in the most effective manner. In general, the wisest course of action is to seek the advice of a mental health professional or an individual with experience assessing the best course of action in such situations. Unfortunately, an officer who responds to a call involving a person who appears to have a mental illness usually does not have the option of consulting with experts at the scene. The situation may involve an emotional outburst, a threatened suicide, or a person barricaded inside a building. These volatile situations too often end in tragedy, and more training is needed so that officers better understand the behaviour of those with mental health issues.

Situations such as the above can be unpredictable, and the safety of all individuals at the scene is paramount. Officers must be alert and aware at all times, and ensure that they understand crisis intervention techniques, such as how to communicate effectively with a distraught person. Should it be necessary to take the person into custody, the officer should follow standard procedure, including searching the person thoroughly.

An officer's duties under the MHA are threefold: enforcement, intervention, and referral.

- *Enforcement:* A police officer may be asked to enforce an order for a psychiatric assessment or examination made by a physician, a justice of the peace, or the "officer in charge" of a psychiatric facility, who is a doctor. The police officer must not have had any previous contact with the subject of the order. Before carrying out the order, the officer should collect as much information as possible about the subject from such sources as police occurrence files, CPIC (Canadian Police Information Centre), family, and neighbours.

- *Intervention:* When an officer is called to the scene of an incident, he or she may need to assess whether the MHA applies, with the assistance of those already present, including family and neighbours. If it is determined that the Act applies, the officer must first ensure the safety of everyone involved before attempting to de-escalate the situation. An officer may also be called to assist when someone (often a senior citizen) lives alone, has not been heard from, and is unable to care for themselves. Police intervention may be needed to ensure their safety and well-being.
- *Referral:* Family members often do not know whom to turn to or what steps to take when someone displays mental health problems, and so the police are called. The MHA is designed to provide resources in non-emergency situations, and it is important that officers be aware of the criteria required for each remedy and be able to offer appropriate advice.

TERMINOLOGY

Informal Patient

An "informal patient" is a person who is a patient in a psychiatric facility, having been admitted with the consent of another person under s. 24 of the *Health Care Consent Act, 1996.*

Involuntary Patient

An "involuntary patient" is a person detained in a psychiatric facility under a certificate of involuntary admission or a certificate of renewal.

Mental Disorder

A "mental disorder" is any disease or disability of the mind.

Officer in Charge

The "officer in charge" is the officer responsible for the administration and management of a psychiatric facility.

Physician

A "physician" is a legally qualified medical practitioner.

Psychiatric Facility

A "psychiatric facility" is a facility designated by regulation for the observation, care, and treatment of persons suffering from mental disorders.

COMMON OFFENCES AND/OR PROVISIONS

There are no offences set out under the MHA, only provisions for the apprehension of those requiring examination.

ARREST POWERS

There are no arrest powers under the MHA. However, the Act does authorize the apprehension of those who meet the defined criteria for being taken to an appropriate facility for an examination by a physician.

Four kinds of professionals may authorize a person to be taken into custody under the MHA: a physician, a justice of the peace, a police officer, and a judge.

Order of a Physician for Psychiatric Assessment of a Person

Section 15(1) of the MHA stipulates that a physician may sign an order for an assessment of a person at a psychiatric facility where the person may be detained for up to 72 hours. To have sufficient grounds to sign such an order, the physician must have examined the person and must

1. have reasonable grounds to believe that the person is suffering from a mental disorder, and
2. believe the person is a danger to him- or herself or others, or
3. believe the person shows a lack of competence to care for him- or herself.

An additional power is given to the physician under s. 15(1.1) for circumstances in which a patient has already received treatment for a mental disorder that is ongoing or recurring and, when not treated, could result in the same grounds as listed in 2 and 3 above. The order is valid for seven days from the date on which it is signed, and the physician must sign the order within seven days of the date of the examination.

Order of a Justice of the Peace for Psychiatric Examination by a Physician

The power conferred on a justice of the peace (JP) under s. 16 is similar to that of a physician, without the examination. Anyone can appear before a JP and, under oath, give information that a person within the JP's jurisdiction meets all of the grounds that a physician requires, is suffering from a mental disorder that threatens anyone in the manner outlined, or has been treated in the past for a mental disorder and appears to require treatment for the same disorder to prevent harm to any person, but cannot consent to the treatment him- or herself. A JP may then issue an order for examination by a physician, which must take place within seven days of the signing of the order, including the day the order is signed.

> Both a physician and a JP have the authority to make an order requiring that a person be given a psychiatric assessment or examination. In both cases, the same grounds must be met and the order is valid for seven days. However, the physician issues an order based on his or her own examination of the person, and the person can be detained for up to 72 hours for a psychiatric assessment. The JP relies on information given under oath in court, and the duration of an examination is not specified but is left up to a physician.

Apprehension of a Person by a Police Officer

Section 17 of the MHA authorizes a police officer to apprehend a person and take him or her for an examination by a physician if certain conditions are met. The police officer must have reasonable and probable grounds to believe that the person is acting or has acted in a disorderly manner and have reasonable cause to believe that the person

1. has threatened or attempted, or is threatening or attempting, to cause bodily harm to himself or herself;
2. has behaved or is behaving violently toward another person or has caused or is causing another person to fear bodily harm; or
3. has shown or is showing an inability to care for him- or herself.

In addition, the officer must believe that the person is suffering from a mental disorder that will likely result in serious bodily harm to the person or another person, or in serious physical impairment of the person (that is, because of some risk the person is exposing him- or herself to because their illness prevents them from understanding the risk), and must believe that it is too dangerous to wait to obtain an order from a JP.

If these conditions apply, the police officer may apprehend and take the person to an appropriate place for an examination by a physician. The police officer must stay with the person until he or she is accepted by a psychiatric facility (or is released without an order for examination).

Order by a Judge for Examination at a Psychiatric Facility

If warranted, ss. 21 and 22 of the MHA authorize a judge to order that a charged person brought before him or her be taken to a psychiatric facility for examination.

If the charged person is not in custody (is out on bail) at the time of his or her court appearance, the senior physician of the facility must make a report in writing to the judge about the mental condition of the person.

If the charged person is in custody (has been denied bail) at the time of his or her court appearance, a judge may order the person to be admitted as a patient to a psychiatric facility for a period of not more than two months.

Before making such an order, a judge must first ascertain whether the services of the psychiatric facility are available.

Apprehension of an Involuntary Patient Who Leaves a Facility Without Permission

A police officer or any other person empowered by an order of the officer in charge of a psychiatric facility may return an involuntary patient who has left the facility without authorization. The order is valid for a period of one month from the time the absence becomes known to the officer in charge. If the patient is not apprehended within that month, he or she is deemed to be discharged.

SEARCH POWERS

There are no search powers under the MHA.

USE OF FORCE

There are no provisions in the MHA regarding use of force in the enforcement of the Act. Refer to *Criminal Code* s. 25 or POA s. 146 for general provisions on the use of force.

LIMITATION PERIOD

The MHA does not deal with laying charges, so the usual limitation periods do not apply. However, in each case where it authorizes apprehension, a time limit is provided:

1. *Physician's order.* This order is valid for seven days from and including the day on which it is signed by a physician. The order must also be signed within seven days of the examination by a physician. Once a physician's order is executed, the psychiatric facility is authorized to restrain, observe, and examine the patient for up to 72 hours.
2. *Justice of the peace order.* This order is valid for a period of seven days from and including the day that it is made. It authorizes any peace officer to apprehend a person and transfer him or her to an appropriate place to be examined by a physician.

3. *Police officer's apprehension.* A police officer who has reasonable and probable grounds to believe that a person is acting in a disorderly manner as a result of a mental illness that may cause harm to him- or herself or to others is authorized to apprehend the person and take him or her to an appropriate place for examination. This authority does not extend beyond the time required for the officer to locate and apprehend the person.
4. *Judge's order.* A judge has two authorities for making an order for the apprehension of a person who appears to be suffering from a mental disorder. If the person appears out of custody before a judge, the judge may make an order for him or her to be examined by a physician. If the person appears in custody before a judge, the judge may make an order of remand to a psychiatric facility for a period not exceeding two months. Both orders must be made at the time of the appearance before the judge.
5. *Involuntary patient absent without leave.* If not apprehended within one month, the patient is deemed to be discharged from the psychiatric facility.

NON-POLICE AGENCIES INVOLVED

1. Judges, who may issue orders for examination from the bench in relation to those appearing in court
2. Justices of the peace, who may also sign orders for apprehension
3. Local mental health care agencies, for after-care treatment and support
4. Physicians, who are the main source of orders for apprehension when required
5. Regional mental health facilities, for on-site treatment

PROVINCIAL OFFENCES GRID COMPLETION

Common Offences and/or Provisions

None.

Arrest Powers

None; only orders of apprehension for examination by a physician, or orders by a physician or a judge for involuntary admission to a psychiatric facility, or an order by an officer in charge of a psychiatric facility who becomes aware of an unauthorized absence of an involuntary patient.

Search Powers

None.

Use of Force

No specific use of force authority under the MHA (refer to *Criminal Code* s. 25 or POA s. 146).

Limitation Period

1. Physician order valid for seven days from and including the date it is signed.
2. Justice of the peace order valid for seven days from and including the date it is signed.
3. Police officer apprehension authority valid for the time it takes to locate and apprehend.
4. Judge's order for both in custody and out of custody apprehensions must be made at the time of the appearance before the judge.

Non-Police Agencies Involved

1. Judges
2. Justices of the peace
3. Local mental health care agencies
4. Physicians
5. Regional mental health facilities

Mental Health Act

RSO 1990, c. M.7

1(1) **Definitions**—In this Act,

"attending physician" means a physician to whom responsibility for the observation, care and treatment of a patient has been assigned;

"Board" means the Consent and Capacity Board continued under the *Health Care Consent Act, 1996*;

"community treatment plan" means a plan described in section 33.7 that is a required part of a community treatment order;

"Deputy Minister" means the deputy minister of the Minister;

"health practitioner" has the same meaning as in the *Health Care Consent Act, 1996*;

"informal patient" means a person who is a patient in a psychiatric facility, having been admitted with the consent of another person under section 24 of the *Health Care Consent Act, 1996*;

"involuntary patient" means a person who is detained in a psychiatric facility under a certificate of involuntary admission or a certificate of renewal;

"local board of health" has the same meaning as board of health in the *Health Protection and Promotion Act*;

"medical officer of health" has the same meaning as in the *Health Protection and Promotion Act*;

"mental disorder" means any disease or disability of the mind;

"Minister" means the Minister of Health and Long-Term Care or such other member of the Executive Council as the Lieutenant Governor in Council designates;

"Ministry" means the Ministry of the Minister;

"officer in charge" means the officer who is responsible for the administration and management of a psychiatric facility;

"out-patient" means a person who is registered in a psychiatric facility for observation or treatment or both, but who is not admitted as a patient and is not the subject of an application for assessment;

"patient" means a person who is under observation, care and treatment in a psychiatric facility;

"personal health information" has the same meaning as in the *Personal Health Information Protection Act, 2004*;

"physician" means a legally qualified medical practitioner and, when referring to a community treatment order, means a legally qualified medical practitioner who meets the qualifications prescribed in the regulations for the issuing or renewing of a community treatment order;

"plan of treatment" has the same meaning as in the *Health Care Consent Act, 1996*;

"prescribed" means prescribed by the regulations;

"psychiatric facility" means a facility for the observation, care and treatment of persons suffering from mental disorder, and designated as such by the Minister;

"psychiatrist" means a physician who holds a specialist's certificate in psychiatry issued by The Royal College of Physicians and Surgeons of Canada or equivalent qualification acceptable to the Minister;

"record of personal health information," in relation to a person, means a record of personal health information that is compiled in a psychiatric facility in respect of the person;

"regulations" means the regulations made under this Act;

"restrain" means place under control when necessary to prevent serious bodily harm to the patient or to another person by the minimal use of such force, mechanical means or chemicals as is reasonable having regard to the physical and mental condition of the patient;

"rights adviser" means a person, or a member of a category of persons, qualified to perform the functions of a rights adviser under this Act and designated by a psychiatric facility, the Minister or by the regulations to perform those functions, but does not include,

(a) a person involved in the direct clinical care of the person to whom the rights advice is to be given, or

(b) a person providing treatment or care and supervision under a community treatment plan;

"senior physician" means the physician responsible for the clinical services in a psychiatric facility;

"substitute decision-maker," in relation to a patient, means the person who would be authorized under the *Health Care Consent Act, 1996* to give or refuse consent to a treatment on behalf of the patient, if the patient were incapable with respect to the treatment under that Act, unless the context requires otherwise;

"treatment" has the same meaning as in the *Health Care Consent Act, 1996.*

(2) **Meaning of "explain"**—A rights adviser or other person whom this Act requires to explain a matter satisfies that requirement by explaining the matter to the best of his or her ability and in a manner that addresses the special needs of the person receiving the explanation, whether that person understands it or not.

2. Repealed.

3. Repealed.

4. Repealed.

5. Repealed.

6. Effect of Act on rights and privileges—Nothing in this Act shall be deemed to affect the rights or privileges of any person except as specifically set out in this Act.

PART I
STANDARDS

7. Application of Act—This Act applies to every psychiatric facility.

8. Conflict—Every psychiatric facility has power to carry on its undertaking as authorized by any Act, but, where the provisions of any Act conflict with the provisions of this Act or the regulations, the provisions of this Act and the regulations prevail.

9(1) **Advisory officers**—The Minister may designate officers of the Ministry or appoint persons who shall advise and assist medical officers of health, local boards of health, hospitals and other bodies and persons in all matters pertaining to mental health and who shall have such other duties as are assigned to them by this Act or the regulations.

(2) **Powers**—Any such officer or person may at any time, and shall be permitted so to do by the authorities thereat, visit and inspect any psychiatric facility, and in so doing may interview patients, examine books, records and other documents relating to patients, examine the condition of the psychiatric facility and its equipment, and inquire into the adequacy of its staff, the range of services provided and any other matter he or she considers relevant to the maintenance of standards of patient care.

10. Provincial aid—The Minister may pay psychiatric facilities provincial aid in such manner, in such amounts and on such conditions as he or she considers appropriate.

PART II
HOSPITALIZATION

11. Where admission may be refused—Despite this or any other Act, admission to a psychiatric facility may be refused where the immediate needs in the case of the proposed patient are such that hospitalization is not urgent or necessary.

12. Admission of informal or voluntary patients—Any person who is believed to be in need of the observation, care and treatment provided in a psychiatric facility may be admitted thereto as an informal or voluntary patient upon the recommendation of a physician.

13(1) **Child as informal patient**—A child who is twelve years of age or older but less than sixteen years of age, who is an informal patient in a psychiatric facility and who has not so applied within the preceding three months may apply in the approved form to the Board to inquire into whether the child needs observation, care and treatment in the psychiatric facility.

(2) **Application deemed made**—Upon the completion of six months after the later of the child's admission to the psychiatric facility as an informal patient or the child's last application under subsection (1), the child shall be deemed to have applied to the Board in the approved form under subsection (1).

(3) **Considerations**—In determining whether the child needs observation, care and treatment in the psychiatric facility, the Board shall consider,

(a) whether the child needs observation, care and treatment of a kind that the psychiatric facility can provide;

(b) whether the child's needs can be adequately met if the child is not an informal patient in the psychiatric facility;

(c) whether there is an available alternative to the psychiatric facility in which the child's needs could be more appropriately met;

(d) the child's views and wishes, where they can be reasonably ascertained; and

(e) any other matter that the Board considers relevant.

(4) **Powers of Board**—The Board by an order in writing may,

(a) direct that the child be discharged from the psychiatric facility; or

(b) confirm that the child may be continued as an informal patient in the psychiatric facility.

(5) **No limitation**—Nothing in this section prevents a physician from completing a certificate of involuntary admission in respect of the child.

(6) **Panels of three or five members**—Despite subsection 73(1) of the *Health Care Consent Act, 1996*, the chair shall assign the members of the Board to sit in panels of three or five members to deal with applications under this section.

(7) **Procedure**—Subsection 39(6) and section 42 of this Act and clause 73(3)(a), subsection 73(4), and sections 74 to 80 of the *Health Care Consent Act, 1996* apply to an application under this section, with necessary modifications.

14. Informal or voluntary patient—Nothing in this Act authorizes a psychiatric facility to detain or to restrain an informal or voluntary patient.

15(1) **Application for psychiatric assessment**—Where a physician examines a person and has reasonable cause to believe that the person,

(a) has threatened or attempted or is threatening or attempting to cause bodily harm to himself or herself;

(b) has behaved or is behaving violently towards another person or has caused or is causing another person to fear bodily harm from him or her; or

(c) has shown or is showing a lack of competence to care for himself or herself, and if in addition the physician is of the opinion that the person is apparently suffering from mental disorder of a nature or quality that likely will result in,

(d) serious bodily harm to the person;

(e) serious bodily harm to another person; or

(f) serious physical impairment of the person,

the physician may make application in the prescribed form for a psychiatric assessment of the person.

(1.1) **Same**—Where a physician examines a person and has reasonable cause to believe that the person,

(a) has previously received treatment for mental disorder of an ongoing or recurring nature that, when not treated, is of a nature or quality that likely will result in serious bodily harm to the person or to another person or substantial mental or physical deterioration of the person or serious physical impairment of the person; and

(b) has shown clinical improvement as a result of the treatment, and if in addition the physician is of the opinion that the person,

(c) is apparently suffering from the same mental disorder as the one for which he or she previously received treatment or from a mental disorder that is similar to the previous one;

(d) given the person's history of mental disorder and current mental or physical condition, is likely to cause serious bodily harm to himself or herself or to another person or is likely to suffer substantial mental or physical deterioration or serious physical impairment; and

(e) is incapable, within the meaning of the *Health Care Consent Act, 1996*, of consenting to his or her treatment in a psychiatric facility and the consent of his or her substitute decision-maker has been obtained,

the physician may make application in the prescribed form for a psychiatric assessment of the person.

In 2000, the MHA was amended in a number of key ways by Brian's Law, which was passed partly in response to the murder of broadcaster Brian Smith by an individual with untreated delusions. In that year, ss. 1.1 of s. 15 was introduced to address individuals with a history of repeated hospital admissions. It is intended to allow physicians to intervene during a new episode before there is substantial mental or physical deterioration, which the physician has reasonable cause to believe will occur due to knowledge of the individual's past treatment history.

(2) **Contents of application**—An application under subsection (1) or (1.1) shall set out clearly that the physician who signs the application personally examined the person who is the subject of the application and made careful inquiry into all of the facts necessary for him or her to form his or her opinion as to the nature and quality of the mental disorder of the person.

(3) **Idem**—A physician who signs an application under subsection (1) or (1.1),

(a) shall set out in the application the facts upon which he or she formed his or her opinion as to the nature and quality of the mental disorder;

(b) shall distinguish in the application between the facts observed by him or her and the facts communicated to him or her by others; and

(c) shall note in the application the date on which he or she examined the person who is the subject of the application.

(4) **Signing of application**—An application under subsection (1) or (1.1) is not effective unless it is signed by the physician within seven days after he or she examined the person who is the subject of the examination.

(5) **Authority of application**—An application under subsection (1) or (1.1) is sufficient authority for seven days from and including the day on which it is signed by the physician,

(a) to any person to take the person who is the subject of the application in custody to a psychiatric facility forthwith; and

(b) to detain the person who is the subject of the application in a psychiatric facility and to restrain, observe and examine him or her in the facility for not more than 72 hours.

16(1) **Justice of the peace's order for psychiatric examination**—Where information upon oath is brought before a justice of the peace that a person within the limits of the jurisdiction of the justice,

(a) has threatened or attempted or is threatening or attempting to cause bodily harm to himself or herself;

(b) has behaved or is behaving violently towards another person or has caused or is causing another person to fear bodily harm from him or her; or

(c) has shown or is showing a lack of competence to care for himself or herself, and in addition based upon the information before him or her the justice of the peace has reasonable cause to believe that the person is apparently suffering from mental disorder of a nature or quality that likely will result in,

(d) serious bodily harm to the person;

(e) serious bodily harm to another person; or

(f) serious physical impairment of the person, the justice of the peace may issue an order in the prescribed form for the examination of the person by a physician.

(1.1) **Same**—Where information upon oath is brought before a justice of the peace that a person within the limits of the jurisdiction of the justice,

(a) has previously received treatment for mental disorder of an ongoing or recurring nature that, when not treated, is of a nature or quality that likely will result in serious bodily harm to the person or to another person or substantial mental or physical deterioration of the person or serious physical impairment of the person; and

(b) has shown clinical improvement as a result of the treatment, and in addition based upon the information before him or her the justice of the peace has reasonable cause to believe that the person,

(c) is apparently suffering from the same mental disorder as the one for which he or she previously received treatment or from a mental disorder that is similar to the previous one;

(d) given the person's history of mental disorder and current mental or physical condition, is likely to cause serious bodily harm to himself or herself or to another person or is likely to suffer substantial mental or physical deterioration or serious physical impairment; and

(e) is apparently incapable, within the meaning of the *Health Care Consent Act, 1996*, of consenting to his or her treatment in a psychiatric facility and the consent of his or her substitute decision-maker has been obtained, the justice of the peace may issue an order in the prescribed form for the examination of the person by a physician.

(2) **Idem**—An order under this section may be directed to all or any police officers of the locality within which the justice has jurisdiction and shall name or otherwise describe the person with respect to whom the order has been made.

(3) **Authority of order**—An order under this section shall direct, and, for a period not to exceed seven days from and including the day that it is made, is sufficient authority for any police officer to whom it is addressed to take the person named or described therein in custody forthwith to an appropriate place where he or she may be detained for examination by a physician.

(4) **Manner of bringing information before justice**—For the purposes of this section, information shall be brought before a justice of the peace in the prescribed manner.

17. Action by police officer—Where a police officer has reasonable and probable grounds to believe that a person is acting or has acted in a disorderly manner and has reasonable cause to believe that the person,

(a) has threatened or attempted or is threatening or attempting to cause bodily harm to himself or herself;

(b) has behaved or is behaving violently towards another person or has caused or is causing another person to fear bodily harm from him or her; or

(c) has shown or is showing a lack of competence to care for himself or herself,

and in addition the police officer is of the opinion that the person is apparently suffering from mental disorder of a nature or quality that likely will result in,

(d) serious bodily harm to the person;

(e) serious bodily harm to another person; or

(f) serious physical impairment of the person,

and that it would be dangerous to proceed under section 16, the police officer may take the person in custody to an appropriate place for examination by a physician.

18. Place of psychiatric examination—An examination under section 16 or 17 shall be conducted by a physician forthwith after receipt of the person at the place of examination and where practicable the place shall be a psychiatric facility or other health facility.

19. Change from informal or voluntary patient to involuntary patient—Subject to subsections 20(1.1) and (5), the attending physician may change the status of an informal or voluntary patient to that of an involuntary patient by completing and filing with the officer in charge a certificate of involuntary admission.

20(1) Duty of attending physician—The attending physician, after observing and examining a person who is the subject of an application for assessment under section 15 or who is the subject of an order under section 32,

(a) shall release the person from the psychiatric facility if the attending physician is of the opinion that the person is not in need of the treatment provided in a psychiatric facility;

(b) shall admit the person as an informal or voluntary patient if the attending physician is of the opinion that the person is suffering from mental disorder of such a nature or quality that the person is in need of the treatment provided in a psychiatric facility and is suitable for admission as an informal or voluntary patient; or

(c) shall admit the person as an involuntary patient by completing and filing with the officer in charge a certificate of involuntary admission if the attending physician is of the opinion that the conditions set out in subsection (1.1) or (5) are met.

(1.1) **Conditions for involuntary admission**—The attending physician shall complete a certificate of involuntary admission or a certificate of renewal if, after examining the patient, he or she is of the opinion that the patient,

(a) has previously received treatment for mental disorder of an ongoing or recurring nature that, when not treated, is of a nature or quality that likely will result in serious bodily harm to the person or to another person or substantial mental or physical deterioration of the person or serious physical impairment of the person;

(b) has shown clinical improvement as a result of the treatment;

(c) is suffering from the same mental disorder as the one for which he or she previously received treatment or from a mental disorder that is similar to the previous one;

(d) given the person's history of mental disorder and current mental or physical condition, is likely to cause serious bodily harm to himself or herself or to another person or is likely to suffer substantial mental or physical deterioration or serious physical impairment;

Section 17 authorizes a police officer to take an individual to a physician for examination where the officer has "reasonable and probable grounds to believe" that a person is behaving *or has behaved* in a disorderly manner and appears to be suffering from a mental disorder. Before amendments to the MHA in 2000, officers had to observe "disorderly conduct" firsthand before they could act, but the current version allows officers to act on reliable information from third parties where the officer believes there are "reasonable and probable grounds" to do so. Because it is common for police to arrive *following* an act that gives rise to the call that brings them to the scene, the old requirement was often not effective.

Note that the harm under ss. 17(a) and (b) must be serious *bodily* harm—that is, the person must be physically dangerous. Psychological harm and other types of harm do not meet the criteria. This causes many individuals with psychoses and those experiencing manic states, for instance, *not* to be admitted to hospitals for treatment. In

continued next page

continued . . .

many cases, it has resulted in tragedies such as homicide and suicide, and other lesser harms, which have occurred while individuals waited for friends or family members to become dangerous enough to be hospitalized. In addition, it is extremely difficult to predict the dangerous behaviour of many individuals with mental disorders, and tragic situations can occur unexpectedly.

Although the Ontario Act includes the bodily harm criteria, a number of provinces, such as British Columbia, do not.

(e) has been found incapable, within the meaning of the *Health Care Consent Act, 1996*, of consenting to his or her treatment in a psychiatric facility and the consent of his or her substitute decision-maker has been obtained; and

(f) is not suitable for admission or continuation as an informal or voluntary patient.

(2) **Physician who completes certificate of involuntary admission**—The physician who completes a certificate of involuntary admission pursuant to clause (1)(c) shall not be the same physician who completed the application for psychiatric assessment under section 15.

(3) **Release of person by officer in charge**—The officer in charge shall release a person who is the subject of an application for assessment under section 15 or who is the subject of an order under section 32 upon the completion of 72 hours of detention in the psychiatric facility unless the attending physician has released the person, has admitted the person as an informal or voluntary patient or has admitted the person as an involuntary patient by completing and filing with the officer in charge a certificate of involuntary admission.

(4) **Authority of certificate**—An involuntary patient may be detained, restrained, observed and examined in a psychiatric facility,

(a) for not more than two weeks under a certificate of involuntary admission; and

(b) for not more than,

(i) one additional month under a first certificate of renewal,

(ii) two additional months under a second certificate of renewal, and

(iii) three additional months under a third or subsequent certificate of renewal,

that is completed and filed with the officer in charge by the attending physician.

(5) **Conditions for involuntary admission**—The attending physician shall complete a certificate of involuntary admission or a certificate of renewal if, after examining the patient, he or she is of the opinion both,

(a) that the patient is suffering from mental disorder of a nature or quality that likely will result in,

(i) serious bodily harm to the patient,

(ii) serious bodily harm to another person, or

(iii) serious physical impairment of the patient,

unless the patient remains in the custody of a psychiatric facility; and

(b) that the patient is not suitable for admission or continuation as an informal or voluntary patient.

(6) **Change of status, where period of detention has expired**—An involuntary patient whose authorized period of detention has expired shall be deemed to be an informal or voluntary patient.

(7) **Idem, where period of detention has not expired**—An involuntary patient whose authorized period of detention has not expired may be continued as an informal or voluntary patient upon completion of the approved form by the attending physician.

(8) **Examination of certificate by officer in charge**—Forthwith following completion and filing of a certificate of involuntary admission or of a certificate of renewal, the officer in charge or his or her delegate shall review the certification documents to ascertain whether or not they have been completed in compliance with the criteria outlined in this Act and where, in his or her opinion, the documents are not properly completed, the officer in charge shall so inform the attending physician and, unless the person is re-examined and released or admitted in accordance with this section, the officer in charge shall release the person.

21(1) **Judge's order for examination**—Where a judge has reason to believe that a person who appears before him or her charged with or convicted of an offence suffers from mental disorder, the judge may order the person to attend a psychiatric facility for examination.

(2) **Senior physician's report**—Where an examination is made under this section, the senior physician shall report in writing to the judge as to the mental condition of the person.

22(1) **Judge's order for admission**—Where a judge has reason to believe that a person in custody who appears before him or her charged with an offence suffers from mental disorder, the judge may, by order, remand that person for admission as a patient to a psychiatric facility for a period of not more than two months.

(2) **Senior physician's report**—Before the expiration of the time mentioned in such order, the senior physician shall report in writing to the judge as to the mental condition of the person.

23. Condition precedent to judge's order—A judge shall not make an order under section 21 or 22 until he or she ascertains from the senior physician of a psychiatric facility that the services of the psychiatric facility are available to the person to be named in the order.

24. Contents of senior physician's report—Despite this or any other Act or any regulation made under any other Act, the senior physician may report all or any part of the information compiled by the psychiatric facility to any person where, in the opinion of the senior physician, it is in the best interests of the person who is the subject of an order made under section 21 or 22.

25. Detention under the *Criminal Code* (Canada)—Any person who is detained in a psychiatric facility under Part XX.1 of the *Criminal Code* (Canada) may be restrained, observed and examined under this Act and provided with treatment under the *Health Care Consent Act, 1996*.

26(1) **Communications to and from patients**—Except as provided in this section, no communication written by a patient or sent to a patient shall be opened, examined or withheld, and its delivery shall not in any way be obstructed or delayed.

(2) **Where communication may be withheld**—Where the officer in charge or a person acting under his or her authority has reasonable and probable cause to believe,

(a) that the contents of a communication written by a patient would,

(i) be unreasonably offensive to the addressee, or

(ii) prejudice the best interests of the patient; or

(b) that the contents of a communication sent to a patient would,

(i) interfere with the treatment of the patient, or

(ii) cause the patient unnecessary distress,

the officer in charge or a person acting under his or her authority may open and examine the contents thereof and, if any condition mentioned in clause (a) or (b), as the case may be, exists, may withhold such communication from delivery.

(3) **Exceptions**—Subsection (2) does not apply to a communication written by a patient to, or appearing to be sent to a patient by,

(a) a barrister and solicitor;

(b) a member of the Board; or

(c) a member of the Assembly.

27(1) **Leave of absence**—The attending physician may, subject to subsection (3), place a patient on a leave of absence from the psychiatric facility for a designated period of not more than three months if the intention is that the patient shall return to the facility.

(2) **Same**—The officer in charge may, upon the advice of the attending physician, place a patient on a leave of absence from the psychiatric facility for a designated period of not more than three months.

(3) **Terms and conditions**—The attending physician and the patient shall comply with such terms and conditions for the leave of absence as the officer in charge may prescribe.

(4) **Exception**—This section does not authorize the placing of a patient on a leave of absence where he or she is subject to detention otherwise than under this Act.

28(1) **Unauthorized absence**—Where a person who is subject to detention is absent without leave from a psychiatric facility, a police officer or any other person to whom the officer in charge has issued an order for return shall make reasonable attempts to return the person and may, within one month after the absence becomes known to the officer in charge, return the person to the psychiatric facility or take the person to the psychiatric facility nearest to the place where the person is apprehended.

(2) **Detention during return**—A patient who is being returned under subsection (1) may be detained in an appropriate place in the course of his or her return.

(3) **Period of detention upon return**—For the purposes of this Act, a patient who is returned under subsection (1) may be detained for the remainder of the period of detention to which he or she was subject when his or her absence became known to the officer in charge.

(4) **Where not returned**—Where a patient is not returned within one month after his or her absence became known to the officer in charge, he or she shall, unless subject to detention otherwise than under this Act, be deemed to be discharged from the psychiatric facility.

(5) **Prohibitions**—No person shall do or omit to do any act for the purpose of aiding, assisting, abetting or counselling a patient in a psychiatric facility to be absent without authorization. . . .

33. Duty to remain and retain custody—A police officer or other person who takes a person in custody to a psychiatric facility shall remain at the facility and retain custody of the person until the facility takes custody of him or her in the prescribed manner.

33.1(1) **Community treatment order**—A physician may issue or renew a community treatment order with respect to a person for a purpose described in subsection (3) if the criteria set out in subsection (4) are met.

> Before Brian's Law was passed in 2000, community-based treatment was not addressed in the MHA. Today, rather than remaining in the hospital, certain individuals can receive treatment for mental illness outside of the hospital through a community treatment order (CTO). CTOs are contracts that outline treatment programs and are signed by both the physician and the individual who will receive the treatment. After consenting, the individual must comply with the order. A physician who believes that an individual is not complying with a CTO may sign an order that authorizes the police to deliver the person named in the order to the signing physician or to a physician authorized to act in that physician's place for examination.

(2) **Same**—The community treatment order must be in the prescribed form.

(3) **Purposes**—The purpose of a community treatment order is to provide a person who suffers from a serious mental disorder with a comprehensive plan of community-based treatment or care and supervision that is less restrictive than being detained in a psychiatric facility. Without limiting the generality of the foregoing, a purpose is to provide such a plan for a person who, as a result of his or her serious mental disorder, experiences this pattern: The person is admitted to a psychiatric facility where his or her condition is usually stabilized; after being released from the facility, the person often stops the treatment or care and supervision; the person's condition changes and, as a result, the person must be re-admitted to a psychiatric facility.

(4) **Criteria for order**—A physician may issue or renew a community treatment order under this section if,

(a) during the previous three-year period, the person,

(i) has been a patient in a psychiatric facility on two or more separate occasions or for a cumulative period of 30 days or more during that three-year period, or

(ii) has been the subject of a previous community treatment order under this section;

(b) the person or his or her substitute decision-maker, the physician who is considering issuing or renewing the community treatment order and any other health practitioner or person involved in the person's treatment or care and supervision have developed a community treatment plan for the person;

(c) within the 72-hour period before entering into the community treatment plan, the physician has examined the person and is of the opinion, based on the examination and any other relevant facts communicated to the physician, that,

(i) the person is suffering from mental disorder such that he or she needs continuing treatment or care and continuing supervision while living in the community,

(ii) the person meets the criteria for the completion of an application for psychiatric assessment under subsection 15(1) or (1.1) where the person is not currently a patient in a psychiatric facility,

(iii) if the person does not receive continuing treatment or care and continuing supervision while living in the community, he or she is likely, because of mental disorder, to cause serious bodily harm to himself or herself or to another person or to suffer substantial mental or physical deterioration of the person or serious physical impairment of the person,

(iv) the person is able to comply with the community treatment plan contained in the community treatment order, and

(v) the treatment or care and supervision required under the terms of the community treatment order are available in the community;

(d) the physician has consulted with the health practitioners or other persons proposed to be named in the community treatment plan;

(e) subject to subsection (5), the physician is satisfied that the person subject to the order and his or her substitute decision-maker, if any, have consulted with a rights adviser and have been advised of their legal rights; and

(f) the person or his or her substitute decision-maker consents to the community treatment plan in accordance with the rules for consent under the *Health Care Consent Act, 1996.*

(5) **Exception**—Clause (4)(e) does not apply in any of the following circumstances:

1. If a rights adviser has made best efforts to locate the person subject to the order, the person could not be located and the rights adviser so informs the physician.
2. If the person subject to the order refuses to consult with a rights adviser and the rights adviser so informs the physician.
3. If, for the renewal of the order, the Public Guardian and Trustee is the substitute decision-maker for the person subject to the order.

(6) **Content of order**—A community treatment order shall indicate,

(a) the date of the examination referred to in clause (4)(c);

(b) the facts on which the physician formed the opinion referred to in clause (4)(c);

(c) a description of the community treatment plan referred to in clause (4)(b); and

(d) an undertaking by the person to comply with his or her obligations as set out in subsection (9) or an undertaking by the person's substitute decision-maker to use his or her best efforts to ensure that the person complies with those obligations.

(7) **Protection from liability, substitute decision-maker**—The substitute decision-maker who, in good faith, uses his or her best efforts to ensure the person's compliance and believes, on reasonable grounds, that the person is in compliance is not liable for any default or neglect of the person in complying.

(8) **Legal advice**—The person who is being considered for a community treatment order, or who is subject to such an order, and that person's substitute decision-maker, if any, have a right to retain and instruct counsel and to be informed of that right.

(9) **Obligations of person**—If a person or his or her substitute decision-maker consents to a community treatment plan under this section, the person shall,

(a) attend appointments with the physician who issued or renewed the community treatment order, or with any other health practitioner or other person referred to in the community treatment plan, at the times and places scheduled from time to time; and

(b) comply with the community treatment plan described in the community treatment order.

(10) **To whom copies of order and plan to be given**—The physician who issues or renews a community treatment order under this section shall ensure that a copy of the order, including the community treatment plan, is given to,

(a) the person, along with a notice that he or she has a right to a hearing before the Board under section 39.1;

(b) the person's substitute decision-maker, where applicable;

(c) the officer in charge, where applicable; and

(d) any other health practitioner or other person named in the community treatment plan.

(11) **Expiry of order**—A community treatment order expires six months after the day it is made unless,

(a) it is renewed in accordance with subsection (12); or

(b) it is terminated earlier in accordance with section 33.2, 33.3 or 33.4.

(12) **Renewals**—A community treatment order may be renewed for a period of six months at any time before its expiry and within one month after its expiry.

(13) **Subsequent plans**—Upon the expiry or termination of a community treatment order, the parties may enter into a subsequent community treatment plan if the criteria set out in subsection (4) are met.

33.2(1) **Early termination of order pursuant to request**—At the request of a person who is subject to a community treatment order or of his or her substitute decision-maker, the physician who issued or renewed the order shall review the person's condition to determine if the person is able to continue to live in the community without being subject to the order.

(2) **Same**—If the physician determines, upon reviewing the person's condition, that the circumstances described in subclauses 33.1(4)(c)(i), (ii) and (iii) no longer exist, the physician shall,

(a) terminate the community treatment order;

(b) notify the person that he or she may live in the community without being subject to the community treatment order; and

(c) notify the persons referred to in clauses 33.1(10)(b), (c) and (d) that the community treatment order has been terminated.

33.3(1) **Early termination of order for failure to comply**—If a physician who issued or renewed a community treatment order has reasonable cause to believe that the person subject to the order has failed to comply with his or her obligations under subsection 33.1(9), the physician may, subject to subsection (2), issue an order for examination of the person in the prescribed form.

(1.1) **Community treatment order not terminated**—A community treatment order is not terminated by the issuance of an order for examination under this section.

(2) **Conditions for issuing order for examination**—The physician shall not issue an order for examination under subsection (1) unless,

(a) he or she has reasonable cause to believe that the criteria set out in subclauses 33.1(4)(c)(i), (ii) and (iii) continue to be met; and

(b) reasonable efforts have been made to,

(i) locate the person,

(ii) inform the person of the failure to comply or, if the person is incapable within the meaning of the *Health Care Consent Act, 1996*, inform the person's substitute decision-maker of the failure,

(iii) inform the person or the substitute decision-maker of the possibility that the physician may issue an order for examination and of the possible consequences; and

(iv) provide assistance to the person to comply with the terms of the order.

(3) **Return to physician**—An order for examination issued under subsection (1) is sufficient authority, for 30 days after it is issued, for a police officer to take the person named in it into custody and then promptly to the physician who issued the order.

(4) **Assessment on return**—The physician shall promptly examine the person to determine whether,

(a) the physician should make an application for a psychiatric assessment of the person under section 15;

(b) the physician should issue another community treatment order where the person, or his or her substitute decision-maker, consents to the community treatment plan; or

(c) the person should be released without being subject to a community treatment order.

33.4(1) **Early termination of order on withdrawal of consent**—A person who is subject to a community treatment order, or his or her substitute decision-maker, may withdraw his or her consent to the community treatment plan by giving the physician who issued or renewed the order a notice of intention to withdraw consent.

(2) **Duty of physician**—Within 72 hours after receipt of the notice, the physician shall review the person's condition to determine if the person is able to continue to live in the community without being subject to the order.

(3) **Order for examination**—If the person subject to the community treatment order fails to permit the physician to review his or her condition, the physician may, within the 72-hour period, issue in the prescribed form an order for examination of the person if he or she has reasonable cause to believe that the criteria set out in subclauses 33.1(4)(c)(i), (ii) and (iii) continue to be met.

(4) **Return to physician**—An order for examination issued under subsection (3) is sufficient authority, for 30 days after it is issued, for a police officer to take the person named in it into custody and then promptly to the physician who issued the order.

(5) **Assessment on return**—The physician shall promptly examine the person to determine whether,

(a) the physician should make an application for a psychiatric assessment of the person under section 15;

(b) the physician should issue another community treatment order where the person, or his or her substitute decision-maker, consents to the community treatment plan; or

(c) the person should be released without being subject to a community treatment order.

33.5(1) **Accountability**—A physician who issues or renews a community treatment order, or a physician who is appointed under subsection (2), is responsible for the general supervision and management of the order.

(2) **Appointment of other physician**—If the physician who issues or renews a community treatment order is absent or, for any other reason, is unable to carry out his or her responsibilities under subsection (1) or under section 33.2, 33.3 or 33.4, the physician may appoint another physician to act in his or her place, with the consent of that physician.

(3) **Responsibility, named providers**—A person who agrees to provide treatment or care and supervision under a community treatment plan shall indicate his or her agreement in the plan and is responsible for providing the treatment or care and supervision in accordance with the plan.

(4) **Responsibility of other persons**—All persons named in a community treatment plan, including the person subject to the plan and the person's substitute decision-maker, if any, are responsible for implementing the plan to the extent indicated in it.

33.6(1) **Protection from liability, issuing physician**—If the physician who issues or renews a community treatment order or a physician appointed under subsection 33.5(2) believes, on reasonable grounds and in good faith, that the persons who are responsible for providing treatment or care and supervision under a community treatment plan are doing so in accordance with the plan, the physician is not liable for any default or neglect by those persons in providing the treatment or care and supervision.

(2) **Same, other persons involved in treatment**—If a person who is responsible for providing an aspect of treatment or care and supervision under a community treatment plan believes, on reasonable grounds and in good faith, that a person who is responsible for providing another aspect of treatment or care and supervision under the plan is doing so in accordance with the plan, the person is not liable for any default or neglect by that person in providing that aspect of treatment or care and supervision.

(3) **Same, physician**—If a person who is responsible for providing an aspect of treatment or care and supervision under a community treatment plan believes, on reasonable grounds and in good faith, that the physician who issued or renewed the community treatment order or a physician appointed under subsection 33.5(2) is providing treatment or care and supervision in accordance with the plan, the person is not liable for any default or neglect by the physician in providing the treatment or care and supervision.

(4) **Reports**—The physician who issues or renews a community treatment order or a physician appointed under subsection 33.5(2) may require reports on the condition of the person subject to the order from the persons who are responsible for providing treatment or care and supervision under the community treatment plan.

33.7 Community treatment plans—A community treatment plan shall contain at least the following:

1. A plan of treatment for the person subject to the community treatment order.
2. Any conditions relating to the treatment or care and supervision of the person.
3. The obligations of the person subject to the community treatment order.
4. The obligations of the substitute decision-maker, if any.
5. The name of the physician, if any, who has agreed to accept responsibility for the general supervision and management of the community treatment order under subsection 33.5(2).
6. The names of all persons or organizations who have agreed to provide treatment or care and supervision under the community treatment plan and their obligations under the plan.

33.8 No limitation—Nothing in sections 33.1 to 33.7 prevents a physician, a justice of the peace or a police officer from taking any of the actions that they may take under section 15, 16, 17 or 20.

ASSIGNMENT: MENTAL HEALTH ACT

1. While on patrol, you receive information over the radio concerning an escapee from the mental health wing of your local hospital. The person is described as being an involuntary patient who was in the facility for assessment and is not known to be dangerous. The hospital is processing a "form 1" under the MHA for the person's return and it will be on the system sometime today. A short time later, you observe a pedestrian who resembles this person. You stop and investigate. The person provides verbal identification and denies having anything to do with a hospital. Do you have the authority to take this person back to the facility?

2. You are called to a location where a woman is on the outside of a guardrail on a bridge over a highway. Passersby have called police because it appears that she is contemplating suicide. The drop to the roadway is considerable. After a successful negotiation, you talk her down from the edge and into your cruiser. You take her to the nearest mental health facility—in this case, your local hospital. You attend the emergency wing with her and speak to the head nurse. She advises you that the doctor in charge of the mental health wing will be down to examine her. In the meantime, you are requested to wait in a room with her for what may be an hour or so. Are you required to stay with the woman as requested? Explain your answer.

3. Regarding question 2, do you as the officer on the scene have the grounds to take the woman to the hospital under the MHA? Explain your grounds in four parts.

4. Residents in a neighbourhood of mostly older people call the police because they are concerned about an elderly man who lives alone. He has not been seen outside or in his yard for three days and the doors and windows to his home are shut. The residents advise you that he has been in poor health for a while and has not answered the phone or the door when they have tried to check on him. He is not known to have any family. You attend the residence and knock on the door. No one answers. Looking around, you find that one door is not locked. You enter. Inside, you locate an elderly man sleeping in his bathrobe on the floor. There are remnants of spoiled food in the kitchen and the whole place is filthy. The man awakens to your voice, and while trying to speak with him you notice that he does not follow your questions. You observe that he is stained with his own waste. Are you able to reach the opinion that he is suffering from a mental illness and his safety is at risk? Explain your answer and detail your subsequent actions.

5. Some citizens come to the front desk of the police station seeking advice. They have a relative in a nearby town and they are concerned about her well-being—in particular, her mental health. She has been talking and acting abnormally. Until now, she has not done anything to endanger herself, but they are worried that she may. Because this person lives outside your jurisdiction, you are powerless to act, but you can offer them advice on what action(s) they can take when they visit her. Family and friends have two ways of having a person examined. Describe the two ways, citing to whom these people should speak and what criteria must exist for an assessment to be made.

6. While on patrol, you observe a female pedestrian known to you from previous encounters. She is standing on a street near a park, apparently talking to some people. You recall that on your shift three days earlier there was a radio broadcast advising that she had left the psychiatric wing of the local hospital without being discharged, and she is to be located and returned. You request a check of the person over the radio and the dispatcher advises you that there are no warrants for this person. Are you authorized to apprehend her and take her back to the hospital? Explain your answer.

7. While on a radio call, you have cause to investigate and run a check on the occupants of a house. The dispatcher advises you that one of the parties is wanted on an outstanding mental health warrant issued by a doctor from the local hospital. When you challenge the person on this warrant, he admits that he had some psychiatric problems over a month ago and was a patient in that hospital. He felt he was over the problem and just walked out, although the staff told him he could not leave. He provides you with the date that he left the facility; it was 38 days ago. A check with dispatch confirms that the issue date of the warrant was the same day he left the facility. What do you do?

8. You are called to a home and speak to a distraught husband who is concerned for the safety of his wife. You are told that she had been receiving psychiatric treatment over the past year and had just returned home that month. She has withdrawn from the family, acts paranoid to strangers, and doesn't seem to follow anyone's conversation. This morning, she tried taking all the miscellaneous pills in the medicine cabinet but was stopped by her eldest son. Since then, she has threatened to wait until no one is around and then kill herself. While speaking to her, you notice that she is aloof and calm as she answers your questions. The family, in her presence, states that they are concerned for her safety. What can you do?

9. You are the investigating officer in a domestic assault and at the request of the Crown are present in court for the defendant's bail hearing. The lawyer for the defendant tells the judge and Crown that his client was and is suffering from a mental illness. The illness was the main cause for the assault, and his client lacked the intent necessary to constitute the charge. What choice does the presiding judge have?

10. A family doctor and a justice of the peace receive information about a person and, through different processes, develop grounds to issue an order for the person's assessment. However, orders from both of these professionals have something in common other than the subject and his or her situation. What is the common factor?

CHAPTER 7

Coroners Act

INTRODUCTION

The tiers associated with the *Coroners Act* are enforcement, Intervention, and referral.

The *Coroners Act* (CA) ensures that society can conduct full investigations into deaths that require examination and can respond with safeguards to prevent future loss of life. The investigation can be as simple as a coroner attending the scene and confirming the circumstances surrounding the death, or it can take the form of a full coroner's inquest, with the corresponding power to subpoena witnesses and seize evidence.

The CA imposes a duty on the public to report sudden or unexpected deaths or the death of an inmate in a specified institution, such as a prison or psychiatric facility. These reporting requirements act as a public mechanism to ensure that certain deaths are subject to a compulsory investigation.

Inquests are mandatory when someone dies in police custody, in a correctional institution, or in a facility for young offenders. They are also required when a death occurs at a construction or mining site.

The CA also establishes procedures for inquests, for appeals of inquest decisions, and for appeals of a coroner's decision not to call an inquest should a member of the public feel that there are grounds that require one. It also ensures that inquests do not interfere with possibly simultaneous criminal investigations or trials.

A coroner's inquest is held before a jury of five persons, and unanimous findings are not required; a majority decision is valid. The jury is asked for recommendations that it feels will help prevent future deaths under similar circumstances. The jury is prevented by the CA from making any findings of legal responsibility or from expressing any conclusion of law; these decisions are reserved for the criminal courts.

Police officers may be involved in the inquest process from the seizure of a body to the hearing itself. Section 9(1) of the CA directs the local police service to assist the coroner as required. Section 48(2) further directs that the local police force shall provide an officer to assist the coroner in his or her duties. This officer becomes the coroner's constable and exercises much of the coroner's authority.

An officer's duties under the CA are threefold: enforcement, intervention, and referral.

- *Enforcement:* Under the CA, the coroner may appoint a police officer as a constable. In this case, the officer functions not as an officer but as a designated coroner's constable, carrying out duties specified by the coroner and assisting in an inquest.
- *Intervention:* When attending the scene of a sudden death, an officer must intervene and notify the coroner if required, preserve the scene, secure valuables and the premises, and notify next of kin of the deceased person.
- *Referral:* An officer may refer the family of a deceased person to the Act and its provisions to help them pursue answers concerning the death.

TERMINOLOGY

Chief Coroner

The term "chief coroner" refers to the chief coroner of Ontario.

Mine

A "mine," according to the *Occupational Health and Safety Act*, means any work or undertaking for the purpose of opening up, proving, removing, or extracting any metallic or non-metallic mineral or mineral-bearing substance, rock, earth, clay, sand, or gravel.

Mining Plant

A "mining plant," according to the *Occupational Health and Safety Act*, means any roasting or smelting furnace, concentrator, mill, or place used for or in connection with washing, crushing, grinding, sifting, reducing, leaching, roasting, smelting, refining, treating, or research on any substance mentioned in the definition of "mine."

Minister

The term "minister" refers to the solicitor general for Ontario.

Spouse

A "spouse" is a person

1. to whom the deceased was married immediately before his or her death, or
2. with whom the deceased was living in a conjugal relationship outside marriage immediately before his or her death, if the deceased and the other person
   a. had cohabited for at least one year,
   b. were together the parents of a child, or
   c. had together entered into a cohabitation agreement under s. 53 of the *Family Law Act*.

COMMON OFFENCES AND/OR PROVISIONS

There are only four sections that involve offences in the CA:

1. s. 10: duty to report a death to a coroner,
2. s. 11: interference with the body of a deceased person,
3. s. 13: shipment of a body outside Ontario without a certificate from a coroner, and
4. s. 16(2): obstructing a coroner or a person authorized by the coroner to carry out an investigation.

These provisions are seldom used but can be enforced, if necessary. More important are the duty to report a death and the purposes of an inquest.

Circumstances Requiring Coroner To Be Notified

One of the primary purposes of the CA is to establish the requirement to contact a coroner whenever deaths occur in certain circumstances or in certain locations. These reporting requirements ensure that society has a mechanism to examine certain deaths with a view to establishing whether or not they could have been prevented and to provide a method of making recommendations to prevent similar deaths in the future. Once the coroner is notified, he or she will investigate the circumstances of the death and determine whether or not an inquiry should be called.

The first criterion that requires a coroner to be notified involves deaths by certain causes outlined in s. 10(1) of the CA. This subsection requires that a coroner or a police officer shall immediately be notified by any person who has reason to believe that a death has occurred as a result of violence, misadventure, negligence, misconduct, or malpractice; by unfair means; during or following pregnancy, in circumstances that might reasonably be attributable to the pregnancy; from disease or sickness for which he or she was not treated by a legally qualified medical practitioner; from any cause other than disease; or under such circumstances as may require investigation (for example, a sudden or unexpected death). If a police officer is notified of such a death, that officer must notify a coroner. Essentially, any death except one in which the person died from disease or sickness for which they were being treated by a legally qualified medical practitioner is reportable.

The second criterion requiring that a coroner be notified of a death involves deaths that occur while the deceased was a resident or inmate of one of the following types of facilities:

1. a charitable institution as defined in the *Charitable Institutions Act*;
2. a children's residence under part IX ("Licensing") of the *Child and Family Services Act* or premises approved under s. 9(1) of part I ("Flexible Services") of the same act;
3. a facility as defined in the *Developmental Services Act*;
4. a psychiatric facility designated under the *Mental Health Act*;
5. an institution under the *Mental Hospitals Act*;

6. a public or private hospital to which the person was transferred from a facility, institution, or home referred to in the previous categories; or
7. a nursing home or home for the aged.

The person in charge of such a facility is responsible for notifying the coroner.

A final criterion, established by ss. 10(3) to 10(5), requires the coroner to call an inquest when a death occurs while a person is an inmate of a psychiatric facility or correctional institution, or is under secure or open custody under the *Young Offenders Act* (replaced by the *Youth Criminal Justice Act*), in the custody of a police officer, or when a death occurs while the deceased was working at a construction project, mining plant, or mine. The coroner has no discretion in these circumstances; an inquest must be called to investigate the death.

The requirement with regard to inmates of psychiatric facilities, correctional institutions, or youth custody facilities applies even if an inmate is not actually on the premises or in the actual custody of the institution at the time of death. This applies to such situations as when the inmate is transferred to a local hospital or is transported to or from court. In addition, a person does not have to be in the physical custody of an officer to be covered by the requirement.

Purposes of a Coroner's Inquest

There are five purposes of a coroner's inquest as established in the CA. The inquest is to determine

1. who the deceased was,
2. how the deceased came to his or her death,
3. when the deceased came to his or her death,
4. where the deceased came to his or her death, and
5. by what means the deceased came to his or her death.

In spite of the fifth point, the coroner's inquest is prohibited by s. 31(2) from making any determination of legal responsibility for the death, or from expressing any conclusion of law on any matter referred to in the five purposes above. In short, the coroner's inquest cannot rule on who was responsible for the death, only on what circumstances contributed to it.

ARREST POWERS

There are no arrest powers under the CA.

SEARCH POWERS

The CA authorizes the coroner, or a police officer or a medical practitioner authorized by the coroner, to

1. view or take possession of any dead body, or both; and

2. enter and inspect any place where a dead body is found and any place from which the coroner has reasonable grounds to believe the body was removed.

The CA goes further and also authorizes a coroner (or a police officer or medical practitioner authorized by the coroner), where the coroner believes on reasonable and probable grounds that to do so is necessary for the purposes of the investigation, to

1. inspect any place in which the deceased person was, or in which the coroner has reasonable grounds to believe the deceased person was, before his or her death;
2. inspect and extract information from any records or writings relating to the deceased or his or her circumstances and reproduce such copies of the records or writings as the coroner believes necessary; and
3. seize anything that the coroner has reasonable grounds to believe is material to the purposes of the investigation.

Where the coroner authorizes a medical practitioner or a police officer to exercise his or her powers in any of these three circumstances, the required grounds to believe must be those of the coroner personally.

USE OF FORCE

The role of the coroner is not one that specifically requires the use of force. For the purpose of maintaining order during a hearing, however, s. 47 of the CA authorizes the coroner to call upon peace officers to enforce order. While performing this role, the designated peace officers are authorized to use "as much force as is reasonably required."

There are no provisions in the CA regarding use of force in the enforcement of the Act. Refer to *Criminal Code* s. 25 or POA s. 146 for general provisions on the use of force.

LIMITATION PERIOD

The CA does not extend the general limitation period contained in the POA; therefore, the limitation period of six months applies.

NON-POLICE AGENCIES INVOLVED

1. Centre of Forensic Sciences
2. Coroners

If a police officer is obstructed by another person while carrying out his or her duties as a coroner's constable, s. 16(6) of the Act is used to address the obstruction, not s. 129 of the *Criminal Code*.

PROVINCIAL OFFENCES GRID COMPLETION

Common Offences and/or Provisions

Four offences are created:

1. failure to report a death to a coroner,
2. interference with the body of a deceased person,
3. shipment of a body outside Ontario without a certificate from the coroner, and
4. obstructing a coroner or a person authorized by the coroner to carry out an investigation.

Arrest Powers

None.

Search Powers

Coroners have powers to

1. view and seize any body;
2. enter and inspect any place where the body was, or the coroner believes the body was, before death;
3. inspect and extract information from any records or writings relating to the deceased or his or her circumstances, and to make copies from those records or writings as the coroner feels necessary; and
4. seize anything that the coroner has reasonable grounds to believe is material to the purposes of the investigation.

Use of Force

No specific use of force authority is contained in the CA, although the coroner may call on police officers to maintain order at an inquest; also, refer to *Criminal Code* s. 25 or POA s. 146.

Limitation Period

Six months from the date of the offence.

Non-Police Agencies Involved

1. Centre of Forensic Sciences
2. Coroners

Coroners Act

RSO 1990, c. C.37

1(1) **Definitions**—In this Act,

"Chief Coroner" means the Chief Coroner for Ontario;

"Chief Forensic Pathologist" means the Chief Forensic Pathologist for Ontario;

"Deputy Chief Coroner" means a Deputy Chief Coroner for Ontario;

"Deputy Chief Forensic Pathologist" means a Deputy Chief Forensic Pathologist for Ontario;

"forensic pathologist" means a pathologist who has been certified by the Royal College of Physicians and Surgeons of Canada in forensic pathology or has received equivalent certification in another jurisdiction;

"mine" means a mine as defined in the *Occupational Health and Safety Act*;

"mining plant" means a mining plant as defined in the *Occupational Health and Safety Act*;

"Minister" means the Solicitor General;

"Oversight Council" means the Death Investigation Oversight Council established under section 8;

"pathologist" means a physician who has been certified by the Royal College of Physicians and Surgeons of Canada as a specialist in anatomical or general pathology or has received equivalent certification in another jurisdiction;

"pathologists register" means the register of pathologists maintained under section 7.1;

"spouse" means a person,

(a) to whom the deceased was married immediately before his or her death,

(b) with whom the deceased was living in a conjugal relationship outside marriage immediately before his or her death, if the deceased and the other person,

(i) had cohabited for at least one year,

(ii) were together the parents of a child, or

(iii) had together entered into a cohabitation agreement under section 53 of the *Family Law Act*.

"tissue" includes an organ or part of an organ.

(2) **Interpretation of body**—A reference in this Act to the body of a person includes part of the body of a person.

Effect of Act

2(1) **Repeal of common law functions**—In so far as it is within the jurisdiction of the Legislature, the common law as it relates to the functions, powers and duties of coroners within Ontario is repealed.

(2) **Inquest not criminal court of record**—The powers conferred on a coroner to conduct an inquest shall not be construed as creating a criminal court of record.

3(1) **Appointment of coroners**—The Lieutenant Governor in Council may appoint one or more legally qualified medical practitioners to be coroners for Ontario who, subject to subsections (2), (3) and (4), shall hold office during pleasure.

(2) **Tenure**—A coroner ceases to hold office,

(a) upon attaining the age of seventy years; or

(b) upon ceasing to be a legally qualified medical practitioner.

(3) **Chief Coroner to be notified**—The College of Physicians and Surgeons of Ontario shall forthwith notify the Chief Coroner where the licence of a coroner for the practice of medicine is revoked, suspended or cancelled.

(4) **Resignation**—A coroner may resign his or her office in writing.

(5) **Residential areas**—The Lieutenant Governor in Council may by regulation establish areas of Ontario and the appointment and continuation in office of a coroner is subject to the condition that he or she is ordinarily resident in the area named in the appointment.

(6) **Crown Attorney notified of appointment**—A copy of the order appointing a coroner shall be sent by the Minister to the Crown Attorney of any area in which the coroner will ordinarily act.

(7) **Appointments continued**—All persons holding appointments as coroners under *The Coroners Act*, being chapter 87 of the Revised Statutes of Ontario, 1970, shall be deemed to have been appointed in accordance with this Act.

4(1) **Chief Coroner and duties**—The Lieutenant Governor in Council may appoint a coroner to be Chief Coroner for Ontario who shall,

(a) administer this Act and the regulations;

(b) supervise, direct and control all coroners in Ontario in the performance of their duties;

(c) conduct programs for the instruction of coroners in their duties;

(d) bring the findings and recommendations of coroners' investigations and coroners' juries to the attention of appropriate persons, agencies and ministries of government;

(e) prepare, publish and distribute a code of ethics for the guidance of coroners;

(f) perform such other duties as are assigned to him or her by or under this or any other Act or by the Lieutenant Governor in Council.

(2) **Deputy Chief Coroners**—The Lieutenant Governor in Council may appoint one or more coroners to be Deputy Chief Coroners for Ontario and a Deputy Chief Coroner shall act as and have all the powers and authority of the Chief Coroner if the Chief Coroner is absent or unable to act or if the Chief Coroner's position is vacant.

(3) **Delegation**—The Chief Coroner may delegate in writing any of his or her powers and duties under this Act to a Deputy Chief Coroner, subject to any limitations, conditions and requirements set out in the delegation.

5(1) **Regional coroners**—The Lieutenant Governor in Council may appoint a coroner as a regional coroner for such region of Ontario as is described in the appointment.

(2) **Duties**—A regional coroner shall assist the Chief Coroner in the performance of his or her duties in the region and shall perform such other duties as are assigned to him or her by the Chief Coroner.

6. Ontario Forensic Pathology Service—The Minister shall establish the Ontario Forensic Pathology Service, to be known in French as Service de médecine légale de l'Ontario, the function of which shall be to facilitate the provision of pathologists' services under this Act.

7(1) **Chief Forensic Pathologist and Deputies**—The Lieutenant Governor in Council may appoint a forensic pathologist to be Chief Forensic Pathologist for Ontario who shall,

(a) be responsible for the administration and operation of the Ontario Forensic Pathology Service;

(b) supervise and direct pathologists in the provision of services under this Act;

(c) conduct programs for the instruction of pathologists who provide services under this Act;

(d) prepare, publish and distribute a code of ethics for the guidance of pathologists in the provision of services under this Act;

(e) perform such other duties as are assigned to him or her by or under this or any other Act or by the Lieutenant Governor in Council.

(2) **Deputy Chief Forensic Pathologists**—The Lieutenant Governor in Council may appoint one or more forensic pathologists to be Deputy Chief Forensic Pathologists for Ontario and a Deputy Chief Forensic Pathologist shall act as and have all the powers and authority of the Chief Forensic Pathologist if the Chief Forensic Pathologist is absent or unable to act or if the Chief Forensic Pathologist's position is vacant.

(3) **Delegation**—The Chief Forensic Pathologist may delegate in writing any of his or her powers and duties under this Act to a Deputy Chief Forensic Pathologist, subject to any limitations, conditions and requirements set out in the delegation.

7.1(1) **Pathologists register**—The Chief Forensic Pathologist shall maintain a register of pathologists who are authorized by the Chief Forensic Pathologist to provide services under this Act.

(2) **Notification re loss of medical licence**—The College of Physicians and Surgeons of Ontario shall forthwith notify the Chief Forensic Pathologist if the licence for the practice of medicine of a pathologist who is on the pathologists register is revoked, suspended or cancelled.

8(1) **Oversight Council**—There is hereby established a council to be known in English as the Death Investigation Oversight Council and in French as Conseil de surveillance des enquêtes sur les décès.

(2) **Membership**—The composition of the Oversight Council shall be as provided in the regulations, and the members shall be appointed by the Lieutenant Governor in Council.

(3) **Chair, vice-chairs**—The Lieutenant Governor in Council may designate one of the members of the Oversight Council to be the chair and one or more members of the Oversight Council to be vice-chairs and a vice-chair shall act as and have all the powers and authority of the chair if the chair is absent or unable to act or if the chair's position is vacant.

(4) **Employees**—Such employees as are considered necessary for the proper conduct of the affairs of the Oversight Council may be appointed under Part III of the *Public Service of Ontario Act, 2006*.

(5) **Delegation**—The chair may authorize one or more members of the Oversight Council to exercise any of the Oversight Council's powers and perform any of its duties.

(6) **Quorum**—The chair shall determine the number of members of the Oversight Council that constitutes a quorum for any purpose.

(7) **Annual report**—At the end of each calendar year, the Oversight Council shall submit an annual report on its activities, including its activities under subsection 8.1(1), to the Minister, who shall submit the report to the Lieutenant Governor in Council and shall then lay the report before the Assembly.

(8) **Additional reports**—The Minister may request additional reports from the Oversight Council on its activities, including its activities under subsection 8.1(1), at any time and the Oversight Council shall submit such reports as requested and may also submit additional reports on the same matters at any time on its own initiative.

(9) **Expenses**—The money required for the Oversight Council's purposes shall be paid out of the amounts appropriated by the Legislature for that purpose.

Functions of Oversight Council

8.1(1) **Advice and recommendations to Chief Coroner and Chief Forensic Pathologist**—The Oversight Council shall oversee the Chief Coroner and the Chief Forensic Pathologist by advising and making recommendations to them on the following matters:

1. Financial resource management.
2. Strategic planning.
3. Quality assurance, performance measures and accountability mechanisms.
4. Appointment and dismissal of senior personnel.

5. The exercise of the power to refuse to review complaints under subsection 8.4(10).
6. Compliance with this Act and the regulations.
7. Any other matter that is prescribed.

(2) **Reports to Oversight Council**—The Chief Coroner and the Chief Forensic Pathologist shall report to the Oversight Council on the matters set out in subsection (1), as may be requested by the Oversight Council.

(3) **Advice and recommendations to Minister**—The Oversight Council shall advise and make recommendations to the Minister on the appointment and dismissal of the Chief Coroner and the Chief Forensic Pathologist.

8.2(1) **Complaints committee**—There shall be a complaints committee of the Oversight Council composed, in accordance with the regulations, of members of the Oversight Council appointed by the chair of the Oversight Council.

(2) **Chair**—The chair of the Oversight Council shall designate one member of the complaints committee to be the chair of the committee.

(3) **Delegation**—The chair of the complaints committee may delegate any of the functions of the committee to one or more members of the committee.

(4) **Quorum**—The chair of the complaints committee shall determine the number of members of the complaints committee that constitutes a quorum for any purpose, and may determine that one member constitutes a quorum.

8.3(1) **Confidentiality**—Every member and employee of the Oversight Council and of the complaints committee shall keep confidential all information that comes to his or her knowledge in the course of performing his or her duties under this Act.

(2) **Exception**—An individual described in subsection (1) may disclose confidential information for the purposes of the administration of this Act or the *Regulated Health Professions Act, 1991* or as otherwise required by law.

Complaints

8.4(1) **Right to make a complaint**—Any person may make a complaint to the complaints committee about a coroner, a pathologist or a person, other than a coroner or pathologist, with powers or duties under section 28.

(2) **Form of complaint**—The complaint must be in writing.

(3) **Matters that may not be the subject of a complaint**—A complaint about the following matters shall not be dealt with under this section:

1. A coroner's decision to hold an inquest or to not hold an inquest.
2. A coroner's decision respecting the scheduling of an inquest.
3. A coroner's decision relating to the conduct of an inquest, including a decision made while presiding at the inquest.

(4) **Complaints about coroners**—Subject to subsection (8), the complaints committee shall refer every complaint about a coroner, other than the Chief Coroner, to the Chief Coroner and the Chief Coroner shall review every such complaint.

(5) **Complaints about pathologists**—Subject to subsection (8), the complaints committee shall refer every complaint about a pathologist, other than the Chief Forensic Pathologist, to the Chief Forensic Pathologist and the Chief Forensic Pathologist shall review every such complaint.

(6) **Complaints about Chiefs**—Subject to subsection (8), the complaints committee shall review every complaint made about the Chief Coroner or the Chief Forensic Pathologist.

(7) **Referral to other persons or bodies**—The complaints committee shall refer every complaint about a person, other than a coroner or pathologist, with powers or duties under section 28 to a person or organization that has power to deal with the complaint

and that the committee considers is the appropriate person or organization to deal with the complaint.

(8) **Same**—If the complaints committee is of the opinion that a complaint about a coroner or pathologist is more appropriately dealt with by the College of Physicians and Surgeons of Ontario or another person or organization that has power to deal with the complaint, the complaints committee shall refer the complaint to the College or that other person or organization.

(9) **Notice of referral**—If the complaints committee refers a complaint to the College of Physicians and Surgeons of Ontario or another person or organization under subsection (8), the committee shall promptly give notice in writing to the complainant, the coroner or pathologist who is the subject of the complaint, and the Oversight Council.

(10) **Refusal to review a complaint**—Despite subsections (4) and (5), the Chief Coroner and the Chief Forensic Pathologist may refuse to review a complaint referred to him or her if, in his or her opinion,

(a) the complaint is trivial or vexatious or not made in good faith;

(b) the complaint does not relate to a power or duty of a coroner or a pathologist under this Act; or

(c) the complainant was not directly affected by the exercise or performance of, or the failure to exercise or perform, the power or duty to which the complaint relates.

(11) **Same**—Despite subsection (6), the complaints committee may refuse to review a complaint if, in its opinion,

(a) the complaint is trivial or vexatious or not made in good faith;

(b) the complaint does not relate to a power or duty of the Chief Coroner or the Chief Forensic Pathologist; or

(c) the complainant was not directly affected by the exercise or performance of, or the failure to exercise or perform, the power or duty to which the complaint relates.

(12) **Reports after review or decision to not review**—The Chief Coroner and the Chief Forensic Pathologist shall, promptly after completing his or her review of a complaint referred to him or her or deciding to not review the complaint, report in writing to the complainant, the person who is the subject of the complaint and the complaints committee on the results of the review or the decision to not review the complaint, as the case may be.

(13) **Same**—The complaints committee shall, promptly after completing its review of a complaint or deciding to not review the complaint, report in writing to the complainant, the person who is the subject of the complaint, the Oversight Council and the Minister on the results of the review or the decision to not review the complaint, as the case may be.

(14) **Request for review by complaints committee**—If a complaint is made about a coroner or pathologist, other than the Chief Coroner or the Chief Forensic Pathologist, and the complainant or the coroner or pathologist who is the subject of the complaint is not satisfied with the results of the review of the complaint or the decision to not review the complaint by the Chief Coroner or the Chief Forensic Pathologist, he or she may request in writing that the complaints committee review the complaint and the complaints committee shall review the complaint and shall, promptly after completing its review or deciding to not review the complaint, report in writing to the complainant, the person who is the subject of the complaint and the Chief Coroner or the Chief Forensic Pathologist, as appropriate, on the results of the review or the decision to not review the complaint, as the case may be.

(15) **Refusal to review a complaint on request**—The complaints committee may refuse to review a complaint pursuant to a request made under subsection (14) if, in its opinion,

(a) the complaint is trivial or vexatious or not made in good faith;

(b) the complaint does not relate to a power or duty of a coroner or a pathologist under this Act; or

(c) the complainant was not directly affected by the exercise or performance of, or the failure to exercise or perform, the power or duty to which the complaint relates.

(16) **Annual reports to Oversight Council**—The complaints committee shall submit an annual report on its activities to the Oversight Council at the end of each calendar year.

(17) **Additional reports**—The Oversight Council may request additional reports from the complaints committee on its activities or on a specific complaint or complaints about a specific person at any time and the complaints committee shall submit such reports as requested and may also submit additional reports as described at any time on its own initiative.

Section 9(1) provides the authority for a police officer to be appointed as a coroner's constable.

9(1) **Police assistance**—The police force having jurisdiction in the locality in which a coroner has jurisdiction shall make available to the coroner the assistance of such police officers as are necessary for the purpose of carrying out the coroner's duties.

(2) **Same**—The Chief Coroner in any case he or she considers appropriate may request that another police force or the criminal investigation branch of the Ontario Provincial Police provide assistance to a coroner in an investigation or inquest.

10(1) **Duty to give information**—Every person who has reason to believe that a deceased person died,

(a) as a result of,

(i) violence,

(ii) misadventure,

(iii) negligence,

(iv) misconduct, or

(v) malpractice;

(b) by unfair means;

(c) during pregnancy or following pregnancy in circumstances that might reasonably be attributable thereto;

(d) suddenly and unexpectedly;

(e) from disease or sickness for which he or she was not treated by a legally qualified medical practitioner;

(f) from any cause other than disease; or

(g) under such circumstances as may require investigation,

shall immediately notify a coroner or a police officer of the facts and circumstances relating to the death, and where a police officer is notified he or she shall in turn immediately notify the coroner of such facts and circumstances.

(2) **Deaths to be reported**—Where a person dies while resident or an in-patient in,

(a) Repealed.

(b) a children's residence under Part IX (Licensing) of the *Child and Family Services Act* or premises approved under subsection 9(1) of Part I (Flexible Services) of that Act;

(c) Repealed.

(d) a supported group living residence or an intensive support residence under the *Services and Supports to Promote the Social Inclusion of Persons with Developmental Disabilities Act, 2008*;

(e) a psychiatric facility designated under the *Mental Health Act*;

(f) Repealed.

(g) Repealed.

(h) a public or private hospital to which the person was transferred from a facility, institution or home referred to in clauses (a) to (g),

the person in charge of the hospital, facility, institution, residence or home shall immediately give notice of the death to a coroner, and the coroner shall investigate the circumstances of the death and, if as a result of the investigation he or she is of the opinion that an inquest ought to be held, the coroner shall hold an inquest upon the body.

(2.1) Where a person dies while resident in a long-term care home to which the *Long-Term Care Homes Act, 2007* applies, the person in charge of the home shall immediately give notice of the death to a coroner and, if the coroner is of the opinion that the death ought to be investigated, he or she shall investigate the circumstances of the death and if, as a result of the investigation, he or she is of the opinion that an inquest ought to be held, the coroner shall hold an inquest upon the body.

(3) **Deaths off premises of psychiatric facilities, correctional institutions, youth custody facilities**—Where a person dies while,

(a) a patient of a psychiatric facility;

(b) committed to a correctional institution;

(c) committed to a place of temporary detention under the *Youth Criminal Justice Act* (Canada); or

(d) committed to secure or open custody under section 24.1 of the *Young Offenders Act* (Canada), whether in accordance with section 88 of the *Youth Criminal Justice Act* (Canada) or otherwise,

but while not on the premises or in actual custody of the facility, institution or place, as the case may be, subsection (2) applies as if the person were a resident of an institution named in subsection (2).

(4) **Death on premises of detention facility or lock-up**—Where a person dies while detained in and on the premises of a detention facility established under section 16.1 of the *Police Services Act* or a lock-up, the officer in charge of the facility or lock-up shall immediately give notice of the death to a coroner and the coroner shall hold an inquest upon the body.

(4.1) **Death on premises of place of temporary detention**—Where a person dies while committed to and on the premises of a place of temporary detention under the *Youth Criminal Justice Act* (Canada), the officer in charge of the place shall immediately give notice of the death to a coroner and the coroner shall hold an inquest upon the body.

(4.2) **Death on premises of place of secure custody**—Where a person dies while committed to and on the premises of a place or facility designated as a place of secure custody under section 24.1 of the Young Offenders Act (Canada), whether in accordance with section 88 of the Youth Criminal Justice Act (Canada) or otherwise, the officer in charge of the place or facility shall immediately give notice of the death to a coroner and the coroner shall hold an inquest upon the body.

(4.3) **Death on premises of correctional institution**—Where a person dies while committed to and on the premises of a correctional institution, the officer in charge of the institution shall immediately give notice of the death to a coroner and the coroner shall investigate the circumstances of the death and shall hold an inquest upon the body if as a result of the investigation he or she is of the opinion that the person may not have died of natural causes.

(4.4) **Non-application of subs. (4.3)**—If a person dies in circumstances referred to in subsection (4), (4.1) or (4.2) on the premises of a lock-up, place of temporary detention or place or facility designated as a place of secure custody that is located in a correctional institution, subsection (4.3) does not apply.

(4.5) **Death in custody off premises of correctional institution**—Where a person dies while committed to a correctional institution, while off the premises of the institution and while in the actual custody of a person employed at the institution, the officer in charge of the institution shall immediately give notice of the death to a coroner and the coroner shall investigate the circumstances of the death and shall hold an inquest upon the body if as a result of the investigation he or she is of the opinion that the person may not have died of natural causes.

(4.6) **Other deaths in custody**—If a person dies while detained by or in the actual custody of a peace officer and subsections (4), (4.1), (4.2), (4.3) and (4.5) do not apply, the peace officer shall immediately give notice of the death to a coroner and the coroner shall hold an inquest upon the body.

(4.7) **Death while restrained on premises of psychiatric facility, etc.**—Where a person dies while being restrained and while detained in and on the premises of a psychiatric facility within the meaning of the *Mental Health Act* or a hospital within the meaning of Part XX.1 (Mental Disorder) of the *Criminal Code* (Canada), the officer in charge of the psychiatric facility or the person in charge of the hospital, as the case may be, shall immediately give notice of the death to a coroner and the coroner shall hold an inquest upon the body.

(4.8) **Death while restrained in secure treatment program**—Where a person dies while being restrained and while committed or admitted to a secure treatment program within the meaning of Part VI of the *Child and Family Services Act*, the person in charge of the program shall immediately give notice of the death to a coroner and the coroner shall hold an inquest upon the body.

(5) **Notice of death resulting from accident at or in construction project, mining plant or mine**—Where a worker dies as a result of an accident occurring in the course of the worker's employment at or in a construction project, mining plant or mine, including a pit or quarry, the person in charge of such project, mining plant or mine shall immediately give notice of the death to a coroner and the coroner shall hold an inquest upon the body.

(6) **Certificate as evidence**—A statement as to the notification or non-notification of a coroner under this section, purporting to be certified by the coroner is without proof of the appointment or signature of the coroner, receivable in evidence as proof, in the absence of evidence to the contrary of the facts stated therein for all purposes in any action, proceeding or prosecution.

11. Interference with body—No person who has reason to believe that a person died in any of the circumstances mentioned in section 10 shall interfere with or alter the body or its condition in any way until the coroner so directs by a warrant.

12(1) **Power of coroner to take charge of wreckage**—Where a coroner has issued a warrant to take possession of the body of a person who has met death by violence in a wreck, the coroner may, with the approval of the Chief Coroner, take charge of the wreckage and place one or more police officers in charge of it so as to prevent persons from disturbing it until the jury at the inquest has viewed it, or the coroner has made such examination as he or she considers necessary.

(2) **View to be expedited**—The jury or coroner, as the case may be, shall view the wreckage at the earliest moment possible.

13(1) **Shipment of bodies outside Ontario**—Subject to section 14, no person shall accept for shipment or ship or take a dead body from any place in Ontario to any place outside Ontario unless a certificate of a coroner has been obtained certifying that there exists no reason for further examination of the body.

(2) **Fee for certificate**—An applicant for a certificate under subsection (1) shall pay to the coroner such fee as is prescribed therefor.

(3) **Embalming, etc., prohibited**—No person who has reason to believe that a dead body will be shipped or taken to a place outside Ontario shall embalm or make any alteration to the body or apply any chemical to the body, internally or externally, until the certificate required by subsection (1) has been issued.

14. Transportation of a body out of Ontario for *post mortem*—A coroner may in writing authorize the transportation of a body out of Ontario for *post mortem* examination and, in such case a provision in any Act or regulation requiring embalming and preparation by a funeral director does not apply.

15(1) **Coroner's investigation**—Where a coroner is informed that there is in his or her jurisdiction the body of a person and that there is reason to believe that the person died in any of the circumstances mentioned in section 10, the coroner shall issue a warrant to take possession of the body and shall examine the body and make such investigation as, in the opinion of the coroner, is necessary in the public interest to enable the coroner,

(a) to determine the answers to the questions set out in subsection 31(1);

(b) to determine whether or not an inquest is necessary; and

(c) to collect and analyze information about the death in order to prevent further deaths in similar circumstances.

(2) **Idem**—Where the Chief Coroner has reason to believe that a person died in any of the circumstances mentioned in section 10 and no warrant has been issued to take possession of the body, he or she may issue the warrant or direct any coroner to do so.

(3) **Jurisdiction**—After the issue of the warrant, no other coroner shall issue a warrant or interfere in the case, except the Chief Coroner.

(4) **Expert assistance**—Subject to the approval of the Chief Coroner, a coroner may obtain assistance or retain expert services for all or any part of his or her investigation or inquest.

(5) **No warrant**—A coroner may proceed with an investigation without taking possession of the body where the body has been destroyed in whole or in part or is lying in a place from which it cannot be recovered or has been removed from Ontario.

16(1) **Investigative powers**—A coroner may,

Section 16 gives the coroner wide authority for search and seizure without requiring a warrant.

(a) examine or take possession of any dead body, or both; and

(b) enter and inspect any place where a dead body is and any place from which the coroner has reasonable grounds for believing the body was removed.

(2) **Idem**—A coroner who believes on reasonable and probable grounds that to do so is necessary for the purposes of the investigation may,

(a) inspect any place in which the deceased person was, or in which the coroner has reasonable grounds to believe the deceased person was, prior to his or her death;

(b) inspect and extract information from any records or writings relating to the deceased or his or her circumstances and reproduce such copies therefrom as the coroner believes necessary;

(c) seize anything that the coroner has reasonable grounds to believe is material to the purposes of the investigation.

(3) **Delegation of powers**—A coroner may authorize a legally qualified medical practitioner or a police officer to exercise all or any of the coroner's powers under subsection (1).

The powers referred to in s. 16(3) are extended to the coroner's constable.

(4) **Idem**—A coroner may, where in his or her opinion it is necessary for the purposes of the investigation, authorize a legally qualified medical practitioner or a police officer to exercise all or any of the coroner's powers under clauses (2)(a), (b) and (c) but, where such power is conditional on the belief of the coroner, the requisite belief shall be that of the coroner personally.

(5) **Return of things seized**—Where a coroner seizes anything under clause (2)(c), he or she shall place it in the custody of a police officer for safekeeping and shall return it to the person from whom it was seized as soon as is practicable after the conclusion of the investigation or, where there is an inquest, of the inquest, unless the coroner is authorized or required by law to dispose of it otherwise.

(6) **Obstruction of coroner**—No person shall knowingly,

(a) hinder, obstruct or interfere with or attempt to hinder, obstruct or interfere with; or

(b) furnish with false information or refuse or neglect to furnish information to, a coroner in the performance of his or her duties or a person authorized by the coroner in connection with an investigation.

16.1(1) **Appointment of persons with coroners' investigative powers and duties**—The Chief Coroner may appoint any person, in accordance with the regulations, to exercise the investigative powers and duties of a coroner.

(2) **Same**—Subject to subsection (3) and the regulations, this Act applies with necessary modifications to a person appointed under subsection (1) as if he or she were a coroner.

(3) **Limitation**—A person appointed under subsection (1) cannot determine whether or not an inquest is necessary or hold an inquest.

(4) **Report**—A person appointed under subsection (1) shall report his or her findings to the Chief Coroner or a coroner specified by the Chief Coroner, who shall then determine whether or not an inquest is necessary.

17(1) **Transfer of investigation**—A coroner may at any time transfer an investigation to another coroner where in his or her opinion the investigation may be continued or conducted more conveniently by that other coroner or for any other good and sufficient reason.

(2) **Investigation and inquest**—The coroner to whom an investigation is transferred shall proceed with the investigation in the same manner as if he or she had issued the warrant to take possession of the body.

(3) **Notification of Chief Coroner**—The coroner who transfers an investigation to another coroner shall notify the Chief Coroner of the transfer, and the Chief Coroner shall assist in the transfer upon request.

(4) **Transmitting results of first investigation**—The coroner who transfers an investigation to another coroner shall transmit to that other coroner the report of the *post mortem* examination of the body, if any, and his or her signed statement setting forth briefly the result of his or her investigation and any evidence to prove the fact of death and the identity of the body.

18(1) **Inquest unnecessary**—Where the coroner determines that an inquest is unnecessary, the coroner shall forthwith transmit to the Chief Coroner a signed statement setting forth briefly the results of the investigation, and shall also forthwith transmit to the division registrar a notice of the death in the form prescribed by the *Vital Statistics Act*.

(2) **Recommendations**—The coroner may make recommendations to the Chief Coroner with respect to the prevention of deaths in circumstances similar to those of the death that was the subject of the coroner's investigation.

(3) **Disclosure to the public**—The Chief Coroner shall bring the findings and recommendations of a coroner's investigation, which may include personal information as defined in the *Freedom of Information and Protection of Privacy Act*, to the attention of the public, or any segment of the public, if the Chief Coroner reasonably believes that it is necessary in the interests of public safety to do so.

(4) **Record of investigations**—Every coroner shall keep a record of the cases reported in which an inquest has been determined to be unnecessary, showing for each case the coroner's findings of facts to determine the answers to the questions set out in subsection 31(1), and such findings, including the relevant findings of the post mortem examination and of any other examinations or analyses of the body carried out, shall be available to the spouse, parents, children, brothers and sisters of the deceased and to his or her personal representative, upon request.

18.1 Coroner's report if death suspected not of natural causes—If the coroner is of the opinion, based on his or her investigation, that the deceased person may not have died of natural causes, the coroner shall advise the regional coroner of that opinion and the regional coroner shall so advise the Crown Attorney.

19. Determination to hold an inquest—Where the coroner determines that an inquest is necessary, the coroner shall,

(a) forthwith notify the Chief Coroner of that determination and give the Chief Coroner a brief summary of the results of the investigation and of the grounds upon which the coroner made that determination; and

(b) hold an inquest.

20. What coroner shall consider and have regard to—When making a determination whether an inquest is necessary or unnecessary, the coroner shall have regard to whether the holding of an inquest would serve the public interest and, without restricting the generality of the foregoing, shall consider,

(a) whether the matters described in clauses 31(1)(a) to (e) are known;

(b) the desirability of the public being fully informed of the circumstances of the death through an inquest; and

(c) the likelihood that the jury on an inquest might make useful recommendations directed to the avoidance of death in similar circumstances.

21. Where body destroyed or removed from Ontario—Where a coroner has reason to believe that a death has occurred in circumstances that warrant the holding of an inquest but, owing to the destruction of the body in whole or in part or to the fact that the body is lying in a place from which it cannot be recovered, or that the body has been removed from Ontario, an inquest cannot be held except by virtue of this section, he or she shall report the facts to the Chief Coroner who may direct an inquest to be held touching the death, in which case an inquest shall be held by the coroner making the report or by such other coroner as the Chief Coroner directs, and the law relating to coroners and coroners' inquests applies with such modifications as are necessary in consequence of the inquest being held otherwise than on or after a view of the body.

22. Repealed.

22.1 Inquest mandatory—A coroner shall hold an inquest under this Act into the death of a child upon learning that the child died in the circumstances described in clauses 72.2(a), (b) and (c) of the *Child and Family Services Act.*

23. Repealed.

24. Chief Coroner may direct that body be disinterred—Despite anything in the *Cemeteries Act*, the Chief Coroner may, at any time where he or she considers it necessary for the purposes of an investigation or an inquest, direct that a body be disinterred under and subject to such conditions as the Chief Coroner considers proper.

> Note: On a day to be named by proclamation of the Lieutenant Governor, section 24 is amended by the Statutes of Ontario, 2002, chapter 33, section 142 by striking out "*Cemeteries Act*" and substituting "*Funeral, Burial and Cremation Services Act, 2002* or a regulation made under that Act."

25(1) Direction by Chief Coroner—The Chief Coroner may direct any coroner in respect of any death to issue a warrant to take possession of the body, conduct an investigation or hold an inquest, or may direct any other coroner to do so or may intervene to act as coroner personally for any one or more of such purposes.

(2) **Inquest into multiple deaths**—Where two or more deaths appear to have occurred in the same event or from a common cause, the Chief Coroner may direct that one inquest be held into all of the deaths.

(3) **Direction to replace coroner**—If the Chief Coroner is of the opinion that a coroner is unable to continue presiding over an inquest for any reason, the Chief Coroner may direct another coroner to continue the inquest.

26(1) **Request by relative for inquest**—Where the coroner determines that an inquest is unnecessary, the spouse, same-sex partner, parent, child, brother, sister or personal representative of the deceased person may request the coroner in writing to hold an inquest, and the coroner shall give the person requesting the inquest an opportunity to state his or her reasons, either personally, by the person's agent or in writing, and the coroner shall advise the person in writing within sixty days of the receipt of the request of the coroner's final decision and where the decision is to not hold an inquest shall deliver the reasons therefor in writing.

(2) **Review of refusal**—Where the final decision of a coroner under subsection (1) is to not hold an inquest, the person making the request may, within twenty days after the receipt of the decision of the coroner, request the Chief Coroner to review the decision and the Chief Coroner shall review the decision of the coroner after giving the person requesting the inquest an opportunity to state his or her reasons either personally, by the person's agent or in writing.

(3) **Decision final**—The decision of the Chief Coroner is final.

27(1) **Where criminal offence charged**—Where a person is charged with an offence under the *Criminal Code* (Canada) arising out of a death, an inquest touching the death shall be held only upon the direction of the Chief Coroner and, when held, the person charged is not a compellable witness.

(2) **Idem**—Where during an inquest a person is charged with an offence under the *Criminal Code* (Canada) arising out of the death, the coroner shall discharge the jury and close the inquest, and shall then proceed as if he or she had determined that an inquest was unnecessary, but the Chief Coroner may direct that the inquest be reopened.

(3) **Where charge or appeal finally disposed of**—Despite subsections (1) and (2), where a person is charged with an offence under the *Criminal Code* (Canada) arising out of the death and the charge or any appeal from a conviction or an acquittal of the offence charged has been finally disposed of or the time for taking an appeal has expired, the coroner may hold an inquest and the person charged is a compellable witness at the inquest.

28(1) ***Post mortem* examination**—A coroner may at any time during an investigation issue a warrant for a pathologist to perform a post mortem examination of the body.

(2) **Other examinations and analyses**—A coroner may at any time during an investigation conduct examinations and analyses that the coroner considers appropriate in the circumstances or direct any person, other than the pathologist to whom the warrant is issued, to conduct such examinations and analyses.

(3) **Pathologist's duty**—The pathologist to whom the warrant is issued shall perform the post mortem examination of the body.

(4) **Power to examine body**—The pathologist to whom the warrant is issued or, if no warrant has been issued, a pathologist who has been notified of the death by a coroner or police officer and who reasonably believes that a coroner's warrant will be issued to him or her under subsection (1) may,

(a) enter and inspect any place where the dead body is and examine the body; and

(b) enter and inspect any place from which the pathologist has reasonable grounds for believing the body was removed.

(5) **Notice to coroner**—A pathologist who exercises a power under subsection (4) shall notify,

(a) the coroner who issued the warrant; or

(b) if no warrant has been issued, the coroner by whom the pathologist believes the warrant will be issued.

(6) **Other examinations and analyses**—The pathologist who performs the post mortem examination may conduct or direct any person other than a coroner to conduct

such other examinations and analyses as he or she considers appropriate in the circumstances.

(7) **Direction of Chief Forensic Pathologist**—The Chief Forensic Pathologist may direct a pathologist or any other person, other than a coroner, to conduct any examinations and analyses that the Chief Forensic Pathologist considers appropriate in the circumstances.

(8) **Assistance** The pathologist who performs the post mortem examination may obtain the assistance of any person or persons in performing the post mortem examination and in conducting any other examinations and analyses.

(9) **Pathologist from register**—The coroner may issue a warrant under subsection (1) only to a pathologist whose name is on the pathologists register.

(10) **Assignment to another pathologist**—The Chief Forensic Pathologist may at any time during an investigation assign another pathologist whose name is on the pathologists register to perform the post mortem examination in place of the pathologist named on the coroner's warrant, and in that case, every reference in this section to the pathologist to whom the warrant is issued applies to the pathologist assigned to the investigation by the Chief Forensic Pathologist.

29(1) **Reports of post mortem findings**—The pathologist who performed the post mortem examination of a body under section 28 shall forthwith report in writing his or her findings from the post mortem examination and from any other examinations or analyses that he or she conducted to the coroner who issued the warrant, the regional coroner and, if the pathologist who performed the post mortem examination is not the Chief Forensic Pathologist, the Chief Forensic Pathologist.

(2) **Same**—A person, other than the pathologist who performed the post mortem examination, who conducted any other examination or analysis under section 28 shall forthwith report his or her findings in writing to the pathologist who performed the post mortem examination, the coroner who issued the warrant, the regional coroner and, if the pathologist who performed the post mortem examination is not the Chief Forensic Pathologist, the Chief Forensic Pathologist.

(3) **Further post mortems**—If, after a post mortem examination of a body is performed, the Chief Forensic Pathologist is of the opinion that a second or further post mortem examination of the body is necessary, he or she shall so advise the Chief Coroner, and the Chief Coroner shall issue a warrant for a second or further post mortem examination of the body.

30(1) **Crown counsel**—Every coroner before holding an inquest shall notify the Crown Attorney of the time and place at which it is to be held and the Crown Attorney or a barrister and solicitor or any other person designated by him or her shall attend the inquest and shall act as counsel to the coroner at the inquest.

(2) **Counsel for Minister**—The Minister may be represented at an inquest by counsel and shall be deemed to be a person with standing at the inquest for the purpose.

31(1) **Purposes of inquest**—Where an inquest is held, it shall inquire into the circumstances of the death and determine,

(a) who the deceased was;
(b) how the deceased came to his or her death;
(c) when the deceased came to his or her death;
(d) where the deceased came to his or her death; and
(e) by what means the deceased came to his or her death.

(2) **Idem**—The jury shall not make any finding of legal responsibility or express any conclusion of law on any matter referred to in subsection (1).

Section 31(2) precludes a coroner's jury from addressing any criminal or legal liability in the death being investigated. Any questions beyond those stated in s. 31(1) are a matter for criminal or civil court.

(3) **Authority of jury to make recommendations**—Subject to subsection (2), the jury may make recommendations directed to the avoidance of death in similar circumstances or respecting any other matter arising out of the inquest.

(4) Repealed.

(5) **Failure to make proper finding**—Where a jury fails to deliver a proper finding it shall be discharged.

32. Inquest public—An inquest shall be open to the public except where the coroner is of the opinion that national security might be endangered or where a person is charged with an indictable offence under the *Criminal Code* (Canada) in which cases the coroner may hold the hearing concerning any such matters in the absence of the public.

Section 33(1) sets the number of jurors in an inquest at 5, in contrast to the 12 that comprise the jury in a criminal trial.

33(1) **Juries**—Except as provided in subsection (4), every inquest shall be held with a jury composed of five persons.

(2) **Jurors**—The coroner shall direct a constable to select from the list of names of persons provided under subsection 34(2) five persons who in his or her opinion are suitable to serve as jurors at an inquest and the constable shall summon them to attend the inquest at the time and place appointed.

(3) **Idem**—Where fewer than five of the jurors so summoned attend at the inquest, the coroner may name and appoint so many persons then present or who can be found as will make up a jury of five.

(4) **Inquest without jury in territorial district**—With the consent of the Chief Coroner, an inquest in a territorial district may be held without a jury.

Jurors in coroners' inquests are drawn from the same pool as those in criminal trials—the jury roll prepared under the *Juries Act*.

34(1) **List of jurors**—A coroner may by his or her warrant require the sheriff for the area in which an inquest is to be held to provide a list of the names of such number of persons as the coroner specifies in the warrant taken from the jury roll prepared under the *Juries Act*.

(2) **Idem**—Upon receipt of the warrant, the sheriff shall provide the list containing names of persons in the number specified by the coroner, taken from the jury roll prepared under the *Juries Act*, together with their ages, places of residence and occupations.

(3) **Eligibility**—No person who is ineligible to serve as a juror under the *Juries Act* shall be summoned to serve or shall serve as a juror at an inquest.

(4) **Idem**—An officer, employee or inmate of a hospital or an institution referred to in subsection 10(2) or (3) shall not serve as a juror at an inquest upon the death of a person who died therein.

(5) **Excusing from service**—The coroner may excuse any person on the list from being summoned or from serving as a juror on the grounds of illness or hardship.

(6) **Exclusion of juror with interest**—The coroner presiding at an inquest may exclude a person from being sworn as a juror where the coroner believes there is a likelihood that the person, because of interest or bias, would be unable to render a verdict in accordance with the evidence.

(7) **Excusing of juror for illness**—Where in the course of an inquest the coroner is satisfied that a juror should not, because of illness or other reasonable cause, continue to act, the coroner may discharge the juror.

(8) **Continuation with reduced jury**—Where in the course of an inquest a member of the jury dies or becomes incapacitated from any cause or is excluded or discharged by the coroner under subsection (6) or (7) or is found to be ineligible to serve, the jury shall, unless the coroner otherwise directs and if the number of jurors is not reduced below three, be deemed to remain properly constituted for all purposes of the inquest.

35. Report to sheriff re jury service—On or before the 31st day of December in each year, the coroner shall advise the sheriff of the names of persons who have received fees for service as jurors at inquests and the number of each such name on the jury roll.

36. Jury irregularities not to affect outcome—The omission to observe any of the provisions of this Act or the regulations respecting the eligibility and selection of jurors is not a ground for impeaching or quashing a verdict.

Jury, Viewing Body and Asking Questions

37(1) **View of body**—The jury shall view the body where the coroner directs them to do so.

(2) **Questions**—The jurors are entitled to ask relevant questions of each witness.

38. Majority verdict—A verdict or finding may be returned by a majority of the jurors sworn.

39. Service of summonses—A summons to a juror or to a witness may be served by personal service or by sending it by registered mail addressed to the usual place of abode of the person summoned.

40(1) **Summonses**—A coroner may require any person by summons,

(a) to give evidence on oath or affirmation at an inquest; and

(b) to produce in evidence at an inquest documents and things specified by the coroner,

relevant to the subject-matter of the inquest and admissible.

(2) **Form and service of summonses**—A summons issued under subsection (1) shall be in the prescribed form and shall be signed by the coroner.

(3) **Bench warrants**—Upon proof to the satisfaction of a judge of the Ontario Court (General Division) of the service of a summons under this section upon a person and that,

(a) such person has failed to attend or to remain in attendance at an inquest in accordance with the requirements of the summons; and

(b) the person's presence is material to the inquest,

the judge may, by a warrant in the prescribed form, directed to any sheriff or police officer, cause such witness to be apprehended anywhere within Ontario and forthwith to be brought to the inquest and to be detained in custody as the judge may order until the person's presence as a witness at the inquest is no longer required, or, in the discretion of the judge, to be released on a recognizance (with or without sureties) conditioned for appearance to give evidence.

(4) **Proof of service**—Service of a summons may be proved by affidavit in an application under subsection (3).

(5) **Certificate of facts**—Where an application under subsection (3) is made on behalf of a coroner, the coroner may certify to the judge the facts relied on to establish that the presence of the person summoned is material for the purposes of the inquest and such certificate may be accepted by the judge as proof of such facts.

41(1) **Persons with standing at inquest**—On the application of any person before or during an inquest, the coroner shall designate the person as a person with standing at the inquest if the coroner finds that the person is substantially and directly interested in the inquest.

(2) **Rights of persons with standing at inquest**—A person designated as a person with standing at an inquest may,

(a) be represented by counsel or an agent;

(b) call and examine witnesses and present arguments and submissions;

(c) conduct cross-examinations of witnesses at the inquest relevant to the interest of the person with standing and admissible.

42(1) **Protection for witnesses**—A witness at an inquest shall be deemed to have objected to answer any question asked the witness upon the ground that his or her answer may tend to criminate the witness or may tend to establish his or her liability to civil proceedings at the instance of the Crown, or of any person, and no answer given by a witness at an inquest shall be used or be receivable in evidence against the witness in any trial or other proceedings against him or her thereafter taking place, other than a prosecution for perjury in giving such evidence.

Jurors in a coroner's inquest play an interactive role, unlike the passive role they assume in a criminal trial.

Unlike in a criminal trial where the jury must reach a unanimous verdict, a coroner's inquest requires a majority.

Section 42(1) of the Act allows a witness at a coroner's inquest to be charged with perjury under the *Criminal Code* and face a trial in a criminal court. This is the only instance where evidence given by a witness in coroner's court can be used against that witness in subsequent proceedings brought against him or her.

Section 42(2) requires that a witness be informed of his or her rights under the *Evidence Act* when it appears that the witness is about to give evidence that would criminate him or her. In this case, although the witness must still answer the question, the witness's answer may not be used against him or her in any subsequent criminal trial or proceeding other than a prosecution for perjury in the giving of that evidence or for the giving of contradictory evidence.

(2) **Right to object under *Canada Evidence Act***—Where it appears at any stage of the inquest that the evidence that a witness is about to give would tend to criminate the witness, it is the duty of the coroner and of the Crown Attorney to ensure that the witness is informed of his or her rights under section 5 of the *Canada Evidence Act*.

43(1) **Rights of witnesses to counsel**—A witness at an inquest is entitled to be advised by his or her counsel or agent as to his or her rights but such counsel or agent may take no other part in the inquest without leave of the coroner.

(2) **Idem**—Where an inquest is held in the absence of the public, a counsel or agent for a witness is not entitled to be present except when that witness is giving evidence.

Admissibility of Evidence

44(1) **What is admissible in evidence at inquest**—Subject to subsections (2) and (3), a coroner may admit as evidence at an inquest, whether or not admissible as evidence in a court,

(a) any oral testimony; and

(b) any document or other thing,

relevant to the purposes of the inquest and may act on such evidence, but the coroner may exclude anything unduly repetitious or anything that the coroner considers does not meet such standards of proof as are commonly relied on by reasonably prudent persons in the conduct of their own affairs and the coroner may comment on the weight that ought to be given to any particular evidence.

(2) **What is inadmissible in evidence at inquest**—Nothing is admissible in evidence at an inquest,

(a) that would be inadmissible in a court by reason of any privilege under the law of evidence; or

(b) that is inadmissible by the statute under which the proceedings arise or any other statute.

(3) **Conflicts**—Nothing in subsection (1) overrides the provisions of any Act expressly limiting the extent to or purposes for which any oral testimony, documents or things may be admitted or used in evidence.

(4) **Copies**—Where the coroner is satisfied as to their authenticity, a copy of a document or other thing may be admitted as evidence at an inquest.

(5) **Photocopies**—Where a document has been filed in evidence at an inquest, the coroner may, or the person producing it or entitled to it may with the leave of the coroner, cause the document to be photocopied and the coroner may authorize the photocopy to be filed in evidence in the place of the document filed and release the document filed, or may furnish to the person producing it or the person entitled to it a photocopy of the document filed certified by the coroner.

45(1) **Taking evidence**—The evidence upon an inquest or any part of it shall be recorded by a person appointed by the coroner and approved by the Crown Attorney and who before acting shall make oath or affirmation that he or she will truly and faithfully record the evidence.

(2) **Transcription of evidence**—It is not necessary to transcribe the evidence unless the Minister, Chief Coroner or Crown Attorney orders it to be done or unless any other person requests a copy of the transcript and pays the fees therefor except that the coroner may prohibit the transcribing of all or any part of evidence taken in the absence of the public.

46. Adjournments—An inquest may be adjourned from time to time by the coroner of his or her own motion or where it is shown to the satisfaction of the coroner that the adjournment is required to permit an adequate hearing to be held.

47. Maintenance of order at inquest—A coroner may make such orders or give such directions at an inquest as he or she considers necessary for the maintenance of order at the inquest, and, if any person disobeys or fails to comply with any such order or direction, the coroner may call for the assistance of any peace officer to enforce the order or direction, and every peace officer so called upon shall take such action as is necessary to enforce the order or direction and may use such force as is reasonably required for that purpose.

Interpreters and Constables

48(1) **Interpreters**—A coroner may, and if required by the Crown Attorney or requested by the witness shall, employ a person to act as interpreter for a witness at an inquest, and such person may be summoned to attend the inquest and before acting shall make oath or affirm that he or she will truly and faithfully translate the evidence.

(2) **Constables**—A coroner may appoint such persons as constables as the coroner considers necessary for the purpose of assisting the coroner in an inquest and, on the request of the coroner, the police force having jurisdiction in the locality in which an inquest is held shall provide a police officer for the purpose and, before acting, every such constable shall take oath or affirm that he or she will faithfully perform his or her duties.

49. Administration of oaths—The coroner conducting an inquest has power to administer oaths and affirmations for the purpose of the inquest.

Further Powers of Coroner

50(1) **Abuse of processes**—A coroner may make such orders or give such directions at an inquest as the coroner considers proper to prevent abuse of its processes.

(2) **Limitation on cross-examination**—A coroner may reasonably limit further cross-examination of a witness where the coroner is satisfied that the cross-examination of the witness has been sufficient to disclose fully and fairly the facts in relation to which the witness has given evidence.

(3) **Exclusion of agents**—A coroner may exclude from a hearing anyone, other than a barrister and solicitor qualified to practise in Ontario, appearing as an agent advising a witness if the coroner finds that such person is not competent properly to advise the witness or does not understand and comply at the inquest with the duties and responsibilities of an adviser.

51. Contempt proceedings—Where any person without lawful excuse,

(a) on being duly summoned as a witness or a juror at an inquest makes default in attending at the inquest; or

(b) being in attendance as a witness at an inquest, refuses to take an oath or to make an affirmation legally required by the coroner to be taken or made, or to produce any document or thing in his or her power or control legally required by the coroner to be produced by the person or to answer any question to which the coroner may legally require an answer; or

(c) does any other thing that would, if the inquest had been a court of law having power to commit for contempt, have been contempt of that court,

the coroner may state a case to the Divisional Court setting out the facts and that court may, on application on behalf of and in the name of the coroner, inquire into the matter and, after hearing any witnesses who may be produced against or on behalf of that person and after hearing any statement that may be offered in defence, punish or take steps for the punishment of that person in like manner as if he or she had been guilty of contempt of the court.

A coroner's court has no authority when issues of contempt, perjury, or any criminality in the death being investigated are revealed during an inquest. Such matters must be referred to Divisional Court to be addressed.

Conclusion of Inquest

52(1) **Return of verdict**—The coroner shall forthwith after an inquest return the verdict or finding, with the evidence where the Minister, Crown Attorney or Chief Coroner has ordered it to be transcribed, to the Chief Coroner, and shall transmit a copy of the verdict and recommendations to the Crown Attorney.

(2) **Release of exhibits**—After an inquest is concluded, the coroner shall, upon request, release documents and things put in evidence at the inquest to the lawful owner or person entitled to possession thereof.

53. Protection from liability—No action or other proceeding for damages lies or shall be instituted against a coroner or any person acting under the coroner's authority for an act done by him or her in good faith in the performance or intended performance of any power or duty under this Act or the regulations, or for any neglect or default in the performance in good faith of any such power or duty.

54. Seals not necessary—In proceedings under this Act, it is not necessary for a person to affix a seal to a document, and no document is invalidated by reason of the lack of a seal, even though the document purports to be sealed.

55. Offences—Any person who contravenes section 10, 11, 13 or subsection 16(6) is guilty of an offence and on conviction is liable to a fine of not more than $1,000 or to imprisonment for a term of not more than six months, or to both.

56(1) **Regulations and fees**—The Lieutenant Governor in Council may make regulations,

(a) prescribing powers and duties of the Chief Coroner;

(b) Repealed.

(c) Repealed.

(d) providing for the selecting, recording, summoning, attendance and service of persons as jurors at inquests;

(e) prescribing the contents of oaths and affirmations required or authorized by this Act;

(f) prescribing matters that may be grounds for disqualification because of interest or bias of jurors for the purposes of subsection 34(6);

(g) Repealed.

(h) prescribing additional rules of procedure for inquests.

(2) **Same**—The Minister may make regulations,

(a) prescribing forms and providing for their use;

(b) prescribing fees and allowances that shall be paid to persons rendering services in connection with coroners' investigations and inquests and providing for the adjustment of such fees and allowances in special circumstances.

(3) **Coroners' fees and allowances**—The Minister may set fees and allowances for coroners for services performed under this or any other Act and may provide for the adjustment of such fees and allowances in special circumstances.

ASSIGNMENT: CORONERS ACT

1. You receive a call to attend at an incident where a pedestrian was struck by a subway train. When you arrive, you find that the train has been emptied and the cars separated to reveal the body. A quick visual examination reveals that the body has fallen across the tracks and has been transected, or cut in half. The ambulance staff is on location and wants to know what you require of them with respect to the deceased. This situation is clearly one where death may be presumed. When can the body be moved?

2. As part of your duties in this incident you interview bystanders and subway staff. Their stories are consistent; it appeared as though there was no foul play—no one pushed this person. The person had been standing there and suddenly fell forward onto the tracks as the train arrived at the platform. About a week after you submit your report, the sergeant advises you that you will be assigned to the coroners court office as the coroner's constable for the purposes of an inquest into this occurrence. What will your duties and authorities be while serving in this position?

3. One of your first duties will be to send summonses to potential jurors to sit on the inquest. How many people will constitute the jury once it is selected?

4. If some members of the jury have to withdraw due to illness or financial hardship, the coroner may proceed with a minimum number of jurors. What is that number?

5. Inquest juries are different from criminal trial juries. What are two primary ways in which they differ (other than the number of members)?

6. The primary function of an inquest is to address five specific points concerning the death of a person. What are the five points?

7. A juror or witness at an inquest has certain obligations. For instance, the juror must attend the hearing and the witness must answer legal questions that are put to him or her. Failure to do so results in a contempt proceeding. Where is this proceeding held and how is the process initiated?

8. There are certain deaths of which a coroner must be notified. As a result of an investigation into a death, the coroner may be of the opinion that an inquest should be held. Give five examples of situations where the coroner may order an inquest.

9. In certain situations where a death has occurred, the coroner does not have discretion as to whether or not an inquest will be held, because an inquest into the matter is mandatory. Give examples of five such situations.

10. As the coroner's constable you attend a scene that is believed to have been connected to the death of the subject. In seeking admittance to examine it, the occupant refuses to admit you. You are being obstructed in your duty. Is this offence related to the *Criminal Code* offence of "obstructing an officer"? Explain your answer.

CHAPTER 8

Child and Family Services Act

INTRODUCTION

The primary tier associated with the *Child and Family Services Act* is enforcement, through the execution of a warrant of apprehension or through accompanying a child protection worker who is acting under the authority of a warrant. Intervention and referral are secondary tiers.

The *Child and Family Services Act* (CFSA) is designed to offer protection to the children of Ontario. Because it often deals with the relationship between children and their parents, its application requires sensitivity and sound judgment. Officers must remember that imposing the will of the province on a family unit requires strict adherence to the legislation. In recent cases in Aylmer, Ontario, children were removed from their families on the grounds that they were being physically abused. The parents' behaviour was later determined by the courts to be a reasonable application of parental discipline. Such rulings must be taken into consideration when applying the provisions of the CFSA.

TERMINOLOGY

Child

There are actually two definitions of "child" within the CFSA: one that deals with the Act generally in s. 3(1) and another that deals with a "child in need of care and protection" under s. 37(1). Under s. 3(1), a "child" is a person under 18 years of age. Under s. 37(1), a "child" does not include a child as defined in s. 3(1) who is actually or apparently 16 years of age or older, unless the child is the subject of an order made under the child protection provisions of the CFSA.

Child in Need of Protection

The definition of "child in need of protection" is the essence of the CFSA, which defines, quite extensively, those situations in which a child may be deemed to be in need of care and protection. (See ss. 37(2)(a)–(l) for complete definitions.)

Parent

In the CFSA, a reference to a child's "parent," except where the CFSA provides otherwise, is deemed to be a reference to

1. both parents, where both have custody of the child;
2. one parent, where that parent has lawful custody of the child or the other parent is unavailable or unable to act, as the context requires; or
3. another individual, where that individual has lawful custody of the child.

Place of Safety

A "place of safety" is a foster home, a hospital, and a place or one of a class of places designated as such by a director or local director under s. 18 of part I ("Flexible Services") but does not include

1. a place of secure custody as defined in part IV ("Youth Justice"), or
2. a place of secure temporary detention as defined in part IV.

Service

"Service" includes

1. a child development service,
2. a child treatment service,
3. a child welfare service,
4. a community support service, or
5. a youth justice service.

Service Provider

A "service provider" is

1. a minister (of a government ministry),
2. an approved agency,
3. a society (such as a children's aid society),
4. a licensee (licensed by a government ministry), or
5. a person who provides an approved service or provides a service purchased by a minister or an approved agency but does not include a foster parent.

Society

A "society" is an approved agency designated as a children's aid society under s. 15(2) of part I ("Flexible Services").

COMMON OFFENCES AND/OR PROVISIONS

Section 72 of the CFSA states that anyone who has reasonable grounds to believe that a child is or may be in need of protection must forthwith report that belief to a children's aid society. If the person with the belief is a professional as outlined in s. 72(5), then that person is also liable to be charged if he or she fails to report the suspected abuse discovered while carrying out his or her professional duties. Professionals with this responsibility are

1. health care professionals, including physicians, nurses, dentists, pharmacists, and psychologists;
2. teachers, school principals, social workers, family counsellors, priests, rabbis, members of the clergy, operators or employees of day nurseries, youth and recreation workers, and early childhood educator;
3. peace officers and coroners;
4. solicitors, arbitrators, and mediators; and
5. service providers and employees of a service provider.

ARREST POWERS

There are no arrest powers under the CFSA, but the statute does authorize a peace officer (including a police officer) to apprehend a child without a warrant in four circumstances

1. where a child is in need of care and protection and it is too dangerous for the child to wait to obtain a warrant to apprehend the child (s. 40(7));
2. where a child is under 16 years of age and has left a society's lawful care and custody without its consent, and it is too dangerous for the child to wait to obtain a warrant to apprehend the child (s. 41(4));
3. where a child is detained under the provisions of part III of the CFSA in a place of safety that has been designated as a place of open temporary detention as referred to in part IV ("Youth Justice") and leaves the place without the consent of the society that has the care, custody, and control of the child and of the person in charge of the place of safety (s. 41(5)); and
4. where a peace officer believes on reasonable and probable grounds that a child actually or apparently under 12 years of age has committed an offence for which a person 12 or older could be found guilty. On apprehension, the officer may return the child to the parent or person having charge of the child. Where this is not possible, the officer may take the child to a place of safety.

SEARCH POWERS

Under s. 40(6), a child protection worker or a police officer authorized by a warrant or an order of the court to bring a child to a place of safety may at any time enter any premises specified in the warrant or order, by force if necessary, and may search for and remove the child.

If a child protection worker or a police officer is authorized to apprehend a child without a warrant under s. 40(7), and he or she has reasonable and probable grounds to believe that the child is in need of protection, that worker or police officer is authorized by s. 40(11) to enter the premises without warrant, by force if necessary, and search for and remove the child. If a child protection worker or police officer is authorized to apprehend a child under a warrant issued under s. 44(1)—when the child has run away from the care of the children's aid society—or is authorized to apprehend a child under a warrant issued under s. 43(2)—when a child has run away from a parent—that child protection worker or police officer may enter any premises specified in the warrant, using force if necessary, and return the child to a place of safety in the first instance or to the parents in the second instance.

When a young person has left a place of temporary detention despite still being subject to detention in the facility, a justice of the peace may issue a warrant for the return of the child and may authorize a police officer, a person in charge of the detention facility, or a person authorized by the person in charge of the facility to apprehend the child. Under s. 98(5), when the police officer, person in charge, or person authorized has reasonable and probable grounds to believe that the child named in the warrant is in any premises, that person may, with or without a warrant, enter the premises, using force if necessary, and search for and remove the child.

USE OF FORCE

As indicated above, police officers or other authorized persons are permitted to use force, if necessary, when they have reasons to search for and remove a child.

LIMITATION PERIOD

The CFSA does not extend the general limitation period contained in the POA; therefore, the limitation period of six months applies.

NON-POLICE AGENCIES INVOLVED

Children's aid societies are the primary agencies responsible for ensuring child safety. They carry out their own investigations, but frequently assist police services with joint investigations, particularly in child abuse situations.

PROVINCIAL OFFENCES GRID COMPLETION

Common Offences and/or Provisions

1. Powers to apprehend children in need of care and protection.
2. Requirement for certain professionals to report suspected child abuse.

Arrest Powers

No arrest powers given under the CFSA, but there are four categories of apprehension without warrant:

1. where a child is in need of care and protection, and it is too dangerous to wait for an order;
2. where a child leaves the care and custody of a society given authority for the child's custody, and it is too dangerous to wait for an order;
3. where a child leaves the care and custody of a place of open temporary detention without the consent of the society that has custody and of the person in charge of the place of safety; and
4. where a child under 12 years of age has apparently committed an offence for which a person 12 or older could be found guilty.

Search Powers

1. A peace officer or child protection worker may enter any place, and search for and remove a child, when authorized by an order under s. 40(6).
2. A peace officer or child protection worker may enter any premises without a warrant when there are reasonable and probable grounds to believe that a child is in need of care and protection and it is too dangerous to wait for a warrant, and may search for and remove such a child (s. 40(11)).
3. A peace officer or child protection worker acting on a warrant to return a runaway child may enter any place named in the warrant and search for and remove such a child (s. 44(1)).

Use of Force

Whenever the CFSA authorizes apprehension of a child by warrant, by order, or without a warrant, the Act also authorizes the person to use force if necessary to enter a premises, to search for the child, and/or to remove the child.

Limitation Period

Six months from the date of the offence.

Non-Police Agency Involved

Children's aid societies.

Child and Family Services Act

RSO 1990, c. C.11

Paramount Purpose and Other Purposes

1(1) **Paramount purpose**—The paramount purpose of this Act is to promote the best interests, protection and well being of children.

(2) **Other purposes**—The additional purposes of this Act, so long as they are consistent with the best interests, protection and well being of children, are:

1. To recognize that while parents may need help in caring for their children, that help should give support to the autonomy and integrity of the family unit and, wherever possible, be provided on the basis of mutual consent.
2. To recognize that the least disruptive course of action that is available and is appropriate in a particular case to help a child should be considered.
3. To recognize that children's services should be provided in a manner that,
   i. respects a child's need for continuity of care and for stable relationships within a family and cultural environment,
   ii. takes into account physical, cultural, emotional, spiritual, mental and developmental needs and differences among children,
   iii. provides early assessment, planning and decision-making to achieve permanent plans for children in accordance with their best interests, and
   iv. includes the participation of a child, his or her parents and relatives and the members of the child's extended family and community, where appropriate.
4. To recognize that, wherever possible, services to children and their families should be provided in a manner that respects cultural, religious and regional differences.
5. To recognize that Indian and native people should be entitled to provide, wherever possible, their own child and family services, and that all services to Indian and native children and families should be provided in a manner that recognizes their culture, heritage and traditions and the concept of the extended family.

Note: Despite the proclamation of the Statutes of Ontario, 1999, chapter 2, section 1, section 1 of this Act, as it read before March 31, 2000, continues to apply with respect to any proceeding under Part III, including a status review proceeding, that was commenced before March 31, 2000.

Duties of Service Providers

2(1) **French language services**—Service providers shall, where appropriate, make services to children and their families available in the French language.

(2) **Duties of service providers**—Service providers shall ensure,

(a) that children and their parents have an opportunity where appropriate to be heard and represented when decisions affecting their interests are made and to be heard when they have concerns about the services they are receiving; and

(b) that decisions affecting the interests and rights of children and their parents are made according to clear, consistent criteria and are subject to procedural safeguards.

Interpretation

3(1) **Definitions**—In this Act,

"agency" means a corporation;

"approved agency" means an agency that is approved under subsection 8(1) of Part I (Flexible Services);

"approved service" means a service provided,

(a) under subsection 7(1) of Part I or with the support of a grant or contribution made under subsection 7(2) of that Part,

(b) by an approved agency, or

(c) under the authority of a licence;

"band" has the same meaning as in the *Indian Act*(Canada);

"Board" means the Child and Family Services Review Board continued under Part IX (Licensing);

"child" means a person under the age of eighteen years;

"child development service" means a service for a child with a developmental disability or physical disability, for the family of a child with a developmental disability or physical disability, or for the child and the family;

Note: On a day to be named by proclamation of the Lieutenant Governor, subsection (1) is amended by the Statutes of Ontario, 2008, chapter 21, section 1 by adding the following definition:

"child pornography" means,

(a) a photographic, film, video or other visual representation, whether or not it was made by electronic or mechanical means,

(i) that shows a child engaged in, or depicted as engaged in, explicit sexual activity, or

(ii) the dominant characteristic of which is the depiction, for a sexual purpose, of a sexual organ of a child or the anal region of a child,

(b) any written material or visual representation that advocates or counsels sexual activity with a child that would be an offence under the *Criminal Code* (Canada),

(c) any written material whose dominant characteristic is the description, for a sexual purpose, of sexual activity with a child that would be an offence under the *Criminal Code* (Canada), or

(d) any audio recording that has as its dominant characteristic, the description, presentation or representation, for a sexual purpose, of sexual activity with a child that would be an offence under the *Criminal Code* (Canada);

"child treatment service" means a service for a child with a mental or psychiatric disorder, for the family of a child with a mental or psychiatric disorder, or for the child and the family;

"child welfare service" means,

(a) a residential or non-residential service, including a prevention service,

(b) a service provided under Part III (Child Protection),

(c) a service provided under Part VII (Adoption), or

(d) individual or family counselling;

"community support service" means a support service or prevention service provided in the community for children and their families;

"court" means the Ontario Court of Justice or the Family Court of the Superior Court of Justice;

"developmental disability" means a condition of mental impairment present or occurring in a person's formative years that is associated with limitations in adaptive behaviour;

"Director" means a Director appointed under subsection 5(1) of Part I (Flexible Services);

"extended family" means persons to whom a child is related by blood, through a spousal relationship or through adoption and, in the case of a child who is an Indian or native person, includes any member of the child's band or native community;

"federal Act" means the *Youth Criminal Justice Act* (Canada);

"foster care" means the provision of residential care to a child, by and in the home of a person who,

(a) receives compensation for caring for the child, except under the *Ontario Works Act, 1997*, the *Ontario Disability Support Program Act, 1997* or the *Family Benefits Act*, and

> Note: On a day to be named by proclamation of the Lieutenant Governor, clause (a) is repealed by the Statutes of Ontario, 1999, chapter 2, subsection 2(3) and the following substituted:
>
> (a) receives compensation for caring for the child, except under the *Ontario Works Act, 1997* or the *Ontario Disability Support Program Act, 1997*, and

(b) is not the child's parent or a person with whom the child has been placed for adoption under Part VII,

and "foster home" and "foster parent" have corresponding meanings;

"Indian" has the same meaning as in the *Indian Act* (Canada);

"licence" means a licence issued under Part IX (Licensing), and "licensed" and "licensee" have corresponding meanings;

"local director" means a local director appointed under section 16 of Part I (Flexible Services);

"Minister" means the Minister of Children and Youth Services or such other member of the Executive Council as may be designated under the *Executive Council Act* to administer this Act;"municipality" does not include a lower-tier municipality that is situated within a regional municipality;

"native community" means a community designated by the Minister under section 209 of Part X (Indian and Native Child and Family Services);

"native person" means a person who is a member of a native community but is not a member of a band, and "native child" has a corresponding meaning;

"order" includes a refusal to make an order;

"place of open custody" means a place or facility designated as a place of open custody under subsection 24.1(1) of the *Young Offenders Act* (Canada), whether in accordance with section 88 of the federal Act or otherwise;

"place of open temporary detention" means a place of temporary detention in which the Minister has established an open detention program;

"place of secure custody" means a place or facility designated for the secure containment or restraint of young persons under subsection 24.1(1) of the *Young Offenders Act* (Canada), whether in accordance with section 88 of the federal Act or otherwise;

"place of secure temporary detention" means a place of temporary detention in which the Minister has established a secure detention program;

"place of temporary detention" means a place or facility designated as a place of temporary detention under the *Young Offenders Act* (Canada) or under the federal Act;

"program supervisor" means a program supervisor appointed under subsection 5(2) of Part I (Flexible Services);

"provincial director" means,

(a) a person, the group or class of persons or the body appointed or designated by the Lieutenant Governor in Council or his or her delegate to perform any of the duties or functions of a provincial director under the *Young Offenders Act* (Canada) or under the federal Act, or

(b) a person as appointed under clause 90(1)(a);

"regulations" means the regulations made under this Act;

"relative" means, with respect to a child, a person who is the child's grandparent, great-uncle, great-aunt, uncle or aunt, whether by blood, through a spousal relationship or through adoption;

"residential service" means boarding, lodging and associated supervisory, sheltered or group care provided for a child away from the home of the child's parent, other than boarding, lodging or associated care for a child who has been placed in the lawful care and custody of a relative or member of the child's extended family or community, and "residential care" and "residential placement" have corresponding meanings;

"service" means,

(a) a child development service,
(b) a child treatment service,
(c) a child welfare service,
(d) a community support service, or
(e) a youth justice service;

"service provider" means,

(a) the Minister,
(b) an approved agency,
(c) a society,
(d) a licensee, or
(e) a person who provides an approved service or provides a service purchased by the Minister or an approved agency,

but does not include a foster parent;

"society" means an approved agency designated as a children's aid society under subsection 15(2) of Part I (Flexible Services);

"Tribunal" means the Licence Appeal Tribunal;

"young person" means a person who is or, in the absence of evidence to the contrary, appears to be 12 years of age or older but less than 18 years old and, if the context requires, includes any person who is charged under the federal Act with having committed an offence while he or she was a young person or who is found guilty of an offence under the federal Act;

"youth justice service" means a service provided under Part IV (Youth Justice) or under a program established under that Part.

(2) **Idem: "parent"**—In this Act, a reference to a child's parent shall be deemed to be a reference to,

(a) both parents, where both have custody of the child;

(b) one parent, where that parent has lawful custody of the child or the other parent is unavailable or unable to act as the context requires; or

(c) another individual, where that individual has lawful custody of the child,

except where this Act provides otherwise. . . .

Children's Aid Societies

15(1) **Children's Aid Society**—In this section,

"prescribed" means prescribed in a regulation made by the Minister under subsection 214(4) of Part XI (Regulations).

(2) **Designation of children's aid society**—The Minister may designate an approved agency as a children's aid society for a specified territorial jurisdiction and for any or all of the functions set out in subsection (3), may impose terms and conditions on a designation and may vary, remove or amend the terms and conditions or impose new terms and conditions at any time, and may at any time amend a designation to provide that the society is no longer designated for a particular function set out in subsection (3) or to alter the society's territorial jurisdiction.

(3) **Functions of society**—The functions of a children's aid society are to,

(a) investigate allegations or evidence that children who are under the age of sixteen years or are in the society's care or under its supervision may be in need of protection;

(b) protect, where necessary, children who are under the age of sixteen years or are in the society's care or under its supervision;

(c) provide guidance, counselling and other services to families for protecting children or for the prevention of circumstances requiring the protection of children;

(d) provide care for children assigned or committed to its care under this Act;

(e) supervise children assigned to its supervision under this Act;

(f) place children for adoption under Part VII; and

(g) perform any other duties given to it by this or any other Act.

(4) **Prescribed standards, etc.**—A society shall,

(a) provide the prescribed standard of services in its performance of its functions; and

(b) follow the prescribed procedures and practices.

(5) Repealed.

(6) **Protection from personal liability**—No action shall be instituted against an officer or employee of a society for an act done in good faith in the execution or intended execution of the person's duty or for an alleged neglect or default in the execution in good faith of the person's duty.

16. Appointment of local director—Every society shall appoint a local director with the prescribed qualifications, powers and duties.

17(1) **Duties of Director with respect to societies**—A Director,

(a) shall advise and supervise societies;

(b) shall inspect or direct and supervise the inspection of the operation and records of societies;

(c) shall exercise the powers and duties of a society in any area in which no society is functioning;

(d) shall inspect or direct and supervise the inspection of places in which children in the care of societies are placed; and

(e) shall ensure that societies provide the standard of services and follow the procedures and practices required by subsection 15(4).

(2) Repealed. . . .

Offences

25. Offence—A person who knowingly,

(a) fails to furnish a report required by the Minister under subsection 5(5);

(b) contravenes subsection 6(2) or (3) (obstructing program supervisor, etc.); or

(c) furnishes false information in an application under this Part or in a report or return required under this Part or the regulations,

and a director, officer or employee of a corporation who authorizes, permits or concurs in such a contravention or furnishing by the corporation, is guilty of an offence and is liable upon conviction to a fine of not more than $2,000. . . .

PART III
CHILD PROTECTION

37(1) Interpretation—In this Part,

"child" does not include a child as defined in subsection 3(1) who is actually or apparently sixteen years of age or older, unless the child is the subject of an order under this Part;

The Act applies to children under 16 years of age. If a child is a ward of the state or is governed by a court order, the Act applies until the child is 18 years of age.

"child protection worker" means a Director, a local director or a person authorized by a Director or local director for the purposes of section 40 (commencing child protection proceedings);

"parent," when used in reference to a child, means each of,

(a) the child's mother,

(b) an individual described in one of paragraphs 1 to 6 of subsection 8(1) of the *Children's Law Reform Act*, unless it is proved on a balance of probabilities that he is not the child's natural father,

(c) the individual having lawful custody of the child,

(d) an individual who, during the twelve months before intervention under this Part, has demonstrated a settled intention to treat the child as a child of his or her family, or has acknowledged parentage of the child and provided for the child's support,

(e) an individual who, under a written agreement or a court order, is required to provide for the child, has custody of the child or has a right of access to the child, and

(f) an individual who has acknowledged parentage of the child in writing under section 12 of the *Children's Law Reform Act*,

but does not include a foster parent;

"place of safety" means a foster home, a hospital, a person's home that satisfies the requirements of subsection (5) or a place or one of a class of places designated as a place of safety by a Director or local director under section 18, but does not include,

When an officer apprehends a child who is in need of protection, the child must be kept somewhere safe until the family or children's aid society can be contacted. A jail cell or a locked room are not considered places of safety, but placing the child in the company of a responsible person is acceptable.

(a) a place of secure custody as defined in Part IV, or

(b) a place of secure temporary detention as defined in Part IV.

(2) Child in need of protection—A child is in need of protection where,

(a) the child has suffered physical harm, inflicted by the person having charge of the child or caused by or resulting from that person's,

(i) failure to adequately care for, provide for, supervise or protect the child, or

(ii) pattern of neglect in caring for, providing for, supervising or protecting the child;

(b) there is a risk that the child is likely to suffer physical harm inflicted by the person having charge of the child or caused by or resulting from that person's,

Section 37(2)(a-d) is unique in that it addresses both past acts and acts that are likely to occur in the future based on a pattern of behaviour. Considering future acts underscores the importance the law places on the well-being of children, in response to cases where children have fallen through the "cracks" in the system.

(i) failure to adequately care for, provide for, supervise or protect the child, or

(ii) pattern of neglect in caring for, providing for, supervising or protecting the child;

(c) the child has been sexually molested or sexually exploited, including by child pornography, by the person having charge of the child or by another person where the person having charge of the child knows or should know of the possibility of sexual molestation or sexual exploitation and fails to protect the child;

Note: On a day to be named by proclamation of the Lieutenant Governor, clause (c) is repealed by the Statutes of Ontario, 2008, chapter 21, section 2 and the following substituted:

(c) the child has been sexually molested or sexually exploited, including by child pornography, by the person having charge of the child or by another person where the person having charge of the child knows or should know of the possibility of sexual molestation or sexual exploitation and fails to protect the child;

(d) there is a risk that the child is likely to be sexually molested or sexually exploited as described in clause (c);

As an example of a situation where s. 37(2)(e) would apply, there have been cases where parents have refused blood transfusions for their children on religious grounds. If refusing medical treatment endangers a child's health or life, the state, through the children's aid society, may apply to have the child designated as being in need of protection. If the application is successful, the child will be placed in the care of the state and the care will be provided.

(e) the child requires medical treatment to cure, prevent or alleviate physical harm or suffering and the child's parent or the person having charge of the child does not provide, or refuses or is unavailable or unable to consent to, the treatment;

(f) the child has suffered emotional harm, demonstrated by serious,

(i) anxiety,

(ii) depression,

(iii) withdrawal,

(iv) self-destructive or aggressive behaviour, or

(v) delayed development,

and there are reasonable grounds to believe that the emotional harm suffered by the child results from the actions, failure to act or pattern of neglect on the part of the child's parent or the person having charge of the child;

(f.1) the child has suffered emotional harm of the kind described in subclause (f)(i), (ii), (iii), (iv) or (v) and the child's parent or the person having charge of the child does not provide, or refuses or is unavailable or unable to consent to, services or treatment to remedy or alleviate the harm;

(g) there is a risk that the child is likely to suffer emotional harm of the kind described in subclause (f)(i), (ii), (iii), (iv) or (v) resulting from the actions, failure to act or pattern of neglect on the part of the child's parent or the person having charge of the child;

(g.1) there is a risk that the child is likely to suffer emotional harm of the kind described in subclause (f)(i), (ii), (iii), (iv) or (v) and that the child's parent or the person having charge of the child does not provide, or refuses or is unavailable or unable to consent to, services or treatment to prevent the harm;

(h) the child suffers from a mental, emotional or developmental condition that, if not remedied, could seriously impair the child's development and the child's parent or the person having charge of the child does not provide, or refuses or is unavailable or unable to consent to, treatment to remedy or alleviate the condition;

(i) the child has been abandoned, the child's parent has died or is unavailable to exercise his or her custodial rights over the child and has not made adequate provision for the child's care and custody, or the child is in a residential placement and the parent refuses or is unable or unwilling to resume the child's care and custody;

(j) the child is less than twelve years old and has killed or seriously injured another person or caused serious damage to another person's property, services or treatment are necessary to prevent a recurrence and the child's parent or the person having charge of the child does not provide, or refuses or is unavailable or unable to consent to, those services or treatment;

(k) the child is less than twelve years old and has on more than one occasion injured another person or caused loss or damage to another person's property, with the encouragement of the person having charge of the child or because of that person's failure or inability to supervise the child adequately; or

In cases where young children who lack proper supervision have injured others or damaged property, a problematic situation may be improved when an officer explains the ramifications of s. 37(2)(k).

(l) the child's parent is unable to care for the child and the child is brought before the court with the parent's consent and, where the child is twelve years of age or older, with the child's consent, to be dealt with under this Part.

(3) **Best interests of child**—Where a person is directed in this Part to make an order or determination in the best interests of a child, the person shall take into consideration those of the following circumstances of the case that he or she considers relevant:

1. The child's physical, mental and emotional needs, and the appropriate care or treatment to meet those needs.
2. The child's physical, mental and emotional level of development.
3. The child's cultural background.
4. The religious faith, if any, in which the child is being raised.
5. The importance for the child's development of a positive relationship with a parent and a secure place as a member of a family.
6. The child's relationships and emotional ties to a parent, sibling, relative, other member of the child's extended family or member of the child's community.
7. The importance of continuity in the child's care and the possible effect on the child of disruption of that continuity.
8. The merits of a plan for the child's care proposed by a society, including a proposal that the child be placed for adoption or adopted, compared with the merits of the child remaining with or returning to a parent.
9. The child's views and wishes, if they can be reasonably ascertained.
10. The effects on the child of delay in the disposition of the case.
11. The risk that the child may suffer harm through being removed from, kept away from, returned to or allowed to remain in the care of a parent.
12. The degree of risk, if any, that justified the finding that the child is in need of protection.
13. Any other relevant circumstance.

(4) **Where child an Indian or native person**—Where a person is directed in this Part to make an order or determination in the best interests of a child and the child is an Indian or native person, the person shall take into consideration the importance, in recognition of the uniqueness of Indian and native culture, heritage and traditions, of preserving the child's cultural identity.

(5) **Place of safety**—For the purposes of the definition of "place of safety" in subsection (1), a person's home is a place of safety for a child if,

(a) the person is a relative of the child or a member of the child's extended family or community; and

(b) a society or, in the case of a child who is an Indian or native person, an Indian or native child and family service authority designated under section 211 of Part X has conducted an assessment of the person's home in accordance with the prescribed procedures and is satisfied that the person is willing and able to provide a safe home environment for the child.

Note: Despite the proclamation of the Statutes of Ontario, 1999, chapter 2, section 9, section 37 of this Act, as it read before March 31, 2000, continues to apply with respect to any proceeding under Part III, including a status review proceeding, that was commenced before March 31, 2000.

Legal Representation

38(1) **Legal representation of child**—A child may have legal representation at any stage in a proceeding under this Part.

(2) **Court to consider issue**—Where a child does not have legal representation in a proceeding under this Part, the court,

(a) shall, as soon as practicable after the commencement of the proceeding; and

(b) may, at any later stage in the proceeding,

determine whether legal representation is desirable to protect the child's interests.

(3) **Direction for legal representation**—Where the court determines that legal representation is desirable to protect a child's interests, the court shall direct that legal representation be provided for the child.

(4) **Criteria**—Where,

(a) the court is of the opinion that there is a difference of views between the child and a parent or a society, and the society proposes that the child be removed from a person's care or be made a society or Crown ward under paragraph 2 or 3 of subsection 57(1);

(b) the child is in the society's care and,

(i) no parent appears before the court, or

(ii) it is alleged that the child is in need of protection within the meaning of clause 37(2)(a), (c), (f), (f.1) or (h); or

(c) the child is not permitted to be present at the hearing,

legal representation shall be deemed to be desirable to protect the child's interests, unless the court is satisfied, taking into account the child's views and wishes if they can be reasonably ascertained, that the child's interests are otherwise adequately protected.

(5) **Where parent a minor**—Where a child's parent is less than eighteen years of age, the Children's Lawyer shall represent the parent in a proceeding under this Part unless the court orders otherwise.

Note: Despite the proclamation of the Statutes of Ontario, 1999, chapter 2, section 10, section 38 of this Act, as it read before March 31, 2000, continues to apply with respect to any proceeding under Part III, including a status review proceeding, that was commenced before March 31, 2000.

Parties and Notice

39(1) **Parties**—The following are parties to a proceeding under this Part:

1. The applicant.
2. The society having jurisdiction in the matter.
3. The child's parent.
4. Where the child is an Indian or a native person, a representative chosen by the child's band or native community. . . .

Commencing Child Protection Proceedings

40(1) **Application**—A society may apply to the court to determine whether a child is in need of protection.

(2) **Warrant to apprehend child**—A justice of the peace may issue a warrant authorizing a child protection worker to bring a child to a place of safety if the justice of the peace is satisfied on the basis of a child protection worker's sworn information that there are reasonable and probable grounds to believe that,

(a) the child is in need of protection; and

(b) a less restrictive course of action is not available or will not protect the child adequately.

(3) **Idem**—A justice of the peace shall not refuse to issue a warrant under subsection (2) by reason only that the child protection worker may bring the child to a place of safety under subsection (7).

(4) **Order to produce or apprehend child**—Where the court is satisfied, on a person's application upon notice to a society, that there are reasonable and probable grounds to believe that,

(a) a child is in need of protection, the matter has been reported to the society, the society has not made an application under subsection (1), and no child protection worker has sought a warrant under subsection (2) or apprehended the child under subsection (7); and

(b) the child cannot be protected adequately otherwise than by being brought before the court,

the court may order,

(c) that the person having charge of the child produce him or her before the court at the time and place named in the order for a hearing under subsection 47(1) to determine whether he or she is in need of protection; or

(d) where the court is satisfied that an order under clause (c) would not protect the child adequately, that a child protection worker employed by the society bring the child to a place of safety.

(5) **Child's name, location not required**—It is not necessary, in an application under subsection (1), a warrant under subsection (2) or an order made under subsection (4), to describe the child by name or to specify the premises where the child is located.

(6) **Authority to enter, etc.**—A child protection worker authorized to bring a child to a place of safety by a warrant issued under subsection (2) or an order made under clause (4)(d) may at any time enter any premises specified in the warrant or order, by force if necessary, and may search for and remove the child.

(7) **Apprehension without warrant**—A child protection worker who believes on reasonable and probable grounds that,

(a) a child is in need of protection; and

(b) there would be a substantial risk to the child's health or safety during the time necessary to bring the matter on for a hearing under subsection 47(1) or obtain a warrant under subsection (2),

may without a warrant bring the child to a place of safety.

(8) **Police assistance**—A child protection worker acting under this section may call for the assistance of a peace officer.

> An officer's primary role when accompanying a child protection worker who is executing a warrant is to keep the peace.

(9) **Consent to examine child**—A child protection worker acting under subsection (7) or under a warrant issued under subsection (2) or an order made under clause (4)(d) may authorize the child's medical examination where a parent's consent would otherwise be required.

(10) **Place of open temporary detention**—Where a child protection worker who brings a child to a place of safety under this section believes on reasonable and probable grounds that no less restrictive course of action is feasible, the child may be detained in a place of safety that is a place of open temporary detention as defined in Part IV (Youth Justice).

(11) **Right of entry, etc.**—A child protection worker who believes on reasonable and probable grounds that a child referred to in subsection (7) is on any premises may without a warrant enter the premises, by force, if necessary, and search for and remove the child.

(12) **Regulations re power of entry**—A child protection worker authorized to enter premises under subsection (6) or (11) shall exercise the power of entry in accordance with the regulations.

(13) **Peace officer has powers of child protection worker**—Subsections (2), (6), (7), (10), (11) and (12) apply to a peace officer as if the peace officer were a child protection worker.

(14) **Protection from personal liability**—No action shall be instituted against a peace officer or child protection worker for any act done in good faith in the execution or intended execution of that person's duty under this section or for an alleged neglect or default in the execution in good faith of that duty.

Special Cases of Apprehension of Children

41(1) **Warrant to apprehend child in care**—A justice of the peace may issue a warrant authorizing a peace officer or child protection worker to bring a child to a place of safety if the justice of the peace is satisfied on the basis of a peace officer's or child protection worker's sworn information that,

(a) the child is actually or apparently under the age of sixteen years and has left or been removed from a society's lawful care and custody without its consent; and

(b) there are reasonable and probable grounds to believe that there is no course of action available other than bringing the child to a place of safety that would adequately protect the child.

(2) **Idem**—A justice of the peace shall not refuse to issue a warrant to a person under subsection (1) by reason only that the person may bring the child to a place of safety under subsection (4).

(3) **No need to specify premises**—It is not necessary in a warrant under subsection (1) to specify the premises where the child is located.

(4) **Apprehension of child in care without warrant**—A peace officer or child protection worker who believes on reasonable and probable grounds that,

(a) a child is actually or apparently under the age of sixteen years and has left or been removed from a society's lawful care and custody without its consent; and

(b) there would be a substantial risk to the child's health or safety during the time necessary to obtain a warrant under subsection (1),

may without a warrant bring the child to a place of safety.

(5) **Apprehension of child absent from place of open temporary detention**—Where a child is detained under this Part in a place of safety that has been designated as a place of open temporary detention as defined in Part IV (Youth Justice) and leaves the place without the consent of,

(a) the society having care, custody and control of the child; or

(b) the person in charge of the place of safety,

a peace officer, the person in charge of the place of safety or that person's delegate may apprehend the child without a warrant.

(6) **Idem**—A person who apprehends a child under subsection (5) shall,

(a) take the child to a place of safety to be detained until the child can be returned to the place of safety the child left; or

(b) return the child or arrange for the child to be returned to the place of safety the child left.

Under s. 42(1), an officer may apprehend a child who has committed an offence and whom the officer believes is under 12 years of age, and treat the child as a child in need of protection.

42(1) **Apprehension of child under twelve**—A peace officer who believes on reasonable and probable grounds that a child actually or apparently under twelve years of age has committed an act in respect of which a person twelve years of age or older could be found guilty of an offence may apprehend the child without a warrant and on doing so,

(a) shall return the child to the child's parent or other person having charge of the child as soon as practicable; or

(b) where it is not possible to return the child to the parent or other person within a reasonable time, shall take the child to a place of safety to be detained there until the child can be returned to the parent or other person.

(2) **Notice to parent, etc.**—The person in charge of a place of safety in which a child is detained under subsection (1) shall make reasonable efforts to notify the child's parent or other person having charge of the child of the child's detention so that the child may be returned to the parent or other person.

(3) **Where child not returned to parent, etc., within twelve hours**—Where a child detained in a place of safety under subsection (1) cannot be returned to the child's parent or other person having charge of the child within twelve hours of being taken to the place of safety, the child shall be dealt with as if the child had been taken to a place of safety under subsection 40(7) and not apprehended under subsection (1).

43(1) **Runaways**—In this section,

"parent" includes,

(a) an approved agency that has custody of the child,

(b) a person who has care and control of the child.

(2) **Warrant to apprehend runaway child**—A justice of the peace may issue a warrant authorizing a peace officer or child protection worker to apprehend a child if the justice of the peace is satisfied on the basis of the sworn information of a parent of the child that,

(a) the child is under the age of sixteen years;

(b) the child has withdrawn from the parent's care and control without the parent's consent; and

(c) the parent believes on reasonable and probable grounds that the child's health or safety may be at risk if the child is not apprehended.

When a justice of the peace issues a warrant to apprehend a runaway child, the warrant is placed on the CPIC (Canadian Police Information Centre) system, allowing any officer who finds the child to apprehend him or her. The officer does not need grounds of endangerment to make an apprehension. As well, a child from another province who is found in Ontario can be apprehended under a warrant.

(3) **Idem**—A person who apprehends a child under subsection (2) shall return the child to the child's parent as soon as practicable and where it is not possible to return the child to the parent within a reasonable time, take the child to a place of safety.

(4) **Notice to parent, etc.**—The person in charge of a place of safety to which a child is taken under subsection (3) shall make reasonable efforts to notify the child's parent that the child is in the place of safety so that the child may be returned to the parent.

(5) **Where child not returned to parent within twelve hours**—Where a child taken to a place of safety under subsection (3) cannot be returned to the child's parent within twelve hours of being taken to the place of safety, the child shall be dealt with as if the child had been taken to a place of safety under subsection 40(2) and not apprehended under subsection (2).

(6) **Where custody enforcement proceedings more appropriate**—A justice of the peace shall not issue a warrant under subsection (2) where a child has withdrawn from the care and control of one parent with the consent of another parent under circumstances where a proceeding under section 36 of the *Children's Law Reform Act* would be more appropriate.

(7) **No need to specify premises**—It is not necessary in a warrant under subsection (2) to specify the premises where the child is located.

(8) **Child protection proceedings**—Where a peace officer or child protection worker believes on reasonable and probable grounds that a child apprehended under this section is in need of protection and there may be a substantial risk to the health or safety of the child if the child were returned to the parent,

(a) the peace officer or child protection worker may take the child to a place of safety under subsection 40(7); or

(b) where the child has been taken to a place of safety under subsection (5), the child shall be dealt with as if the child had been taken there under subsection 40(7).

Power of Entry and Other Provisions for Special Cases of Apprehension

44(1) **Authority to enter, etc.**—A person authorized to bring a child to a place of safety by a warrant issued under subsection 41(1) or 43(2) may at any time enter any premises specified in the warrant, by force, if necessary, and may search for and remove the child.

(2) **Right of entry, etc.**—A person authorized under subsection 41(4) or (5) or 42(1) who believes on reasonable and probable grounds that a child referred to in the relevant subsection is on any premises may without a warrant enter the premises, by force, if necessary, and search for and remove the child.

(3) **Regulations re power of entry**—A person authorized to enter premises under this section shall exercise the power of entry in accordance with the regulations.

(4) **Police assistance**—A child protection worker acting under section 41 or 43 may call for the assistance of a peace officer.

(5) **Consent to examine child**—A child protection worker who deals with a child under subsection 42(3) or 43(5) as if the child had been taken to a place of safety may authorize the child's medical examination where a parent's consent would otherwise be required.

(6) **Place of open temporary detention**—Where a person who brings a child to a place of safety under section 41 or 42 believes on reasonable and probable grounds that no less restrictive course of action is feasible, the child may be detained in a place of safety that is a place of open temporary detention as defined in Part IV (Youth Justice).

(7) **Protection from personal liability**—No action shall be instituted against a peace officer or child protection worker for any act done in good faith in the execution or intended execution of that person's duty under this section or section 41, 42 or 43 or for an alleged neglect or default in the execution in good faith of that duty.

Hearings and Orders

...

Section 45(8) prohibits identifying any child or family involved in a proceeding under the Act.

45(8) **Prohibition: identifying child**—No person shall publish or make public information that has the effect of identifying a child who is a witness at or a participant in a hearing or the subject of a proceeding, or the child's parent or foster parent or a member of the child's family.

(9) **Idem: order re adult**—The court may make an order prohibiting the publication of information that has the effect of identifying a person charged with an offence under this Part.

46(1) **Time of detention limited**—As soon as practicable, but in any event within five days after a child is brought to a place of safety under section 40 or subsection 79(6) or a homemaker remains or is placed on premises under subsection 78(2),

(a) the matter shall be brought before a court for a hearing under subsection 47(1) (child protection hearing);

(b) the child shall be returned to the person who last had charge of the child or, where there is an order for the child's custody that is enforceable in Ontario, to the person entitled to custody under the order; or

(c) a temporary care agreement shall be made under subsection 29(1) of Part II (Voluntary Access to Services).

(2) **Idem: place of open temporary detention**—Within twenty-four hours after a child is brought to a place of safety that is a place of open temporary detention, or as soon thereafter as is practicable, the matter shall be brought before a court for a hearing and the court shall,

(a) where it is satisfied that no less restrictive course of action is feasible, order that the child remain in the place of open temporary detention for a period or periods not exceeding an aggregate of thirty days and then be returned to the care and custody of the society;

(b) order that the child be discharged from the place of open temporary detention and returned to the care and custody of the society; or

(c) make an order under subsection 51(2) (temporary care and custody).

47(1) **Child protection hearing**—Where an application is made under subsection 40(1) or a matter is brought before the court to determine whether the child is in need of protection, the court shall hold a hearing to determine the issue and make an order under section 57.

(2) **Child's name, age, etc.**—As soon as practicable, and in any event before determining whether a child is in need of protection, the court shall determine,

(a) the child's name and age;

(b) the religious faith, if any, in which the child is being raised;

(c) whether the child is an Indian or a native person and, if so, the child's band or native community; and

(d) where the child was brought to a place of safety before the hearing, the location of the place from which the child was removed.

(3) **Where sixteenth birthday intervenes**—Despite anything else in this Part, where the child was under the age of sixteen years when the proceeding was commenced or when the child was apprehended, the court may hear and determine the matter and make an order under this Part as if the child were still under the age of sixteen years. . . .

57(1) **Order where child in need of protection**—Where the court finds that a child is in need of protection and is satisfied that intervention through a court order is necessary to protect the child in the future, the court shall make one of the following orders or an order under section 57.1, in the child's best interests:

1. **Supervision order**—That the child be placed in the care and custody of a parent or another person, subject to the supervision of the society, for a specified period of at least three months and not more than 12 months.
2. **Society wardship**—That the child be made a ward of the society and be placed in its care and custody for a specified period not exceeding twelve months.
3. **Crown wardship**—That the child be made a ward of the Crown, until the wardship is terminated under section 65.2 or expires under subsection 71(1), and be placed in the care of the society.
4. **Consecutive orders of society wardship and supervision**—That the child be made a ward of the society under paragraph 2 for a specified period and then be returned to a parent or another person under paragraph 1, for a period or periods not exceeding an aggregate of twelve months. . . .

(9) **Where no court order necessary**—Where the court finds that a child is in need of protection but is not satisfied that a court order is necessary to protect the child in the future, the court shall order that the child remain with or be returned to the person who had charge of the child immediately before intervention under this Part.

Note: Despite the proclamation of the Statutes of Ontario, 1999, chapter 2, section 15, section 57 of this Act, as it read before March 31, 2000, continues to apply with respect to any proceeding under Part III, including a status review proceeding, that was commenced before March 31, 2000. . . .

Duty to Report

An officer who becomes aware of a child in need of protection is required, under the Act, to write a report and issue a copy to the children's aid society. Failure to do so may constitute neglect of duty.

72(1) **Duty to report child in need of protection**—Despite the provisions of any other Act, if a person, including a person who performs professional or official duties with respect to children, has reasonable grounds to suspect one of the following, the person shall forthwith report the suspicion and the information on which it is based to a society:

1. The child has suffered physical harm, inflicted by the person having charge of the child or caused by or resulting from that person's,
   i. failure to adequately care for, provide for, supervise or protect the child, or
   ii. pattern of neglect in caring for, providing for, supervising or protecting the child.
2. There is a risk that the child is likely to suffer physical harm inflicted by the person having charge of the child or caused by or resulting from that person's,
   i. failure to adequately care for, provide for, supervise or protect the child, or
   ii. pattern of neglect in caring for, providing for, supervising or protecting the child.
3. The child has been sexually molested or sexually exploited, by the person having charge of the child or by another person where the person having charge of the child knows or should know of the possibility of sexual molestation or sexual exploitation and fails to protect the child.

Note: On a day to be named by proclamation of the Lieutenant Governor, paragraph 3 is repealed by the Statutes of Ontario, 2008, chapter 21, subsection 3(1) and the following substituted:

3. The child has been sexually molested or sexually exploited, including by child pornography, by the person having charge of the child or by another person where the person having charge of the child knows or should know of the possibility of sexual molestation or sexual exploitation and fails to protect the child.

4. There is a risk that the child is likely to be sexually molested or sexually exploited as described in paragraph 3.
5. The child requires medical treatment to cure, prevent or alleviate physical harm or suffering and the child's parent or the person having charge of the child does not provide, or refuses or is unavailable or unable to consent to, the treatment.
6. The child has suffered emotional harm, demonstrated by serious,
   i. anxiety,
   ii. depression,
   iii. withdrawal,
   iv. self-destructive or aggressive behaviour, or
   v. delayed development,

   and there are reasonable grounds to believe that the emotional harm suffered by the child results from the actions, failure to act or pattern of neglect on the part of the child's parent or the person having charge of the child.
7. The child has suffered emotional harm of the kind described in subparagraph i, ii, iii, iv or v of paragraph 6 and the child's parent or the person having charge of the child does not provide, or refuses or is unavailable or unable to consent to, services or treatment to remedy or alleviate the harm.
8. There is a risk that the child is likely to suffer emotional harm of the kind described in subparagraph i, ii, iii, iv or v of paragraph 6 resulting from the actions, failure to act or pattern of neglect on the part of the child's parent or the person having charge of the child.

9. There is a risk that the child is likely to suffer emotional harm of the kind described in subparagraph i, ii, iii, iv or v of paragraph 6 and that the child's parent or the person having charge of the child does not provide, or refuses or is unavailable or unable to consent to, services or treatment to prevent the harm.
10. The child suffers from a mental, emotional or developmental condition that, if not remedied, could seriously impair the child's development and the child's parent or the person having charge of the child does not provide, or refuses or is unavailable or unable to consent to, treatment to remedy or alleviate the condition.
11. The child has been abandoned, the child's parent has died or is unavailable to exercise his or her custodial rights over the child and has not made adequate provision for the child's care and custody, or the child is in a residential placement and the parent refuses or is unable or unwilling to resume the child's care and custody.
12. The child is less than 12 years old and has killed or seriously injured another person or caused serious damage to another person's property, services or treatment are necessary to prevent a recurrence and the child's parent or the person having charge of the child does not provide, or refuses or is unavailable or unable to consent to, those services or treatment.
13. The child is less than 12 years old and has on more than one occasion injured another person or caused loss or damage to another person's property, with the encouragement of the person having charge of the child or because of that person's failure or inability to supervise the child adequately.

Note: On a day to be named by proclamation of the Lieutenant Governor, section 72 is amended by the Statutes of Ontario, 2008, chapter 21, subsection 3(2) by adding the following subsections:

(1.1) **Reporting child pornography**—In addition to the duty to report under subsection (1), any person who reasonably believes that a representation or material is, or might be, child pornography shall promptly report the information to an organization, agency or person designated by a regulation made under clause 216(c.3).

(1.2) **Seeking out child pornography not required or authorized**—Nothing in this section requires or authorizes a person to seek out child pornography.

(1.3) **Protection of informant**—No action lies against a person for providing information in good faith in compliance with subsection (1.1).

(1.4) **Identity of informant**—Except as required or permitted in the course of a judicial proceeding, in the context of the provision of child welfare services, otherwise by law or with the written consent of an informant, no person shall disclose,

(a) the identity of an informant under subsection (1) or (1.1),

(i) to the family of the child reported to be in need of protection, or

(ii) to the person who is believed to have caused the child to be in need of protection; or

(b) the identity of an informant under subsection (1.1) to the person who possessed or accessed the representation or material that is or might be child pornography.

(1.5) **Retaliation against informant prohibited**—No person shall dismiss, suspend, demote, discipline, harass, interfere with or otherwise disadvantage an informant under this section.

(2) **Ongoing duty to report**—A person who has additional reasonable grounds to suspect one of the matters set out in subsection (1) shall make a further report under subsection (1) even if he or she has made previous reports with respect to the same child.

When a child is in need of protection, an officer's original report is not sufficient if further grounds for concern arise after the original report was written. Section 72(2) places an ongoing duty on officers to submit a new report with each occurrence.

Note: On a day to be named by proclamation of the Lieutenant Governor, subsection (2) is repealed by the Statutes of Ontario, 2008, chapter 21, subsection 3(3) and the following substituted:

(2) **Ongoing duty to report**—A person who has additional reasonable grounds to suspect one of the matters set out in subsection (1) or to believe that a representation or material is, or might be, child pornography under subsection (1.1) shall make a further report under subsection (1) or (1.1) even if he or she has made previous reports with respect to the same child.

(3) **Person must report directly**—A person who has a duty to report a matter under subsection (1) or (2) shall make the report directly to the society and shall not rely on any other person to report on his or her behalf.

Note: On a day to be named by proclamation of the Lieutenant Governor, subsection (3) is repealed by the Statutes of Ontario, 2008, chapter 21, subsection 3(3) and the following substituted:

(3) **Person to report directly**—A person who has a duty to report under subsection (1) or (2) shall make the report directly to the society, a person who has a duty to report under subsection (1.1) shall make the report directly to any organization, agency or person designated by regulation to receive such reports, and such persons shall not rely on any other person to report on their behalf.

(4) **Offence**—A person referred to in subsection (5) is guilty of an offence if,

(a) he or she contravenes subsection (1) or (2) by not reporting a suspicion; and

(b) the information on which it was based was obtained in the course of his or her professional or official duties.

Note: On a day to be named by proclamation of the Lieutenant Governor, section 72 is amended by the Statutes of Ontario, 2008, chapter 21, subsection 3(4) by adding the following subsections:

(4.1) **Same**—A person is guilty of an offence if the person fails to report information as required under subsection (1.1).

(4.2) **Same**—A person is guilty of an offence if the person,

(a) discloses the identity of an informant in contravention of subsection (1.4); or

(b) dismisses, suspends, demotes, disciplines, harasses, interferes with or otherwise disadvantages an informant in contravention of subsection (1.5).

(5) **Same**—Subsection (4) applies to every person who performs professional or official duties with respect to children including,

(a) a health care professional, including a physician, nurse, dentist, pharmacist and psychologist;

(b) a teacher, person appointed to a position designated by a board of education as requiring an early childhood educator, school principal, social worker, family counsellor, operator or employee of a day nursery and youth and recreation worker;

(b.1) a religious official, including a priest, a rabbi and a member of the clergy;

(b.2) a mediator and an arbitrator;

(c) a peace officer and a coroner;

(d) a solicitor; and

(e) a service provider and an employee of a service provider.

(6) **Same**—In clause (5)(b),

"youth and recreation worker" does not include a volunteer.

(6.1) **Same**—A director, officer or employee of a corporation who authorizes, permits or concurs in a contravention of an offence under subsection (4) by an employee of the corporation is guilty of an offence.

> Note: On a day to be named by proclamation of the Lieutenant Governor, subsection (6.1) is repealed by the Statutes of Ontario, 2008, chapter 21, subsection 3(5) and the following substituted:
>
> (6.1) **Same**—A director, officer or employee of a corporation who authorizes, permits or concurs in a contravention of an offence under subsection (4) or (4.1) by an employee of the corporation is guilty of an offence.

(6.2) **Same**—A person convicted of an offence under subsection (4) or (6.1) is liable to a fine of not more than $1,000.

> Note: On a day to be named by proclamation of the Lieutenant Governor, subsection (6.2) is repealed by the Statutes of Ontario, 2008, chapter 21, subsection 3(6) and the following substituted:
>
> (6.2) **Penalty**—A person convicted of an offence under subsection (4), (4.1), (4.2) or (6.1) is liable to a fine of not more than $50,000 or to imprisonment for a term of not more than two years, or to both.

(7) **Section overrides privilege**—This section applies although the information reported may be confidential or privileged, and no action for making the report shall be instituted against a person who acts in accordance with this section unless the person acts maliciously or without reasonable grounds for the suspicion.

(8) **Exception: solicitor client privilege**—Nothing in this section abrogates any privilege that may exist between a solicitor and his or her client.

(9) **Conflict**—This section prevails despite anything in the *Personal Health Information Protection Act, 2004.*

> Note: On a day to be named by proclamation of the Lieutenant Governor, the Act is amended by the Statutes of Ontario, 2008, chapter 21, section 4 by adding the following section:

> **72.0.1**(1) **Action by organization receiving report of child pornography**—An organization, agency or person that obtains information on child pornography under subsection 72(1.1) shall review the report and, if it reasonably believes that the representation or material is or might be child pornography, it shall report the matter to a society or a law enforcement agency, or to both as necessary.
>
> (2) **Annual report**—The organization, agency or person shall prepare and submit to the Minister an annual report with respect to its activities and actions relating to information it obtains on child pornography, and the Minister shall submit the report to the Lieutenant Governor in Council and then table the report in the Assembly if it is in session or, if not, at the next session.

72.1(1) **Duty of society**—A society that obtains information that a child in its care and custody is or may be suffering or may have suffered abuse shall forthwith report the information to a Director.

(2) **Definition**—In this section and sections 73 and 75,

"to suffer abuse," when used in reference to a child, means to be in need of protection within the meaning of clause 37(2)(a), (c), (e), (f), (f.1) or (h).

> Note: On a day to be named by proclamation of the Lieutenant Governor, subsection 72.1(2) is amended by the Statutes of Ontario, 1999, chapter 2, subsection 23(2) by striking out "sections 73 and 75" and substituting "section 73."

72.2 **Duty to report child's death**—A person or society that obtains information that a child has died shall report the information to a coroner if,

(a) a court made an order under this Act denying access to the child by a parent of the child or making the access subject to supervision;

(b) on the application of a society, a court varied the order to grant the access or to make it no longer subject to supervision; and

(c) the child subsequently died as a result of a criminal act committed by a parent or family member who had custody or charge of the child at the time of the act.

. . .

Offences, Restraining Orders, Recovery on Child's Behalf

> Officers may encounter individuals who appear to be under 16 years of age in a place described in s. 79(5), between the hours of midnight and 6 a.m., loitering, engaging in disruptive behaviour, and/or engaging in acts of vandalism, such as "tagging." Instead of seeking a remedy by applying the *Criminal Code*, where all of the elements of the offence may not be satisfied, s. 79(6) may very well provide an officer with another response option. Interestingly, the phrase "apparently less than sixteen" solves the problem of having to establish the age of the subject in a definitive sense. Young persons may not carry or even have adequate identification. The officer must only satisfy that the young person *appears* to be less than 16 years of age.

Abuse, failure to provide for reasonable care, etc.

79(1) **Definition**—In this section,

"abuse" means a state or condition of being physically harmed, sexually molested or sexually exploited.

(2) **Child abuse**—No person having charge of a child shall,

(a) inflict abuse on the child; or

(b) by failing to care and provide for or supervise and protect the child adequately,

(i) permit the child to suffer abuse, or

(ii) permit the child to suffer from a mental, emotional or developmental condition that, if not remedied, could seriously impair the child's development.

(3) **Leaving child unattended**—No person having charge of a child less than sixteen years of age shall leave the child without making provision for his or her supervision and care that is reasonable in the circumstances.

(4) **Reverse onus**—Where a person is charged with contravening subsection (3) and the child is less than ten years of age, the onus of establishing that the person made provision for the child's supervision and care that was reasonable in the circumstances rests with the person.

(5) **Allowing child to loiter, etc.**—No parent of a child less than sixteen years of age shall permit the child to,

(a) loiter in a public place between the hours of midnight and 6 a.m.; or

(b) be in a place of public entertainment between the hours of midnight and 6 a.m., unless the parent accompanies the child or authorizes a specified individual eighteen years of age or older to accompany the child.

(6) **Police may take child home or to place of safety**—Where a child who is actually or apparently less than sixteen years of age is in a place to which the public has access between the hours of midnight and 6 a.m. and is not accompanied by a person described in clause (5)(b), a peace officer may apprehend the child without a warrant and proceed as if the child had been apprehended under subsection 42(1).

(7) **Child protection hearing**—The court may, in connection with a case arising under subsection (2), (3) or (5), proceed under this Part as if an application had been made under subsection 40(1) (child protection proceeding) in respect of the child.

80(1) **Restraining order**—Instead of making an order under subsection 57(1) or section 65.2 or in addition to making a temporary order under subsection 51(2) or an order under subsection 57(1) or section 65.2, the court may make one or more of the following orders in the child's best interests:

1. An order restraining or prohibiting a person's access to or contact with the child, and may include in the order such directions as the court considers appropriate for implementing the order and protecting the child.

2. An order restraining or prohibiting a person's contact with the person who has lawful custody of the child following a temporary order under subsection 51(2) or an order under subsection 57(1) or clause 65.2(1)(a) or (b).

(2) **Idem: notice**—An order shall not be made under subsection (1) unless notice of the proceeding has been served personally on the person to be named in the order.

(3) **Duration of the order**—An order made under subsection (1) shall continue in force for such period as the court considers in the best interests of the child and,

(a) if the order is made in addition to a temporary order under subsection 51(2) or an order made under subsection 57(1) or clause 65.2(1)(a), (b) or (c), the order may provide that it continues in force, unless it is varied, extended or terminated by the court, as long as the temporary order under subsection 51(2) or the order under subsection 57(1) or clause 65.2(1)(a), (b) or (c), as the case may be, remains in force; or

(b) if the order is made instead of an order under subsection 57(1) or clause 65.2(1)(a), (b) or (c) or if the order is made in addition to an order under clause 65.2(1)(d), the order may provide that it continues in force until it is varied or terminated by the court....

83. Offence—If a child is the subject of an order for society wardship under subsection 57(1) or an order for society supervision or Crown wardship under that subsection or subsection 65.2(1), no person shall,

(a) induce or attempt to induce the child to leave the care of the person with whom the child is placed by the court or by the society, as the case may be;

(b) detain or harbour the child after the person or society referred to in clause (a) requires that the child be returned;

(c) interfere with the child or remove or attempt to remove the child from any place; or

(d) for the purpose of interfering with the child, visit or communicate with the person referred to in clause (a).

84. Offence—No person shall,

(a) knowingly give false information in an application under this Part; or

(b) obstruct, interfere with or attempt to obstruct or interfere with a child protection worker or a peace officer who is acting under section 40, 41, 42, 43 or 44.

85(1) **Offences**—A person who contravenes,

(a) an order for access made under subsection 58(1);

(b) Repealed.

(c) subsection 74(5) (disclosure of information obtained by court order);

(d) subsection 75(6) or (10) (confidentiality of child abuse register);

Note: On a day to be named by proclamation of the Lieutenant Governor, clause (d) is repealed by the Statutes of Ontario, 1999, chapter 2, subsection 30(2).

(e) an order made under subsection 76(8) (amendment of society's records);

Note: On a day to be named by proclamation of the Lieutenant Governor, clause (e) is repealed by the Statutes of Ontario, 1999, chapter 2, subsection 30(3).

(f) subsection 79(3) or (5) (leaving child unattended, etc.);

(g) a restraining order made under subsection 80(1);

(h) section 82 (unauthorized placement);

(i) any provision of section 83 (interference with child, etc.); or

(j) clause 84(a) or (b),

and a director, officer or employee of a corporation who authorizes, permits or concurs in such a contravention by the corporation is guilty of an offence and on conviction is liable to a fine of not more than $1,000 or to imprisonment for a term of not more than one year, or to both.

(2) **Idem**—A person who contravenes subsection 79(2) (child abuse), and a director, officer or employee of a corporation who authorizes, permits or concurs in such a contravention by the corporation is guilty of an offence and on conviction is liable to a fine of not more than $2,000 or to imprisonment for a term of not more than two years, or to both.

(3) **Idem**—A person who contravenes subsection 45(8) or 76(11) (publication of identifying information) or an order prohibiting publication made under clause 45(7)(c) or subsection 45(9), and a director, officer or employee of a corporation who authorizes, permits or concurs in such a contravention by the corporation, is guilty of an offence and on conviction is liable to a fine of not more than $10,000 or to imprisonment for a term of not more than three years, or to both. . . .

Note: On a day to be named by proclamation of the Lieutenant Governor, subsection (3) is amended by the Statutes of Ontario, 1999, chapter 2, subsection 30(5) by striking out "or 76(11)."

PART IV
YOUTH JUSTICE

...

Apprehension of Young Persons Who Are Absent from Custody Without Permission

98(1) **Apprehension of young person absent from place of temporary detention**—A peace officer, the person in charge of a place of temporary detention or that person's delegate, who believes on reasonable and probable grounds that a young person detained under the *Young Offenders Act* (Canada) or the federal Act or the *Provincial Offences Act* in a place of temporary detention has left the place without the consent of the person in charge and fails or refuses to return there may apprehend the young person with or without a warrant and take the young person or arrange for the young person to be taken to a place of temporary detention.

(2) **Idem: place of open custody**—A peace officer, the person in charge of a place of open custody or that person's delegate, who believes on reasonable and probable grounds that a young person held in a place of open custody as described in section 95,

(a) has left the place without the consent of the person in charge and fails or refuses to return there; or

(b) fails or refuses to return to the place of open custody upon completion of a period of reintegration leave under clause 95(b),

may apprehend the young person with or without a warrant and take the young person or arrange for the young person to be taken to a place of open custody or a place of temporary detention.

(3) **Young person to be returned within forty-eight hours**—A young person who is apprehended under this section shall be returned to the place from which he or she is absent within forty-eight hours after being apprehended unless the provincial director detains the young person in secure temporary detention under paragraph 2 of subsection 93(2).

(4) **Warrant to apprehend young person**—A justice of the peace who is satisfied on the basis of a sworn information that there are reasonable and probable grounds to believe that a young person held in a place of temporary detention or open custody,

(a) has left the place without the consent of the person in charge and fails or refuses to return there; or

(b) fails or refuses to return to a place of open custody upon completion of a period of reintegration leave under clause 95(b),

may issue a warrant authorizing a peace officer, the person in charge of the place of temporary detention or open custody or that person's delegate to apprehend the young person.

(5) **Authority to enter, etc.**—Where a person authorized to apprehend a young person under subsection (1) or (2) believes on reasonable and probable grounds that a young person referred to in the relevant subsection is on any premises, the person may with or without a warrant enter the premises, by force, if necessary, and search for and remove the young person.

(6) **Regulations re exercise of power of entry**—A person authorized to enter premises under subsection (5) shall exercise the power of entry in accordance with the regulations. . . .

PART V
RIGHTS OF CHILDREN

. . .

Locking Up

100(1) **Locking up restricted**—No service provider shall detain a child or permit a child to be detained in locked premises in the course of the provision of a service to the child, except as Part IV (Youth Justice) and Part VI (Extraordinary Measures) authorize.

(2) **Application of subs. (1)**—Subsection (1) does not prohibit the routine locking of premises for security at night.

Corporal Punishment

101. No corporal punishment—No service provider or foster parent shall inflict corporal punishment on a child or permit corporal punishment to be inflicted on a child in the course of the provision of a service to the child. . . .

ASSIGNMENT: CHILD AND FAMILY SERVICES ACT

1. The term "child" in the CFSA refers to anyone under 18 years of age. The age of a child in need of protection under the CFSA varies. What is the usual age and what is the exception to this rule?

2. There are three circumstances in which a child may be in need of protection. Two of these situations deal with factual occurrences and with possible risk situations. The third deals with a physical health issue. Describe these situations.

3. Certain professionals who witness or become aware of a child in need of protection have certain duties imposed on them by their knowledge. Give examples of five of these professionals and describe the duties imposed on them.

4. While on patrol, you are dispatched to a residence with a crying child. At the scene, you speak to neighbours, who inform you that a child has been heard crying from the residence for over two hours. You are told that a young couple, believed to be in their early teens, and an infant live as a family in the residence. The mother and father were seen leaving about three hours earlier in the family car and have not been seen since. All doors and windows to the residence are secure, and the crying seems to be coming from the upstairs area, which you can't see into. What do you do and by what authority?

5. The CFSA refers to "a place of safety" where a child in need of protection may be taken. Give two examples of places of safety. Is a police station cell one such place?

6. In response to a shoplifter call from a variety store, you find that the suspect is a young boy. He appears to be about 10 years old, but he says that he is 11. The store owner states that he has been trying to call the parents of the boy, but there is no answer. At your request, a fellow officer attends the residence and is unable to locate anyone there. Because the *Criminal Code* does not to apply to children under 12, the option of arrest is not available to you. What action can you take, and what authority will allow you to tend to this child?

7. While on foot patrol in an area of the city known for its prostitutes and runaway street kids, you are approached by the parents of a young girl. They ask if you have seen their daughter, who is 14 years old, and show you a picture of her. They recently moved to this city and their daughter was having trouble making friends. She has been seen on the street in this area with a male who is apparently a lot older than she. They have imposed curfews and restrictions on her, but she just runs away. They have always located her, but this time they have spent four days searching without result. They know about the prostitution and drug use in the area and are genuinely concerned for her well-being. These potential dangers to her safety and the influence that the older male may have on her are valid concerns. In an effort to assist these people, you explain that you will take a copy of her picture and keep an eye out for her. You advise the parents to see a justice of the peace and obtain a warrant to apprehend her. With a warrant on file, any officer will have the authority to exercise it. What will the parents have to present to the JP to get such a warrant? Use details provided in this scenario to support your answer.

8. Any officer who apprehends the girl described in question 7 under the authority of a warrant has a duty to fulfill. Describe that duty.

9. In the CFSA, there are specific hours when and set places where a child may not loiter. What are the hours and the places?

10. There are two exceptions to the loitering section. One involves a child in the company of a parent. What is the second, and how is it specific?

CHAPTER 9

Family Law Act

INTRODUCTION

The primary tier associated with the *Family Law Act* is enforcement—specifically, of a court order for exclusive possession of the matrimonial home. The Act authorizes arrest without a warrant of any person whom a police officer has reasonable grounds to believe has contravened such an order. Intervention and referral are secondary tiers.

Provisions of the *Family Law Act* (FLA) authorize police officers to intervene in some domestic dispute situations. In addition to providing for orders of exclusive possession of the matrimonial home for couples who are separating or who are already separated, the FLA provides a mechanism for one spouse to obtain a restraining order against the other, and there is an arrest power, on reasonable and probable grounds, authorizing the arrest of anyone contravening such a restraining order.

Once a domestic dispute has advanced to the point where it falls under the jurisdiction of the Act, an officer's duties go beyond negotiation and diffusing conflict to enforcing the provisions of the law. Officers must understand those provisions so that they can explain them to the parties, as this may help resolve a conflict. Remaining calm, unbiased, and professional is critical, as is remembering that disputes that have reached such an advanced stage always carry the potential for violence.

TERMINOLOGY

Child

A "child" includes a person whom a parent has demonstrated a settled intention to treat as a child of his or her family, except under an arrangement where the child is placed for valuable consideration (payment) in a foster home by a person having lawful custody.

Cohabit

To "cohabit" means to live together in a conjugal relationship, whether within or outside marriage.

Matrimonial Home

A "matrimonial home" is every property in which a person has an interest and that is or, if the spouses have separated, was at the time of separation ordinarily occupied by the person and his or her spouse as the family residence.

Parent

A "parent" includes a person who has demonstrated a settled intention to treat a child as a child of his or her family, except under an arrangement where the child is placed for valuable consideration (payment) in a foster home by a person having lawful custody.

Spouse

A "spouse" is either of two persons who (1) are married to each other, or (2) have together entered into a marriage that is voidable or void, in good faith on the part of a person relying on this clause to assert any right.

COMMON OFFENCES AND/OR PROVISIONS

Under the FLA, a court may make an order giving one spouse exclusive rights to possession of the matrimonial home. The other spouse must abide by that order. A spouse suspected of violating the order is subject to arrest without warrant and to a penalty of $5,000 or three months' incarceration or both on the first offence, and a maximum of $10,000 or two years' imprisonment or both for second or subsequent offences.

Under s. 24(1), the court may make an order in one or more of the following ways. It may

1. provide for the delivery, safekeeping, and preservation of the matrimonial home and its contents;
2. direct that one spouse be given exclusive possession of the matrimonial home or part of it for the period that the court directs and release other property contained in a matrimonial home from the application;
3. direct a spouse to whom exclusive possession of the matrimonial home is given to make periodic payments to the other spouse;
4. direct that the contents of the matrimonial home, or any part of them, either remain in the home for the use of the spouse given possession, or be removed from the home for the use of a spouse or child;
5. order a spouse to pay for all or part of the repair or maintenance of the matrimonial home and of other liabilities arising in respect of it, or to make periodic payments to the other spouse for those purposes;
6. authorize the disposition or encumbrance of a spouse's interest in the matrimonial home, subject to the other spouse's right of exclusive possession as ordered; and
7. where a false statement is made under s. 21(3), direct the person who made the false statement, or a person who knew at the time he or she acquired an

interest in the property that the statement was false and afterward conveyed the interest, to substitute other real property for the matrimonial home; or direct the person to set aside money or security to stand in place of it, subject to any conditions that the court considers appropriate.

Section 24(1) also provides the court with a wide range of powers to order who has the right of possession of what in a variety of combinations. The order is to ensure that the spouse so authorized continues to have the possession of the home or its contents or a portion thereof.

If a spouse contravenes the order, that spouse is subject to arrest without warrant and fines and/or imprisonment as outlined above. A police officer responding to a domestic dispute must be aware of these provisions. If there are reasonable and probable grounds to believe that a violation of the order has taken place, the officer may arrest and/or charge the spouse suspected of the violation.

An additional provision in s. 46(1) provides the option for one spouse to obtain a restraining order against the other spouse in circumstances where there are grounds for the court to believe that the spouse must be restrained from molesting, annoying, harassing, or communicating with the applicant or children in the applicant's lawful custody, except as the order provides.

Non-compliance with a restraining order should be addressed in Family Court, usually before the judge who imposed the order. An application can be made by the lawyer for the complainant to bring the matter back to court.

A restraining order should be viewed as a way to overcome minor conflict and distress in the initial stages of marital breakdown, but it is certainly not a safeguard against injury or intimidation. Officers should always look at *all* of the circumstances in a complaint regarding a restraining order, and should be on the lookout for evidence that suggests a criminal offence could take place. There may be grounds to proceed with a charge of threatening or criminal harassment.

ARREST POWERS

Under s. 24(6), a police officer who has reasonable and probable grounds to believe that an order of exclusive possession of the matrimonial home has been contravened may arrest the offender without a warrant. This power may be used in situations where one spouse satisfies the officer that there are grounds to believe that there is an order in place and that the other spouse has contravened it.

Section 24(6) provides the only circumstances under the Act where an officer may make an arrest without a warrant.

SEARCH POWERS

There are no search powers under the FLA.

USE OF FORCE

There are no provisions in the FLA regarding the use of force in the enforcement of the Act. Refer to *Criminal Code* s. 25 or POA s. 146 for general provisions on the use of force.

LIMITATION PERIOD

The FLA does not extend the general limitation period contained in the POA; therefore, the limitation period of six months applies.

NON-POLICE AGENCIES INVOLVED

1. Counselling services
2. Mediation services

PROVINCIAL OFFENCES GRID COMPLETION

Common Offences and/or Provisions

1. Order for exclusive possession of matrimonial home.
2. Order restraining spouse from molesting, annoying, harassing, or communicating with the other spouse or children in that spouse's legal custody.

Arrest Powers

Reasonable and probable grounds to believe that there has been a violation of an order for exclusive possession of the matrimonial home.

Search Powers

None.

Use of Force

No specific use of force authority under the FLA (refer to *Criminal Code* s. 25 or POA s. 146).

Limitation Period

Six months from the date of the offence.

Non-Police Agencies Involved

1. Counselling services
2. Mediation services

Family Law Act

RSO 1990, c. F.3

1(1) **Definitions**—In this Act,

"child" includes a person whom a parent has demonstrated a settled intention to treat as a child of his or her family, except under an arrangement where the child is placed for valuable consideration in a foster home by a person having lawful custody;

"child support guidelines" means the guidelines established by the regulations made under subsections 69(2) and (3);

"cohabit" means to live together in a conjugal relationship, whether within or outside marriage;

"court" means the Ontario Court of Justice, the Family Court of the Superior Court of Justice or the Superior Court of Justice;

"domestic contract" means a domestic contract as defined in Part IV (Domestic Contracts);

"parent" includes a person who has demonstrated a settled intention to treat a child as a child of his or her family, except under an arrangement where the child is placed for valuable consideration in a foster home by a person having lawful custody;

"paternity agreement" means a paternity agreement as defined in Part IV (Domestic Contracts);

"spouse" means either of two persons who,

(a) are married to each other, or

(b) have together entered into a marriage that is voidable or void, in good faith on the part of a person relying on this clause to assert any right.

(2) **Polygamous marriages**—In the definition of "spouse", a reference to marriage includes a marriage that is actually or potentially polygamous, if it was celebrated in a jurisdiction whose system of law recognizes it as valid. . . .

PART I
FAMILY PROPERTY

4(1) **Definitions**—In this Part,

"court" means a court as defined in subsection 1(1), but does not include the Ontario Court of Justice;

"matrimonial home" means a matrimonial home under section 18 and includes property that is a matrimonial home under that section at the valuation date;

"net family property" means the value of all the property, except property described in subsection (2), that a spouse owns on the valuation date, after deducting,

(a) the spouse's debts and other liabilities, and

(b) the value of property, other than a matrimonial home, that the spouse owned on the date of the marriage, after deducting the spouse's debts and other liabilities, other than debts or liabilities related directly to the acquisition or significant improvement of a matrimonial home, calculated as of the date of the marriage;

"property" means any interest, present or future, vested or contingent, in real or personal property and includes,

(a) property over which a spouse has, alone or in conjunction with another person, a power of appointment exercisable in favour of himself or herself,

(b) property disposed of by a spouse but over which the spouse has, alone or in conjunction with another person, a power to revoke the disposition or a power to consume or dispose of the property, and

(c) in the case of a spouse's rights under a pension plan, the imputed value, for family law purposes, of the spouse's interest in the plan, as determined in accordance with section 10.1, for the period beginning with the date of the marriage and ending on the valuation date;

"valuation date" means the earliest of the following dates:

1. The date the spouses separate and there is no reasonable prospect that they will resume cohabitation.
2. The date a divorce is granted.
3. The date the marriage is declared a nullity.
4. The date one of the spouses commences an application based on subsection 5(3) (improvident depletion) that is subsequently granted.
5. The date before the date on which one of the spouses dies leaving the other spouse surviving.

(1.1) **Net family property, liabilities**—The liabilities referred to in clauses (a) and (b) of the definition of "net family property" in subsection (1) include any applicable contingent tax liabilities in respect of the property.

Under s. 4(2), property given to or inherited by a spouse from a third person after the date the marriage took place is not part of the spouse's net family property, unless the gift or inheritance was jointly used by the family.

(2) **Excluded property**—The value of the following property that a spouse owns on the valuation date does not form part of the spouse's net family property:

1. Property, other than a matrimonial home, that was acquired by gift or inheritance from a third person after the date of the marriage.
2. Income from property referred to in paragraph 1, if the donor or testator has expressly stated that it is to be excluded from the spouse's net family property.
3. Damages or a right to damages for personal injuries, nervous shock, mental distress or loss of guidance, care and companionship, or the part of a settlement that represents those damages.
4. Proceeds or a right to proceeds of a policy of life insurance, as defined under the *Insurance Act*, that are payable on the death of the life insured.
5. Property, other than a matrimonial home, into which property referred to in paragraphs 1 to 4 can be traced.
6. Property that the spouses have agreed by a domestic contract is not to be included in the spouse's net family property.
7. Unadjusted pensionable earnings under the *Canada Pension Plan*. . . .

Equalization of net family properties

5(1) **Divorce, etc.**—When a divorce is granted or a marriage is declared a nullity, or when the spouses are separated and there is no reasonable prospect that they will resume cohabitation, the spouse whose net family property is the lesser of the two net family properties is entitled to one-half the difference between them.

(2) **Death of spouse**—When a spouse dies, if the net family property of the deceased spouse exceeds the net family property of the surviving spouse, the surviving spouse is entitled to one-half the difference between them.

(3) **Improvident depletion of spouse's net family property**—When spouses are cohabiting, if there is a serious danger that one spouse may improvidently deplete his or her net family property, the other spouse may on an application under section 7 have the difference between the net family properties divided as if the spouses were separated and there were no reasonable prospect that they would resume cohabitation. . . .

18(1) **Matrimonial home**—Every property in which a person has an interest and that is or, if the spouses have separated, was at the time of separation ordinarily occupied by the person and his or her spouse as their family residence is their matrimonial home. . . .

19(1) **Possession of matrimonial home**—Both spouses have an equal right to possession of a matrimonial home.

(2) **Idem**—When only one of the spouses has an interest in a matrimonial home, the other spouse's right of possession,

(a) is personal as against the first spouse; and

(b) ends when they cease to be spouses, unless a separation agreement or court order provides otherwise. . . .

24(1) **Order for possession of matrimonial home**—Regardless of the ownership of a matrimonial home and its contents, and despite section 19 (spouse's right of possession), the court may on application, by order,

(a) provide for the delivering up, safekeeping and preservation of the matrimonial home and its contents;

(b) direct that one spouse be given exclusive possession of the matrimonial home or part of it for the period that the court directs and release other property that is a matrimonial home from the application of this Part;

(c) direct a spouse to whom exclusive possession of the matrimonial home is given to make periodic payments to the other spouse;

(d) direct that the contents of the matrimonial home, or any part of them,

(i) remain in the home for the use of the spouse given possession, or

(ii) be removed from the home for the use of a spouse or child;

(e) order a spouse to pay for all or part of the repair and maintenance of the matrimonial home and of other liabilities arising in respect of it, or to make periodic payments to the other spouse for those purposes;

(f) authorize the disposition or encumbrance of a spouse's interest in the matrimonial home, subject to the other spouse's right of exclusive possession as ordered; and

(g) where a false statement is made under subsection 21(3), direct,

(i) the person who made the false statement, or

(ii) a person who knew at the time he or she acquired an interest in the property that the statement was false and afterwards conveyed the interest,

to substitute other real property for the matrimonial home, or direct the person to set aside money or security to stand in place of it, subject to any conditions that the court considers appropriate.

(2) **Temporary or interim order**—The court may, on motion, make a temporary or interim order under clause (1)(a), (b), (c), (d) or (e).

(3) **Order for exclusive possession: criteria**—In determining whether to make an order for exclusive possession, the court shall consider,

(a) the best interests of the children affected;

(b) any existing orders under Part I (Family Property) and any existing support orders;

(c) the financial position of both spouses;

(d) any written agreement between the parties;

(e) the availability of other suitable and affordable accommodation; and

(f) any violence committed by a spouse against the other spouse or the children.

(4) **Best interests of child**—In determining the best interests of a child, the court shall consider,

(a) the possible disruptive effects on the child of a move to other accommodation; and

(b) the child's views and preferences, if they can reasonably be ascertained.

(5) **Offence**—A person who contravenes an order for exclusive possession is guilty of an offence and upon conviction is liable,

(a) in the case of a first offence, to a fine of not more than $5,000 or to imprisonment for a term of not more than three months, or to both; and

(b) in the case of a second or subsequent offence, to a fine of not more than $10,000 or to imprisonment for a term of not more than two years, or to both.

(6) **Arrest without warrant**—A police officer may arrest without warrant a person the police officer believes on reasonable and probable grounds to have contravened an order for exclusive possession.

(7) **Existing orders**—Subsections (5) and (6) also apply in respect of contraventions, committed on or after the 1st day of March, 1986, of orders for exclusive possession made under Part III of the *Family Law Reform Act*, being chapter 152 of the Revised Statutes of Ontario, 1980. . . .

PART III
SUPPORT OBLIGATIONS

. . .

31(1) **Obligation of parent to support child**—Every parent has an obligation to provide support for his or her unmarried child who is a minor or is enrolled in a full time program of education, to the extent that the parent is capable of doing so.

(2) **Idem**—The obligation under subsection (1) does not extend to a child who is sixteen years of age or older and has withdrawn from parental control.

32. Obligation of child to support parent—Every child who is not a minor has an obligation to provide support, in accordance with need, for his or her parent who has cared for or provided support for the child, to the extent that the child is capable of doing so.

33(1) **Order for support**—A court may, on application, order a person to provide support for his or her dependants and determine the amount of support. . . .

(7) **Purposes of order for support of child**—An order for the support of a child should,

(a) recognize that each parent has an obligation to provide support for the child;

(b) apportion the obligation according to the child support guidelines. . . .

43(1) **Arrest of absconding debtor**—If an application is made under section 33 or 37 and the court is satisfied that the respondent is about to leave Ontario and that there are reasonable grounds for believing that the respondent intends to evade his or her responsibilities under this Act, the court may issue a warrant for the respondent's arrest for the purpose of bringing him or her before the court. . . .

Section 43(1) allows a court to grant an arrest warrant in cases where it is believed that a spouse plans to leave the province and evade his or her legal responsibilities. This is different from the authority officers have under the Act to make an arrest without a warrant in cases where an order of exclusive possession of the matrimonial home has been violated.

46(1) **Restraining order**—On application, the court may make an interim or final restraining order against a person described in subsection (2) if the applicant has reasonable grounds to fear for his or her own safety or for the safety of any child in his or her lawful custody.

(2) **Same**—A restraining order under subsection (1) may be made against,

(a) a spouse or former spouse of the applicant; or

(b) a person other than a spouse or former spouse of the applicant, if the person is cohabiting with the applicant or has cohabited with the applicant for any period of time.

(3) **Provisions of order**—A restraining order made under subsection (1) shall be in the form prescribed by the rules of court and may contain one or more of the following provisions, as the court considers appropriate:

1. Restraining the respondent, in whole or in part, from directly or indirectly contacting or communicating with the applicant or any child in the applicant's lawful custody.
2. Restraining the respondent from coming within a specified distance of one or more locations.
3. Specifying one or more exceptions to the provisions described in paragraphs 1 and 2.
4. Any other provision that the court considers appropriate.

(4) **Transition**—This section, as it read immediately before the day section 35 of the *Family Statute Law Amendment Act, 2009* came into force, continues to apply to,

(a) any prosecution or other proceeding begun under this section before that day; and

(b) any order made under this section that was in force immediately before that day. . . .

50. Repealed.

ASSIGNMENT: FAMILY LAW ACT

1. Attending a call regarding a domestic dispute, you are confronted by two irate people. They have been married for 10 years and have one child. In the past four months the tension in the home has increased so significantly that the husband left; he has been staying with friends for the past two weeks. The wife tells you that the marriage is headed for divorce, and, in fact, she attended Family Court in that regard just yesterday. She produces an interim order of possession issued by the court. How do you explain the situation to the husband?

2. Regarding question 1, what is your legal obligation if the husband insists on entering the home despite the order?

3. A woman attends the police station and lodges a complaint against her estranged husband. She produces a current and valid restraining order granted by the local Family Court against him. Her allegation is that he repeatedly calls her to the point where she cannot carry on a regular routine. To support her allegations, she produces a cassette on which there are 10 answering machine messages from a person she identifies as her husband. In your investigation of the matter, you interview the husband as a matter of course. Can you arrest the husband under the FLA? What course of action would you recommend?

4. While on a domestic complaint call, you encounter a man who is upset. He explains that he and his wife are separated. Furthermore, she has "exclusive possession" of the family home by agreement, which is supported by a court order. She has threatened to damage his collection of hunting trophies, which were to remain in the home until the conclusion of the divorce (he did not have a place to store them). It appears that she is becoming less compliant with the agreed-upon parts of the separation agreement. To mediate the situation, you attend the residence and speak with the wife. What advice do you give her regarding her responsibility as stipulated by the exclusive possession order?

CHAPTER 10
Children's Law Reform Act

INTRODUCTION

The *Children's Law Reform Act* (CLRA) deals with child custody and access situations. It contains provisions for resolving disputes concerning custody and access, such as visitation. Contrary to popular belief, police officers cannot take action when a parent appears to be in violation of a custody agreement and refuses to allow a visitation to occur. Officers must refer conflicting parties to Family Court for an order of apprehension before an officer may forcibly remove a child from one parent and surrender the child to the other parent.

The primary tier associated with the *Children's Law Reform Act* is enforcement, through an order to apprehend a child and turn the child over to the person named in the order. Intervention and referral are secondary tiers.

Removal of a child should be avoided if at all possible. An officer's negotiation skills and ability to resolve conflicts, backed by the authority of the court, can lessen the distress of such an event.

The question of jurisdiction must also be addressed. Where does the child reside? What happens if one parent appears from another jurisdiction with a court order allowing access to the child? The CLRA contains provisions that answer those questions.

TERMINOLOGY

Court

"Court" means the Ontario Court of Justice, the Family Court, or the Superior Court of Justice.

Extra-provincial Order

An "extra-provincial order" is an order, or that part of an order, of a court or tribunal outside Ontario (an "extra-provincial tribunal") that grants to a person custody of or access to a child.

Extra-provincial Tribunal

An "extra-provincial tribunal" is a court or tribunal outside Ontario that has the jurisdiction to grant to a person custody of or access to a child.

Separation Agreement

A "separation agreement" is a valid separation agreement, as defined under the *Family Law Act*, between estranged spouses.

COMMON OFFENCES AND/OR PROVISIONS

Section 36(4) of the CLRA is very clear in directing police officers on how to enforce an order of apprehension. Officers have no discretion when enforcing such an order.

An order of apprehension may be issued where there are reasonable and probable grounds to believe that a person is unlawfully withholding a child from the applicant or proposes to remove the child from Ontario in contravention of a court order or separation agreement. An order is also issued where there are reasonable and probable grounds to believe that a person who is entitled to access to a child proposes to remove the child from Ontario and the child is unlikely to return. Under an order of apprehension, police officers are directed to locate, apprehend, and deliver the child to the person named in the order.

In situations involving apprehension orders, police officers should also attempt to ensure that the child is not in any danger. The *Child and Family Services Act* provides police officers with the power to apprehend any child who is "in need of care and protection" in order to safeguard the child (see chapter 8).

ARREST POWERS

Section 36(2), which allows a court to order the apprehension of a child, seems to be similar to an arrest order in that the child is being physically controlled by a police officer. But because the officer is carrying out a court order that specifies apprehension and delivery, the legal process usual for an arrest is avoided.

SEARCH POWERS

Sections 36(5) and 36(6) set out the search powers with respect to a child who is the subject of an order of apprehension issued under s. 36(2). A court will issue an order of apprehension if it is satisfied on reasonable and probable grounds that a person is unlawfully withholding a child from the applicant or proposes to remove the child from Ontario in contravention of a court order or separation agreement, or if a person who is entitled to access to a child proposes to remove the child from Ontario and the child is not likely to return.

The CLRA provides that a police officer may enter and search any place where the officer has reasonable and probable grounds to believe that a child named in an order of apprehension is being kept. The officer may also use such assistance and force as is reasonable. The search should be conducted between 0600 hours (6:00 a.m.) and 2100 hours (9:00 p.m.), unless the court, in the order, authorizes entry and search at another time.

USE OF FORCE

As indicated above, an officer authorized by s. 36(5) of the CLRA to enter and search a place for a child named in an order for apprehension is permitted to use such assistance and force as is reasonable.

LIMITATION PERIOD

The CLRA does not extend the general limitation period contained in the POA; therefore, the limitation period of six months applies.

NON-POLICE AGENCIES INVOLVED

Children's aid societies (see chapter 8 on the *Child and Family Services Act*).

PROVINCIAL OFFENCES GRID COMPLETION

Common Offences and/or Provisions

1. Restraining order prohibiting a person from molesting, annoying, or harassing the applicant or children in the applicant's lawful custody.
2. Apprehension of a child who is being unlawfully withheld from the applicant in contravention of a custody order, is being proposed to be moved from the province of Ontario contrary to a court order or separation agreement, or if a child is likely to be removed from the province and is not likely to return.

Arrest Powers

No arrest authority.

Search Powers

A police officer may enter and search any place that the officer has reasonable and probable grounds to believe a child named in an order of apprehension is being held.

Use of Force

A police officer who is authorized by an order of apprehension for a child who is being unlawfully withheld may use such force as is necessary to execute the order.

Limitation Period

Six months from the date of the offence.

Non-Police Agencies Involved

Children's aid societies.

Children's Law Reform Act

RSO 1990, c. C.12

...

PART III
CUSTODY, ACCESS AND GUARDIANSHIP

Interpretation

18(1) **Definitions, Part III**—In this Part,

"court" means the Ontario Court of Justice, the Family Court or the Superior Court of Justice;

"extra-provincial order" means an order, or that part of an order, of an extra-provincial tribunal that grants to a person custody of or access to a child;

"extra-provincial tribunal" means a court or tribunal outside Ontario that has jurisdiction to grant to a person custody of or access to a child;

"separation agreement" means an agreement that is a valid separation agreement under Part IV of the *Family Law Act*.

(2) **Child**—A reference in this Part to a child is a reference to the child while a minor.

19. Purposes, Part III—The purposes of this Part are,

(a) to ensure that applications to the courts in respect of custody of, incidents of custody of, access to and guardianship for children will be determined on the basis of the best interests of the children;

(b) to recognize that the concurrent exercise of jurisdiction by judicial tribunals of more than one province, territory or state in respect of the custody of the same child ought to be avoided, and to make provision so that the courts of Ontario will, unless there are exceptional circumstances, refrain from exercising or decline jurisdiction in cases where it is more appropriate for the matter to be determined by a tribunal having jurisdiction in another place with which the child has a closer connection;

(c) to discourage the abduction of children as an alternative to the determination of custody rights by due process; and

(d) to provide for the more effective enforcement of custody and access orders and for the recognition and enforcement of custody and access orders made outside Ontario.

Custody and Access

20(1) **Father and mother entitled to custody**—Except as otherwise provided in this Part, the father and the mother of a child are equally entitled to custody of the child.

(2) **Rights and responsibilities**—A person entitled to custody of a child has the rights and responsibilities of a parent in respect of the person of the child and must exercise those rights and responsibilities in the best interests of the child.

(3) **Authority to act**—Where more than one person is entitled to custody of a child, any one of them may exercise the rights and accept the responsibilities of a parent on behalf of them in respect of the child.

(4) **Where parents separate**—Where the parents of a child live separate and apart and the child lives with one of them with the consent, implied consent or acquiescence of the other of them, the right of the other to exercise the entitlement of custody and the incidents of custody, but not the entitlement to access, is suspended until a separation agreement or order otherwise provides.

(5) **Access**—The entitlement to access to a child includes the right to visit with and be visited by the child and the same right as a parent to make inquiries and to be given information as to the health, education and welfare of the child.

(6) **Marriage of child**—The entitlement to custody of or access to a child terminates on the marriage of the child.

(7) **Entitlement subject to agreement or order**—Any entitlement to custody or access or incidents of custody under this section is subject to alteration by an order of the court or by separation agreement.

21(1) **Application for custody or access**—A parent of a child or any other person may apply to a court for an order respecting custody of or access to the child or determining any aspect of the incidents of custody of the child.

(2) **Affidavit**—An application under subsection (1) for custody of or access to a child shall be accompanied by an affidavit, in the form prescribed for the purpose by the rules of court, of the person applying for custody or access, containing,

(a) the person's proposed plan for the child's care and upbringing;

(b) information respecting the person's current or previous involvement in any family proceedings, including proceedings under Part III of the *Child and Family Services Act* (child protection), or in any criminal proceedings; and

(c) any other information known to the person that is relevant to the factors to be considered by the court under subsections 24(2), (3) and (4) in determining the best interests of the child.

21.1(1) **Police records checks, non-parents**—Every person who applies under section 21 for custody of a child and who is not a parent of the child shall file with the court the results of a recent police records check respecting the person in accordance with the rules of court.

(2) **Admissibility**—The results obtained by the court under subsection (1) and any information, statement or document derived from the information contained in the results are admissible in evidence in the application, if the court considers it to be relevant.

(3) **Use of evidence**—Subject to subsection 24(3), evidence that is determined by the court to be admissible under subsection (2) shall be considered in determining the best interests of the child under section 24.

(4) **Regulations**—The Lieutenant Governor in Council may make regulations defining "police records check" for the purposes of subsection (1).

CAS records search, non-parents

21.2(1) **Definition**—In this section,

"society" means an approved agency designated as a children's aid society under the *Child and Family Services Act.*

(2) **Request for report**—Every person who applies under section 21 for custody of a child and who is not a parent of the child shall submit a request, in the form provided by the Ministry of the Attorney General, to every society or other body or person prescribed by the regulations, for a report as to,

(a) whether a society has records relating to the person applying for custody; and

(b) if there are records and the records indicate that one or more files relating to the person have been opened, the date on which each file was opened and, if the file was closed, the date on which the file was closed.

(3) **Request to be filed**—A copy of each request made under subsection (2) shall be filed with the court.

(4) **Report required**—Within 30 days of receiving a request under subsection (2), a society or other body or person shall provide the court in which the application was filed with a report, in the form provided by the Ministry of the Attorney General, containing

the information required under that subsection, and shall provide a copy of the report to the requesting party.

(5) **Duty of clerk**—Subject to subsection (6), if the report indicates that there are records relating to the requesting party, the clerk of the court shall, 20 days after all of the reports that were requested by the party have been received by the court,

(a) give a copy of the report to every other party and to counsel, if any, representing the child; and

(b) file the report in the court file.

(6) **Exception**—The court may, on motion by the requesting party, order,

(a) that the time period referred to in subsection (5) be lengthened; or

(b) that all or part of the report be sealed in the court file and not disclosed if,

(i) the court determines that some or all of the information contained in the report is not relevant to the application, or

(ii) the party withdraws the application.

(7) **Admissibility**—A report that is filed under subsection (5) and any information, statement or document derived from the information contained in the report is admissible in evidence in the application, if the court considers it to be relevant.

(8) **Use of evidence**—Subject to subsection 24(3), evidence that is determined by the court to be admissible under subsection (7) shall be considered in determining the best interests of the child under section 24.

(9) **Interpretation**—Nothing done under this section constitutes publication of information or making information public for the purposes of subsection 45(8) of the *Child and Family Services Act* or an order under clause 70(1)(b).

(10) **Regulations**—The Lieutenant Governor in Council may make regulations for the purposes of subsection (2),

(a) specifying one or more societies or other bodies or persons to whom a request must be submitted;

(b) governing the manner and scope of the search required to be undertaken in response to a request;

(c) specifying classes of files that shall be excluded from the report.

Other proceedings

21.3(1) **Application by non-parent**—Where an application for custody of a child is made by a person who is not a parent of the child, the clerk of the court shall provide to the court and to the parties information in writing respecting any current or previous family proceedings involving the child or any person who is a party to the application and who is not a parent of the child.

(2) **Same**—Where an application for custody of a child is made by a person who is not a parent of the child, the court may require the clerk of the court to provide to the court and to the parties information in writing respecting any current or previous criminal proceedings involving any person who is a party to the application and who is not a parent of the child.

(3) **Same**—Written information provided under subsection (1) or (2) shall also be provided to counsel, if any, representing the child who is the subject of the application.

(4) **Admissibility**—Written information that is provided to the court under subsection (1) or (2) and any information, statement or document derived from that information is admissible in evidence in the application, if the court considers it to be relevant.

(5) **Use of evidence**—Subject to subsection 24(3), evidence that is determined by the court to be admissible under subsection (4) shall be considered in determining the best interests of the child under section 24.

(6) **Interpretation**—Nothing done under this section constitutes publication of information or making information public for the purposes of subsection 45(8) of the *Child and Family Services Act* or an order under clause 70(1)(b).

(7) **Regulations**—The Attorney General may make regulations for the purposes of this section,

(a) defining "family proceeding" and "criminal proceeding";

(b) prescribing the scope, content and form of the written information that shall or may be provided under this section;

(c) providing for a process for removing from the written information provided under subsection (1) or (2) information respecting a proceeding that does not involve the child who is the subject of the application or a person who is a party and is not a parent of the child, as the case may be.

22(1) **Jurisdiction**—A court shall only exercise its jurisdiction to make an order for custody of or access to a child where,

(a) the child is habitually resident in Ontario at the commencement of the application for the order;

(b) although the child is not habitually resident in Ontario, the court is satisfied,

(i) that the child is physically present in Ontario at the commencement of the application for the order,

(ii) that substantial evidence concerning the best interests of the child is available in Ontario,

(iii) that no application for custody of or access to the child is pending before an extra-provincial tribunal in another place where the child is habitually resident,

(iv) that no extra-provincial order in respect of custody of or access to the child has been recognized by a court in Ontario,

(v) that the child has a real and substantial connection with Ontario, and

(vi) that, on the balance of convenience, it is appropriate for jurisdiction to be exercised in Ontario.

(2) **Habitual residence**—A child is habitually resident in the place where he or she resided,

(a) with both parents;

(b) where the parents are living separate and apart, with one parent under a separation agreement or with the consent, implied consent or acquiescence of the other or under a court order; or

(c) with a person other than a parent on a permanent basis for a significant period of time,

whichever last occurred.

(3) **Abduction**—The removal or withholding of a child without the consent of the person having custody of the child does not alter the habitual residence of the child unless there has been acquiescence or undue delay in commencing due process by the person from whom the child is removed or withheld.

23. Serious harm to child—Despite sections 22 and 41, a court may exercise its jurisdiction to make or to vary an order in respect of the custody of or access to a child where,

(a) the child is physically present in Ontario; and

(b) the court is satisfied that the child would, on the balance of probabilities, suffer serious harm if,

(i) the child remains in the custody of the person legally entitled to custody of the child,

(ii) the child is returned to the custody of the person legally entitled to custody of the child, or

(iii) the child is removed from Ontario. . . .

Custody and Access—Enforcement

34(1) **Supervision of custody or access**—Where an order is made for custody of or access to a child, a court may give such directions as it considers appropriate for the supervision of the custody or access by a person, a children's aid society or other body.

(2) **Consent to act**—A court shall not direct a person, a children's aid society or other body to supervise custody or access as mentioned in subsection (1) unless the person, society or body has consented to act as supervisor.

35(1) **Restraining order**—On application, the court may make an interim or final restraining order against any person if the applicant has reasonable grounds to fear for his or her own safety or for the safety of any child in his or her lawful custody.

(2) **Provisions of order**—A restraining order made under subsection (1) shall be in the form prescribed by the rules of court and may contain one or more of the following provisions, as the court considers appropriate:

1. Restraining the respondent, in whole or in part, from directly or indirectly contacting or communicating with the applicant or any child in the applicant's lawful custody.
2. Restraining the respondent from coming within a specified distance of one or more locations.
3. Specifying one or more exceptions to the provisions described in paragraphs 1 and 2.
4. Any other provision that the court considers appropriate.

(3) **Transition**—This section, as it read immediately before the day section 15 of the *Family Statute Law Amendment Act, 2009* came into force, continues to apply to,

(a) any prosecution or other proceeding begun under this section before that day; and

(b) any order made under this section that was in force immediately before that day.

36(1) **Order where child unlawfully withheld**—Where a court is satisfied upon application by a person in whose favour an order has been made for custody of or access to a child that there are reasonable and probable grounds for believing that any person is unlawfully withholding the child from the applicant, the court by order may authorize the applicant or someone on his or her behalf to apprehend the child for the purpose of giving effect to the rights of the applicant to custody or access, as the case may be.

(2) **Order to locate and take child**—Where a court is satisfied upon application that there are reasonable and probable grounds for believing,

(a) that any person is unlawfully withholding a child from a person entitled to custody of or access to the child;

(b) that a person who is prohibited by court order or separation agreement from removing a child from Ontario proposes to remove the child or have the child removed from Ontario; or

(c) that a person who is entitled to access to a child proposes to remove the child or to have the child removed from Ontario and that the child is not likely to return,

the court by order may direct a police force, having jurisdiction in any area where it appears to the court that the child may be, to locate, apprehend and deliver the child to the person named in the order.

(3) **Application without notice**—An order may be made under subsection (2) upon an application without notice where the court is satisfied that it is necessary that action be taken without delay.

(4) **Duty to act**—The police force directed to act by an order under subsection (2) shall do all things reasonably able to be done to locate, apprehend and deliver the child in accordance with the order.

Anyone who prevents a police officer from enforcing a court-ordered apprehension may be charged with obstructing an officer in the execution of his or her duties under s. 129 of the *Criminal Code*.

(5) **Entry and search**—For the purpose of locating and apprehending a child in accordance with an order under subsection (2), a member of a police force may enter and search any place where he or she has reasonable and probable grounds for believing that the child may be with such assistance and such force as are reasonable in the circumstances.

(6) **Time**—An entry or a search referred to in subsection (5) shall be made only between 6 a.m. and 9 p.m. standard time unless the court, in the order, authorizes entry and search at another time.

(7) **Expiration of order**—An order made under subsection (2) shall name a date on which it expires, which shall be a date not later than six months after it is made unless the court is satisfied that a longer period of time is necessary in the circumstances.

(8) **When application may be made**—An application under subsection (1) or (2) may be made in an application for custody or access or at any other time.

Court orders, removal and return of children

37(1) **To prevent unlawful removal of child**—Where a court, upon application, is satisfied upon reasonable and probable grounds that a person prohibited by court order or separation agreement from removing a child from Ontario proposes to remove the child from Ontario, the court in order to prevent the removal of the child from Ontario may make an order under subsection (3).

(2) **To ensure return of child**—Where a court, upon application, is satisfied upon reasonable and probable grounds that a person entitled to access to a child proposes to remove the child from Ontario and is not likely to return the child to Ontario, the court in order to secure the prompt, safe return of the child to Ontario may make an order under subsection (3).

(3) **Order by court**—An order mentioned in subsection (1) or (2) may require a person to do any one or more of the following:

1. Transfer specific property to a named trustee to be held subject to the terms and conditions specified in the order.
2. Where payments have been ordered for the support of the child, make the payments to a specified trustee subject to the terms and conditions specified in the order.
3. Post a bond, with or without sureties, payable to the applicant in such amount as the court considers appropriate.
4. Deliver the person's passport, the child's passport and any other travel documents of either of them that the court may specify to the court or to an individual or body specified by the court.

(4) **Idem, Ontario Court of Justice**—The Ontario Court of Justice shall not make an order under paragraph 1 of subsection (3).

(5) **Terms and conditions**—In an order under paragraph 1 of subsection (3), the court may specify terms and conditions for the return or the disposition of the property as the court considers appropriate.

(6) **Safekeeping**—A court or an individual or body specified by the court in an order under paragraph 4 of subsection (3) shall hold a passport or travel document delivered in accordance with the order in safekeeping in accordance with any directions set out in the order.

(7) **Directions**—In an order under subsection (3), a court may give such directions in respect of the safekeeping of the property, payments, passports or travel documents as the court considers appropriate.

ASSIGNMENT: CHILDREN'S LAW REFORM ACT

1. You attend a residence to help settle a dispute between estranged parents over access to a child. The husband is outside the home and shows you a court order that allows him to visit with his child on this day of the week. He explains that his estranged wife refuses to let him leave with the child. You examine the order and determine that it is valid and current. The wife confirms that the order is valid but flatly refuses to give the husband access to the child. Do you have the authority to remove the child and turn him over to the husband?

2. Regarding the situation in question 1, what would you advise the husband to do to remedy the problem?

3. In another dispute over access to a child, the estranged parents have two different court orders from Family Court. The wife has an order that is dated for the previous month, and the husband has an order that has been varied and is dated for the current month. Which order is in force?

4. In another dispute over access to a child, the estranged parents have two different court orders from family courts. The husband, who resides in Calgary, has a current order from a family court in the province of Alberta, and the wife has an order dated three months earlier than the husband's order from Family Court in Ontario. Which order is in force? Why?

5. In a dispute between estranged parents over custody of a child, the wife has a court order that directs the police to apprehend the child and turn her over to the wife. The husband, however, refuses to give up custody of the child. What must you ultimately do in this situation?

CHAPTER 11

Motorized Snow Vehicles Act

INTRODUCTION

The primary tier associated with the *Motorized Snow Vehicles Act* is enforcement, in three areas: the permits/licences required to operate a motorized snow vehicle; the places where such machines may be operated; and the equipment required to operate them lawfully.

The *Motorized Snow Vehicles Act* (MSVA) establishes rules for the operation of snow vehicles in Ontario. The Act covers the areas where snow vehicles may or may not be operated—for example, organized trails and provincial highways. The Act does not cover the operation of a snow vehicle on private property, and it recognizes the authority of municipal councils to control the operation of snow vehicles in their respective jurisdictions.

Standard requirements of registration, equipment usage, and insurance are set out in the MSVA and are common to all areas of operation. Because the snow vehicle is capable of travelling over a variety of terrains, certain restrictions for its use on highways and operator obligations to landowners are incorporated into the Act. The MSVA also holds the owner and operator jointly liable for damage caused by the operation of a snow vehicle.

The Act provides permit requirements for use of snow vehicles on organized trails (see MSVA s. 2.1 and Regulation 185/01 below). It also stipulates different minimum operator ages depending on where the vehicle is being operated.

Fines are outlined in this Act and not the *Provincial Offences Act* (POA). Minimum and maximum fine ranges are similar to those for other provincial offences; however, certain contraventions may result in a driver's licence suspension, as well as the lifetime loss of motor vehicle privileges under the *Highway Traffic Act*.

Law enforcement officers have the authority to stop and arrest under the Act, and operators who refuse to stop or who initiate a chase are subject to notable penalties and fines. The financial penalty for ignoring a request to stop is considerable, and such an action may result in a mandatory jail term for a minimum of 14 days.

TERMINOLOGY

Motorized Snow Vehicle (MSV)

A self-propelled vehicle that is designed primarily to travel over snow and does not include an all-terrain vehicle (ATV) or other "off-road" vehicles. (These are addressed by the *Off-Road Vehicles Act.*)

Operator's Licence

This refers to a specific licence—that is, the motorized snow vehicle operator's licence—issued under the Act. The licence applicant must be at least 12 years of age and meet the requirements of a test as set down within the regulations.

Trail

A trail maintained by a recreational organization, which may include private land and Crown land designated as part of the trail.

Speed Limits

Speed limits for snow vehicles are tied to three specific recreation areas: highways; parks or exhibition grounds; and trails.

HIGHWAYS

On a highway with posted speed limits of 50 km/h or under, the snow vehicle speed limit is 20 km/h.

On a highway where the posted limit is greater than 50 km/h, the snow vehicle speed limit is 50 km/h.

PARKS OR EXHIBITION GROUNDS

In a park or exhibition ground, the snow vehicle speed limit is 20 km/h.

TRAILS

On trails (see definition above), the snow vehicle speed limit is 50 km/h.

COMMON OFFENCES AND/OR PROVISIONS

MSV offences are similar to motor vehicle offences, with some distinct differences.

Specific fines are imposed by the MSVA and vary according to the violation. Notably, a minimum of $200 and a maximum of $1,000 is the norm.

The owner/lessee of a snow vehicle is jointly liable with the operator of the snow vehicle should the operation of it result in damage or personal injury. The owner/lessee is also liable for any charges for which the driver is liable. However, if the vehicle was used or taken without the consent of the owner/lessee, he or she is not considered liable (s. 23).

Permit/Licence Offences

1. It is an offence to drive or allow an MSV to be driven without a permit unless on land owned by the MSV owner. A permit must be displayed as prescribed by regulation (s. 2(8)), and the MSV number must be unobstructed (s. 4).
2. Operators who wish to drive an MSV along a highway or across a highway must be 16 years of age and possess either a valid Ontario driver's licence (G, G, G2) (s. 9(1)) or an MSV operator's licence (s. 9(1)).
3. Operators who wish to drive an MSV on an organized trail must be 12 years of age and possess an MSV operator's licence (s. 9(3)).
4. Relevant licences should be carried when operating an MSV (s. 16(1)) and it is an offence to fail to produce a licence on request (s. 16(2)).
5. All MSVs must be registered. The first registration must be filed by a vendor licensed by the province. For subsequent sales, the onus is on the private vendor each time the machine is sold (s. 3(3)) to forward notice of sale to the ministry. Registration must occur within six days of the sale.
6. As with motor vehicles, permits for MSVs must be validated annually (Reg. 804, s. 18(1)). MSVs operated on the owner's land, reserve land, and in certain areas of northern and northwestern Ontario do not require annual permit validations (Reg. 804, s. 19(3)).
7. It is an offence to drive with a suspended licence (s. 17.1(11)).

   Note that on suspension of a motor vehicle driver's licence, the MSV licence is suspended as well. However, any violations and related convictions resulting from the operation of an MSV do not affect demerit points of a person's driver's licence.

Location Offences

HIGHWAYS

It is an offence to drive on a King's highway or a secondary highway except to cross (s. 5(2)(b); Reg. 803). The province declares which highways are prohibited to snow vehicle travel. Vehicular and population density are primary factors in establishing whether an MSV may be operated on or across a highway. Prohibited highways include the 400-series highways, the Queen Elizabeth Way (QEW), the Ottawa Queensway, and the Kitchener-Waterloo Expressway (see s. 5(2)(b) of Regulation 803 for a complete list).

In areas where highway usage is permitted, two stipulations are imposed. The first establishes that any crossing of a highway must be a route that is 90 degrees to the direction of the roadway (s. 5(1)). The second is that any travel along a highway must not be on the serviced area, which includes the shoulders. That leaves travel on the area between the shoulder and fence line or public boundary line (s. 5(2)).

Where roadways and portions of a highway fall within a municipal boundary, the council of that municipality may permit, restrict, or prohibit snow vehicle travel (s. 7(2)).

TRAILS

Unless on the MSV owner's land, special licensing and permit fees are required for trails that are developed and maintained by a recreational organization such as the Ontario Federation of Snowmobile Clubs (s. 2.1(1)).

Equipment Offences

1. A headlight and tail light are required on an MSV, with the same restrictions as a motor vehicle. They must be used one-half hour before sunset and one-half hour after sunrise or when visibility is reduced as a result of atmospheric conditions (fog, snow, etc.) (Reg. 804, s. 17).
2. Any towed conveyance must bear reflectors to the sides and rear as described in Reg. 804.
3. Helmets are required for all operators and passengers, whether on the machine or on a towed conveyance such as a sled (s. 20(1)).
4. Any connection with a towed conveyance must be by means of a rigid tow bar (s. 19(1)).

Insurance Offences

1. It is an offence to drive or allow one's MSV to be driven unless the vehicle is insured under a motor vehicle liability policy (s. 12(1)).
2. It is an offence to fail to produce evidence of such insurance on request by a law enforcement officer (police or conservation officer) (s. 12(2)).

Driving and Speeding Offences

Operators of snow vehicles are bound by obligations similar to those of motor vehicle operators.

1. The MSV driver must stop when signalled by a law enforcement officer (police or conservation officer) (s. 17.1(1)).

   If an operator wilfully attempts to escape by flight and is pursued by an officer, he or she will be liable for a fine of not less than $5,000 and not more than $25,000, and imprisonment of not less than 14 days and not more than six months, and the suspension of his or her driver's licence or MSV licence for five years. If the driver's conduct results in death or bodily harm, the suspension will be for a period of not less than ten years (ss. 17.1(1)–(3)).
2. The driver of a snow machine being approached by a vehicle displaying a flashing red or combination of red and blue lights must bring the snow vehicle to an immediate stop (s. 17(1)).
3. The driver must produce required documents upon demand—that is, licence, permit, and insurance (s. 16(1)).
4. Rules of operation or "rules of the road" must be obeyed. This includes the signalling of stopping or change of direction, and obeying regulatory signs such as stop signs, speed signs, and passing requirements (Reg. 804).

5. Accidents with damage over $400 must be reported (s. 13(1)).
6. It is an offence to drive an MSV faster than 20 km/h on a highway where the posted speed limit is less than 50 km/h or in any public park or exhibition ground (s. 14(1)(a)).
7. It is an offence to drive an MSV faster than 50 km/h on a highway where the posted limit is greater than 50 km/h or on a trail (s. 14(1)(b)).

COMMONLY ENCOUNTERED PROVISIONS

The most common offences involving the operation of snow vehicles fall into the following categories:

1. *In town or out of town.* This concerns the operation of snow vehicles on prohibited highways and municipal roadways or properties governed under a municipal bylaw.
2. *Permits and licences.* Commonly, driver's licences and operator's licences are required to operate a machine. Ownership with proof of validation and required insurance are required as well. Where applicable, the necessary "trail permit" must be obtained.
3. *Equipment.* Helmets and lights are the most important mandated equipment.
4. *Operating offences.* These are essentially the same as those for motor vehicles. Offences that involve failing to comply with signs controlling movement and speed are in this category.
5. *Trespass.* It is an offence under the *Trespass to Property Act* for MSVs to travel onto private property or areas not designated as "trails."
6. *Impaired Operation.* Offences are the same as those found in the *Criminal Code* for motor vehicles. The same blood alcohol level restrictions are placed on MSV operators as on operators of cars or other vehicles.

ARREST POWERS

An operator stopped by a police officer or conservation officer must produce a valid driver's licence or MSV operating licence, as well as registration for the snow vehicle. If the operator is unable to do so, the operator must provide his or her name and address. If the MSV operator refuses to do so, or the officer believes, on reasonable and probable grounds, that the operator is in contravention of these requirements, he or she may be arrested (s. 16(5)).

SEARCH POWERS

There are no specific search powers contained in the MSVA. If an arrest is made, a search can be conducted under the common-law powers of searching incident to an arrest, in order to protect the officer or the suspect, to preserve any evidence in the possession of the person being arrested, and/or to establish identification.

USE OF FORCE

There is no specific use-of-force authority in relation to an arrest or search.

LIMITATION PERIOD

The MSVA is silent on limitation period, so the general limitation period of six months from the date of the offence, as defined in the POA, applies.

NON-POLICE AGENCIES INVOLVED

Ministry of Natural Resources

This refers to conservation officers (that is, game wardens). Their involvement is logical because most snow vehicle operation is conducted in areas regularly patrolled by conservation officers who are, by legislation, empowered to enforce this Act (ss. 16(5) and 17(3)).

Environment Canada

An officer from this department is the federal counterpart of the provincial conservation officer and the province grants him or her the same authorities as a provincial conservation officer has.

Ontario Federation of Snowmobile Clubs (OFSC)

These clubs are recognized by provincial legislation as overseeing the approved trail system. Part of this responsibility is to ensure users do not operate on closed trails or fail to have a trail permit. Because these lands may consist of Crown and private lands, it is the practice for these clubs to act as agents for both the Crown and private landowners. This authorization is recognized and applied by way of the *Trespass to Property Act.*

Members of the OFSC may be appointed by law, under the *Police Services Act*, as "special constables" for a specific time period and geographic area, such as a particular organized trail. This initiative is known as STOP—Snowmobile Trail Officer Patrol. These individuals have the same authorities as a constable in this application. For more information on this program, visit the "Get Involved" section of the OFSC's website at www.ofsc.on.ca.

PROVINCIAL OFFENCES GRID COMPLETION

Common Offences and/or Provisions

The most common offences involving the operation of snow vehicles fall into the following categories:

1. operation of snow vehicles on prohibited highways and municipal roadways or properties governed under a municipal bylaw;
2. the requirement for valid licences, permits, and insurance;
3. mandated equipment—that is, helmets and lights;
4. various operating offences, which are essentially the same as those for motor vehicles—that is, failure to comply with laws controlling movement and speed;
5. offences under the *Trespass to Property Act*; and
6. offences regarding impairment under the *Criminal Code*.

Arrest Powers

They are the same as those under the *Highway Traffic Act*, *Trespass to Property Act*, and *Criminal Code*, as well as s. 16(5) of the MSVA for the failure to produce requested documents.

Search Powers

There are no specific search powers contained in the MSVA. If an arrest is made, a search may be conducted under the common-law powers of searching incident to an arrest.

Use of Force

There is no specific use-of-force authority under the MSVA. Use *Criminal Code* s. 25 or POA s. 146.

Limitation Period

Six months from the date of the offence.

Non-Police Agencies Involved

1. Conversation offices (Ministry of Natural Resources and Environment Canada)
2. Special constables (OFSC)

Motorized Snow Vehicle Act

RSO 1990, c. M.44

1. Definitions—In this Act,

"conservation officer" means a conservation officer under the *Fish and Wildlife Conservation Act, 1997*;

"driver's licence" means a valid and subsisting licence to drive a motor vehicle on a highway issued under the authority of the *Highway Traffic Act*;

"highway" includes a common and public highway, street, avenue, parkway, driveway, square, place, bridge, viaduct or trestle, designed and intended for, or used by, the general public for the passage of vehicles;

"median strip" means the portion of a highway so constructed as to separate traffic travelling in one direction from traffic travelling in the opposite direction by a physical barrier or an unpaved strip of ground;

"Minister" means the Minister of Transportation;

"Ministry" means the Ministry of Transportation;

"motorized snow vehicle" means a self-propelled vehicle designed to be driven primarily on snow;

"permit" means a permit issued under section 2;

"registration number" means a number or combination of letters and numbers allocated to a motorized snow vehicle by the Ministry on the registration thereof;

"regulations" means the regulations made under this Act;

"school bus" means a school bus as defined in section 175 of the *Highway Traffic Act*;

"serviced roadway" means the part of highway that is improved, designed or ordinarily used for vehicular traffic, and includes the ploughed portion of the shoulder, and, where a highway includes two or more separate serviced roadways, the term "serviced roadway" refers to any one serviced roadway separately and not to all of the serviced roadways collectively;

"trail" means the whole of any trail established and maintained by a recreational organization for the use of motorized snow vehicles;

"trail permit" means a permit issued under section 2.1;

"validate" means render in force for the period of time prescribed by the regulations, and "validation" and "validated" have corresponding meanings.

2(1) Permit Required—The owner of a motorized snow vehicle shall not,

(a) drive the motorized snow vehicle; or

(b) cause or permit the motorized snow vehicle to be driven,

except under the authority of a permit for the motorized snow vehicle issued or validated under subsection (3) or except on lands occupied by the owner of the motorized snow vehicle.

(2) **Dealer shall register**—Every dealer in motorized snow vehicles who sells a new motorized snow vehicle shall register the motorized snow vehicle on behalf of the purchaser thereof with the Ministry within six days following the sale.

(3) **Issuance of permits**—Upon registration of a motorized snow vehicle by a dealer pursuant to subsection (2) or by the owner of the motorized snow vehicle and upon payment of the fee prescribed by the regulations, the Minister or any person authorized by the Minister shall issue for the motorized snow vehicle a numbered permit in accordance

with the regulations, bearing the registration number of the motorized snow vehicle and provide such evidence of the issue of the permit for display upon the motorized snow vehicle as may be prescribed by the regulations.

(4) **Issuance of validations of permits**—Upon the application of the owner of a motorized snow vehicle for which a permit has been issued and upon payment of the fee prescribed by the regulations, the Minister or any person authorized by the Minister shall validate the permit and provide such evidence of validation as may be prescribed by the regulations.

(5) **Records**—The Ministry shall maintain,

(a) a numerical index record of all permits issued and in force under this section; and

(b) an alphabetical index record of the names and addresses of all persons to whom permits that are in force have been issued.

(6) **Term of permit**—A permit that is issued or validated is in force during the period of time prescribed by the regulations.

(7) **Registration number to be displayed**—Every motorized snow vehicle, unless exempted under this Act or the regulations, shall have attached to or painted on both sides of the cowling in a clearly visible position a sign showing the registration number of the motorized snow vehicle in the form and manner prescribed in the regulations.

(8) **Display of evidence of permit**—Every driver of a motorized snow vehicle shall display evidence of the issue or validation of the permit on the motorized snow vehicle in the form and manner prescribed by the regulations.

(8.1) **Offence for failing to have a permit**—Every driver of a motorized snow vehicle who contravenes subsection (1) is guilty of an offence and on conviction is liable

(9) **Exceptions as to manufacturers, dealers, non-residents**—This section does not apply,

(a) to manufacturers of motorized snow vehicles or to dealers in motorized snow vehicles in relation to motorized snow vehicles,

(i) that are kept for sale and are not driven or permitted to be driven upon a highway, or

(ii) that are not rented or leased or kept for renting or leasing to any person;

(b) to a motorized snow vehicle owned by a person who does not reside in Ontario if the vehicle is registered in some other jurisdiction and has attached to it the number plate furnished by the other jurisdiction.

(10) **Local issuance of permits**—The Minister may give authority to any person to issue permits, to validate permits and to provide evidence of such issue or validation of permits for motorized snow vehicles and may define the duties and powers of such person and, despite section 2 of the *Financial Administration Act*, may authorize and fix the fee to be retained by the person so authorized for each permit issued or validated. . . .

2.1(1) **Trail permit required**—No person shall drive a motorized snow vehicle upon a prescribed trail except under the authority of, and in accordance with, a trail permit for the motorized snow vehicle issued under subsection (2) or except on lands occupied by the owner of the motorized snow vehicle.

(2) **Issuance of trail permits**—Upon the application of the owner of a motorized snow vehicle and payment of the required fee, the Minister or any person authorized by the Minister shall,

(a) issue for the motorized snow vehicle a numbered trail permit in accordance with the regulations; and

(b) provide such evidence of the issue of the trail permit for display upon the motorized snow vehicle as may be prescribed by the regulations.

(3) **Validity of trail permit**—A trail permit is valid during the period of time prescribed by the regulations.

(4) **Display of evidence of trail permit**—Every driver of a motorized snow vehicle upon a prescribed trail shall display evidence of the issue of the trail permit on the motorized snow vehicle in the form and manner prescribed by the regulations.

(5) **Local issuance of trail permits**—The Minister may give authority to any person to issue trail permits and to provide evidence of such issue of trail permits and may define the duties and powers of such person and, despite section 2 of the *Financial Administration Act*, may authorize the fee to be retained by the person so authorized for each trail permit issued.

(6) **Offence**—Every person who contravenes subsection (1) is guilty of an offence and on conviction is liable to a fine of not less than $200 and not more than $1,000. . . .

(8) **Regulations re trail permits**—The Lieutenant Governor in Council may make regulations respecting any matter ancillary to the provisions of this section with respect to trail permits and in particular,

(a) prescribing trails or classes of trails, or parts of trails or classes of trails, on which trail permits are required;

(b) respecting the issuance and replacement of trail permits;

(c) prescribing the term of validity of trail permits;

(d) governing the form and manner of displaying evidence of the issue of trail permits on motorized snow vehicles;

(e) prescribing records to be kept by the Ministry, or by a person authorized under subsection (5) to issue trail permits, with respect to the issuance of trail permits.

3(1) **False statement**—No person shall knowingly make a false statement of fact in any application, declaration, affidavit or paper-writing required by this Act or the regulations.

(2) **Change of address**—Where an owner of a motorized snow vehicle changes his, her or its address as stated in an application for a permit or for a validation of a permit or in a previous notice sent or filed under this subsection, the owner shall within six days send by registered mail to or file with the Ministry notice of the new address.

(3) **Change of ownership**—Every person who sells or purchases a motorized snow vehicle shall, within six days of the sale or purchase, forward to the Ministry on the prescribed form a notice of the sale or purchase.

4. Registration number to be kept clean, unobstructed—When a motorized snow vehicle is being driven, the registration number required to be displayed under subsection 2(7) shall be kept free of dirt, snow and ice, in good repair and the view thereof shall not be obscured or obstructed by any part of the motorized snow vehicle or any equipment or attachment thereon or by the load carried thereon.

5(1) **Driving on King's Highway or secondary highway**—Subject to subsection (2), no person shall drive a motorized snow vehicle upon the serviced roadway of the King's Highway or of a secondary highway except to cross.

(2) **Regulations**—The Minister may make regulations designating any part or parts of the King's Highway or a secondary highway,

(a) across the serviced roadway of which no motorized snow vehicle may be driven;

(b) upon which motorized snow vehicles may be driven; or

(c) upon which motorized snow vehicles may not be driven.

6(1) **Duty of driver when school bus stopped on highway**—Every driver of a motorized snow vehicle, when approaching or overtaking on a highway a stopped school bus that has two red signal-lights flashing, shall stop the motorized snow vehicle before reaching the school bus and shall not proceed until the signal-lights are no longer operating.

(2) **Exception to subs. (1)**—Subsection (1) does not apply to a driver of a motorized snow vehicle on a highway with a median strip who is approaching a school bus that is stopped on the other side of the median strip.

7(1) Repealed.

(2) **Local municipality may pass by-laws**—The council of a local municipality may pass by-laws regulating, governing or prohibiting the operation of motorized snow vehicles within the municipality including any highways therein or any part or parts thereof.

(3) **Application of subs. (2)**—Where a by-law is passed under subsection (2), the provisions regulating or governing the operation of motorized snow vehicles under the by-law do not apply to highways or any part or parts thereof that are not under the jurisdiction of the local municipality.

(4) **Upper-tier municipality may pass by-laws**—The council of an upper-tier municipality may pass by-laws regulating and governing the operation of motorized snow vehicles along or across any highway or part of a highway under its jurisdiction.

(5) **Upper-tier municipality may pass prohibiting by-laws**—Where the operation of motorized snow vehicles is not prohibited on a highway under the jurisdiction of an upper-tier municipality by a by-law passed under subsection (4), the council of the municipality may pass by-laws prohibiting the operation of motorized snow vehicles along or across the highway or any part thereof. . . .

8. Crossing roadway—No person shall drive a motorized snow vehicle across a serviced roadway except at an angle of approximately 90 degrees to the direction of the serviced roadway.

9(1) **Driving along highway**—Subject to subsection (2), no person shall drive a motorized snow vehicle along a highway unless,

(a) the person has attained the full age of sixteen years; and

(b) the person holds a driver's licence; or

(c) the person holds a motorized snow vehicle operator's licence; or

(d) the person is a resident of any other province, country or state and holds a licence issued by such province, country or state which authorizes the person to drive a motorized snow vehicle.

(2) **Driving across highway**—No person shall drive a motorized snow vehicle across a highway unless,

(a) the person has attained the full age of sixteen years; and

(b) the person holds a driver's licence, a motorized snow vehicle operator's licence or is a resident of any other province, country or state and holds a licence issued by such province, country or state which authorizes the person to drive a motorized snow vehicle.

(3) **Driving on trails**—No person shall drive a motorized snow vehicle upon a trail unless,

(a) the person has obtained the full age of twelve years; and

(b) the person holds a driver's licence, a motorized snow vehicle operator's licence or is a resident of any other province, country or state and holds a licence issued by such province, country or state which authorizes the person to drive a motorized snow vehicle.

10(1) **Operator's licences**—The Minister may issue a motorized snow vehicle operator's licence to any person who has attained the full age of twelve years and who meets the requirements of this Act and the regulations authorizing the person to drive a motorized snow vehicle, subject to any conditions and for the period of time prescribed by the regulations. . . .

11. Application of certain Acts—The *Highway Traffic Act*, except Part XII, and the *Motor Vehicle Accident Claims Act*, except section 6, do not apply to a motorized snow vehicle or to the driving thereof.

12(1) **Insurance**—No person shall drive a motorized snow vehicle unless the vehicle is insured under a motor vehicle liability policy in accordance with the *Insurance Act*, and

What happens when a person under 12 years of age is found operating a snow vehicle on a trail and does not have a "motorized snow vehicle operator's permit"? Contacting a parent and arranging the parent's attendance are the preferable solution. However, if the parent is not available, s. 42(1) of the *Child and Family Services Act* may be applied. A person over 12 years of age is required to have an MSV operator's licence, and failing to present one is an offence under the Act. Therefore, anyone over 12 could be charged. This requirement gives an officer the legal authority to prevent the unsafe practice from continuing. While such a situation may be rare, it is important for an officer to understand the law and be able to apply its provisions.

the owner of a motorized snow vehicle shall not permit any person to drive the vehicle unless the vehicle is so insured.

(2) **Production of evidence of insurance**—The driver of a motorized snow vehicle who drives or permits the driving of the motorized snow vehicle shall, upon the request of a police officer or conservation officer, produce evidence that the vehicle is insured under a motor vehicle liability policy in accordance with the *Insurance Act*.

(3) **Offence for failure to have insurance**—Every person who contravenes subsection (1) is guilty of an offence and on conviction is liable to a fine of not less than $200 and not more than $1,000.

(4) **Offence for producing false evidence**—Every driver of a motorized snow vehicle who produces false evidence when required to produce evidence under subsection (2) is guilty of an offence and on conviction is liable to a fine of not less than $200 and not more than $1,000.

(5) **Exemption**—This section does not apply to a person driving a motorized snow vehicle on land occupied by the owner of the vehicle.

(6) **Application of Part VI of *Insurance Act***—A motorized snow vehicle shall be deemed to be a motor vehicle for the purposes of Part VI of the *Insurance Act*.

There is no exemption from this requirement on "private land."

13(1) **Duty to report accident**—Every person in charge of a motorized snow vehicle who is directly or indirectly involved in an accident shall, if the accident results in personal injuries or in damage to property apparently exceeding $400, report the accident forthwith to the nearest police officer and furnish the police officer with information in respect of,

(a) the names and addresses of the persons involved;

(b) the date and location of the occurrence; and

(c) the circumstances under which the accident occurred.

(2) **Disposition of report**—A police officer receiving a report of an accident under subsection (1) shall forward the report to the Registrar of Motor Vehicles within ten days of receiving it.

14(1) **Speed limit**—No person shall drive a motorized snow vehicle at a greater rate of speed than,

(a) 20 kilometres per hour,

(i) on a highway where the speed limit established pursuant to the *Highway Traffic Act* is 50 kilometres per hour or less, or

(ii) in any public park or exhibition grounds; or

(b) 50 kilometres per hour,

(i) on any highway which is open to motor vehicle traffic, where the speed limit established pursuant to the *Highway Traffic Act* is greater than 50 kilometres per hour, or

(ii) on a trail.

(2) **Municipality may prescribe different rate of speed**—The council of a municipality may by by-law prescribe,

(a) a lower rate of speed for motorized snow vehicles upon any highway or part thereof under its jurisdiction; and

(b) a higher or lower rate of speed for motorized snow vehicles upon a trail, public park or exhibition ground under its jurisdiction,

than is prescribed in subsection (1).

(3) **Minister may prescribe different rate of speed**—The Minister may by regulation prescribe a higher or lower rate of speed upon any trail or any part thereof, public park or exhibition ground not under the jurisdiction of a municipality, than is prescribed in subsection (1).

(4) **By-law effective**—No by-law passed under subsection (2) or regulation made pursuant to subsection (3) becomes effective until signs are erected in accordance with the regulations.

(5) **Exception**—Speed limits prescribed by this section or any regulation made or by-law passed under this section do not apply to a motorized snow vehicle operated by a police officer or conservation officer in the lawful performance of his or her duties.

15. Careless driving—Every person is guilty of the offence of driving carelessly who drives a motorized snow vehicle without due care and attention or without reasonable consideration for other persons.

16(1) **Driver to carry documents**—Subject to subsection (2), every driver of a motorized snow vehicle shall carry his or her driver's licence or motorized snow vehicle operator's licence and evidence of the motorized snow vehicle's registration at all times while operating a motorized snow vehicle and shall produce them when demanded by a police officer or conservation officer.

(2) **Exception**—A person shall not be required to carry any document referred to in subsection (1) while operating a motorized snow vehicle on lands occupied by the owner of the motorized snow vehicle.

(3) **Driver to identify self**—Every person who is unable or refuses to produce a document in accordance with subsection (1) or (2), when requested by a police officer or conservation officer, shall give his or her correct name and address to the police officer or conservation officer.

(4) **Stopping on request**—Upon the request of the owner or occupier of land upon which a person is operating a motorized snow vehicle, the person operating the motorized snow vehicle shall stop and give his or her correct name and address.

This section authorizes a landowner/agent to stop the driver of a snow vehicle from operating on his or her property, and requires the operator to provide his or her name and address.

(5) **Constable may arrest without warrant**—Every police officer or conservation officer, who, on reasonable and probable grounds, believes that a contravention of subsection (3) or (4) has been committed, may arrest without warrant any person whom the police officer or conservation officer, on reasonable and probable grounds, believes has committed the contravention.

17(1) **Stopping for vehicles with red or red and blue lights**—Every driver of a motorized snow vehicle shall immediately bring the motorized snow vehicle to a standstill for the purpose of complying with section 16 when approached by,

(a) a motorized snow vehicle with a flashing red light;

(b) a motorized snow vehicle with flashing red and blue lights;

(c) a motor vehicle with a flashing red light, operated by a police officer or conservation officer; or

(d) a motor vehicle with flashing red and blue lights, operated by a police officer.

(2) **Where on a roadway**—Where a driver to whom subsection (1) applies is on a roadway, he or she shall bring the vehicle to a standstill as near as is practicable to the right-hand edge of the roadway and clear of any intersection.

(3) **Red light**—No person except a police officer or conservation officer shall operate a motorized snow vehicle that is equipped with a lamp that produces flashes of red light.

(4) **Red and blue lights**—No person except a police officer shall operate a motorized snow vehicle that is equipped with lamps that produce flashes of red and blue lights.

17.1(1) **Power of police officer to stop**—A police officer, in the lawful execution of his or her duties and responsibilities, may require the driver of a motorized snow vehicle to stop and the driver of a motorized snow vehicle, when signalled or requested to stop by a police officer, shall immediately come to a safe stop.

(2) **Offence**—Every person who contravenes subsection (1) is guilty of an offence and on conviction is liable, subject to subsection (3),

(a) to a fine of not less than $1,000 and not more than $10,000;

(b) to imprisonment for a term of not more than six months; or

(c) to both a fine and imprisonment.

(3) **Escape by flight**—If a person is convicted of an offence under subsection (2) and the court is satisfied on the evidence that the person wilfully continued to avoid police when a police officer gave pursuit,

(a) the person is liable to a fine of not less than $5,000 and not more than $25,000, instead of the fine described in clause (2) (a);

(b) the court shall make an order imprisoning the person for a term of not less than 14 days and not more than six months, instead of the term described in clause (2)(b); and

(c) the court shall make an order suspending the person's driver's licence or motorized snow vehicle's operator's licence,

(i) for a period of five years, unless subclause (ii) applies, or

(ii) for a period of not less than 10 years, if the court is satisfied on the evidence that the person's conduct or the pursuit resulted in the death of or bodily harm to any person.

(4) **Lifetime suspension**—An order under subclause (3)(c)(ii) may suspend the person's driver's licence or motorized snow vehicle operator's licence for the remainder of the person's life.

(5) **Suspension in addition**—Except in the case of a suspension for the remainder of the person's life, a suspension of a driver's licence under clause (3)(c) is in addition to any other period for which the person's driver's licence is suspended and is consecutive to that period.

(6) **Notice of suspension**—Subject to subsection (7), in a proceeding for a contravention of subsection (1) in which it is alleged that the person wilfully continued to avoid police when a police officer gave pursuit, the clerk or registrar of the court, before the court accepts the plea of the defendant, shall orally give a notice to the person to the following effect:

> *"The Motorized Snow Vehicles Act provides that upon conviction of the offence with which you are charged, in the circumstances indicated therein, your driver's licence or motorized snow vehicle operator's licence shall be suspended for five years."*

(7) **Same: death or bodily harm**—In a proceeding for a contravention of subsection (1) in which it is alleged that the person wilfully continued to avoid police when a police officer gave pursuit and that the person's conduct or the pursuit resulted in the death of or bodily harm to any person, the clerk or registrar of the court, before the court accepts the plea of the defendant, shall orally give a notice to the person to the following effect:

> *"The Motorized Snow Vehicles Act provides that upon conviction of the offence with which you are charged, in the circumstances indicated therein, your driver's licence or motorized snow vehicle operator's licence shall be suspended for not less than 10 years and that it may be suspended for the remainder of your life."*

(8) **Same**—The suspension of a driver's licence or motorized snow vehicle operator's licence shall not be held to be invalid by reason of failure to give the notice provided for in subsection (6) or (7).

(9) **Appeal of suspension**—An appeal may be taken from an order under clause (3)(c) or a decision to not make the order in the same manner as from a conviction or an acquittal under subsection (2). . . .

Suspension of a driver's licence also prohibits the operation of a snow vehicle.

(11) **Driving while licence suspended**—Every person who drives a motorized snow vehicle while his or her driver's licence is suspended under this section or under any other Act or while his or her motorized snow vehicle operator's licence is suspended under this section is guilty of an offence and on conviction is liable,

(a) for a first offence, to a fine of not less than $1,000 and not more than $5,000; and

(b) for each subsequent offence, to a fine of not less than $2,000 and not more than $5,000,

or to imprisonment for a term of not more than six months, or to both. . . .

18(1) **Muffler in working order**—No person shall drive a motorized snow vehicle unless it is equipped with a muffler in good working order and in constant operation and no person shall drive a motorized snow vehicle which has a muffler cut-out, straight exhaust, gutted muffler, hollywood muffler, by-pass or similar device upon the motorized snow vehicle.

(2) **Removing or modifying any component**—No person shall drive or permit to be driven any motorized snow vehicle upon which any component or device, which was required under the provisions of the *Motor Vehicle Safety Act* (Canada) at the time that the motorized snow vehicle was manufactured or imported into Canada, has been removed, modified or rendered inoperative.

(3) **Exception in racing area**—Subsections (1) and (2) do not apply to a motorized snow vehicle while it is driven in a racing area sanctioned as such by the council of the municipality within which the racing area is located.

19(1) **By means of a rigid tow bar**—No person shall drive a motorized snow vehicle which is towing a cutter, toboggan, sled or similar conveyance except by means of a rigid tow bar.

(2) **On serviced roadway prohibited**—No person shall drive a motorized snow vehicle which is towing a person or conveyance on a serviced roadway except to cross the serviced roadway at an angle of approximately 90 degrees to the direction of the serviced roadway.

(3) **Exception for unditching, etc.**—This section does not apply to a person while driving a motorized snow vehicle for the sole purpose of unditching a stuck vehicle or conveyance or under an emergency rescue situation or while operating trail maintenance equipment.

20(1) **Driver shall wear helmet**—No person shall drive a motorized snow vehicle or ride on a motorized snow vehicle or on a cutter, toboggan, sled or similar conveyance towed by a motorized snow vehicle unless he or she is wearing a helmet that complies with the regulations and the chin strap of the helmet is securely fastened under the chin.

(2) **Exemption**—This section does not apply to a person driving a motorized snow vehicle on land occupied by the owner of the vehicle. . . .

> Requirements concerning documents, helmets, and equipment do not apply to snow vehicles operated on land occupied by the owner of the vehicle. The exemption for passengers does not apply. An administrative oversight, perhaps?

22. **Risks willingly assumed**—Every person who is driving or riding on a motorized snow vehicle or is being towed by a motorized snow vehicle on any premises shall be deemed, for the purposes of subsection 4(1) of the *Occupiers' Liability Act*, to have willingly assumed all risks where,

(a) no fee is paid for the entry or activity of the person, other than a benefit or payment received from a government or government agency or a non-profit recreation club or association; and

(b) the person is not being provided with living accommodation by the occupier.

23(1) **Liability of owner**—Where the driver of a motorized snow vehicle who is not the owner thereof is liable for damages respecting damage or injury arising out of the operation by the driver of the motorized snow vehicle with the consent of the owner, the owner is jointly and severally liable.

> Section 23(1) clearly sets out the liability for damage or injury. Both the owner and operator are liable. In contrast, under s. 11 of the *Trespass to Property Act*, such liability defaults to the operator alone once he or she is identified.

(2) **Idem**—Where a motorized snow vehicle is leased, the consent of the lessee of the motorized snow vehicle to the operation or possession thereof by some person other than the lessee shall, for the purposes of subsection (1), be deemed to be the consent of the owner of the motorized snow vehicle.

The comparison to s. 11 of the *Trespass to Property* Act continues in this section. Logically, if the machine is being operated without the owner's consent, he or she is deemed not to be liable—for example, if the machine were stolen or taken without consent.

24. Owner may be convicted—The owner of a motorized snow vehicle may be charged with and convicted of an offence under this Act or the regulations or any municipal by-law regulating, governing or prohibiting the operation of motorized snow vehicles, for which the driver of the motorized snow vehicle is subject to be charged unless, at the time of the offence, the motorized snow vehicle was in the possession of a person other than the owner without the owner's consent and on conviction the owner is liable to the penalty prescribed for the offence.

25. Offences and fines—Every person who contravenes any of the provisions of this Act or the regulations is guilty of an offence and on conviction where a fine for the contravention is not otherwise provided for herein is liable to a fine not exceeding $1,000.

Regulations . . .

26(2.2) **Classes**—A regulation made under any provision of this Act may create different classes of persons and motorized snow vehicles and may apply differently to each class created.

(3) **Driver shall obey signs**—Every driver of a motorized snow vehicle shall obey the instructions and directions indicated on any sign erected pursuant to regulations made under clause (1)(g).

Ontario Regulation 185/01

Trail Permits

1(1) **Definitions**—For the purpose of section 2.1 of the Act and this Regulation,

"prescribed trail" means a trail or part of a trail on which a trail permit is required by section 2.1 of the Act and that is operated or maintained by or on behalf of the Ontario Federation of Snowmobile Clubs, and includes such a trail or part of a trail that is on Crown land or other public land, but excludes any Crown land or other public land where the operation of motorized snow vehicles is prohibited by law.

(2) In this Regulation,

"immediate family members" means a person's spouse, sibling, father, mother, grandfather, grandmother, son, daughter, grandson, granddaughter, son-in-law, daughter-in-law, father-in-law or mother-in-law;

"spouse" has the same meaning as in Part III of the *Family Law Act*.

2(1) **Signs on prescribed trails**—Prescribed trails shall be identified by signs bearing the letters "OFSC" in letters not less than 4.5 centimetres high and the words "Prescribed Trail" in letters not less than 1 centimetre high that are posted,

(a) not more than 5 kilometres from any point along every prescribed trail; and

(b) at every intersection of prescribed trails with any other trail, highway, railway crossing or other crossing.

(2) The signs shall be retro-reflective and not less than 20 centimetres by 10 centimetres.

(3) A trail or part of a trail is a prescribed trail whether or not the signs described in this section are posted.

3(1) **Trail permits**—A person shall not be issued a trail permit unless the person completes the application in full and pays the fee established by the Minister.

(2) A trail permit is valid until the 31st day of May after the date the permit is issued.

(3) A trail permit shall be affixed to the motorized snow vehicle,

(a) at the bottom edge of the centre of the windshield; or

(b) on top of and to the left of centre of the engine cowling as close as possible to the centre of the windshield, without obscuring or being obscured by the registration number required to be displayed on the vehicle.

4. Exemptions—Subsections 2.1(1) and (4) of the Act do not apply to a person belonging to a class of persons listed in Column 1 of the Table only in the circumstances set out opposite the class in Column 2 of the Table and only if the person carries with him or her while driving the motorized snow vehicle on the prescribed trail the documents listed opposite the class in Column 3 of the Table.

Item	Column 1	Column 2	Column 3
1.	Police officers, emergency workers including ambulance and medical workers, search and rescue workers, firefighters as defined in subsection 1(1) of the *Fire Protection and Prevention Act, 1997*, employees of the Ministry of Natural Resources or the Ministry of Northern Development and Mines, employees of the federal Department of National Defence.	While engaged in duties required by their employer.	Identification issued by their employer.
2.	Aboriginal peoples of Canada.	While on treaty or traditional lands.	None.
3.	(a) Licensed bait harvesters and their designates.	(a) While engaged in bait harvesting within the bait harvest area or while travelling directly to or from the bait harvest area to engage in bait harvesting, if the trail is the only access route from the closest road to the bait harvest area or is the only safe access route to the bait harvest area.	(a) An original or a legible copy of a valid bait harvester licence.
	(b) Licensed bait harvesters' helpers.	(b) While accompanying a licensed bait harvester or designate in the circumstances described in clause (a).	(b) None.
4.	Licensed commercial fish harvesters and their designates.	While engaged in commercial fishing activities within the commercial fishing area or while travelling directly to or from the commercial fishing area to engage in commercial fishing, if the trail is the only access route from the closest road to the commercial fishing area or is the only safe access route to the commercial fishing area.	An original or a legible copy of a valid commercial fishing licence.
5.	Tenants of Crown land and such tenants' immediate family members.	While travelling directly to or from the Crown land, if the trail is the only access route from the closest road to the Crown land or is the only safe access route to the Crown land.	A legible copy of a land use permit, licence of occupation or lease, issued under the *Public Lands Act* or a regulation under that Act.

Item	Column 1	Column 2	Column 3
6.	Forest workers, including the employees or agents of any forest or timber company.	While engaged in forestry activities pursuant to a licence under the *Crown Forest Sustainability Act, 1994* or a private land forest harvesting contract within the location of the forestry operation or while travelling directly to or from the location of the forestry operation, if the trail is the only access route from the closest road to the location of the forestry operation or is the only safe access route to the location of the forestry operation.	A valid forest resource licence or a letter prepared within the previous 240 days by the forest or timber company on stationery bearing the company's letterhead, setting out, (i) the company name, address, phone number and the date on which the letter was prepared, (ii) the name, address and phone number for each contractor or agent working on the operation, (iii) the name of each employee working on operation for both the company and any contractor or agent, (iv) a description of the location of the operation, including the name of any municipality within which the operation is located, and (v) the signature, name, title, address and phone number of the person who prepared the letter.
7.	Landowners, their tenants and the immediate family members of landowners and of their tenants.	While travelling directly to or from the property owned by the landowner, if the trail is the only access route from the closest road to the property or is the only safe access route to the property.	Proof of ownership of or title to the property that is a government form, deed, registry or other document of land transfer, or in the case of tenancy, a copy of the lease for the property if one exists or a letter from the landowner prepared within the previous 240 days identifying the property by its municipal description and address and identifying the owner and the tenant by name, address and phone number.
8.	The immediate family members of the owners of land on which there is a prescribed trail and the guests of such landowners and of their immediate family members.	While on the trail on the owned property.	None.

Item	Column 1	Column 2	Column 3
9.	(a) Licensed trappers.	While engaged in trapping activities within the trapping area, or while travelling directly to or from the trapping area, if the trail is the only access route from the closest road to the trapping area or is the only safe access route to the trapping area.	(a) An original valid trapper's licence and either a registered trapline map issued by the Ministry of Natural Resources or a description of the resident trapline area, including its municipal location, lot number and size.
	(b) Licensed trappers' helpers.		(b) An original valid trapper's licence or a legible copy of it and either a registered trapline map issued by the Ministry of Natural Resources or a description of the resident trapline area, including its municipal location, lot number and size.
10.	Workers for utility companies including telephone, cable, hydro-electric, gas or other pipeline companies or service providers, and their contractors.	While engaged in activities pursuant to employment at the location of the installation, or when travelling directly to or from the location of the installation, if the trail is the only access route from the closest road to the location of the installation or is the only safe access route to the location of the installation.	A copy of the contract or work order, if any, or a letter prepared within the previous 240 days from the utility company, on stationery bearing the company's letterhead, setting out, (i) the company name, address and phone number and the date on which the letter was prepared, (ii) the name, address and phone number of each contractor working on the project, (iii) the name and employee identification number, if any, for each employee working on the project for both the company and the contractor, (iv) the description of the location of the project, including the name of any municipality within which the project is located, and (v) the signature, name, title, address and phone number of the person who prepared the letter.

Item	Column 1	Column 2	Column 3
11.	(a) Licensed prospectors and their helpers 18 years old or older.	While staking or working claims within a claim area, or while travelling directly to or from a claim area, if the trail is the only access route from the closest road to the claim area or is the only safe access route to the claim area. While working for a mining or exploration company, a contractor or field service supplier, within a claim area, or while travelling directly to or from a claim area, if the trail is the only access route from the closest road to the claim area or is the only safe access route to the claim area.	(a) An original valid prospectors licence or a legible copy of it and either, (i) mining claim tags, or (ii) a claim map or a legible copy of a claim map, showing the property or part of the property on which the trail is situate and a claim abstract or a legible copy of a claim abstract for the claim area.
	(b) Licensed prospectors' helpers, under the age of 18, accompanying a licensed prospector.		(b) None.
12.	Employees of a mining or exploration company, and the employees of any contractor, driller, claim staker, land surveyor or geotechnical surveyor that is engaged by such a company, or any field service supplier of any of these persons.	Within the mining or exploration project area or while travelling directly to or from the project area, if the trail is the only access route from the closest road to the project area or is the only safe access route to the project area.	A valid trail permit exemption form issued by the Ministry of Northern Development and Mines or a letter prepared within the previous 240 days on stationery bearing the mining or exploration company's letterhead, setting out, (i) the company name, address and phone number and the date on which the letter was prepared, (ii) the contractor name, address and phone number for each contractor working on the project, (iii) the name and employee identification number, if any, for each employee working on project for both the company and the contractor, (iv) the description of the location of the project, including the name of any municipality within which the project is located, and (v) the signature, name, title, address and phone number of the person who prepared the letter.

Item	Column 1	Column 2	Column 3
13.	(a) Licensed anglers.	While engaged in angling activities during open season, as defined in the Ontario Fishery Regulations made under the *Fisheries Act* (Canada), pursuant to a valid fishing or fishing/hunting outdoors card and a valid sport fishing validation tag, both issued under the *Fish and Wildlife Conservation Act, 1997*, and while travelling on Crown or other public land directly to or from the area open for angling, within the meaning of the *Fisheries Act* (Canada), if the trail is the only access route from the closest road to the area open for angling or is the only safe access route to the area open for angling.	(a) A valid fishing or fishing/hunting outdoors card and a valid sport fishing validation tag, both issued under the *Fish and Wildlife Conservation Act, 1997*.
	(b) Anglers 65 years old or older or under 18 years old.		(b) A valid fishing or fishing/hunting outdoors card issued under the *Fish and Wildlife Conservation Act, 1997* or, (i) a driver's licence, (ii) a motorized snow vehicle operator's licence, or (iii) a birth certificate.
14.	Licensed hunters.	While engaged in hunting activities and carrying hunting equipment on land other than the trail, during open season, as defined in the *Fish and Wildlife Conservation Act, 1997*, pursuant to a valid outdoors card and a valid licence to hunt, both issued under that Act, and while travelling on Crown or other public land directly to or from the hunting area and carrying hunting equipment, if the trail is the only access route from the closest road to the hunting area or is the only safe access route to the hunting area.	A valid outdoors card and a valid licence to hunt, both issued under the *Fish and Wildlife Conservation Act, 1997*.

RRO 1990, Regulation 803

Designations

[For a complete list and description of highways that restrict or allow snow vehicle operation, refer to Reg. 803 either electronically (e-Laws—Ontario) or in hard copy through the Queen's Printer, Toronto.]

RRO 1990, Regulation 804

General

1. In this Regulation,

"roadway" means roadway as defined in the *Highway Traffic Act*;

"vehicle" means a vehicle as defined in the *Highway Traffic Act*.

2. Where, in order to,

(a) ensure orderly movement of traffic;

(b) prevent injury or damage to persons or property; or

(c) permit proper action in an emergency,

a conservation officer or police officer, who considers it necessary to take control of the situation and direct traffic, may do so and, despite this Regulation, every driver of a motorized snow vehicle who is in a position to obey his or her directions shall do so.

3. A driver of a motorized snow vehicle approaching an intersection shall yield the right of way to a vehicle or motorized snow vehicle that has entered the intersection from a different highway and when a motorized snow vehicle and vehicle or motorized snow vehicle enter an intersection from different highways at approximately the same time the driver on the left shall yield the right of way to the vehicle or motorized snow vehicle on the right.

4. Every driver of a motorized snow vehicle shall obey the instructions or directions indicated on any official sign as defined in the *Highway Traffic Act*.

5(1) Except as provided in sections 3 and 9, the driver of a motorized snow vehicle about to enter or cross a roadway from property adjoining the roadway shall,

(a) bring the motorized snow vehicle to a complete stop; and

(b) upon entering the roadway yield the right of way to all oncoming traffic that constitutes a hazard..

(2) The driver referred to in subsection (1) shall enter or cross at an angle of approximately 90 degrees to the direction of the roadway.

6(1) The driver of a motorized snow vehicle intending to turn to the right into an intersecting highway shall approach the intersection and turn as closely as practicable to the right curb or edge of the roadway.

(2) The driver of a motorized snow vehicle within an intersection intending to turn to the left across the path of any vehicle or motorized snow vehicle approaching from the opposite direction shall not make the left turn until he or she has afforded a reasonable opportunity to the driver of the other vehicle or motorized snow vehicle to avoid a collision.

(3) The driver of a motorized snow vehicle intending to turn to the left into an intersecting highway at an intersection where traffic is permitted to move in both directions on each highway entering the intersection shall approach the intersection as closely as practicable to the centre line of the highway and the left turn shall be made by passing to the right of the centre line where it enters the intersection, and upon leaving the intersection by passing to the right of the centre line of the highway then entered.

(4) The driver of a motorized snow vehicle intending to turn to the left from a highway designated for use of one-way traffic into an intersecting highway on which traffic is permitted to move in both directions shall approach the intersection as closely as practi-

cable to the left curb or edge of the roadway and on entering the intersection shall pass to the right of and as closely as practicable to the centre line of the highway being entered where it enters the intersection.

(5) The driver of a motorized snow vehicle intending to turn to the left from a highway on which traffic is permitted to move in both directions into an intersecting highway designated for the use of one-way traffic shall approach the intersection as closely as practicable to the centre line of the highway and on entering the intersection the left turn shall be made by passing as closely as practicable to the left hand curb or edge of the roadway designated for the use of one-way traffic.

(6) The driver of a motorized snow vehicle intending to turn to the left from a highway designated for use of one-way traffic into an intersecting highway designated for use of one-way traffic shall approach the intersection as closely as practicable to the left-hand curb or edge of the roadway and on entering the intersection the left turn shall be made by passing as closely as practicable to the left-hand curb or edge of the roadway being entered.

7(1) The driver of a motorized snow vehicle upon a highway before turning to the left or right at any intersection or into a private road or driveway or from one lane for traffic to another lane for traffic or to leave the roadway shall first see that the movement can be made in safety, and if the operation of any other vehicle or motorized snow vehicle may be affected by the movement shall give a signal plainly visible to the driver of the other vehicle or motorized snow vehicle of the intention to make the movement.

(2) The driver of a motorized snow vehicle parked or stopped on the highway before setting the motorized snow vehicle in motion shall first see that the movement can be made in safety, and, if in turning the motorized snow vehicle the operation of any other vehicle or motorized snow vehicle may be affected by the movement, shall give a signal plainly visible to the driver of the other vehicle or motorized snow vehicle of the intention to make the movement.

(3) The signal referred to in subsections (1) and (2) shall be given by means of the hand and arm and the driver shall indicate his or her intention to turn,

(a) to the left, by extending the hand and arm horizontally and beyond the left side of the vehicle; or

(b) to the right, by extending the hand and arm upward and beyond the left side of the vehicle.

(4) The driver of a motorized snow vehicle upon a highway before stopping or suddenly decreasing the speed of the motorized snow vehicle, if the operation of any other vehicle or motorized snow vehicle may be affected by the stopping or decreasing of speed, shall give a signal,

(a) plainly visible to the driver of the other vehicle or motorized snow vehicle of the intention to stop or decrease speed; and

(b) by means of the right hand and arm extended straight upward.

8. No driver of a motorized snow vehicle upon a highway shall turn the motorized snow vehicle so as to proceed in the opposite direction when,

(a) upon a curve where traffic approaching the motorized snow vehicle from either direction cannot be seen by the driver of the motorized snow vehicle within a distance of 150 metres;

(b) on a railway crossing or within 30 metres of a railway crossing;

(c) upon an approach to or near the crest of a grade where the motorized snow vehicle cannot be seen by the driver of another vehicle or motorized snow vehicle approaching from either direction within 150 metres; or

(d) within 150 metres of a bridge, viaduct or tunnel where the driver's view is obstructed within that distance.

9. Every driver of a motorized snow vehicle shall obey the requirements set out in sections 144 and 146 of the *Highway Traffic Act* with respect to an indication of a traffic control signal system or a portable lane control signal system.

10(1) Where a driver of a motorized snow vehicle on a highway meets another vehicle or motorized snow vehicle, he or she shall turn out to the right from the centre of the roadway, allowing to the vehicle or motorized snow vehicle so met one-half of the roadway free.

(2) No driver of a motorized snow vehicle shall pass or attempt to pass another vehicle or motorized snow vehicle going in the same direction on a highway unless the roadway,

(a) in front of and to the left of the vehicle or motorized snow vehicle to be passed is safely free from approaching traffic; and

(b) to the left of the motorized snow vehicle passing or attempting to pass is safely free from overtaking traffic.

11. No motorized snow vehicle shall be driven to the left of the centre of a roadway designed for one or more lines of traffic in each direction, when approaching the crest of a grade or upon a curve in the roadway or within thirty metres of a bridge, viaduct or tunnel where the driver's view is obstructed within that distance as to create a hazard in the event another vehicle or motorized snow vehicle might approach from the opposite direction, but this section does not apply to a highway designated for the use of one-way traffic or to a highway divided into clearly marked lanes where there are more lanes for traffic in one direction than in the other direction.

12(1) Subject to subsection (2), the driver of a motorized snow vehicle may overtake and pass to the right of another vehicle or motorized snow vehicle on a highway only,

(a) when the vehicle or motorized snow vehicle overtaken is making or about to make a left turn or its driver has signalled his or her intention to make a left turn;

(b) upon a highway with unobstructed pavement of sufficient width for two or more lines of vehicles or motorized snow vehicles in each direction; or

(c) upon a highway designed for the use of one-way traffic only.

(2) The driver of a motorized snow vehicle shall not overtake and pass to the right of another vehicle or motorized snow vehicle where the movement cannot be made in safety.

13. The driver of a motorized snow vehicle shall not follow another vehicle or motorized snow vehicle more closely than is reasonable and prudent having due regard for the speed of the vehicle or motorized snow vehicle and the traffic on and the conditions of the highway.

14(1) When the driver of a motorized snow vehicle is approaching a railway, he or she shall stop the motorized snow vehicle and shall not proceed to cross until he or she can do so safely.

(2) The driver referred to in subsection (1) shall enter or cross at an angle of approximately 90 degrees to the direction of the railway.

15(1) No person shall park, stand or stop a motorized snow vehicle on a roadway,

(a) when it is practicable to park, stand or stop the motorized snow vehicle off the roadway; or

(b) when it is not practicable to park, stand or stop the motorized snow vehicle off the roadway unless a clear view of the motorized snow vehicle and of the roadway for at least 125 metres beyond the motorized snow vehicle may be obtained from a distance of at least 125 metres from the motorized snow vehicle in each direction upon the highway.

(2) Subsection (1) does not apply to a roadway within a city, town or village, and the provisions of subsection (1) with respect to parking, standing or stopping do not apply to a portion of a roadway in respect of which a by-law passed by the council of a township or county or by the trustees of a police village prohibiting or regulating parking, standing or stopping on the roadway, as the case may be, is in force.

(3) Where a police officer finds a motorized snow vehicle on a highway in contravention of the provisions of this section, he or she may move the motorized snow vehicle or require the driver or other person in charge of the motorized snow vehicle to move it.

(4) Despite this section, no person shall park or stand a motorized snow vehicle on a highway in such a manner as to interfere with the movement of traffic or the clearing of snow from the highway.

(5) A police officer upon discovery of any motorized snow vehicle parked or standing in contravention of subsection (4) or of a municipal by-law, may cause it to be moved or taken to and placed or stored in a suitable place and all costs and charges for removing, care and storage of it, if any, are a lien upon the motorized snow vehicle, which may be enforced in the manner provided the *Repair and Storage Liens Act.*

16. Subject to section 4, no person shall operate a motorized snow vehicle at a speed greater than is reasonable and prudent under conditions then existing.

17(1) This section applies to every motorized snow vehicle in operation,

(a) at any time from one-half hour before sunset to one-half hour after sunrise; or

(b) when, because of insufficient light or unfavourable atmospheric conditions, persons and vehicles are not clearly visible at a distance of up to 150 metres.

(2) Every vehicle to which this section applies must have,

(a) at least one head lamp on the front of the vehicle showing a white or amber light only; and

(b) one tail lamp on the rear of the vehicle showing a red light only.

(3) Every lamp required by subsection (2) must be clearly visible at a distance of at least 150 metres from the front or rear of the vehicle, as the case may be.

17.1 Every motorized snow vehicle must, at all times, have one working head lamp and one working tail lamp capable of complying with the requirements of section 17.

17.2(1) Every cutter, toboggan, sled or similar conveyance towed by a motorized snow vehicle must have,

(a) one yellow reflex reflector on each side at the front;

(b) one red reflex reflector on each side at the rear; and

(c) one or two red reflex reflectors on the rear.

(2) The reflex reflectors required by subsection (1) must comply with the Society of Automotive Engineers Standard J594May89, Reflex Reflectors.

18(1) A permit for a motorized snow vehicle must be validated each year.

(2) A permit is not valid unless it is properly affixed to the Registration Certificate for the motorized snow vehicle.

(3) A valid permit ceases to be valid when the expiry date shown on the permit has passed, the motorized snow vehicle is transferred or the permit is surrendered to the Ministry or replaced by a permit issued by another jurisdiction.

19(1) In this section,

"new motorized snow vehicle" includes a used vehicle with no previous registration in Ontario;

"resident of Northern Ontario" means a person, other than a corporation, who ordinarily resides in the Territorial District of Algoma, Cochrane, Kenora, Manitoulin, Nipissing, Parry Sound, Rainy River, Sudbury, Timiskaming or Thunder Bay.

(2) The following fees shall be paid to the Ministry:

1.	For the registration of a new motorized snow vehicle	$30
2.	For an annual validation device for a motorized snow vehicle permit	15
3.	For the transfer of a motorized snow vehicle permit	6
4.	For a replacement permit and set of adhesive devices in case of loss or destruction	10
5.	For a copy of any writing, paper or document filed in the Ministry, other than an accident report, or any statement containing information from the records	6
6.	For a copy of an accident report	12
7.	For certification of a copy of any writing, paper or document filed in the Ministry or any statement containing information from the records	6
8.	For each search of motorized snow vehicle records by registration number, vehicle identification number or name or identification number of the registered owner or permit holder	12

(3) Despite subsection (2), no fee is payable for the following:

1. The registration of a new motorized snow vehicle that is to be driven only on lands owned or occupied by the vehicle owner.
2. An annual validation device for a motorized snow vehicle permit if the permit holder is a resident of Northern Ontario.
3. The registration of a new motorized snow vehicle or an annual validation device if the permit holder is an aboriginal person and the vehicle is to be driven only on reserve land.
4. The issue or transfer of a permit or the issue or replacement of a validation device for a motorized snow vehicle owned or leased by the Government of Ontario.

20. The helmet worn by a person who drives a motorized snow vehicle or rides on a motorized snow vehicle or on a cutter, toboggan, sled or similar conveyance towed by a motorized snow vehicle must comply with the standards set out in the regulations made under the *Highway Traffic Act* for helmets used while riding or operating a motorcycle or motor assisted bicycle.

21. Persons in a motorized snow vehicle commonly known as an enclosed personnel carrier are designated a class of persons to whom subsection 20 (1) of the Act does not apply.

22. Upon the registration of a motorized snow vehicle, the Ministry or a person authorized by the Minister shall issue a Registration Certificate bearing the registration number of the motorized snow vehicle.

23(1) The registration number of the motorized snow vehicle shall be,

(a) affixed to both sides of the cowling on decals provided by the Ministry; or

(b) painted on, or affixed to, both sides of the cowling as prescribed in subsection (4).

(2) Decals with a registration number displayed in accordance with clause (1)(a) shall be not less than 10 centimetres and not more than 15 centimetres from the rear of the cowling.

(3) Despite subsection (2), if the design of the motorized snow vehicle makes it impracticable to affix the decals in accordance with that subsection, the decals may be affixed to each side of the tunnel of the vehicle next to or as near as possible to the forward edge of the reflector light.

(4) A registration number displayed in accordance with clause (1)(b) shall,

(a) be painted on, or affixed to, both sides of the cowling with the rear limit of the number being not less than 10 centimetres and not more than 15 centimetres from the rear of the cowling;

(b) be in a colour that contrasts with its background;

(c) be not less than five centimetres and not more than 7.6 centimetres high;

(d) have a stroke width of not less than five millimetres and not more than 13 millimetres;

(e) have digits of uniform style and height; and

(f) where practicable, have the digits separated by spaces that are not more than five centimetres wide.

24(1) If a validation device is issued, its adhesive part must be affixed so that,

(a) for a registration number displayed in accordance with clause 23(1)(a), the adhesive part of the device is on the upper right hand corner of the decal that is on the left side of the motorized snow vehicle; or

(b) for a registration number displayed in accordance with clause 23(1)(b), the adhesive part of the device is to the left side of the cowling of the vehicle between the registration number and the rear of the cowling.

(2) For a validation device issued after June 1, 1997 for a registration number displayed in accordance with clause 23(1)(b), the adhesive part of the device must be affixed to the centre of an area of white background that forms a border of at least one centimetre in width surrounding the adhesive part of the validation device.

25. Revoked.

26. Subsection 19(2) of the Act does not apply to a driver of a motorized snow vehicle which is towing a conveyance on a serviced roadway within the areas designated in Schedule 1 if two red reflectors,

(a) are securely attached to the back of the conveyance;

(b) are located as far apart as practicable and are at the same height; and

(c) are positioned so as to reflect the light from the headlights of a vehicle approaching from the rear.

SCHEDULE 1

1. Those areas in the districts of Kenora and Thunder Bay north of the railway tracks of the Canadian National Railways passing through the municipalities of Malachi, Minaki, Quibell, Sioux Lookout, Savant Lake, Armstrong and Nakina.

2. Those areas in the Territorial District of Cochrane north of 50 degrees latitude.

3. Those areas in the Territorial District of Algoma north of the railway tracks of the Canadian Pacific Limited passing through the municipalities of Amyot, Franz and Missanabie.

4. Those areas in the territorial districts of Rainy River, Kenora, Thunder Bay, Cochrane, Algoma and Sudbury that are not within a city, town, village or police village and not within eight kilometres of a highway designated as a King's Highway or secondary highway under the *Public Transportation and Highway Improvement Act*.

ASSIGNMENT 1: MOTORIZED SNOW VEHICLES ACT

1. Define a snow machine.

2. What requirements must be met by a snow machine and the operator before it can be used on

   a. an approved trail?

   b. a highway?

   c. private property owned by the owner of the snow machine?

3. Describe how the registration for a snow machine must be displayed.

4. What is the maximum speed a snow vehicle can legally travel on a trail?

5. When can an operator of a snow machine cross a highway without a driver's licence?

6. If a driver's licence is suspended, can he or she still operate a snow machine anywhere? Explain.

7. When must the operator of a snow vehicle come to a stop?

ASSIGNMENT 2: MOTORIZED SNOW VEHICLES ACT

You are a police officer in cottage country, assigned to a spot check at a level crossing of a snow vehicle trail and a secondary road. During the previous snow vehicle season, many complaints were received from local snowmobile clubs concerning cottagers using the trails without trail passes or proper equipment. This is the first weekend after a major snowfall and the trails are open. This snow vehicle spot check is a concerted effort that involves local trail wardens, conservation officers, and police.

First Stop

Two vehicles operated by local men are the first to be stopped as they exit the bush on a trail sanctioned by the Ontario Federation of Snowmobile Clubs.

1. What documents will you ask them to produce?

2. What stickers or markings must be found on each machine and where must they be located?

Second Stop

Three other machines exit the bush from an area near your location. They climb the snowbank and proceed to travel along the shoulder of the road facing oncoming traffic. You wave them over to your location and speak to them. When asked where they are going, they say that they had been on the trail and left it about a quarter of a kilometre earlier. They then went cross-country until they came out to the road. They wanted to rejoin the trail, so they were travelling on the road until they could find their way to the trail crossing. Is there a problem with their actions? Describe and provide citation(s).

Third Stop

A single machine crosses the road from the other side. As it nears your location, a club member says he has seen this machine on the trail before and the operator does not have a trail sticker. The member insists this operator should not be allowed to proceed onto the trail. After speaking with the operator, you make a couple of observations:

1. The member is correct—the machine does not have a trail sticker.
2. Instead of a snowmobile suit, the operator is wearing a wool parka and pants. His MSV is carrying a packsack, an ice chisel, and animal traps. The operator says he is a new trapper in the area, licensed by the Ministry of Natural Resources, and that the area of the river where he wants to trap is only accessible this early in the season by crossing the bridge on this trail. He further provides his provincial trapping licence.

How would you assess this complaint? Explain.

Fourth Stop

A single machine comes to the edge of the road on the trail. It is carrying a driver and passenger, both young people. They are towing a toboggan carrying two more young people. The toboggan is attached to the machine by a rope affixed to the rear rail, and the two youths on the toboggan are not wearing helmets. What is your assessment of this situation and what do you propose to do?

Fifth Stop

You become aware that another machine is approaching you along the trail. The snowmobile is extremely loud, suggesting there are problems with the muffler. Once you catch sight of the vehicle, you estimate that it is travelling at about 80 to 90 km/h—an extremely high speed. You signal for the machine to stop and the operator complies. As he slows down, you observe him removing something from his outer pocket and placing it inside his jacket.

The driver is able to produce the documents you request, but you detect the odour of alcohol on his breath. You ask the operator whether he has been drinking and he replies "yes." You also ask him whether he has liquor in his possession and he replies "yes," producing a "mickey" of whisky from inside his jacket. The bottle is about one-third empty.

Describe the problems with this situation and cite what offences have been committed under the MSVA and under the *Liquor Licence Act*.

Sixth Stop

A group of snow vehicles approach and stop. The operators are from Michigan and are visiting a cottage in the area. One member of the party is an Ontario resident who is operating one of the Michigan-registered vehicles. None of the machines has a trail pass from the Ontario Federation of Snowmobile Clubs. On checking documents, you find that the Ontario resident has a suspended Ontario driver's licence. The suspension, which was issued for unpaid fines, is confirmed as valid.

How would you follow through with this investigation?

Seventh Stop

A group of MSVs arrive at your crossing and are waiting to proceed across the road. The operator of one of the machines in the back of the group yells to you. He wants you to stop the Ski-Doo now approaching your location because the operator was trespassing on his property. You wave the Ski-Doo operator out of the line and speak to him while awaiting the arrival of the complainant.

The complainant identifies himself as a local landowner who allows members of the club to pass over his land as part of the trail. His land is a raspberry farm and he allows the machines to travel on a clearly marked trail along the edge of his raspberry field. He alleges that the Ski-Doo operator broke off the trail, accelerated rapidly, and cut a course through his raspberry canes, destroying many of them. He happened to be near his outbuildings at the time and saw what was happening. He mounted his own machine and sped toward this driver with his arm outstretched and palm up. The driver turned away and sped across the field, back onto the trail, where the owner followed him until arriving at this point.

The Ski-Doo operator has all of his required documents, including a trail sticker and an ownership document indicating that the vehicle is owned by his father.

1. Describe what offences are alleged to have occurred.

2. Who will be liable for the damages to the raspberry crop?

3. Can the driver be charged with trespassing? Explain.

CHAPTER 12

Off-Road Vehicles Act

INTRODUCTION

The primary tier associated with the *Off-Road Vehicles Act* is enforcement, in three areas: the permits/licences required to operate an all-terrain vehicle, or ATV; the places where such machines may be operated; and the equipment required to operate them lawfully.

The *Off-Road Vehicles Act* (ORVA) establishes rules for the operation of vehicles commonly referred to as ATVs. The popularity and versatility of these machines are the result of two distinct designs. The first, which is operated on all terrains, has three or more wheels, and the driver straddles the seat and steers using handlebars. The second, also operated on all terrains, has a utility function, allowing it to transport cargo, and a bench seat, and is capable of carrying a passenger. The ORVA regulates only the first type of vehicle.

The operation of these vehicles is regulated according to where they are driven. The ORVA is supplemented by Ontario Regulation 863. The Act addresses the recreational use of ATVs on Crown land and on land with trails that are organized by the Ontario Federation of All Terrain Vehicle Clubs (OFATV), which represents ATV enthusiasts. The ORVA does not cover the operation of ATVs on owner-occupied property.

The most restrictive regulation of ATVs applies to provincial and municipal highways. It is in this application that the *Highway Traffic Act* (HTA) is recognized through Reg. 316/03. This regulation controls when ATVs may be operated on or across highway property, operator licences, equipment permits, and rules of the road.

Because an ATV is capable of travelling over a variety of terrains, certain restrictions for use on highways and operator obligations to landowners are incorporated into the Act. As with motorized snow vehicles, the owner/lessee and the operator are held jointly liable for damage caused by the operation of an off-road vehicle (ORVA, s. 12(1)), unless the vehicle was being operated without the owner's consent (ORVA, s. 14(2)).

ATV trails are not as extensive as those used by motorized snow vehicles. Unlike legislation governing snow vehicles, the ORVA does not regulate trail permits and special youth operator permits.

The legislation addresses damage to the environment caused by ATVs (Reg. 316/03, s. 23). Because ATVs can be used on terrain that is not frozen, forest lands can be damaged, taking several years to repair. Section 23 of the regulation is designed to protect sensitive environmental areas, both on land and in water.

The fine system falls within the ORVA, not the *Provincial Offences Act* (POA). There is no organized schedule of offences and corresponding fines, as in many other pieces of legislation. Instead, each section of the Act deals with a violation and sets fine parameters. Certain contraventions of the law, such as impaired operation of an ATV, may result in a driver's licence suspension. The ATV is classified as a motor vehicle under the *Criminal Code*. Therefore, impaired operation of an ATV results in a suspension, just as it would for driving a car or other motor vehicle while impaired.

Both landowners and law enforcement officers have the authority to stop an ATV. Officers have the authority to make an arrest under the Act, and operators who refuse to stop or initiate a chase are subject to penalties and fines.

TERMINOLOGY

All-Terrain Vehicle (ATV)

An ATV is an off-road vehicle designed for use on all terrains. It has four wheels; steering handlebars; a seat that is straddled by the driver or that can carry a driver only and no passengers; and meets the requirements of the federal *Motor Vehicle Safety Act*. Mini bikes, dirt bikes, and moto-cross bikes are not off-road vehicles.

Contract Lands

Contract lands are owned both privately and by the Crown, where specific use has been contracted by an organization such as the OFATV.

Dune Buggy

A dune buggy is a self-propelled vehicle with four or more wheels that has been manufactured or modified for off-road use but does not include an amphibious vehicle with six or more wheels.

Occupier

An occupier is a person who is in physical possession of the land, or a person who is responsible for and has control over the land or the activities that take place on the land, or has control over those allowed to enter upon the land.

Off-Road Vehicle

An off-road vehicle is not propelled or driven by muscular power or wind, and is designed to travel on no more than three wheels, or on more than three wheels and is a prescribed class of vehicle.

Peace Officer

A peace officer can be a police officer, a conservation officer, or someone who is employed to preserve and maintain the public peace, or any officer appointed for enforcing the provisions of the ORVA.

COMMON OFFENCES AND/OR PROVISIONS

ORVA offences are similar to snow vehicle and motor vehicle offences, with some distinct differences.

Permit/Licence Offences

1. It is an offence to drive or allow an ATV to be driven without a permit unless on land owned by the ATV owner. A permit must be displayed as prescribed by regulation and the ATV plate number must be unobstructed (ORVA, s. 5; Reg. 316/03, s. 16).
2. Operators who wish to drive an ATV along a highway or across a highway must be 16 years of age and possess either a valid Ontario driver's licence (G, G2) or a motorcycle operator's licence (M, M2) (Reg. 316/03, s. 18).
3. No owner of an ATV may permit a child under 12 to drive the vehicle, unless on land occupied by the ATV owner or under the close supervision of an adult (ORVA, s. 4).
4. Relevant permits should be carried when operating an ATV and it is an offence to fail to produce a permit on request (Reg. 863, s. 8).
5. All ATVs must be registered each time the machine is sold. The time period for registration is within six days after the sale. A change of address of the owner is also required. The new owner must obtain his or her own plate (ORVA, ss. 7 and 8).
6. On the sale of an ATV, the vendor removes the plate and keeps it for use on a new, similar machine, which must be re-registered on purchase (ORVA, s. 8).
7. Any change of address by the owner must be reported within six days (ORVA, s. 6).

Location Offences

This Act deals with the operation of an ATV in three settings. As with snow vehicles, private and Crown lands are considered. There are, however, fewer organized trails and contract lands for ATVs than for snow vehicles.

1. In some situations, the Ontario Federation of All Terrain Vehicle Clubs has developed its own trail system, and the use of these trails requires federation membership. Limited shared use with the Ontario Federation of Snowmobile Clubs is available and must be identified by the landowner or agency having authority to do so. An example of this relationship is the "rail trail" system in Ontario. Some trails may be

approved for multi-seasonal use, but consideration for ice crossing and crop planting may prohibit ATV access.

2. Essentially, the restrictions imposed on the operator of an ATV on public land do not apply on private land when the owner of the vehicle is also the owner of the land. This exemption applies to production of permits (ORVA, s. 3(3)), helmet use (ORVA, s. 19), and vehicle insurance (ORVA, s. 15(9)).
3. Generally, ATVs are not allowed on highways (Reg. 316/03, s. 2). However, travel on Crown land contained within the definition of a highway may be allowed (Reg. 316/03, s. 29(1)).

   Under the ORVA, ATVs are not allowed on the travelled portion of the road or on the shoulder unless safe operation or common sense makes this necessary. Land beyond the maintained shoulder may be used by an ATV.

   Under Reg. 316/03 of the HTA, all of the requirements for a motor vehicle—for example, driver's licence, insurance, registration, and helmet (Reg. 316/03, s. 24)—must be met to operate an ATV on highways where ATV use is permitted (Schedule B highways).

   Where lands, roadways, and portions of a highway fall within a municipal boundary, the council of that municipality may permit, restrict, or prohibit ATV travel (HTA, s. 191.8(3)).

Equipment Offences

The following applies only to ATVs operated on or across a highway:

1. A headlight and tail light are required on an ATV with the same restrictions as a motor vehicle—that is, with a white light to the front and a red to the rear. These lamps must be operated whenever an ATV is on the highway (Reg. 316/03, ss. 13(1) and (2)).
2. Helmets, securely fastened under the chin, are required for all operators and passengers—whether on an ATV or on a towed conveyance (ORVA, s. 19(1); Reg. 316/03, s. 19).
3. All tires used on an ATV must be low-pressure bearing (Reg. 316/03, s. 8).
4. An operator of an ATV must have an unobstructed view (ORVA, s. 15).

Insurance Offences

1. It is an offence to drive an ATV or allow an ATV to be driven unless the vehicle is insured under a motor vehicle liability policy (ORVA, s. 15; Reg. 316/03, s. 17).
2. It is an offence to fail to produce evidence of such insurance on request by a law enforcement officer (police or conservation officer) (ORVA, s. 15(3)).

Driving and Speeding Offences

Operators of ATVs are bound by obligations similar to those of motor vehicle operators.

1. The ATV driver must stop when signalled by a law enforcement officer (police or conservation officer) or a landowner (ORVA, s. 17).
2. The driver of an ATV that is approached by a vehicle displaying a flashing red or combination of red and blue lights must immediately stop the ATV (ORVA, s. 18(1)).
3. The driver must produce required documents upon demand—a licence (Reg. 316/03, s. 18), permit (ORVA, s. 3(2)), and proof of insurance (ORVA, s. 15(3)).
4. Rules of operation or "rules of the road" must be obeyed. They include signalling when stopping or changing direction, and obeying regulatory signs such as stop signs, speed signs, and passing requirements (Reg. 316/03, s. 24).
5. Because there is no specific designation in the ORVA for accident reporting, HTA provisions apply—damage in excess of $1,000 or any personal injury must be reported (HTA, s. 199(1); Reg. 316/03, s. 20).
6. It is an offence to drive an ATV faster than 20 km/h on a highway where the posted speed limit is less than 50 km/h, or faster than 50 km/h on a highway where the posted limit is greater than 50 km/h (Reg. 316/03, s. 22).

Environmental Offence

It is an offence to operate an ATV in a way that disrupts or destroys the natural environment, including fish habitats, property, and flora and fauna (ORVA, s. 23).

FINES

Insurance

Owners who fail to insure their vehicles are liable to a fine of between $200 and $1,000 (ORVA, s. 15(7)). Fines for owners who fail to produce proof of insurance or produce false proof are also between $200 and $1,000 (ORVA, s. 15(8)).

False Statements

Anyone who knowingly makes a false statement with regard to the paperwork (for example, applications and permits) required under the Act is liable to a fine of between $100 and $500 or to a maximum jail term of 30 days, or both (ORVA, s. 6(1)).

General

Where a specific fine is not provided, a general fine of $300 is levied on anyone who is convicted of contravening the ORVA.

When an ATV is operated on a highway, HTA fines apply (Reg. 316/03, s. 20). Demerit points incurred as a result of ATV operation also affect the operator's driver's licence record.

LIABILITY

The owner/lessee of an ATV is jointly liable with the operator of an ATV who causes damage or personal injury (ORVA, s. 12(1)). The exception to owner liability is if the vehicle was used or taken without the owner's consent (ORVA. s. 14(2)).

ARREST POWERS

An operator stopped by a police officer or conservation officer must produce a driver's licence as well as registration for the ATV. If unable to do so, the operator must provide his or her name and address.

If the operator refuses to do so or the officer believes on reasonable and probable grounds that the operator is violating these requirements, he or she may be arrested (ORVA, s. 17(5)).

SEARCH AND SEIZURE POWERS

The ORVA contains no specific search powers. If an arrest is made, a search may be conducted under the common-law powers of searching incident to an arrest, in order to protect the officer or the suspect, to preserve any evidence in the possession of the person being arrested, and/or to establish identification.

A peace officer who believes that the plate and/or permit presented for an ATV either is not the correct one issued for it, or has been obtained by false pretenses, or is altered/defaced, may seize the plate and/or permit pending an investigation (ORVA, s. 11).

USE OF FORCE

There is no specific use-of-force authority in relation to an arrest or search.

LIMITATION PERIOD

The ORVA does not mention the limitation period, so the general limitation period of six months from the date of the offence, as defined in the POA, applies.

NON-POLICE AGENCIES INVOLVED

- Ministry of Natural Resources: conservation officers (that is, game wardens).
- Environment Canada: an officer from this department is the federal counterpart of the provincial conservation officer and is authorized by the province to have the same authorities as a provincial conservation officer.
- Ontario Federation of All Terrain Vehicle Clubs: an organized group of ATV enthusiasts who engage provincial and local authorities to establish trail systems for ATV users.

PROVINCIAL OFFENCES GRID COMPLETION

Common Offences and/or Provisions

The most common offences involving the operation of ATVs are

1. driving without a licence;
2. failure to produce documents (insurance, permits, etc.);
3. careless driving (operating without "due care and attention or due consideration");
4. driving an ATV with a passenger; and
5. driving without the mandated equipment (that is, helmet and lights).

Arrest Powers

Same as those under the *Highway Traffic Act*, *Trespass to Property Act*, and *Criminal Code*, as well as s. 15(8) of the ORVA for the failure to produce requested documents.

Search Powers

There are no specific search powers contained in the ORVA. If an arrest is made, a search may be conducted under the common-law powers of searching incident to an arrest.

Use of Force

No specific use-of-force authority under the ORVA (refer to *Criminal Code* s. 25 or POA s. 146).

Limitation Period

Six months from the date of the offence.

Non-Police Agencies Involved

Conservation offices (Ministry of Natural Resources and Environment Canada)

Off-Road Vehicles Act

RSO 1990, c. O.4

1. Definitions—In this Act,

"conservation officer" means a conservation officer under the *Fish and Wildlife Conservation Act, 1997* and an officer under the *Provincial Parks and Conservation Reserves Act, 2006*;

"highway" includes a common and public highway, street, avenue, parkway, driveway, square, place, bridge, viaduct or trestle, any part of which is intended for or used by the general public for the passage of vehicles and includes the area between the lateral property lines thereof;

"holder," when used in relation to a permit, means the person in whose name the plate portion of a permit is issued;

"Minister" means the Minister of Transportation;

"Ministry" means the Ministry of Transportation;

"occupier" includes,

(a) a person who is in physical possession of the land, or

(b) a person who has responsibility for and control over the condition of land or the activities there carried on, or control over persons allowed to enter the land,

even if there is more than one occupier of the same land;

"off-road vehicle" means a vehicle propelled or driven otherwise than by muscular power or wind and designed to travel,

(a) on not more than three wheels, or

(b) on more than three wheels and being of a prescribed class of vehicle;

"peace officer" includes a police officer, conservation officer or other person employed for the preservation and maintenance of the public peace or any officer appointed for enforcing or carrying out the provisions of this Act;

"permit," unless otherwise indicated, means a permit issued under section 5 consisting of a vehicle portion and a plate portion;

"prescribed" means prescribed by the regulations;

"Registrar" means the Registrar of Motor Vehicles appointed under the *Highway Traffic Act*;

"regulations" means the regulations made under this Act.

2(1) **Application**—This Act does not apply in respect of off-road vehicles being operated on a highway.

(2) **Exception**—Despite subsection (1), and section 7, subsection 32 (1) and subsections 62 (1), (3) to (26) and (28) to (32) of the *Highway Traffic Act*, a holder of a driver's licence issued under section 32 of the *Highway Traffic Act* who is not contravening any provision of this Act may drive an off-road vehicle,

> Note: On a day to be named by proclamation of the Lieutenant Governor, subsection (2) is amended by the Statutes of Ontario, 1999, chapter 12, Schedule R, section 20 by striking out "Despite subsection (1), and section 7, subsection 32 (1) and subsections 62 (1), (3) to (26) and (28) to (32) of the *Highway Traffic Act*" at the beginning and substituting "Despite subsection (1), and despite section 7, subsections 32 (1), 62 (1), (3) to (26) and (28) to (32) and section 191.8 of the *Highway Traffic Act*." See: 1999, c. 12, Sched. R, ss. 20, 21.

(a) directly across a highway; or

(b) on a highway, if the vehicle is designed to travel on more than two wheels and the driver is,

(i) a farmer using the vehicle for agricultural purposes, or

(ii) a person licensed under the *Fish and Wildlife Conservation Act, 1997* to trap furbearing mammals, if the person is using the vehicle for trapping purposes,

and the vehicle or a vehicle drawn by it bears a slow moving vehicle sign.

(3) **Application**—Subsection (2) does not apply to a motorcycle with a side car, a farm tractor, a self-propelled implement of husbandry or a road-building machine as defined in the *Highway Traffic Act* or to an off-road vehicle designated by regulation as a vehicle of a class of off-road vehicle that is exempt from section 3 of this Act.

3(1) **Permit required**—No person shall drive an off-road vehicle except under the authority of a permit for the vehicle and with the number plate showing the number of the permit displayed on the vehicle in the manner prescribed.

(2) **Permit to be carried**—Every driver of an off-road vehicle shall carry the permit for it or a true copy thereof and shall surrender the permit or copy for inspection upon demand of a peace officer.

(3) **Exception**—Subsection (2) does not apply to a driver of an off-road vehicle on land where the owner of the vehicle is the occupier of the land.

4(1) **Age limit for driving**—No owner of an off-road vehicle shall permit a child under the age of twelve to drive the vehicle.

(2) **Exception**—Subsection (1) does not apply where the child is driving the vehicle,

(a) on land occupied by the vehicle owner; or

(b) under the close supervision of an adult.

This section is interesting because there is no definition of "close supervision." The *Motorized Snow Vehicles Act* provides the age criteria and training in the form of a special licence. The ATV legislation does not provide this to the same degree.

5(1) **Issuance of permits**—Subject to subsection (2), every person who,

(a) is the owner of an off-road vehicle;

(b) is, in the case of an individual, at least sixteen years of age; and

(c) pays the prescribed fee,

is entitled to be issued a numbered permit from the Ministry for the vehicle in accordance with the regulations.

(2) **Permit documentation**—Prior to the issuance of a permit under this section, the person to whom the application is made may require production of such documentation as is considered necessary to establish the requirements set out in subsection (1).

(3) **Use of plates**—The Ministry may authorize number plates in an applicant's possession for use on an off-road vehicle. . . .

(7) **Regulations re permits and permit numbers**—The Lieutenant Governor in Council may make regulations respecting any matter ancillary to the provisions of this section with respect to permits and in particular,

(a) prescribing forms for the purposes of this section and requiring their use;

(b) respecting the issuance of permits and number plates;

(c) governing the manner of displaying number plates on off-road vehicles;

(d) prescribing fees for the issuance and replacement of permits and number plates and for any additional administrative proceedings arising therefrom;

(e) respecting permits and number plates for use, on a temporary basis, on off-road vehicles in the possession of,

(i) manufacturers of off-road vehicles,

(ii) dealers in off-road vehicles, or

(iii) persons in the business of repairing, customizing, modifying or transporting off-road vehicles,

where the vehicles are not kept for private use or for hire and prescribing conditions under which such off-road vehicles may be operated;

(f) prescribing requirements for the purposes of section 8;

(g) prescribing conditions precedent to be met before an issued permit is valid.

6(1) **False statement**—Every person who knowingly makes a false statement in an application, declaration, affidavit or paper writing required by this Act, the regulations or the Ministry, is guilty of an offence and on conviction, in addition to any other penalty to which the person may be liable, is liable to a fine of not less than $100 and not more than $500 or to imprisonment for a term of not more than thirty days, or to both.

(2) **Change of address**—If there is a change in an owner's address as stated in an application for a permit or in a previous notice sent or filed under this subsection, the owner shall, within six days, send by registered mail to or file with the Ministry notice of the owner's new address.

7. **Application where permit held**—Section 3 does not apply if the owner of the vehicle holds a permit for the vehicle issued under section 7 of the *Highway Traffic Act*, the number plate issued thereunder is displayed on the vehicle in accordance with the regulations under that Act and the permit is of such a nature that, were the vehicle driven on a highway, there would be no contravention of the *Highway Traffic Act* with respect to the permit and number plate.

8(1) **Where transfer of ownership**—Where the holder of a permit ceases to be the owner of the off-road vehicle referred to in the permit, the holder shall,

(a) remove the number plate from the vehicle;

(b) on the delivery of the vehicle to the new owner, complete the transfer section of the vehicle portion of the permit including the date of the delivery and give that portion of the permit to the new owner; and

(c) retain the plate portion of the permit.

(2) **Re-issue of permit**—Every person shall, within six days after becoming the owner of an off-road vehicle for which a permit has been issued, apply to the Ministry, on the form provided therefor, for a new permit for the vehicle.

(3) **Temporary use of plate**—Despite subsections 3(1) and 9(1), a person, to whom a number plate has been issued under section 5 for a vehicle the person no longer owns, may affix the number plate to a similar vehicle that the person owns where the person does so in accordance with the prescribed requirements.

> The provisions in this section are noteworthy because they correspond to the provisions for the sale of a motor vehicle. The ownership has a plate and a vehicle portion. Upon sale, the vendor retains the plate and signs over the vehicle portion to the buyer, and the buyer must apply for a new plate. The vendor is allowed six days to use the old plate on a new vehicle, and the registration must be completed within six days. This does not apply to the new owner unless he or she also had a plate from a previous ownership.

(4) **Idem**—Despite section 3, a person may drive an off-road vehicle during the six day period referred to in subsection (2) where he or she complies with the prescribed requirements.

9(1) **Violations as to number**—Every person who,

(a) defaces or alters any number plate furnished by the Ministry;

(b) uses or permits the use of a defaced or altered number plate;

(c) without the authority of the permit holder removes a number plate from an off-road vehicle; or

(d) uses or permits the use of any number plate upon an off-road vehicle other than a number plate authorized for use on that off-road vehicle,

is guilty of an offence and on conviction is liable to a fine of not less than $100 and not more than $1,000 or to imprisonment for not more than thirty days, or to both.

(2) **Property of the Crown**—Every number plate furnished by the Ministry under this Act is the property of the Crown and shall be returned to the Ministry when required by the Ministry.

10(1) **No other number to be exposed and number to be kept clean**—The driver of an off-road vehicle shall ensure that,

(a) no number other than that upon the number plate furnished under this Act shall be exposed on any part of an off-road vehicle in such a position or manner as to confuse the identity of the number plate; and

(b) the number is kept free from dirt and obstruction and is so affixed that the numbers thereon are plainly visible at all times and the view thereof is not obscured by any part of the vehicle or any attachments thereto, or by the load carried.

(2) **Penalty**—Every person who contravenes clause (1)(b) is guilty of an offence and on conviction is liable to a fine of not less than $20 and not more than $50.

11. Improper number—Where a peace officer has reason to believe that a number plate attached to an off-road vehicle or the permit carried by the driver,

(a) was not furnished under this Act for the vehicle;

(b) was obtained by false pretences; or

(c) has been defaced or altered,

the peace officer may take possession of the number plate or permit and retain it until the facts as to the use or furnishing of the number plate or permit for the off-road vehicle have been determined.

12(1) **Liability of owner**—Where the driver of an off-road vehicle, who is not the owner thereof, is liable for damages for injury or damage arising out of the operation by the driver of the vehicle with the consent of the owner, the owner is jointly and severally liable....

14(1) **Owner may be convicted**—The owner of an off-road vehicle may be charged with and convicted of an offence under this Act, the regulations or any municipal by-law regulating, governing or prohibiting the operation of off-road vehicles, for which the driver of the off-road vehicle is subject to be charged and on conviction, the owner is liable to the penalty prescribed for the offence.

(2) **Exception**—Subsection (1) does not apply where, at the time of the offence, the vehicle was in the possession of a person other than the owner without the owner's consent....

(4) **Permit holder deemed owner**—For the purposes of this Act, where a number plate issued under section 5 of this Act or section 7 of the *Highway Traffic Act* is exposed on an off-road vehicle, the holder of the permit corresponding thereto shall be deemed to be the owner of that vehicle unless the number plate was exposed thereon without the holder's consent, the burden of proof of which is on the permit holder.

15(1) **Insurance**—No person shall drive an off-road vehicle unless it is insured under a motor vehicle liability policy in accordance with the *Insurance Act*.

(2) **Idem**—No owner of an off-road vehicle shall permit it to be driven unless it is insured under a motor vehicle liability policy in accordance with the *Insurance Act*.

(3) **Production of evidence of insurance**—Every driver of an off-road vehicle who is not owner thereof shall, upon the request of a peace officer, surrender for inspection evidence that the vehicle is insured under a motor vehicle liability policy in accordance with the *Insurance Act*.

(4) **Idem**—Every owner of an off-road vehicle that is driven on land other than land that the owner occupies shall, upon request of a peace officer, surrender, for inspection, within seventy-two hours after the request is made, evidence that the vehicle was insured under a motor vehicle liability policy in accordance with the *Insurance Act* at the time it was driven.

(5) Time limit—Subsection (4) does not apply unless the request is made within three months after the time the vehicle was driven.

(6) **Driver offences**—Every person, other than the owner of the vehicle involved, who,

(a) contravenes subsection (1);

(b) fails to surrender evidence under subsection (3) when requested to do so; or

(c) produces false evidence when required to surrender evidence under subsection (3),

This is the only seizure authority by a law enforcement officer in this Act.

Note that the driver and owner are jointly liable for damages. This is in contrast to the *Trespass to Property Act*, where, if the driver cannot be identified, the owner is liable if the damage is done with a motor vehicle.

This section precludes the owner's liability if the machine was taken without the owner's consent. In examining the *Criminal Code*, one section notes that there may be a "theft" of a vehicle, as well as the offence of "taking an auto without consent." This seems to indicate that the theft of an ATV does not necessarily have to have occurred. The ATV merely has to be taken, later to be returned.

Note the exception to this when an off-road vehicle is driven on land belonging to the machine's registered owner.

is guilty of an offence and on conviction is liable to a fine of not less than $20 and not more than $200.

(7) **Owner offences**—Every person who, being the owner of an off-road vehicle, drives it in contravention of subsection (1) or permits it to be driven in contravention of subsection (2) is guilty of an offence and on conviction is liable to a fine of not less than $200 and not more than $1,000.

(8) **Owner offence for failure to produce evidence or producing false evidence**—Every person who contravenes subsection (4) or who produces false evidence when required to surrender evidence under subsection (4) is guilty of an offence and on conviction is liable to a fine of not less than $200 and not more than $1,000.

(9) **Exemption**—Subsections (1), (2) and (3) do not apply where the vehicle is driven on land occupied by the owner of the vehicle.

16. Careless driving—Every person who drives an off-road vehicle without due care and attention or without reasonable consideration for other persons is guilty of an offence.

Because this section replicates the phrasing used in the *Highway Traffic Act*, one may reasonably refer to that legislation and case law to define "due care," "attention," and "reasonable consideration."

17(1) **Officer may stop driver**—A peace officer may stop any person driving an off-road vehicle.

(2) **Land owner may stop driver**—The owner or occupier of land may stop any person driving an off-road vehicle on the land.

(3) Duty to stop—Every person who has been signalled to stop by a person authorized to do so under subsection (1) or (2) shall stop forthwith.

(4) **Driver to identify himself**—Every person stopped under this section or subsection 18(1) shall, when so requested, identify himself or herself by giving his or her name and address to the person who stopped him or her.

(5) **Peace officer may arrest without warrant**—A peace officer who, on reasonable and probable grounds, believes that a contravention of subsection (3) or (4) has been committed, may arrest without warrant any person whom he or she, on reasonable and probable grounds, believes has committed the contravention.

This authority to arrest is also found in the *Motorized Snow Vehicles Act* and the *Trespass to Property Act*. The fact that they use the phrase "reasonable and probable grounds" makes them unique within the realm of provincial offences. Usually, "found committing" provides the arrest authority in the POA, while "reasonable and probable grounds" is an authority reserved for federal legislation.

18(1) **Duty to stop**—Every driver of an off-road vehicle shall stop his or her vehicle when approached by another vehicle with a flashing red light or with flashing red and blue lights.

(2) **Red light on vehicle**—No person, except a peace officer, shall operate an off-road vehicle that is equipped with a lamp that produces flashes of red light.

(2.1) **Red and blue lights on vehicle**—No person, except a police officer, shall operate an off-road vehicle that is equipped with lamps that produce flashes of red and blue lights.

(3) **Hazard warning lamps permitted**—Subsection (2) does not apply to prohibit the use of vehicular hazard warning lamps commonly known as four way flashers.

19(1) **Helmet**—No person shall drive an off-road vehicle or ride on an off-road vehicle or on a conveyance towed by an off-road vehicle unless he or she is wearing a helmet that complies with the regulations, securely fastened under his or her chin with a chin strap.

The Act provides an exemption for agricultural activities when carried out by a farmer, and when stipulations such as a driver's licence and slow-moving vehicle sign are met. However, it still insists on helmets.

(2) **Idem**—This section does not apply to a person driving or riding on an off-road vehicle or on a conveyance towed by an off-road vehicle where the owner of the off-road vehicle is the occupier of the land.

In contrast, passengers on a snow machine are not exempt from wearing helmets.

20. Risks willingly assumed—Every person who enters premises on an off-road vehicle or while being towed by an off-road vehicle shall be deemed, for the purpose of subsection 4(1) of the *Occupiers' Liability Act*, to have willingly assumed all risks where,

(a) no fee is paid for the entry or activity of the person, other than a benefit or payment received from a government or government agency or a non-profit recreation club or association; and

(b) the person is not being provided with living accommodation by the occupier.

21. Offences and fines Every person who contravenes any of the provisions of this Act or the regulations is guilty of an offence and on conviction, where a fine for the contravention is not otherwise provided for in this Act, is liable to a fine not exceeding $300.

. . .

RRO 1990, Regulation 863

General

1. In this Regulation,

"dune buggy" means a self-propelled vehicle with four or more wheels that has been manufactured or modified for off-road use but does not include an amphibious vehicle with six or more wheels;

"motorcycle association" means a motorcycle club or association that has or is affiliated with a motorcycle club or association that has a published constitution and a membership roster of more than twenty-four persons;

"road-building machine" means a self propelled vehicle of a design commonly used in the construction or maintenance of highways, including but not limited to,

(a) an asphalt spreader, concrete paving or finishing machine, motor grader, roller, tractor-dozer and motor scraper,

(b) a tracked and wheeled tractor equipped with mowers, post-hole diggers, compactors, weed spraying equipment, snow blowers, snow plow, front-end loader, back-hoe, rock drill or litter collection vehicle, and

(c) a power shovel on tracks and drag lines on tracks,

but not including a commercial motor vehicle;

"self-propelled implement of husbandry" means a self-propelled vehicle manufactured, designed, redesigned, converted or reconstructed for a specific use in farming and used for farming purposes;

"wheelchair" means a chair mounted on wheels propelled or driven otherwise than by muscular power and used for the carriage of a person who has a physical defect or disability.

2(1) The following are designated as classes of vehicles that are exempt from the provisions of the Act and this Regulation:

1. Golf carts.
2. Road-building machines.
3. Self-propelled implements of husbandry.
4. Wheelchairs.
5. Off-road vehicles driven or exhibited at a closed course competition or rally sponsored by a motorcycle association.

(2) Motorcycles, as defined in the *Highway Traffic Act*, that are,

(a) lent to a motorcycle driver training school by a manufacturer or dealer for the purpose of driver training;

(b) used in an area designated for driver training by the school; and

(c) driven by persons enrolled in the driver training course or by course instructors for instruction purposes,

are designated as a class of off-road vehicle to which section 3 of the Act does not apply.

3. For the purposes of the definition of "off-road vehicle" in section 1 of the Act, the following classes of vehicles are prescribed:

1. Dune buggies.

1.1 Vehicles designed for use on all terrains, commonly known as all-terrain vehicles, that have steering handlebars and a seat that is designed to be straddled by the driver.

This is the only reference to ATVs with a bench-style seat and steering wheel, and that carry passengers. Examples are the Kawasaki Mule and the John Deere Gator. The Act does not define machines such as Bombardier's "One-Up," which is designed for a passenger, as all-terrain vehicles.

1.2 Vehicles designed for utility applications or uses on all terrains that have four or more wheels and a seat that is not designed to be straddled by the driver.

2. Suzukis, Model Numbers LT125D, LT50E, LT125E, LT185E, LT250EF and LT250EFF.

3. Hondas, Model Numbers FL250 series and TRX200.

4. Yamahas, Model Number YFM 200N.

4(1) The areas set out in Schedule 1 are designated as areas within which subsection 2(2) of the Act does not apply.

(2) Where a highway is referred to in Schedule 1 by a number or name, the reference is to that part of the King's Highway that is known thereby.

5. The areas set out in Schedule 2 are designated as areas within which subsections 3(1) and (2) of the Act do not apply.

6(1) Off-road vehicles owned by persons not residing in Ontario are designated as a class of vehicle.

(2) Vehicles of a class designated under subsection (1) are exempt from the provisions of section 3 of the Act if they are registered in another jurisdiction and have number plates furnished by the other jurisdiction attached.

7. The number plate for an off-road vehicle,

(a) with three or less wheels, shall be securely mounted on the front of the vehicle in a conspicuous position; or

(b) with more than three wheels, shall be securely mounted in a conspicuous position on the rear of the vehicle.

8(1) For the purposes of subsection 8(3) of the Act, the permit holder of an off-road vehicle is required to have in his or her possession,

(a) the vehicle portion of the permit issued for the vehicle bearing the date of purchase and the signature of the vendor of the used vehicle; and

(b) the plate portion of the permit that corresponds with the number plate affixed to the vehicle.

(2) For the purposes of subsection 8(4) of the Act, a person driving an off-road vehicle is required to carry the documents referred to in subsection (1) or true copies thereof, and to surrender them for inspection upon the demand of a peace officer.

9. A permit for an off-road vehicle may be terminated by surrendering it to the Ministry.

10(1) Dealer and Service permits and number plates may be issued to manufacturers of or dealers in off-road vehicles or to persons engaged in the business of repairing, customizing, modifying or transporting off-road vehicles.

(2) A Dealer and Service number plate may be used only,

(a) on a vehicle in the possession of the person to whom the corresponding permit was issued; and

(b) for purposes related to the sale, repair, customization or modification of the vehicle on which it is used or, in the case of a person engaged in the business of transporting vehicles, for purposes of transporting the vehicles.

(3) The Dealer and Service number plate for an off-road vehicle,

(a) with three or less wheels, shall be securely mounted in a conspicuous position on the front of the vehicle; or

(b) with more than three wheels, shall be securely mounted in a conspicuous position on the rear of the vehicle.

(4) Subsection 8(3) of the Act does not apply to a person referred to in subsection (1) with respect to a vehicle in the person's possession for purposes related to the sale, repair, customization or modification of the vehicle or, in the case of a person engaged in the business of transporting vehicles, for purposes of transporting the vehicle.

11. The requirements for a helmet for the purpose of section 19 of the *Off-Road Vehicles Act* are those set out for motorcycles in Regulation 610 of the Revised Regulations of Ontario, 1990 made under the *Highway Traffic Act.*

General Fees

12(1) The following fees shall be paid to the Ministry:

1.	For a permit for an off-road vehicle	$10
2.	For a permit and number plate for an off-road vehicle	35
3.	For an application for a duplicate permit for an off-road vehicle, in case of loss or destruction	10
4.	For the replacement of a permit and number plate, in case of loss or destruction	20
5.	For a Dealer and Service Permit and number plate	55
6.	For a copy of any writing, paper or document, other than an accident report, related to an off-road vehicle filed in the Ministry or any statement containing information from the records	6
7.	For a copy of an accident report	12
8.	For certification of a copy of any writing, paper or document related to an off-road vehicle filed in the Ministry or any statement containing information from the records	6
9.	For administrative costs for processing a cheque that is not honoured	10
10.	For each search of off-road vehicle records by vehicle identification number, plate number or name or identification number of registered owner or permit holder	12

(2) The fees set out in subsection (1) do not apply to an off-road vehicle owned by the Government of the Province of Ontario.

Ontario Regulation 316/03
Operation of Off-Road Vehicles on Highways

PART I
DEFINITIONS

1. Definitions—In this Regulation,

"all-terrain vehicle" means an off-road vehicle that,

(a) has four wheels, the tires of all of which are in contact with the ground,
(b) has steering handlebars,
(c) has a seat that is designed to be straddled by the driver, and
(d) is designed to carry a driver only and no passengers;

"off-road vehicle" has the same meaning as in the *Off-Road Vehicles Act.*

This definition does not include vehicles designed to carry passengers, where the seat is not meant to be straddled.

PART II
OPERATION ON CLASSES OF HIGHWAYS

2. Operation on highways generally prohibited—An off-road vehicle shall not be driven on any highway except,

(a) as specified in this Part;

(b) as permitted by Part IV; or

(c) as permitted by clause 2(2)(a) of the *Off-Road Vehicles Act.*

3. Prohibited highways—Except as permitted by section 28, no off-road vehicle shall be driven on a highway listed in Schedule A.

4(1) **Permitted highways for ATVs**—Subject to subsection (2), no off-road vehicle shall be driven on a highway listed in Schedule B.

(2) All-terrain vehicles may be driven on a highway listed in Schedule B only if, in addition to meeting the requirements of Part III, there is only one driver and no passenger on the all-terrain vehicle at the time.

The definition of an ATV concerns only those vehicles with a seat designed to be straddled. This specific section implies that passengers are allowed on a vehicle with the "bench" style seat (for example, the Mule and Gator).

5. Highways in parks—An off-road vehicle may be driven on a highway that is within a provincial park or public park if the road authority or governing body of the park permits the operation of off-road vehicles in the park.

PART III
REGULATION OF OFF-ROAD VEHICLES ON HIGHWAYS

6. Conditions for off-road vehicles to be operated on highways—An off-road vehicle shall not be operated on a highway unless it meets the requirements of sections 7 to 15 and it is operated in accordance with sections 16 to 24.

Equipment Requirements

7(1) **Weight and dimensions**—The off-road vehicle must weigh 450 kilograms or less.

(2) The off-road vehicle must have an overall width not greater than 1.35 metres, excluding mirrors.

8. Tires—All the tires on the off-road vehicle must be low pressure bearing tires.

9. Motor vehicle safety standards—The off-road vehicle must meet the motor vehicle safety standards prescribed for restricted-use motorcycles in the *Motor Vehicle Safety Regulations* made under the *Motor Vehicle Safety Act* (Canada) applicable when the vehicle was manufactured.

10(1) **Equipment configuration and performance requirements**—If the off-road vehicle was manufactured after May 31, 1991 and before January 1, 2002, it must meet the equipment configuration and performance requirements set out in the American National Standards Institute/Specialty Vehicle Institute of America publication entitled *Four Wheel All-Terrain Vehicles ANSI/SVIA-1-1990* or *Four Wheel All-Terrain Vehicles—Equipment, Configuration and Performance Requirements ANSI/SVIA-1-2001.*

(2) If the off-road vehicle was manufactured after December 31, 2001, it must meet the equipment configuration and performance requirements set out in the American National Standards Institute/Specialty Vehicle Institute of America publication entitled *Four Wheel All-Terrain Vehicles—Equipment, Configuration and Performance Requirements ANSI/SVIA-1-2001.*

11. Equipment must be operating properly—A component, equipment or other feature of the off-road vehicle that was part of the vehicle when manufactured and that is required by section 9 or 10 must operate properly and must not be missing, rendered partly or wholly inoperable or modified so as to reduce its effectiveness.

12. Braking system—The off-road vehicle must be equipped with a service brake, parking brake and parking mechanism that comply with section 4 of the American National Standards Institute/Specialty Vehicle Institute of America publication entitled *Four Wheel All-Terrain Vehicles—Equipment, Configuration and Performance Requirements ANSI/SVIA-1-2001.*

13(1) **Lamps**—Despite subsection 62 (1) of the Act, the off-road vehicle must be equipped with one or two lamps that emit a white light on the front of the vehicle and one or two lamps that emit a red light at the rear of the vehicle.

(2) The lamps required by subsection (1) must be lit at all times the off-road vehicle is operated on the highway.

(3) The subsections of section 62 of the Act that refer to lamps required under subsections (1), (2) or (3) of that section shall be read as if referring to the lamps required under subsection (1) of this section.

(4) The lamps required on the front of an off-road vehicle by subsection (1) must be aimed such that the high intensity portion of the beam is directed below the horizontal line through the centre of the lamp from which it comes, at a distance of 7.6 metres ahead of the lamp, when the vehicle is not loaded.

(5) If the off-road vehicle was manufactured after January 1, 1998, it must be equipped with a stop lamp or lamps on the rear of the vehicle that emit a red light when any brake is applied.

(6) A stop lamp required under subsection (5) may be incorporated with a rear lamp or may be a separate lamp.

(7) The off-road vehicle must be equipped with,

(a) one yellow reflex reflector on each side at the front;

(b) one red reflex reflector on each side at the rear; and

(c) one or two red reflex reflectors on the rear.

(8) The reflex reflectors required by subsection (7) must comply with the requirements of the *Motor Vehicle Safety Regulations* made under the *Motor Vehicle Safety Act* (Canada) applicable when the vehicle was manufactured.

14. Windshield—The off-road vehicle need not be equipped with a windshield, but if it is, the windshield must satisfy the requirements prescribed for a motorcycle windshield under subsection 1(10) of Schedule 6 to Regulation 611 of the Revised Regulations of Ontario, 1990.

15(1) **No obstruction of view**—There must not be any object or non-transparent material placed on or attached to the off-road vehicle that obstructs the driver's view of traffic approaching from any direction at an intersection, or of traffic approaching from the rear of the vehicle.

(2) If the off-road vehicle is towing a trailer, the trailer or load must not obstruct the driver's view of traffic approaching from any direction at an intersection, or of traffic approaching from the rear of the vehicle.

Operation Requirements

16(1) **Permit**—The off road vehicle shall be operated under the authority of a permit issued under section 5 of the *Off-Road Vehicles Act* and a number plate showing the number of the permit shall be displayed on the vehicle as required under that Act.

(2) Subsection (1) does not apply to an off-road vehicle operated under the authority of a permit issued under section 7 of the *Highway Traffic Act*, as provided by section 7 of the *Off-Road Vehicles Act.*

17. Insurance—The off-road vehicle shall be insured in accordance with section 2 of the *Compulsory Automobile Insurance Act* and section 15 of the *Off-Road Vehicles Act.*

18. Driver's licence—The driver of the off-road vehicle shall hold a valid Class A, B, C, D, E, F, G, G2, M or M2 driver's licence issued under the Act unless he or she is exempt, under section 34 of the Act, from the application of section 32 of the Act.

19. Helmet—The driver of the off-road vehicle shall wear a helmet that complies with section 19 of the *Off-Road Vehicles Act*.

20(1) **Application of *Highway Traffic Act***—Except as otherwise provided in this Regulation, the provisions of the Act and its regulations applicable to motor vehicles apply with necessary modifications to the operation of an off-road vehicle on a highway.

(2) Subsection 62 (19), sections 64 and 66 and subsection 76 (1) of the Act do not apply to the operation of an off-road vehicle on a highway.

21. Application of *Off-Road Vehicles Act*—The *Off-Road Vehicles Act* and the regulations made under that Act that apply to the operation of off-road vehicles off the highway apply with necessary modifications to the operation of an off-road vehicle on a highway.

22. Maximum speed—The off-road vehicle shall not be driven at a rate of speed greater than,

(a) 20 kilometres per hour, if the speed limit established under the Act for that part of the highway is not greater than 50 kilometres per hour; or

(b) 50 kilometres per hour, if the speed limit established under the Act for that part of the highway is greater than 50 kilometres per hour.

23(1) **Environmental protection**—The off-road vehicle shall not be operated in such a manner as to,

(a) discharge a contaminant or cause or permit the discharge of a contaminant into the natural environment that may have an adverse effect on the environment or impair the quality of any waters; or

(b) contravene any conditions, restrictions and prohibitions imposed by any legislation and related regulations enacted to protect the environment.

(2) The off-road vehicle shall not be operated in such a manner that it causes or is likely to cause,

(a) a risk to the safety of any person;

(b) harm or material discomfort to any person from dust, emissions or noise;

(c) harm, injury or damage, either directly or indirectly, to any property, flora or fauna; or

(d) alteration, disruption or destruction to the natural environment, including erosion damage or degradation of the right of way.

(3) The off-road vehicle shall not be driven in or through a river, stream or other watercourse on a highway if doing so would or would be likely to alter, disrupt or destroy any fish habitat.

> These are very specific restrictions for ATVs concerning noise, flora and fauna, the environment, and waterways.

24(1) **Rules of the road**—The off-road vehicle shall be driven on the shoulder of the highway in the same direction as the traffic using the same side of the highway.

(2) Despite subsection (1), the off-road vehicle may be driven on the roadway in the same direction as the traffic using the same side of the highway if,

(a) there is no shoulder; or

(b) the shoulder of the highway is obstructed and cannot be used by the off-road vehicle.

(3) Despite subsection (1), the off-road vehicle shall not be driven on the shoulder but shall be driven on the roadway in the same direction as the traffic using the same side of the highway if it is being driven across a level railway crossing.

(4) When driven on the shoulder of the highway, the off-road vehicle shall be driven as close to and parallel with the right edge of the shoulder as can be done practicably and safely.

(5) When driven on the roadway pursuant to subsection (2), the off-road vehicle shall be driven as close to and parallel with the right edge of the roadway as can be done practicably and safely.

(6) When entering the shoulder or the roadway, the off-road vehicle shall yield the right of way to vehicles already using the shoulder or the roadway, as the case may be, and shall enter the shoulder or roadway only when it is safe to do so.

(7) The off-road vehicle shall not be driven in the median strip of the highway.

(8) The off-road vehicle shall not be driven on any part of the highway that is designated as a construction zone under subsection 128(8) of the Act or on any other part of the highway where construction work or highway maintenance is being carried out, unless the off-road vehicle is operating as a vehicle described in subsection 128(13) of the Act or as a road service vehicle.

(9) If part or all of the highway is closed under subsection 134 (2) of the Act, the off-road vehicle shall not be driven on any adjacent part of the highway that may be open, unless the off-road vehicle is operating as a vehicle described in subsection 128(13) of the Act or as a road service vehicle.

(10) The off-road vehicle shall not overtake and pass any moving motor vehicle or motorized snow vehicle at any time when both the off-road vehicle and the other vehicle are travelling on the same shoulder or roadway of the highway.

(11) Despite subsection (10), an off-road vehicle may overtake and pass another off-road vehicle when both are travelling on the shoulder if the movement can be made in safety while remaining on the shoulder and to the left of the off-road vehicle being overtaken and passed.

(12) Despite clause 142(4)(b) of the Act, a person driving an off-road vehicle on the highway may indicate the intention to turn right by extending the right hand and arm horizontally beyond the right side of the vehicle.

(13) Before commencing a left turn in the manner required by subsection 141(5), (6) or (7) of the Act, the off-road vehicle shall, without interfering with the movement of traffic travelling in the same direction as the off-road vehicle, move away from the shoulder or from the right edge of the roadway, as the case may be, and be positioned on the roadway in the position from which the left turn is to be made.

(14) Upon completing a left turn, the off-road vehicle shall, without interfering with the movement of traffic travelling in the same direction as the off-road vehicle, move back to the right edge of the roadway or shoulder, as the case may be.

PART IV
EXEMPTIONS

25. Definitions—In this Part,

"emergency" means a situation that constitutes a danger to life or property;

"employee" means,

(a) a person employed in the service of the Crown or any agency of the Crown,

(b) a police officer, conservation officer or other person appointed for the preservation and maintenance of the public peace or any officer appointed for enforcing or carrying out the provisions of this Act or the *Off-Road Vehicles Act*,

(c) a firefighter as defined in the *Fire Protection and Prevention Act, 1997*,

(d) an employee of an ambulance service as defined in the *Ambulance Act*,

(e) an employee of a municipality or of a local board as defined in the *Municipal Affairs Act*,

(f) an employee of a board, commission or other local authority exercising any power with respect to municipal affairs or purposes, or

(g) an employee or agent of the operator of a water, gas, electric heat, light or power works, telegraph and telephone lines, a railway, a street railway, works for the transmission of gas, oil, water or electrical power or energy or any similar works supplying the general public with necessaries or conveniences.

26. Crossing a highway—Part III of this Regulation does not apply to a person who drives an off-road vehicle directly across a highway pursuant to clause 2(2)(a) of the *Off-Road Vehicles Act.*

27(1) **Farmers and trappers**—Sections 8, 9, 10 and 18 do not apply to the operation of an off-road vehicle as described in clause 2(2)(b) of the *Off-Road Vehicles Act* if,

(a) the driver of the vehicle holds a driver's licence; and

(b) the number of passengers on the off-road vehicle does not exceed the number of places on the vehicle intended for passengers.

(2) Despite section 4, an off-road vehicle may be operated as described in clause 2(2)(b) of the *Off-Road Vehicles Act* on any highway other than a highway listed in Schedule A if the conditions described in clauses (1)(a) and (b) are met. . . .

29(1) **Far northern Ontario and unorganized territory**—A person may operate an off-road vehicle on a highway in an area of the province described in Schedule C in accordance with this Regulation despite any provision that would provide otherwise in Parts II, IV and VI of the Act.

(2) Sections 9, 10, 16 and 18 do not apply to the operation of an off-road vehicle on a highway in an area of the province described in Schedule C if,

(a) the driver of the off-road vehicle is at least 16 years old;

(b) the driver of the off-road vehicle holds a driver's licence or a motorized snow vehicle operator's licence; and

(c) the number of passengers on the off-road vehicle does not exceed the number of places on the vehicle intended for passengers.

(3) Despite section 4, an off-road vehicle may be operated on any highway other than a highway listed in Schedule A in an area of the province described in Schedule C if the conditions described in clauses (2)(a), (b) and (c) are met.

30. Omitted (revokes other Regulations).

31. Omitted (provides for coming into force of provisions of this Regulation).

SCHEDULE A
HIGHWAYS PROHIBITED TO ALL OFF-ROAD VEHICLES

[For a complete listing of all prohibited highways, refer to the Ontario government website.]

ASSIGNMENT: OFF-ROAD VEHICLES ACT

Scenario One

You are on patrol and are dispatched to a semi-rural area in your zone. The call concerns youths operating ATVs. The complainant is concerned because the operators appear to be too young to be driving on a road in the township.

Upon attending the area, you observe two "mini" ATVs pulling out onto the road from a bush area and proceeding down the shoulder of the road in the same direction you are travelling. They fit the description of the subjects in your call, so you pull up beside them and wave them to stop, which they do.

In speaking to them, you discover the following: both boys live in a recently developed area, which borders on a county forest. The parents of both bought them mini ATVs to "play" with. They are wearing helmets, but neither ATV has a plate. One boy is 11 and the other is 13 years old. When you ask whether they are insured, they reply that they do not know.

QUESTIONS

1. What offences have been committed here?
2. Because there has been no serious incident, how will you exercise your discretion in addressing the situation?

Scenario Two

In your patrol area, there is a hydro line that crosses a county road. Informally, many ATV operators have developed a trail following the hydro line to the point where it crosses the county road and continues on the other side.

This spring, your dispatcher received a complaint that operators of ATVs are not crossing the road with caution. Specifically, they seem to race across the road in front of vehicles already travelling on the road, and motorists are concerned.

Upon checking the area, you observe that the ATVs have travelled along the hydro line to a point on the roadway where there is a rock exposure. They have then dropped down into the road allowance, which is quite swampy, and passed through a water trench to a level area, where they have then crossed the roadway.

As you examine the area, you observe three ATVs approaching. They reach the point of crossing and instead of going through the swamp area, they race through a nearby wooded area blooming with the provincial flower, the trillium. Countless numbers of flowers are torn from the ground as the ATVs pass and accelerate through the wooded area. Their passage is marked by deep ruts and mud spattered on nearby trees. You flag down the drivers before they cross the road, and investigate.

QUESTIONS

1. Must the vehicles be registered?
2. Because they are about to cross a secondary road, what documentation must the operators provide?

Scenario Three

It is the fall and the area you patrol is frequented by moose hunters. There are numerous secondary roads interwoven by logging roads and skidder trails.

Since the advent of ATVs, many hunters use these vehicles to travel from one point to another. As you proceed down a secondary road, tow machines merge from a logging road and travel along the shoulder of the secondary road, in the same direction that you are travelling.

Although the hunters are wearing hunter orange and their rifles are in scabbards mounted on the ATVs, you observe that

- each machine is a four-wheel ATV, with handle bars and a seat designed to be straddled by the operator;
- each machine is carrying two people, a driver and a passenger; and
- neither occupant on either machine is wearing a helmet.

Upon stopping the two machines, the drivers produce provincial driver's licences, insurance, and registration for their respective machines.

QUESTION

What offences are being committed in this situation?

Scenario Four

You are patrolling a rural roadway on a hot June day. You observe what appears to be an ATV pull out of a driveway ahead of you. It has four wheels and a bench seat, and is occupied by both a driver and a passenger. As you follow the vehicle, you observe that an Ontario ATV plate is attached to the back of the vehicle and a "slow-moving vehicle" sign is attached to the mesh area behind the driver and passenger. The vehicle pulls into a field lane and stops. You pull in behind and engage the people in conversation. The driver is wearing a John Deere cap and the female passenger is wearing a straw hat. In view are wagons, a hay baler, a hay rake, and numerous round bales of hay. In the background in the same area are numerous horses.

The driver identifies himself with a valid Ontario driver's licence and asks what he has done to warrant the attention of the police on his own property? Further conversation reveals that the driver, who is a farmer, came from the driveway of his house onto the roadway and travelled to his field access gate in order to transport hay to his livestock. The driver also produces a valid insurance policy for the machine.

QUESTION

Is there anything wrong with this scenario and is the driver at fault for any violation concerning the operation of his machine?

Scenario Five

As you travel down the road in your patrol area, you observe two ATVs racing through a field and over a jump made from piled-up earth. One operator is wearing a helmet and the other is not. The whole exercise looks dangerous, so you stop and wave the machines to your location. The driver without the helmet advises you that this is his father's field and his father has made this jump for him. The second machine is operated by a friend who lives down the road. Both boys are 15 years old and neither machine has a plate for an ATV. When asked about insurance, neither boy can produce any evidence of insurance.

QUESTION

Where does each boy stand with regard to the law governing ATVs?

APPENDIX A

Blank Tickets for Assignments and Practice

Blank Certificate of Offence and Enforcement Agency Notes

ICON Location Code / Code d'emplacement du RIII: 3860

Offence Number / N° d'infraction: 6571079A

Form 1 Reg. 950 *Provincial Offences Act* Ontario Court of Justice
Formule 1 Règl. 950 Loi sur les infractions provinciales *Cour de justice de l'Ontario*

Certificate of Offence / *Procès-verbal d'infraction*

I/Je soussigné(e) ______ (Print name/*nom en lettres moulées*)

Believe and certify that on the day of / *Crois et atteste que le* — Y/A 2 0 — M/M — D/J — Time/ *À (Heure)* — M

Name / *Nom* ______ Family/*Nom de famille*

______ Given/*Prénom* — Initials/*Initiales*

Address / *Adresse* ______ Number and street/*Numéro et nom de la rue*

Municipality/*Municipalité* — P.O./C.P. — Province — Postal code/*Code postal*

Driver's licence No./*Numéro de permis de conduire* — Juris *Aut. lég.*

Birthdate/*Date de naissance* Y/A 1 9 — M/M — D/J | Sex / *Sexe* | Motor Vehicle Involved *Véhicule impliqué* ☐ N/N | Collision Involved *Collision* ☐ Y/O | Witnesses *Témoins* ☐ Y/O

At/À ______

______ Municipality/*Municipalité*

Did commit the offence of: / *A commis l'infraction de :* ______

Contrary to: / *Contrairement à :* ______

Sect./*L'art.* ______

Plate number / *N° de plaque d'immatriculation*	Juris / *Aut. lég.*	Commercial / *Utilitaire*	CVOR/*IUVU*	NSC/CNS	Code
		☐ Y/O	☐ Y/O	☐ Y/O	

CVOR No. - NSC No. / *N° de l'IUVU - N° du CNS*

And I further certify that I served an offence notice personally upon the person charged on the offence date.
J'atteste également qu'à la date de l'infraction, j'ai signifié, en mains propres, un avis d'infraction à la personne accusée.

☐ Or other service date of: / *Autre date de signification, le :*

Signature of issuing Provincial Offences Officer / *Signature de l'agent des infractions provinciales*	Officer No. / *N° de l'agent*	Platoon / *Peloton*	Unit / *Unité*

Set fine of / *Amende fixée de*	Total payable	Total payable includes set fine, applicable victim fine surcharge and costs. / *Le montant total exigible comprend l'amende fixée, la suramende compensatoire applicable et les frais.*
$	$ **Montant total exigible**	

Summons issued. You are required to appear in court on / ***Assignation.*** *Vous êtes tenu(e) de comparaître devant le tribunal le* — Y/A 2 0 — M/M — D/J — Time / *À (Heure)* — M

Ct. room/*Salle d'audience* — at the Ontario Court of Justice P.O.A. Office at / *à la Cour de justice de l'Ontario, Bureau des infractions provinciales au*
45 Cedar Pointe Drive, Barrie, Ontario
45, promenade Cedar Pointe, Barrie (Ontario)

Conviction entered pursuant to section 9 of the Provincial Offences Act. Set fine imposed.
Déclaration de culpabilité inscrite conformément à l'article 9 de la Loi sur les infractions provinciales. Amende fixée imposée.

Y/A 2 0 — M/M — D/J

Justice/*Juge* — 03-588

POA 6000 v.1 rev. 01/09

The DATA Group of Companies 373059

Enforcement Agency notes/*Notes de l'agence d'exécution*

Blank Certificate of Offence and Enforcement Agency Notes

ICON Location Code / Code d'emplacement du RIII 3860
Offence Number / N° d'infraction 6571079A

Form 1 Reg. 950 *Provincial Offences Act* Ontario Court of Justice
Formule 1 Règl. 950 Loi sur les infractions provinciales *Cour de justice de l'Ontario*

Certificate of Offence / *Procès-verbal d'infraction*

I/Je soussigné(e) (Print name/nom en lettres moulées)

Believe and certify that on the day of / *Crois et atteste que le* Y/A 2 0 M/M D/J Time/ *À (Heure)* M

Name / *Nom* Family/*Nom de famille*

Given/*Prénom* Initials/*Initiales*

Address / *Adresse* Number and street/*Numéro et nom de la rue*

Municipality/*Municipalité* P.O./C.P. Province Postal code/*Code postal*

Driver's licence No./*Numéro de permis de conduire* Juris / *Aut. lég.*

Birthdate/*Date de naissance* Y/A 1 9 M/M D/J Sex / *Sexe* Motor Vehicle Involved / *Véhicule impliqué* ☐ N/N Collision Involved / *Collision* ☐ Y/O Witnesses / *Témoins* ☐ Y/O

At/*À*

Municipality/*Municipalité*

Did commit the offence of:
A commis l'infraction de :

Contrary to:
Contrairement à :

Sect./*L'art.*

Plate number / *N° de plaque d'immatriculation*	Juris / *Aut. lég.*	Commercial / *Utilitaire*	CVOR/*IUVU*	NSC/CNS	Code
		☐ Y/O	☐ Y/O	☐ Y/O	

CVOR No. - NSC No. / *N° de l'IUVU - N° du CNS*

And I further certify that I served an offence notice personally upon the person charged on the offence date.
J'atteste également qu'à la date de l'infraction, j'ai signifié, en mains propres, un avis d'infraction à la personne accusée.

☐ Or other service date of: / *Autre date de signification, le :*

Signature of issuing Provincial Offences Officer / *Signature de l'agent des infractions provinciales*	Officer No. / *N° de l'agent*	Platoon / *Peloton*	Unit / *Unité*

Set fine of / *Amende fixée de*	**Total payable** / ***Montant total exigible***	
$	$	Total payable includes set fine, applicable victim fine surcharge and costs. *Le montant total exigible comprend l'amende fixée, la suramende compensatoire applicable et les frais.*

Summons issued. You are required to appear in court on
Assignation. *Vous êtes tenu(e) de comparaître devant le tribunal le*
Y/A 2 0 M/M D/J Time / *À (Heure)* M

Ct. room/*Salle d'audience* at the Ontario Court of Justice P.O.A. Office at
à la Cour de justice de l'Ontario, Bureau des infractions provinciales au
45 Cedar Pointe Drive, Barrie, Ontario
45, promenade Cedar Pointe, Barrie (Ontario)

Conviction entered pursuant to section 9 of the *Provincial Offences Act*. Set fine imposed.
Déclaration de culpabilité inscrite conformément à l'article 9 de la Loi sur les infractions provinciales. Amende fixée imposée
Y/A 2 0 M/M D/J

Justice/*Juge*

POA 6000 v.1 rev. 01/09

The DATA Group of Companies 579060

Enforcement Agency notes/*Notes de l'agence d'exécution*

Blank Certificate of Offence and Enforcement Agency Notes

ICON Location Code / Code d'emplacement du RIII 3860 Offence Number / Nº d'infraction 6571079A

Form 1 Reg. 950 *Provincial Offences Act* Ontario Court of Justice
Formule 1 Règl. 950 Loi sur les infractions provinciales *Cour de justice de l'Ontario*

Certificate of Offence / *Procès-verbal d'infraction*

I/Je soussigné(e)

(Print name/nom en lettres moulées)

Believe and certify that on the day of
Crois et atteste que le

Y/A M/M D/J Time/ À (Heure)

2 0 M

Name
Nom

Family/Nom de famille

Given/Prénom Initials/Initiales

Address
Adresse

Number and street/Numéro et nom de la rue

Municipality/Municipalité P.O./C.P. Province Postal code/Code postal

Driver's licence No./*Numéro de permis de conduire* Juris. Aut. lég.

Birthdate/*Date de naissance* Y/A M/M D/J 1 9

Sex *Sexe*

Motor Vehicle Involved *Véhicule impliqué* ☐ N/N

Collision Involved *Collision* ☐ Y/O

Witnesses *Témoins* ☐ Y/O

At/*À*

Municipality/Municipalité

Did commit the offence of:
A commis l'infraction de :

Contrary to:
Contrairement à :

Sect./*L'art.*

Plate number *Nº de plaque d'immatriculation*	Juris *Aut. lég.*	Commercial *Utilitaire*	CVOR/*IUVU*	NSC/CNS	Code
		☐ Y/O	☐ Y/O	☐ Y/O	

CVOR No. - NSC No. / *Nº de l'IUVU - Nº du CNS*

And I further certify that I served an offence notice personally upon the person charged on the offence date.
J'atteste également qu'à la date de l'infraction, j'ai signifié, en mains propres, un avis d'infraction à la personne accusée.

☐ Or other service date of:
Autre date de signification, le :

Signature of issuing Provincial Offences Officer *Signature de l'agent des infractions provinciales*	Officer No. *Nº de l'agent*	Platoon *Peloton*	Unit *Unité*

Set fine of *Amende fixée de*	**Total payable** / ***Montant total exigible***	
$	$	Total payable includes set fine, applicable victim fine surcharge and costs. *Le montant total exigible comprend l'amende fixée, la suramende compensatoire applicable et les frais.*

Summons issued. You are required to appear in court on
Assignation. *Vous êtes tenu(e) de comparaître devant le tribunal le*

Y/A M/M D/J Time / *À (Heure)*

2 0 M

Ct. room/*Salle d'audience*

at the Ontario Court of Justice P.O.A. Office at
à la Cour de justice de l'Ontario, Bureau des infractions provinciales au
45 Cedar Pointe Drive, Barrie, Ontario
45, promenade Cedar Pointe, Barrie (Ontario)

Conviction entered pursuant to section 9 of the *Provincial Offences Act*. Set fine imposed.
Déclaration de culpabilité inscrite conformément à l'article 9 de la Loi sur les infractions provinciales. Amende fixée imposée.

Y/A M/M D/J

2 0

Justice/*Juge*

03-580

POA 6000 v.1 rev. 01/09

The DATA Group of Companies S75059

Enforcement Agency notes/*Notes de l'agence d'exécution*

Blank Certificate of Offence and Enforcement Agency Notes

ICON Location Code / Code d'emplacement du RIII 3860 Offence Number / N° d'infraction 6571079A

Form 1 Reg. 950 *Provincial Offences Act* Ontario Court of Justice
Formule 1 Règl. 950 Loi sur les infractions provinciales *Cour de justice de l'Ontario*

Certificate of Offence / *Procès-verbal d'infraction*

I/Je soussigné(e)
(Print name/*nom en lettres moulées*)

Believe and certify that on the day of / *Crois et atteste que le* Y/A 2 0 M/M D/J Time/ *À (Heure)* M

Name / *Nom* Family/*Nom de famille*
Given/*Prénom* Initials/*Initiales*

Address / *Adresse* Number and street/*Numéro et nom de la rue*
Municipality/*Municipalité* P.O./*C.P.* Province Postal code/*Code postal*

Driver's licence No./*Numéro de permis de conduire* Juris. *Aut. lég.*

Birthdate/*Date de naissance* Y/A 1 9 M/M D/J | Sex *Sexe* | Motor Vehicle Involved *Véhicule impliqué* ☐ N/N | Collision Involved *Collision* ☐ Y/O | Witnesses *Témoins* ☐ Y/O

At/*À*
Municipality/*Municipalité*

Did commit the offence of:
A commis l'infraction de :

Contrary to:
Contrairement à :

Sect./*L'art.*

Plate number *N° de plaque d'immatriculation*	Juris *Aut. lég.*	Commercial *Utilitaire*	CVOR/*IUVU*	NSC/CNS	Code
		☐ Y/O	☐ Y/O	☐ Y/O	

CVOR No. - NSC No. / *N° de l'IUVU - N° du CNS*

And I further certify that I served an offence notice personally upon the person charged on the offence date.
J'atteste également qu'à la date de l'infraction, j'ai signifié, en mains propres, un avis d'infraction à la personne accusée.

☐ Or other service date of:
Autre date de signification, le :

Signature of issuing Provincial Offences Officer / *Signature de l'agent des infractions provinciales* | Officer No. *N° de l'agent* | Platoon *Peloton* | Unit *Unité*

Set fine of / *Amende fixée de* $ | **Total payable** $ **Montant total exigible** | Total payable includes set fine, applicable victim fine surcharge and costs. *Le montant total exigible comprend l'amende fixée, la suramende compensatoire applicable et les frais.*

Summons issued. You are required to appear in court on Y/A 2 0 M/M D/J Time / *À (Heure)* M
Assignation. *Vous êtes tenu(e) de comparaître devant le tribunal le*

Ct. room/*Salle d'audience* at the Ontario Court of Justice P.O.A. Office at
à la Cour de justice de l'Ontario, Bureau des infractions provinciales au
45 Cedar Pointe Drive, Barrie, Ontario
45, promenade Cedar Pointe, Barrie (Ontario)

Conviction entered pursuant to section 9 of the *Provincial Offences Act*. Set fine imposed.
Déclaration de culpabilité inscrite conformément à l'article 9 de la Loi sur les infractions provinciales. Amende fixée imposée.
Y/A 2 0 M/M D/J

Justice/*Juge*

POA 6000 v.1 rev. 01/09

The DATA Group of Companies 573059

Enforcement Agency notes/*Notes de l'agence d'exécution*

Blank Certificate of Offence and Enforcement Agency Notes

ICON Location Code / Code d'emplacement du RIII **3860**
Offence Number / N° d'infraction **6571079A**

Form 1 Reg. 950 *Provincial Offences Act* Ontario Court of Justice
Formule 1 Règl. 950 Loi sur les infractions provinciales *Cour de justice de l'Ontario*

Certificate of Offence / *Procès-verbal d'infraction*

I/Je soussigné(e)
(Print name/nom en lettres moulées)

Believe and certify that on the day of / *Crois et atteste que le* Y/A 2 0 M/M D/J Time/ *À (Heure)* M

Name / *Nom*
Family/*Nom de famille*
Given/*Prénom* Initials/*Initiales*

Address / *Adresse*
Number and street/*Numéro et nom de la rue*
Municipality/*Municipalité* P.O./C.P. Province Postal code/*Code postal*

Driver's licence No./*Numéro de permis de conduire*

Birthdate/*Date de naissance* Y/A 1 9 M/M D/J
Sex / *Sexe*
Motor Vehicle Involved / *Véhicule impliqué* ☐ N/N
Collision Involved / *Collision* ☐ Y/O
Witnesses / *Témoins* ☐ Y/O

At/*À*

Municipality/*Municipalité*

Did commit the offence of:
A commis l'infraction de :

Contrary to:
Contrairement à :

Sect./*L'art.*

Plate number *N° de plaque d'immatriculation*	Juris *Aut. lég.*	Commercial *Utilitaire*	CVOR/*IUVU*	NSC/*CNS*	Code
		☐ Y/O	☐ Y/O	☐ Y/O	

CVOR No. - NSC No. / *N° de l'IUVU - N° du CNS*

And I further certify that I served an offence notice personally upon the person charged on the offence date.
J'atteste également qu'à la date de l'infraction, j'ai signifié, en mains propres, un avis d'infraction à la personne accusée.

☐ Or other service date of: / *Autre date de signification, le :*

Signature of issuing Provincial Offences Officer / *Signature de l'agent des infractions provinciales*	Officer No. / *N° de l'agent*	Platoon / *Peloton*	Unit / *Unité*

Set fine of / *Amende fixée de*	**Total payable** / ***Montant total exigible***	
$ $	$ $	Total payable includes set fine, applicable victim fine surcharge and costs. *Le montant total exigible comprend l'amende fixée, la suramende compensatoire applicable et les frais.*

Summons issued. You are required to appear in court on
Assignation. *Vous êtes tenu(e) de comparaître devant le tribunal le*
Y/A 2 0 M/M D/J Time / *À (Heure)* M

Ct. room/*Salle d'audience* at the Ontario Court of Justice P.O.A. Office at
à la Cour de justice de l'Ontario, Bureau des infractions provinciales au
45 Cedar Pointe Drive, Barrie, Ontario
45, promenade Cedar Pointe, Barrie (Ontario)

Conviction entered pursuant to section 9 of the *Provincial Offences Act*. Set fine imposed.
Déclaration de culpabilité inscrite conformément à l'article 9 de la Loi sur les infractions provinciales. Amende fixée imposée.
Y/A 2 0 M/M D/J

Justice/Juge

POA 6000 v.1 rev. 01/09

The DATA Group of Companies 573059

Enforcement Agency notes/*Notes de l'agence d'exécution*

Blank Certificate of Offence and Enforcement Agency Notes

ICON Location Code
Code d'emplacement du RIII
3860

Offence Number
N° d'infraction
6571079A

Form 1 Reg. 950 *Provincial Offences Act* Ontario Court of Justice
Formule 1 Règl. 950 Loi sur les infractions provinciales *Cour de justice de l'Ontario*

Certificate of Offence / *Procès-verbal d'infraction*

I/Je soussigné(e)

(Print name/*nom en lettres moulées*)

Believe and certify that on the day of
Crois et atteste que le

Y/A M/M D/J Time/ *À (Heure)*

2 0 M

Name
Nom

Family/*Nom de famille*

Given/*Prénom* Initials/*Initiales*

Address
Adresse

Number and street/*Numéro et nom de la rue*

Municipality/*Municipalité* P.O./*C.P.* Province Postal code/*Code postal*

Driver's licence No./*Numéro de permis de conduire*

Juris
Aut. lég.

Birthdate/*Date de naissance*
Y/A M/M D/J
1 9

Sex
Sexe

Motor Vehicle Involved
Véhicule impliqué
☐ N/N

Collision Involved
Collision
☐ Y/O

Witnesses
Témoins
☐ Y/O

At/*À*

Municipality/*Municipalité*

Did commit the offence of:
A commis l'infraction de :

Contrary to:
Contrairement à :

Sect./*L'art.*

Plate number *N° de plaque d'immatriculation*	Juris *Aut. lég.*	Commercial *Utilitaire*	CVOR/*IUVU*	NSC/CNS	Code
		☐ Y/O	☐ Y/O	☐ Y/O	

CVOR No. - NSC No. / *N° de l'IUVU - N° du CNS*

And I further certify that I served an offence notice personally upon the person charged on the offence date.
J'atteste également qu'à la date de l'infraction, j'ai signifié, en mains propres, un avis d'infraction à la personne accusée.

☐ Or other service date of:
Autre date de signification, le :

Signature of issuing Provincial Offences Officer
Signature de l'agent des infractions provinciales

Officer No.
N° de l'agent

Platoon
Peloton

Unit
Unité

Set fine of
Amende fixée de
$ $

Total payable
$ $
Montant total exigible

Total payable includes set fine, applicable victim fine surcharge and costs.
Le montant total exigible comprend l'amende fixée, la suramende compensatoire applicable et les frais.

Summons issued. You are required to appear in court on
Assignation. *Vous êtes tenu(e) de comparaître devant le tribunal le*

Y/A M/M D/J Time / *À (Heure)*

2 0 M

Ct. room/*Salle d'audience*

at the Ontario Court of Justice P.O.A. Office at
à la Cour de justice de l'Ontario, Bureau des infractions provinciales au
45 Cedar Pointe Drive, Barrie, Ontario
45, promenade Cedar Pointe, Barrie (Ontario)

Conviction entered pursuant to section 9 of the *Provincial Offences Act*. Set fine imposed.
Déclaration de culpabilité inscrite conformément à l'article 9 de la Loi sur les infractions provinciales. *Amende fixée imposée.*

Y/A M/M D/J
2 0

03-588

Justice/*Juge*

POA 6000 v.1 rev. 01/09

The DATA Group of Companies S73059

Enforcement Agency notes/***Notes de l'agence d'exécution***

Blank Certificate of Offence and Enforcement Agency Notes

ICON Location Code / Code d'emplacement du RIII 3860
Offence Number / N° d'infraction 6571079A

Form 1 Reg. 950 *Provincial Offences Act* Ontario Court of Justice
Formule 1 Règl. 950 Loi sur les infractions provinciales *Cour de justice de l'Ontario*

Certificate of Offence / *Procès-verbal d'infraction*

I/Je soussigné(e)
(Print name/nom en lettres moulées)

Believe and certify that on the day of / *Crois et atteste que le* Y/A 2 0 M/M D/J Time/ *À (Heure)* M

Name / *Nom*
Family/*Nom de famille*
Given/*Prénom* Initials/*Initiales*

Address / *Adresse*
Number and street/*Numéro et nom de la rue*
Municipality/*Municipalité* P.O./C.P. Province Postal code/*Code postal*

Driver's licence No./*Numéro de permis de conduire* Juris *Aut. lég.*

Birthdate/*Date de naissance* Y/A 1 9 M/M D/J
Sex / *Sexe*
Motor Vehicle Involved / *Véhicule impliqué* N/N
Collision Involved / *Collision* Y/O
Witnesses / *Témoins* Y/O

At/*À*
Municipality/*Municipalité*

Did commit the offence of:
A commis l'infraction de :

Contrary to:
Contrairement à :

Sect./*L'art.*

Plate number *N° de plaque d'immatriculation*	Juris *Aut. lég.*	Commercial *Utilitaire*	CVOR/*IUVU*	NSC/CNS	Code
		Y/O	Y/O	Y/O	

CVOR No. NSC No. / *N° de l'IUVU - N° du CNS*

And I further certify that I served an offence notice personally upon the person charged on the offence date.
J'atteste également qu'à la date de l'infraction, j'ai signifié, en mains propres, un avis d'infraction à la personne accusée.

Or other service date of:
Autre date de signification, le :

Signature of issuing Provincial Offences Officer / *Signature de l'agent des infractions provinciales*
Officer No. / *N° de l'agent* Platoon / *Peloton* Unit / *Unité*

Set fine of / *Amende fixée de* $
Total payable $ **Montant total exigible**
Total payable includes set fine, applicable victim fine surcharge and costs.
Le montant total exigible comprend l'amende fixée, la suramende compensatoire applicable et les frais.

Summons issued. You are required to appear in court on Y/A 2 0 M/M D/J Time / *À (Heure)* M
Assignation. *Vous êtes tenu(e) de comparaître devant le tribunal le*
Ct. room/*Salle d'audience*
at the Ontario Court of Justice P.O.A. Office at
à la Cour de justice de l'Ontario, Bureau des infractions provinciales au
45 Cedar Pointe Drive, Barrie, Ontario
45, promenade Cedar Pointe, Barrie (Ontario)

Conviction entered pursuant to section 9 of the *Provincial Offences Act*. Set fine imposed.
Déclaration de culpabilité inscrite conformément à l'article 9 de la Loi sur les infractions provinciales. Amende fixée imposée.
Y/A 2 0 M/M D/J

Justice/*Juge*

POA 6000 v.1 rev. 01/09

The DATA Group of Companies 573059

Enforcement Agency notes/*Notes de l'agence d'exécution*

Blank Certificate of Offence and Enforcement Agency Notes

ICON Location Code / Code d'emplacement du RIII 3860
Offence Number / N° d'infraction 6571079A

Form 1 Reg. 950 *Provincial Offences Act* Ontario Court of Justice
Formule 1 Règl. 950 Loi sur les infractions provinciales *Cour de justice de l'Ontario*

Certificate of Offence / *Procès-verbal d'infraction*

I/Je soussigné(e)
(Print name/*nom en lettres moulées*)

Believe and certify that on the day of / *Crois et atteste que le* Y/A 2 0 M/M D/J Time/ *À (Heure)* M

Name / *Nom*
Family/*Nom de famille*
Given/*Prénom* Initials/*Initiales*

Address / *Adresse*
Number and street/*Numéro et nom de la rue*
Municipality/*Municipalité* P.O./C.P. Province Postal code/*Code postal*

Driver's licence No./*Numéro de permis de conduire* Juris / *Aut. lég.*

Birthdate/*Date de naissance* Y/A 1 9 M/M D/J
Sex / *Sexe*
Motor Vehicle Involved / *Véhicule impliqué* ☐ N/N
Collision Involved / *Collision* ☐ Y/O
Witnesses / *Témoins* ☐ Y/O

At/*À*

Municipality/*Municipalité*

Did commit the offence of:
A commis l'infraction de :

Contrary to:
Contrairement à :

Sect./*L'art.*

Plate number / *N° de plaque d'immatriculation*	Juris / *Aut. lég.*	Commercial / *Utilitaire*	CVOR/*IUVU*	NSC/*CNS*	Code
		☐ Y/O	☐ Y/O	☐ Y/O	

CVOR No. - NSC No. / *N° de l'IUVU - N° du CNS*

And I further certify that I served an offence notice personally upon the person charged on the offence date.
J'atteste également qu'à la date de l'infraction, j'ai signifié, en mains propres, un avis d'infraction à la personne accusée.

☐ Or other service date of: / *Autre date de signification, le :*

Signature of issuing Provincial Offences Officer / *Signature de l'agent des infractions provinciales*
Officer No. / *N° de l'agent* Platoon / *Peloton* Unit / *Unité*

Set fine of / *Amende fixée de* $
Total payable $ **_Montant total exigible_** $
Total payable includes set fine, applicable victim fine surcharge and costs.
Le montant total exigible comprend l'amende fixée, la suramende compensatoire applicable et les frais.

Summons issued. You are required to appear in court on / ***Assignation.*** *Vous êtes tenu(e) de comparaître devant le tribunal le* Y/A 2 0 M/M D/J Time / *À (Heure)* M

Ct. room/*Salle d'audience* at the Ontario Court of Justice P.O.A. Office at
à la Cour de justice de l'Ontario, Bureau des infractions provinciales au
45 Cedar Pointe Drive, Barrie, Ontario
45, promenade Cedar Pointe, Barrie (Ontario)

Conviction entered pursuant to section 9 of the *Provincial Offences Act*. Set fine imposed.
Déclaration de culpabilité inscrite conformément à l'article 9 de la Loi sur les infractions provinciales. Amende fixée imposée.
Y/A 2 0 M/M D/J

Justice/*Juge*

03-592

POA 6000 v.1 rev. 01/09

The DATA Group of Companies S73059

Enforcement Agency notes/*Notes de l'agence d'exécution*

Blank Certificate of Offence and Enforcement Agency Notes

ICON Location Code / Code d'emplacement du RIII 3860
Offence Number / N° d'infraction 6571079A

Form 1 Reg. 950 *Provincial Offences Act* Ontario Court of Justice
Formule 1 Règl. 950 Loi sur les infractions provinciales *Cour de justice de l'Ontario*

Certificate of Offence / *Procès-verbal d'infraction*

I/Je soussigné(e)
(Print name/nom en lettres moulées)

Believe and certify that on the day of
Crois et atteste que le
Y/A 2 0 M/M D/J Time/ *À (Heure)* M

Name
Nom
Family/*Nom de famille*
Given/*Prénom* Initials/*Initiales*

Address
Adresse
Number and street/*Numéro et nom de la rue*
Municipality/*Municipalité* P.O./C.P. Province Postal code/*Code postal*

Driver's licence No./*Numéro de permis de conduire* Juris *Aut. lég.*

Birthdate/*Date de naissance* Y/A 1 9 M/M D/J
Sex *Sexe*
Motor Vehicle Involved *Véhicule impliqué* N/N
Collision Involved *Collision* Y/O
Witnesses *Témoins* Y/O

At/*À*
Municipality/*Municipalité*

Did commit the offence of:
A commis l'infraction de :

Contrary to:
Contrairement à :

Sect./*L'art.*

Plate number *N° de plaque d'immatriculation*	Juris *Aut. lég.*	Commercial *Utilitaire*	CVOR/*IUVU*	NSC/*CNS*	Code
		Y/O	Y/O	Y/O	

CVOR No. - NSC No. / *N° de l'IUVU - N° du CNS*

And I further certify that I served an offence notice personally upon the person charged on the offence date.
J'atteste également qu'à la date de l'infraction, j'ai signifié, en mains propres, un avis d'infraction à la personne accusée.

Or other service date of:
Autre date de signification, le :

Signature of issuing Provincial Offences Officer
Signature de l'agent des infractions provinciales
Officer No. *N° de l'agent* Platoon *Peloton* Unit *Unité*

Set fine of *Amende fixée de* $
Total payable $ ***Montant total exigible***
Total payable includes set fine, applicable victim fine surcharge and costs.
Le montant total exigible comprend l'amende fixée, la suramende compensatoire applicable et les frais.

Summons issued. You are required to appear in court on
Assignation. *Vous êtes tenu(e) de comparaître devant le tribunal le*
Y/A 2 0 M/M D/J Time / *À (Heure)* M

Ct. room/*Salle d'audience* at the Ontario Court of Justice P.O.A. Office at
à la Cour de justice de l'Ontario, Bureau des infractions provinciales au
45 Cedar Pointe Drive, Barrie, Ontario
45, promenade Cedar Pointe, Barrie (Ontario)

Conviction entered pursuant to section 9 of the *Provincial Offences Act*. Set fine imposed.
Déclaration de culpabilité inscrite conformément à l'article 9 de la Loi sur les infractions provinciales. Amende fixée imposée.
Y/A 2 0 M/M D/J

Justice/*Juge*

POA 6000 v.1 rev. 01/09

The DATA Group of Companies S73050

Enforcement Agency notes/*Notes de l'agence d'exécution*

Blank Certificate of Offence and Enforcement Agency Notes

ICON Location Code / Code d'emplacement du RIII 3860 Offence Number / N° d'infraction 6571079A

Form 1 Reg. 950 *Provincial Offences Act* Ontario Court of Justice
Formule 1 Règl. 950 Loi sur les infractions provinciales *Cour de justice de l'Ontario*

Certificate of Offence / *Procès-verbal d'infraction*

I/Je soussigné(e)
(Print name/*nom en lettres moulées*)

Believe and certify that on the day of
Crois et atteste que le 2 0 Y/A M/M D/J Time/ *À (Heure)* M

Name
Nom
Family/*Nom de famille*
Given/*Prénom* Initials/*Initiales*

Address
Adresse
Number and street/*Numéro et nom de la rue*
Municipality/*Municipalité* P.O./C.P. Province Postal code/*Code postal*

Driver's licence No./*Numéro de permis de conduire*

Birthdate/*Date de naissance* Y/A 1 9 M/M D/J
Sex / *Sexe*
Motor Vehicle Involved / *Véhicule impliqué* ☐ N/N
Collision Involved / *Collision* ☐ Y/O
Witnesses / *Témoins* ☐ Y/O

At/*À*
Municipality/*Municipalité*

Did commit the offence of:
A commis l'infraction de :

Contrary to:
Contrairement à :

Sect./*L'art.*

Plate number / *N° de plaque d'immatriculation*	Juris / *Aut. lég.*	Commercial / *Utilitaire*	CVOR/*IUVU*	NSC/*CNS*	Code
		☐ Y/O	☐ Y/O	☐ Y/O	

CVOR No. - NSC No. / *N° de l'IUVU - N° du CNS*

And I further certify that I served an offence notice personally upon the person charged on the offence date.
J'atteste également qu'à la date de l'infraction, j'ai signifié, en mains propres, un avis d'infraction à la personne accusée.

☐ Or other service date of:
Autre date de signification, le :

Signature of issuing Provincial Offences Officer
Signature de l'agent des infractions provinciales
Officer No. / *N° de l'agent* Platoon / *Peloton* Unit / *Unité*

Set fine of / *Amende fixée de*	**Total payable** / ***Montant total exigible***	Total payable includes set fine, applicable victim fine surcharge and costs. / *Le montant total exigible comprend l'amende fixée, la suramende compensatoire applicable et les frais.*
$	$	

Summons issued. You are required to appear in court on
Assignation. *Vous êtes tenu(e) de comparaître devant le tribunal le*
2 0 Y/A M/M D/J Time / *À (Heure)* M

Ct. room/*Salle d'audience* at the Ontario Court of Justice P.O.A. Office at
à la Cour de justice de l'Ontario, Bureau des infractions provinciales au
45 Cedar Pointe Drive, Barrie, Ontario
45, promenade Cedar Pointe, Barrie (Ontario)

Conviction entered pursuant to section 9 of the *Provincial Offences Act*. Set fine imposed.
Déclaration de culpabilité inscrite conformément à l'article 9 de la Loi sur les infractions provinciales. Amende fixée imposée.
2 0 Y/A M/M D/J

Justice/*Juge*

POA 6000 v.1 rev. 01/09

The DATA Group of Companies 373059

Enforcement Agency notes/*Notes de l'agence d'exécution*

Blank Certificate of Offence and Enforcement Agency Notes

ICON Location Code / Code d'emplacement du RIII 3860

Offence Number / N° d'infraction 6571079A

Form 1 Reg. 950 *Provincial Offences Act* Ontario Court of Justice
Formule 1 Règl. 950 Loi sur les infractions provinciales *Cour de justice de l'Ontario*

Certificate of Offence / *Procès-verbal d'infraction*

I/Je soussigné(e)

(Print name/nom en lettres moulées)

Believe and certify that on the day of
Crois et atteste que le

Y/A 2 0 M/M D/J Time/ *À (Heure)* M

Name
Nom

Family/*Nom de famille*

Given/*Prénom* Initials/*Initiales*

Address
Adresse

Number and street/*Numéro et nom de la rue*

Municipality/*Municipalité* P.O./C.P. Province Postal code/*Code postal*

Driver's licence No./*Numéro de permis de conduire* Juris *Aut. lég.*

Birthdate/*Date de naissance* Y/A 1 9 M/M D/J

Sex *Sexe*

Motor Vehicle Involved *Véhicule impliqué* N/N

Collision Involved *Collision* Y/O

Witnesses *Témoins* Y/O

At/À

Municipality/*Municipalité*

Did commit the offence of:
A commis l'infraction de :

Contrary to:
Contrairement à :

Sect./*L'art.*

Plate number *N° de plaque d'immatriculation*	Juris *Aut. lég.*	Commercial *Utilitaire*	CVOR/*IUVU*	NSC/CNS	Code
		Y/O	Y/O	Y/O	

CVOR No. - NSC No. / *N° de l'IUVU - N° du CNS*

And I further certify that I served an offence notice personally upon the person charged on the offence date.
J'atteste également qu'à la date de l'infraction, j'ai signifié, en mains propres, un avis d'infraction à la personne accusée.

Or other service date of:
Autre date de signification, le :

Signature of issuing Provincial Offences Officer
Signature de l'agent des infractions provinciales

Officer No. *N° de l'agent* Platoon *Peloton* Unit *Unité*

Set fine of
Amende fixée de
$

Total payable $
Montant total exigible

Total payable includes set fine, applicable victim fine surcharge and costs.
Le montant total exigible comprend l'amende fixée, la suramende compensatoire applicable et les frais.

Summons issued. You are required to appear in court on
Assignation. *Vous êtes tenu(e) de comparaître devant le tribunal le*

Y/A 2 0 M/M D/J Time / *À (Heure)* M

Ct. room/*Salle d'audience*

at the Ontario Court of Justice P.O.A. Office at
à la Cour de justice de l'Ontario, Bureau des infractions provinciales au
45 Cedar Pointe Drive, Barrie, Ontario
45, promenade Cedar Pointe, Barrie (Ontario)

Conviction entered pursuant to section 9 of the *Provincial Offences Act*. Set fine imposed.
Déclaration de culpabilité inscrite conformément à l'article 9 de la Loi sur les infractions provinciales. Amende fixée imposée.

Y/A 2 0 M/M D/J

Justice/*Juge*

03-188

POA 6000 v.1 rev. 01/09

The DATA Group of Companies S73060

Enforcement Agency notes/*Notes de l'agence d'exécution*

Blank Certificate of Offence and Enforcement Agency Notes

ICON Location Code / Code d'emplacement du RIII 3860
Offence Number / N° d'infraction 6571079A

Form 1 Reg. 950 *Provincial Offences Act* Ontario Court of Justice
Formule 1 Règl. 950 Loi sur les infractions provinciales *Cour de justice de l'Ontario*

Certificate of Offence / *Procès-verbal d'infraction*

I/Je soussigné(e) ______ (Print name/nom en lettres moulées)

Believe and certify that on the day of / *Crois et atteste que le* Y/A 2 0 __ M/M __ D/J __ Time/ *À (Heure)* __ M

Name / *Nom* ______ Family/*Nom de famille*

______ Given/*Prénom* Initials/*Initiales*

Address / *Adresse* ______ Number and street/*Numéro et nom de la rue*

Municipality/*Municipalité* P.O./C.P. Province Postal code/*Code postal*

Driver's licence No./*Numéro de permis de conduire* Juris / Aut. lég.

Birthdate/*Date de naissance* Y/A 1 9 M/M D/J | Sex / *Sexe* | Motor Vehicle Involved / *Véhicule impliqué* ☐ N/N | Collision Involved / *Collision* ☐ Y/O | Witnesses / *Témoins* ☐ Y/O

At/*À* ______ Municipality/*Municipalité*

Did commit the offence of: / *A commis l'infraction de :* ______

Contrary to: / *Contrairement à :* ______

Sect./*L'art.*

Plate number / *N° de plaque d'immatriculation*	Juris / *Aut. lég.*	Commercial / *Utilitaire*	CVOR/*IUVU*	NSC/CNS	Code
		☐ Y/O	☐ Y/O	☐ Y/O	

CVOR No. - NSC No. / *N° de l'IUVU - N° du CNS*

And I further certify that I served an offence notice personally upon the person charged on the offence date. / *J'atteste également qu'à la date de l'infraction, j'ai signifié, en mains propres, un avis d'infraction à la personne accusée.*

☐ Or other service date of: / *Autre date de signification, le :*

Signature of issuing Provincial Offences Officer / *Signature de l'agent des infractions provinciales* | Officer No. / *N° de l'agent* | Platoon / *Peloton* | Unit / *Unité*

Set fine of / *Amende fixée de* $ | **Total payable** $ ***Montant total exigible*** | Total payable includes set fine, applicable victim fine surcharge and costs. / *Le montant total exigible comprend l'amende fixée, la suramende compensatoire applicable et les frais.*

Summons issued. You are required to appear in court on Y/A 2 0 M/M D/J Time / *À (Heure)* M
Assignation. *Vous êtes tenu(e) de comparaître devant le tribunal le*
Ct. room/*Salle d'audience* at the Ontario Court of Justice P.O.A. Office at / *à la Cour de justice de l'Ontario, Bureau des infractions provinciales au*
45 Cedar Pointe Drive, Barrie, Ontario
45, promenade Cedar Pointe, Barrie (Ontario)

Conviction entered pursuant to section 9 of the *Provincial Offences Act*. Set fine imposed. / *Déclaration de culpabilité inscrite conformément à l'article 9 de la Loi sur les infractions provinciales. Amende fixée imposée.* Y/A 2 0 M/M D/J

Justice/*Juge*

POA 6000 v.1 rev. 01/09

The DATA Group of Companies

Enforcement Agency notes/*Notes de l'agence d'exécution*

Blank Certificate of Offence and Enforcement Agency Notes

ICON Location Code / Code d'emplacement du RIII: 3860
Offence Number / N° d'infraction: 6571079A

Form 1 Reg. 950 *Provincial Offences Act* Ontario Court of Justice
Formule 1 Règl. 950 Loi sur les infractions provinciales *Cour de justice de l'Ontario*

Certificate of Offence / *Procès-verbal d'infraction*

I/Je soussigné(e) ____ (Print name/nom en lettres moulées)

Believe and certify that on the day of / *Crois et atteste que le* 2 0 __ Y/A __ M/M __ D/J __ Time/ *À (Heure)* __ M

Name / *Nom* ____ Family/*Nom de famille*

____ Given/*Prénom* ____ Initials/*Initiales*

Address / *Adresse* ____ Number and street/*Numéro et nom de la rue*

____ Municipality/*Municipalité* ____ P.O./C.P. ____ Province ____ Postal code/*Code postal*

Driver's licence No./*Numéro de permis de conduire* ____ Juris / Aut. lég.

Birthdate/*Date de naissance* 1 9 __ Y/A __ M/M __ D/J | Sex / *Sexe* | Motor Vehicle Involved / *Véhicule impliqué* ☐ N/N | Collision Involved / *Collision* ☐ Y/O | Witnesses / *Témoins* ☐ Y/O

At/*À* ____

____ Municipality/*Municipalité*

Did commit the offence of: / *A commis l'infraction de :* ____

Contrary to: / *Contrairement à :* ____

Sect./*L'art.* ____

Plate number / *N° de plaque d'immatriculation*	Juris / *Aut. lég.*	Commercial / *Utilitaire*	CVOR/*IUVU*	NSC/CNS	Code
		☐ Y/O	☐ Y/O	☐ Y/O	

CVOR No. - NSC No. / *N° de l'IUVU N° du CNS*

And I further certify that I served an offence notice personally upon the person charged on the offence date.
J'atteste également qu'à la date de l'infraction, j'ai signifié, en mains propres, un avis d'infraction à la personne accusée.

☐ Or other service date of: / *Autre date de signification, le :*

Signature of issuing Provincial Offences Officer / *Signature de l'agent des infractions provinciales* | Officer No. / *N° de l'agent* | Platoon / *Peloton* | Unit / *Unité*

Set fine of / *Amende fixée de*	Total payable / *Montant total exigible*	
$ $	$ $	Total payable includes set fine, applicable victim fine surcharge and costs. *Le montant total exigible comprend l'amende fixée, la suramende compensatoire applicable et les frais.*

Summons issued. You are required to appear in court on / ***Assignation.*** *Vous êtes tenu(e) de comparaître devant le tribunal le* 2 0 __ Y/A __ M/M __ D/J __ Time / *À (Heure)* __ M

Ct. room/*Salle d'audience* ____ at the Ontario Court of Justice P.O.A. Office at / *à la Cour de justice de l'Ontario, Bureau des infractions provinciales au* **45 Cedar Pointe Drive, Barrie, Ontario** / ***45, promenade Cedar Pointe, Barrie (Ontario)***

Conviction entered pursuant to section 9 of the *Provincial Offences Act*. Set fine imposed.
Déclaration de culpabilité inscrite conformément à l'article 9 de la Loi sur les infractions provinciales. Amende fixée imposée.

2 0 __ Y/A __ M/M __ D/J

Justice/*Juge* ____

POA 6000 v.1 rev. 01/09

The DATA Group of Companies S73059

Enforcement Agency notes/*Notes de l'agence d'exécution*

Blank Certificate of Offence and Enforcement Agency Notes

ICON Location Code / Code d'emplacement du RIII 3860

Offence Number / N° d'infraction 6571079A

Form 1 Reg. 950 *Provincial Offences Act* Ontario Court of Justice
Formule 1 Règl. 950 Loi sur les infractions provinciales *Cour de justice de l'Ontario*

Certificate of Offence / *Procès-verbal d'infraction*

I/Je soussigné(e) ______ (Print name/nom en lettres moulées)

Believe and certify that on the day of / *Crois et atteste que le* 2 0 __ Y/A __ M/M __ D/J Time/ *À (Heure)* __ M

Name / *Nom* ______ Family/*Nom de famille*

______ Given/*Prénom* Initials/*Initiales*

Address / *Adresse* ______ Number and street/*Numéro et nom de la rue*

______ Municipality/*Municipalité* P.O./C.P. Province Postal code/*Code postal*

Driver's licence No./*Numéro de permis de conduire* ______ Juris *Aut. lég.*

Birthdate/*Date de naissance* 1 9 __ Y/A __ M/M __ D/J

Sex / *Sexe*

Motor Vehicle Involved / *Véhicule impliqué* ☐ N/N

Collision Involved / *Collision* ☐ Y/O

Witnesses / *Témoins* ☐ Y/O

At/*À* ______

______ Municipality/*Municipalité*

Did commit the offence of: / *A commis l'infraction de :* ______

Contrary to: / *Contrairement à :* ______

Sect./*L'art.* ______

Plate number / *N° de plaque d'immatriculation*	Juris / *Aut. lég.*	Commercial / *Utilitaire*	CVOR/*IUVU*	NSC/*CNS*	Code
		☐ Y/O	☐ Y/O	☐ Y/O	

CVOR No. - NSC No. / *N° de l'IUVU - N° du CNS* ______

And I further certify that I served an offence notice personally upon the person charged on the offence date.
J'atteste également qu'à la date de l'infraction, j'ai signifié, en mains propres, un avis d'infraction à la personne accusée.

☐ Or other service date of: / *Autre date de signification, le :*

Signature of issuing Provincial Offences Officer / *Signature de l'agent des infractions provinciales* | Officer No. / *N° de l'agent* | Platoon / *Peloton* | Unit / *Unité*

Set fine of / *Amende fixée de* $ ______ | **Total payable** $ ______ ***Montant total exigible***

Total payable includes set fine, applicable victim fine surcharge and costs.
Le montant total exigible comprend l'amende fixée, la suramende compensatoire applicable et les frais.

Summons issued. You are required to appear in court on 2 0 __ Y/A __ M/M __ D/J Time / *À (Heure)* __ M

Assignation. *Vous êtes tenu(e) de comparaître devant le tribunal le*

Ct. room/*Salle d'audience* ______ at the Ontario Court of Justice P.O.A. Office at
à la Cour de justice de l'Ontario, Bureau des infractions provinciales au
45 Cedar Pointe Drive, Barrie, Ontario
45, promenade Cedar Pointe, Barrie (Ontario)

Conviction entered pursuant to section 9 of the *Provincial Offences Act*. Set fine imposed.
Déclaration de culpabilité inscrite conformément à l'article 9 de la Loi sur les infractions provinciales. Amende fixée imposée.

2 0 __ Y/A __ M/M __ D/J

Justice/*Juge*

POA 6000 v.1 rev. 01/09

The DATA Group of Companies 573059

Enforcement Agency notes/***Notes de l'agence d'exécution***

Blank Certificate of Offence and Enforcement Agency Notes

ICON Location Code / Code d'emplacement du RIIl 3860
Offence Number / N° d'infraction 6571079A

Form 1 Reg. 950 *Provincial Offences Act* Ontario Court of Justice
Formule 1 Règl. 950 Loi sur les infractions provinciales *Cour de justice de l'Ontario*

Certificate of Offence / *Procès-verbal d'infraction*

I/Je soussigné(e)
(Print name/*nom en lettres moulées*)

Believe and certify that on the day of
Crois et atteste que le
Y/A 2 0 M/M D/J Time/ *À (Heure)* M

Name
Nom
Family/*Nom de famille*
Given/*Prénom* Initials/*Initiales*

Address
Adresse
Number and street/*Numéro et nom de la rue*
Municipality/*Municipalité* P.O./C.P. Province Postal code/*Code postal*

Driver's licence No./*Numéro de permis de conduire*

Birthdate/*Date de naissance* Y/A 1 9 M/M D/J
Sex / *Sexe*
Motor Vehicle Involved / *Véhicule impliqué* N/N
Collision Involved / *Collision* Y/O
Witnesses / *Témoins* Y/O

At/*À*
Municipality/*Municipalité*

Did commit the offence of:
A commis l'infraction de :

Contrary to:
Contrairement à :

Sect./*L'art.*

Plate number *N° de plaque d'immatriculation*	Juris *Aut. lég.*	Commercial *Utilitaire*	CVOR/*IUVU*	NSC/*CNS*	Code
		Y/O	Y/O	Y/O	

CVOR No. - NSC No. / *N° de l'IUVU - N° du CNS*

And I further certify that I served an offence notice personally upon the person charged on the offence date.
J'atteste également qu'à la date de l'infraction, j'ai signifié, en mains propres, un avis d'infraction à la personne accusée.

Or other service date of:
Autre date de signification, le :

Signature of issuing Provincial Offences Officer
Signature de l'agent des infractions provinciales
Officer No. / *N° de l'agent* Platoon / *Peloton* Unit / *Unité*

Set fine of / *Amende fixée de* $
Total payable $ ***Montant total exigible***
Total payable includes set fine, applicable victim fine surcharge and costs.
Le montant total exigible comprend l'amende fixée, la suramende compensatoire applicable et les frais.

Summons issued. You are required to appear in court on
Y/A 2 0 M/M D/J Time / *À (Heure)* M
Assignation. *Vous êtes tenu(e) de comparaître devant le tribunal le*
Ct. room/*Salle d'audience*
at the Ontario Court of Justice P.O.A. Office at
à la Cour de justice de l'Ontario, Bureau des infractions provinciales au
45 Cedar Pointe Drive, Barrie, Ontario
45, promenade Cedar Pointe, Barrie (Ontario)

Conviction entered pursuant to section 9 of the *Provincial Offences Act*. Set fine imposed.
Déclaration de culpabilité inscrite conformément à l'article 9 de la Loi sur les infractions provinciales. Amende fixée imposée.
Y/A 2 0 M/M D/J

Justice/*Juge*

POA 6000 v.1 rev. 01/09

The DATA Group of Companies S73059

Enforcement Agency notes/***Notes de l'agence d'exécution***

Blank Certificate of Offence and Enforcement Agency Notes

ICON Location Code / Code d'emplacement du RIII 3860
Offence Number / N° d'infraction 6571079A

Form 1 Reg. 950 *Provincial Offences Act* Ontario Court of Justice
Formule 1 Règl. 950 Loi sur les infractions provinciales *Cour de justice de l'Ontario*

Certificate of Offence / *Procès-verbal d'infraction*

I/Je soussigné(e)

(Print name/nom en lettres moulées)

Believe and certify that on the day of / *Crois et atteste que le* Y/A 2 0 M/M D/J Time/ À (Heure) M

Name / *Nom*

Family/Nom de famille

Given/Prénom Initials/Initiales

Address / *Adresse*

Number and street/Numéro et nom de la rue

Municipality/Municipalité P.O./C.P. Province Postal code/Code postal

Driver's licence No./*Numéro de permis de conduire*

Birthdate/*Date de naissance* Y/A 1 9 M/M D/J

Sex / *Sexe*

Motor Vehicle Involved / *Véhicule impliqué* N/N

Collision Involved / *Collision* Y/O

Witnesses / *Témoins* Y/O

At/À

Municipality/Municipalité

Did commit the offence of:
A commis l'infraction de :

Contrary to:
Contrairement à :

Sect./*L'art.*

Plate number / *N° de plaque d'immatriculation*	Juris / *Aut. lég.*	Commercial / *Utilitaire*	CVOR/*IUVU*	NSC/CNS	Code
		Y/O	Y/O	Y/O	

CVOR No. - NSC No. / *N° de l'IUVU - N° du CNS*

And I further certify that I served an offence notice personally upon the person charged on the offence date.
J'atteste également qu'à la date de l'infraction, j'ai signifié, en mains propres, un avis d'infraction à la personne accusée.

Or other service date of:
Autre date de signification, le :

Signature of issuing Provincial Offences Officer / *Signature de l'agent des infractions provinciales*	Officer No. / *N° de l'agent*	Platoon / *Peloton*	Unit / *Unité*

Set fine of / *Amende fixée de*	Total payable / *Montant total exigible*	Total payable includes set fine, applicable victim fine surcharge and costs.
$	$	*Le montant total exigible comprend l'amende fixée, la suramende compensatoire applicable et les frais.*

Summons issued. You are required to appear in court on Y/A 2 0 M/M D/J Time / À (Heure) M
Assignation. *Vous êtes tenu(e) de comparaître devant le tribunal le*

Ct. room/Salle d'audience at the Ontario Court of Justice P.O.A. Office at
à la Cour de justice de l'Ontario, Bureau des infractions provinciales au
45 Cedar Pointe Drive, Barrie, Ontario
45, promenade Cedar Pointe, Barrie (Ontario)

Conviction entered pursuant to section 9 of the *Provincial Offences Act*. Set fine imposed.
Déclaration de culpabilité inscrite conformément à l'article 9 de la Loi sur les infractions provinciales. Amende fixée imposée
Y/A 2 0 M/M D/J

Justice/Juge

POA 6000 v.1 rev. 01/09

The DATA Group of Companies 573059

Enforcement Agency notes/*Notes de l'agence d'exécution*

Blank Certificate of Offence and Enforcement Agency Notes

ICON Location Code / Code d'emplacement du RIII 3860
Offence Number / N° d'infraction 6571079A

Form 1 Reg. 950 *Provincial Offences Act* Ontario Court of Justice
Formule 1 Règl. 950 Loi sur les infractions provinciales *Cour de justice de l'Ontario*

Certificate of Offence / *Procès-verbal d'infraction*

I/Je soussigné(e) (Print name/nom en lettres moulées)

Believe and certify that on the day of / *Crois et atteste que le* Y/A 2 0 M/M D/J Time/ *À (Heure)* M

Name / *Nom* Family/*Nom de famille*

Given/*Prénom* Initials/*Initiales*

Address / *Adresse* Number and street/*Numéro et nom de la rue*

Municipality/*Municipalité* P.O./C.P. Province Postal code/*Code postal*

Driver's licence No./*Numéro de permis de conduire* Juris *Aut. lég.*

Birthdate/*Date de naissance* Y/A 1 9 M/M D/J | Sex *Sexe* | Motor Vehicle Involved *Véhicule impliqué* N/N | Collision Involved *Collision* Y/O | Witnesses *Témoins* Y/O

At/À

Municipality/*Municipalité*

Did commit the offence of: / *A commis l'infraction de :*

Contrary to: / *Contrairement à :*

Sect./*L'art.*

Plate number *N° de plaque d'immatriculation*	Juris *Aut. lég.*	Commercial *Utilitaire*	CVOR/*IUVU*	NSC/CNS	Code
		Y/O	Y/O	Y/O	

CVOR No. - NSC No. / *N° de l'IUVU - N° du CNS*

And I further certify that I served an offence notice personally upon the person charged on the offence date.
J'atteste également qu'à la date de l'infraction, j'ai signifié, en mains propres, un avis d'infraction à la personne accusée.

Or other service date of: / *Autre date de signification, le :*

Signature of issuing Provincial Offences Officer *Signature de l'agent des infractions provinciales*	Officer No. *N° de l'agent*	Platoon *Peloton*	Unit *Unité*

Set fine of *Amende fixée de*	Total payable / *Montant total exigible*	
$	$	Total payable includes set fine, applicable victim fine surcharge and costs. *Le montant total exigible comprend l'amende fixée, la suramende compensatoire applicable et les frais.*

Summons issued. You are required to appear in court on Y/A 2 0 M/M D/J Time / *À (Heure)* M
Assignation. *Vous êtes tenu(e) de comparaître devant le tribunal le*

Ct. room/*Salle d'audience* at the Ontario Court of Justice P.O.A. Office at
à la Cour de justice de l'Ontario, Bureau des infractions provinciales au
45 Cedar Pointe Drive, Barrie, Ontario
45, promenade Cedar Pointe, Barrie (Ontario)

Conviction entered pursuant to section 9 of the *Provincial Offences Act*. Set fine imposed.
Déclaration de culpabilité inscrite conformément à l'article 9 de la Loi sur les infractions provinciales. Amende fixée imposée.
Y/A 2 0 M/M D/J

Justice/*Juge*

POA 6000 v.1 rev. 01/09

The DATA Group of Companies 573050

Enforcement Agency notes/*Notes de l'agence d'exécution*

Blank Certificate of Offence and Enforcement Agency Notes

ICON Location Code / Code d'emplacement du RIII 3860

Offence Number / N° d'infraction 6571079A

Form 1 Reg. 950 *Provincial Offences Act* Ontario Court of Justice
Formule 1 Règl. 950 Loi sur les infractions provinciales *Cour de justice de l'Ontario*

Certificate of Offence / *Procès-verbal d'infraction*

I/Je soussigné(e) (Print name/*nom en lettres moulées*)

Believe and certify that on the day of / *Crois et atteste que le* Y/A 2 0 M/M D/J Time/ *À (Heure)* M

Name / *Nom* Family/*Nom de famille* Given/*Prénom* Initials/*Initiales*

Address / *Adresse* Number and street/*Numéro et nom de la rue*

Municipality/*Municipalité* P.O./C.P. Province Postal code/*Code postal*

Driver's licence No./*Numéro de permis de conduire* Juris / *Aut. lég.*

Birthdate/*Date de naissance* Y/A 1 9 M/M D/J Sex / *Sexe* Motor Vehicle Involved / *Véhicule impliqué* ☐ N/N Collision Involved / *Collision* ☐ Y/O Witnesses / *Témoins* ☐ Y/O

At/*À*

Municipality/*Municipalité*

Did commit the offence of: / *A commis l'infraction de :*

Contrary to: / *Contrairement à :*

Sect./*L'art.*

Plate number / *N° de plaque d'immatriculation*	Juris / *Aut. lég.*	Commercial / *Utilitaire*	CVOR/*IUVU*	NSC/*CNS*	Code
		☐ Y/O	☐ Y/O	☐ Y/O	

CVOR No. - NSC No. / *N° de l'IUVU - N° du CNS*

And I further certify that I served an offence notice personally upon the person charged on the offence date. / *J'atteste également qu'à la date de l'infraction, j'ai signifié, en mains propres, un avis d'infraction à la personne accusée.*

☐ Or other service date of: / *Autre date de signification, le :*

Signature of issuing Provincial Offences Officer / *Signature de l'agent des infractions provinciales* — Officer No. / *N° de l'agent* — Platoon / *Peloton* — Unit / *Unité*

Set fine of / *Amende fixée de* $ $ — **Total payable** $ $ **Montant total exigible** — Total payable includes set fine, applicable victim fine surcharge and costs. / *Le montant total exigible comprend l'amende fixée, la suramende compensatoire applicable et les frais.*

Summons issued. You are required to appear in court on / ***Assignation.*** *Vous êtes tenu(e) de comparaître devant le tribunal le* Y/A 2 0 M/M D/J Time / *À (Heure)* M

Ct. room/*Salle d'audience* at the Ontario Court of Justice P.O.A. Office at / *à la Cour de justice de l'Ontario, Bureau des infractions provinciales au*
45 Cedar Pointe Drive, Barrie, Ontario
45, promenade Cedar Pointe, Barrie (Ontario)

Conviction entered pursuant to section 9 of the Provincial Offences Act. Set fine imposed. / *Déclaration de culpabilité inscrite conformément à l'article 9 de la Loi sur les infractions provinciales. Amende fixée imposée.* Y/A 2 0 M/M D/J

Justice/*Juge*

POA 6000 v.1 rev. 01/09

The DATA Group of Companies S73059

Enforcement Agency notes/*Notes de l'agence d'exécution*

Blank Summons and Enforcement Agency Notes

ICON Location Code
Code d'emplacement du RIII
3860

Form 6 Reg. 950 *Provincial Offences Act* Ontario Court of Justice
Formule 6 Règl. 950 Loi sur les infractions provinciales *Cour de justice de l'Ontario*

Summons / *Assignation*

Believes and certifies that on the day of
Croit et atteste que le

(Print name/nom en lettres moulées)

Y/A 2 0 | M/M | D/J | Time/ *À (Heure)* M

Name
Nom

Family/*Nom de famille*

Given/*Prénom* Initials/*Initiales*

Address
Adresse

Number and street/*Numéro et nom de la rue*

Municipality/*Municipalité* P.O./C.P. Province Postal code/*Code postal*

Driver's licence No./*Numéro de permis de conduire*

Birthdate/*Date de naissance*
Y/A 1 9 | M/M | D/J

Sex *Sexe*

Motor Vehicle Involved *Véhicule impliqué* ☐ N/N

Collision Involved *Collision* ☐ Y/O

Witnesses *Témoins* ☐ Y/O

At/*À*

Municipality/*Municipalité*

Did commit the offence of:
A commis l'infraction de :

Contrary to:
Contrairement à :

Sect./*L'art.*

Plate number *N° de plaque d'immatriculation*	Juris *Aut. lég.*	Commercial *Utilitaire*	CVOR/*IUVU*	NSC/CNS	Code
		☐ Y/O	☐ Y/O	☐ Y/O	

CVOR No. - NSC No. / *N° de l'IUVU - N° du CNS*

This is therefore to command you in Her Majesty's name to appear before the Ontario Court of Justice.
Pour ces motifs, il vous est enjoint, au nom de Sa Majesté, de comparaître devant la Cour de justice de l'Ontario.

Officer No. *N° de l'agent*	Platoon *Peloton*	Unit *Unité*

Y/A 2 0 | M/M | D/J | Time / *À (Heure)* M

Ct. room/*Salle d'audience* at the Ontario Court of Justice P.O.A. Office at
à la Cour de justice de l'Ontario, Bureau des infractions provinciales au
45 Cedar Pointe Drive, Barrie, Ontario
45, promenade Cedar Pointe, Barrie (Ontario)

And to attend thereafter as required by the court in order to be dealt with according to law, this summons is served under Part I of the *Provincial Offences Act*.
Et d'être présent(e) par la suite selon les exigences du tribunal, afin d'être traité(e) selon la loi. La présente assignation vous est signifiée conformément à la partie I de la Loi sur les infractions provinciales.

Signature of Provincial Offences Officer
Signature de l'agent des infractions provinciales

Enforcement Agency notes/*Notes de l'agence d'exécution*

Blank Summons and Enforcement Agency Notes

ICON Location Code
Code d'emplacement du RIII
3860

Form 6 Reg. 950 *Provincial Offences Act* Ontario Court of Justice
Formule 6 Règl. 950 Loi sur les infractions provinciales *Cour de justice de l'Ontario*

Summons / *Assignation*

Believes and certifies that on the day of
Croit et atteste que le

(Print name/nom en lettres moulées)

Y/A M/M D/J Time/ *À (Heure)*

2 0 M

Name
Nom

Family/*Nom de famille*

Given/*Prénom* Initials/*Initiales*

Address
Adresse

Number and street/*Numéro et nom de la rue*

Municipality/*Municipalité* P.O./C.P. Province Postal code/*Code postal*

Driver's licence No./*Numéro de permis de conduire*

Juris *Aut. lég.*

Birthdate/*Date de naissance*
Y/A M/M D/J
1 9

Sex *Sexe*

Motor Vehicle Involved *Véhicule impliqué* ☐ N/N

Collision Involved *Collision* ☐ Y/O

Witnesses *Témoins* ☐ Y/O

At/*À*

Municipality/*Municipalité*

Did commit the offence of:
A commis l'infraction de :

Contrary to:
Contrairement à :

Sect./*L'art.*

Plate number *N° de plaque d'immatriculation*	Juris *Aut. lég.*	Commercial *Utilitaire*	CVOR/*IUVU*	NSC/CNS	Code
		☐ Y/O	☐ Y/O	☐ Y/O	
CVOR No. - NSC No. / *N° de l'IUVU - N° du CNS*					

This is therefore to command you in Her Majesty's name to appear before the Ontario Court of Justice.
Pour ces motifs, il vous est enjoint, au nom de Sa Majesté, de comparaître devant la Cour de justice de l'Ontario.

Officer No. *N° de l'agent*	Platoon *Peloton*	Unit *Unité*

Y/A M/M D/J Time / *À (Heure)*

2 0 M

Ct. room/*Salle d'audience*

at the Ontario Court of Justice P.O.A. Office at
à la Cour de justice de l'Ontario, Bureau des infractions provinciales au
45 Cedar Pointe Drive, Barrie, Ontario
45, promenade Cedar Pointe, Barrie (Ontario)

And to attend thereafter as required by the court in order to be dealt with according to law, this summons is served under Part I of the *Provincial Offences Act*.
Et d'être présent(e) par la suite selon les exigences du tribunal, afin d'être traité(e) selon la loi. La présente assignation vous est signifiée conformément à la partie I de la Loi sur les infractions provinciales.

Signature of Provincial Offences Officer
Signature de l'agent des infractions provinciales

Enforcement Agency notes/***Notes de l'agence d'exécution***

Blank Summons and Enforcement Agency Notes

ICON Location Code
Code d'emplacement du RIII
3860

Form 6 Reg. 950 *Provincial Offences Act* Ontario Court of Justice
Formule 6 Règl. 950 Loi sur les infractions provinciales *Cour de justice de l'Ontario*

Summons / *Assignation*

Believes and certifies that on the day of
Croit et atteste que le

(Print name/*nom en lettres moulées*)

Y/A M/M D/J Time/ *À (Heure)*

2 0 M

Name
Nom

Family/*Nom de famille*

Given/*Prénom* Initials/*Initiales*

Address
Adresse

Number and street/*Numéro et nom de la rue*

Municipality/*Municipalité* P.O./*C.P.* Province Postal code/*Code postal*

Driver's licence No./*Numéro de permis de conduire*

Birthdate/*Date de naissance* Y/A M/M D/J

1 9

Sex / *Sexe*

Motor Vehicle Involved / *Véhicule impliqué* ☐ N/N

Collision Involved / *Collision* ☐ Y/O

Witnesses / *Témoins* ☐ Y/O

At/*À*

Municipality/*Municipalité*

Did commit the offence of:
A commis l'infraction de :

Contrary to:
Contrairement à :

Sect./*L'art.*

Plate number *N° de plaque d'immatriculation*	Juris *Aut. lég.*	Commercial *Utilitaire*	CVOR/*IUVU*	NSC/CNS	Code
		☐ Y/O	☐ Y/O	☐ Y/O	

CVOR No. - NSC No. / *N° de l'IUVU - N° du CNS*

This is therefore to command you in Her Majesty's name to appear before the Ontario Court of Justice.
Pour ces motifs, il vous est enjoint, au nom de Sa Majesté, de comparaître devant la Cour de justice de l'Ontario.

Officer No. *N° de l'agent*	Platoon *Peloton*	Unit *Unité*

Y/A M/M D/J Time / *À (Heure)*

2 0 M

Ct. room/*Salle d'audience* at the Ontario Court of Justice P.O.A. Office at
à la Cour de justice de l'Ontario, Bureau des infractions provinciales au
45 Cedar Pointe Drive, Barrie, Ontario
45, promenade Cedar Pointe, Barrie (Ontario)

And to attend thereafter as required by the court in order to be dealt with according to law, this summons is served under Part I of the *Provincial Offences Act*.
Et d'être présent(e) par la suite selon les exigences du tribunal, afin d'être traité(e) selon la loi. La présente assignation vous est signifiée conformément à la partie I de la Loi sur les infractions provinciales.

Signature of Provincial Offences Officer
Signature de l'agent des infractions provinciales

Enforcement Agency notes/*Notes de l'agence d'exécution*

Blank Summons and Enforcement Agency Notes

ICON Location Code
Code d'emplacement du RIII
3860

Form 6 Reg. 950 *Provincial Offences Act* Ontario Court of Justice
Formule 6 Règl. 950 Loi sur les infractions provinciales *Cour de justice de l'Ontario*

Summons / *Assignation*

Believes and certifies that on the day of
Croit et atteste que le
(Print name/nom en lettres moulées)
Y/A M/M D/J Time/ *À (Heure)*
2 0 M

Name
Nom
Family/*Nom de famille*
Given/*Prénom* Initials/*Initiales*

Address
Adresse
Number and street/*Numéro et nom de la rue*
Municipality/*Municipalité* P.O./C.P. Province Postal code/*Code postal*

Driver's licence No./*Numéro de permis de conduire*
Juris *Aut. lég.*

Birthdate/*Date de naissance*
Y/A M/M D/J
1 9
Sex *Sexe*
Motor Vehicle Involved *Véhicule impliqué* ☐ N/N
Collision Involved *Collision* ☐ Y/O
Witnesses *Témoins* ☐ Y/O

At/*À*
Municipality/*Municipalité*

Did commit the offence of:
A commis l'infraction de :

Contrary to:
Contrairement à :

Sect./*L'art.*

Plate number *N° de plaque d'immatriculation*	Juris *Aut. lég.*	Commercial *Utilitaire*	CVOR/*IUVU*	NSC/CNS	Code
		☐ Y/O	☐ Y/O	☐ Y/O	

CVOR No. - NSC No. / *N° de l'IUVU - N° du CNS*

This is therefore to command you in Her Majesty's name to appear before the Ontario Court of Justice.
Pour ces motifs, il vous est enjoint, au nom de Sa Majesté, de comparaître devant la Cour de justice de l'Ontario.

Officer No. *N° de l'agent*	Platoon *Peloton*	Unit *Unité*

Y/A M/M D/J Time / *À (Heure)*
2 0 M

Ct. room/*Salle d'audience* at the Ontario Court of Justice P.O.A. Office at
à la Cour de justice de l'Ontario, Bureau des infractions provinciales au
45 Cedar Pointe Drive, Barrie, Ontario
45, promenade Cedar Pointe, Barrie (Ontario)

And to attend thereafter as required by the court in order to be dealt with according to law, this summons is served under Part I of the *Provincial Offences Act*.
Et d'être présent(e) par la suite selon les exigences du tribunal, afin d'être traité(e) selon la loi. La présente assignation vous est signifiée conformément à la partie I de la Loi sur les infractions provinciales.

Signature of Provincial Offences Officer
Signature de l'agent des infractions provinciales

Enforcement Agency notes/*Notes de l'agence d'exécution*

Extra Blank Enforcement Agency Notes

Enforcement Agency notes/*Notes de l'agence d'exécution*

Enforcement Agency notes/*Notes de l'agence d'exécution*

Extra Blank Enforcement Agency Notes

Enforcement Agency notes/*Notes de l'agence d'exécution*

Enforcement Agency notes/*Notes de l'agence d'exécution*

Extra Blank Enforcement Agency Notes

Enforcement Agency notes/*Notes de l'agence d'exécution*

Enforcement Agency notes/*Notes de l'agence d'exécution*

Extra Blank Enforcement Agency Notes

Enforcement Agency notes/*Notes de l'agence d'exécution*

Enforcement Agency notes/*Notes de l'agence d'exécution*

Extra Blank Enforcement Agency Notes

Enforcement Agency notes/*Notes de l'agence d'exécution*

Enforcement Agency notes/*Notes de l'agence d'exécution*

Extra Blank Enforcement Agency Notes

Enforcement Agency notes/*Notes de l'agence d'exécution*

Enforcement Agency notes/*Notes de l'agence d'exécution*

Extra Blank Enforcement Agency Notes

Enforcement Agency notes/*Notes de l'agence d'exécution*

Enforcement Agency notes/*Notes de l'agence d'exécution*

Extra Blank Enforcement Agency Notes

Enforcement Agency notes/*Notes de l'agence d'exécution*

Enforcement Agency notes/*Notes de l'agence d'exécution*

Extra Blank Enforcement Agency Notes

Enforcement Agency notes/*Notes de l'agence d'exécution*

Enforcement Agency notes/*Notes de l'agence d'exécution*

Extra Blank Enforcement Agency Notes

Enforcement Agency notes/*Notes de l'agence d'exécution*

Enforcement Agency notes/*Notes de l'agence d'exécution*

Summons to Defendant

Form 104 Courts of Justice Act R.R.O. 1990 Reg. 200
Formule 104 Loi sur les tribunaux judiciaires L.R.O. 1990, Règl. 200

SUMMONS TO DEFENDANT
SOMMATION ADRESSÉE AU DÉFENDEUR
Under Section 22 of the Provincial Offences Act
Aux termes de l'article 22 de la Loi sur les infractions provinciales

ONTARIO COURT OF JUSTICE PROVINCE OF ONTARIO
COUR DE JUSTICE DE L'ONTARIO PROVINCE DE L'ONTARIO

CD 756516

YOU ARE CHARGED WITH THE FOLLOWING OFFENCE
VOUS ÊTES ACCUSÉ(E) DE L'INFRATION SUIVANTE

On the / *Le* ______ day of ______ yr / *an* ______ at / *à* ______ **M**

NAME / *NOM* ______
LAST/*NOM DE FAMILLE* FIRST/*PRÉNOM* MIDDLE/*INITIALE*

ADDRESS / *ADRESSE* ______
NUMBER AND STREET/*N° ET RUE*

______
MUNICIPALITY/*MUNICIPALITÉ* P.O./*C.P.* PROVINCE POSTAL CODE/*CODE POSTAL*

AT / *À* ______

______
MUNICIPALITY/*MUNICIPALITÉ*

DID COMMIT THE OFFENCE OF
VOUS AVEZ COMMIS L'INFRACTION SUIVANTE ______

______

______

______

CONTRARY TO
PAR DÉROGATION À ______

______ SECTION / *ARTICLE* ______

THEREFORE YOU ARE COMMANDED IN HER MAJESTY'S NAME TO APPEAR BEFORE THE ONTARIO COURT OF JUSTICE

À CES CAUSES, AU NOM DE SA MAJESTÉ, VOUS ÊTES SOMMÉ(E) DE COMPARAÎTRE DEVANT LA COUR DE JUSTICE DE L'ONTARIO

AT / *À* ______

______ On the / *Le* ______ day of ______

yr / *an* ______ at / *à* ______ **M**

Courtroom / *salle d'audience* ______

and to appear thereafter as required by the court in order to be dealt with according to law.

et de comparaître par la suite chaque fois que le tribunal l'exigera de façon à ce que vous soyez jugé(e) selon la Loi.

Issued - *Émis*
this *ce*
day of ______ yr / *an* ______

______
SIGNATURE OF PROVINCIAL OFFENCES OFFICER
SIGNATURE DE L'AGENT D'INFRACTIONS PROVINCIALES

Summons confirmed / *Sommation confirmée* ☐
Summons cancelled / *Sommation annulée* ☐

this / *le* ______ day of ______ yr / *an* ______ by / *par* ______
A judge or justice of the peace in and for the Province of Ontario
Juge ou juge de paix dans et pour la province de l'Ontario

DRIVER'S LICENSE NO. *PERMIS DE CONDUIRE NUMÉRO* CLASS *CATÉGORIE* COND *RESTRICTION*

SEX *SEXE* BIRTHDATE *DATE DE NAISSANCE* DAY *JOUR* MO *MOIS* YEAR *ANNÉE* REGISTRATION NO. *NUMÉRO D'ENREGISTREMENT* YEAR *ANNÉE* PROVINCE MAKE *MARQUE*

OFFICER NO. *AGENT DE POLICE NO* UNIT *GROUPE*

Defendant's Copy
Copie du défendeur

NOTE This summons is issued under Part III of the Provincial Offences Act.
Cette sommation est émise aux termes de la partie III de la Loi sur les infractions provinciales.

AFFIDAVIT OF SERVICE OF SUMMONS UNDER SECTION
26(6) OF THE PROVINCIAL OFFENCES ACT
R.R.O. 1990, REG. 200

ONTARIO COURT
OF JUSTICE

I, ______ ,of ______ ,
a provincial offences officer make oath and say as follows, that on the ______ day of ______ , yr ______ , I did serve the summons in the manner indicated below:
(Check one)

(a) ☐ by delivering it personally on the defendant

(b) ☐ I could not conveniently find the defendant and left the summons for him/her at his/her last known or usual place of abode with ______
______ , an inmate thereof who appeared to be at least sixteen years of age.

Sworn before me at ______
______
this ______ day of ______ , yr ______

______
A Justice of the Peace
in and for the Province of Ontario

______
Signature
No. ______ Div. ______
______

Summons to Defendant

Form 104 Courts of Justice Act R.R.O. 1990 Reg. 200
Formule 104 Loi sur les tribunaux judiciaires L.R.O. 1990, Régl. 200

SUMMONS TO DEFENDANT
SOMMATION ADRESSÉE AU DÉFENDEUR
Under Section 22 of the Provincial Offences Act
Aux termes de l'article 22 de la Loi sur les infractions provinciales

ONTARIO COURT OF JUSTICE PROVINCE OF ONTARIO
COUR DE JUSTICE DE L'ONTARIO PROVINCE DE L'ONTARIO

CD 756516

YOU ARE CHARGED WITH THE FOLLOWING OFFENCE
VOUS ÊTES ACCUSÉ(E) DE L'INFRATION SUIVANTE

On the / *Le* ________ day of ________________ yr / *an* ______ at / *à* ____________ **M**

NAME / *NOM* ________________________________
LAST/*NOM DE FAMILLE* FIRST/*PRÉNOM* MIDDLE/*INITIALE*

ADDRESS / *ADRESSE* ________________________________
NUMBER AND STREET/*N° ET RUE*

____
MUNICIPALITY/*MUNICIPALITÉ* P.O./*C.P.* PROVINCE POSTAL CODE/*CODE POSTAL*

AT / *À* ________________________________

____
MUNICIPALITY/*MUNICIPALITÉ*

DID COMMIT THE OFFENCE OF
VOUS AVEZ COMMIS L'INFRACTION SUIVANTE ________________________________

____

____

____

CONTRARY TO
PAR DÉROGATION À ________________________________

________________ SECTION / *ARTICLE* ________________

THEREFORE YOU ARE COMMANDED IN HER MAJESTY'S NAME TO APPEAR BEFORE THE ONTARIO COURT OF JUSTICE

À CES CAUSES, AU NOM DE SA MAJESTÉ, VOUS ÊTES SOMMÉ(E) DE COMPARAÎTRE DEVANT LA COUR DE JUSTICE DE L'ONTARIO

AT / *À* ________________________________

________________ On the / *Le* ________ day of ________

yr / *an* ________ at / *à* ________ **M** Courtroom / *salle d'audience* ________

and to appear thereafter as required by the court in order to be dealt with according to law.

et de comparaître par la suite chaque fois que le tribunal l'exigera de façon à ce que vous soyez jugé(e) selon la Loi.

Issued · *Émis* this · *ce* day of ________________ yr / *an* ______

____
SIGNATURE OF PROVINCIAL OFFENCES OFFICER
SIGNATURE DE L'AGENT D'INFRACTIONS PROVINCIALES

Summons confirmed / *Summation confirmée* ☐ Summons cancelled / *Sommation annulée* ☐

this / *le* ______ day of ________ yr / *an* ______ by / *par* ________________
A judge or justice of the peace in and for the Province of Ontario
Juge ou juge de paix dans et pour la province de l'Ontario

DRIVER'S LICENSE NO. *PERMIS DE CONDUIRE NUMÉRO* CLASS / *CATÉGORIE* COND / *RESTRICTION*

SEX / *SEXE*	BIRTHDATE / *DATE DE NAISSANCE* DAY / *JOUR* MO / *MOIS* YEAR / *ANNÉE*	REGISTRATION NO. / *NUMÉRO D'ENREGISTREMENT*	YEAR / *ANNÉE*	PROVINCE	MAKE / *MARQUE*

OFFICER NO. / *AGENT DE POLICE NO*	UNIT / *GROUPE*

Defendant's Copy
Copie du défendeur

NOTE This summons is issued under Part III of the Provincial Offences Act.
Cette sommation est émise aux termes de la partie III de la Loi sur les infractions provinciales.

AFFIDAVIT OF SERVICE OF SUMMONS UNDER SECTION
26(6) OF THE PROVINCIAL OFFENCES ACT
R.R.O. 1990, REG. 200

ONTARIO COURT
OF JUSTICE

I, ________________________ ,of ________________________ ,
a provincial offences officer make oath and say as follows, that on the ________ day of ________________ , yr ________ . I did serve the summons in the manner indicated below:
(Check one)

(a) ☐ by delivering it personally on the defendant

(b) ☐ I could not conveniently find the defendant and left the summons for him/her at his/her last known or usual place of abode with ________________________________
________________________________ , an inmate thereof who appeared to be at least sixteen years of age.

Sworn before me at ________________________
____
this ______ day of ________________ . yr ______

____
A Justice of the Peace
in and for the Province of Ontario

____
Signature

No. ________ Div. ________

Summons to Defendant

Form 104 Courts of Justice Act R.R.O. 1990 Reg. 200
Formule 104 Loi sur les tribunaux judiciaires L.R.O. 1990, Régl. 200

SUMMONS TO DEFENDANT
SOMMATION ADRESSÉE AU DÉFENDEUR
Under Section 22 of the Provincial Offences Act
Aux termes de l'article 22 de la Loi sur les infractions provinciales

ONTARIO COURT OF JUSTICE PROVINCE OF ONTARIO
COUR DE JUSTICE DE L'ONTARIO PROVINCE DE L'ONTARIO

CD 756516

YOU ARE CHARGED WITH THE FOLLOWING OFFENCE
VOUS ÊTES ACCUSÉ(E) DE L'INFRACTION SUIVANTE

On the / *Le* ________ day of ________________ yr / *an* ______ at / *à* __________ M

NAME / *NOM* ______________________________
LAST/*NOM DE FAMILLE* FIRST/*PRÉNOM* MIDDLE/*INITIALE*

ADDRESS / *ADRESSE* ______________________________
NUMBER AND STREET/*N° ET RUE*

____
MUNICIPALITY/*MUNICIPALITÉ* P.O./*C.P.* PROVINCE POSTAL CODE/*CODE POSTAL*

AT / *À* ______________________________
MUNICIPALITY/*MUNICIPALITÉ*

DID COMMIT THE OFFENCE OF
VOUS AVEZ COMMIS L'INFRACTION SUIVANTE ______________________________

CONTRARY TO
PAR DÉROGATION À ______________________________

SECTION / *ARTICLE* ______________

THEREFORE YOU ARE COMMANDED IN HER MAJESTY'S NAME TO APPEAR BEFORE THE ONTARIO COURT OF JUSTICE

À CES CAUSES, AU NOM DE SA MAJESTÉ, VOUS ÊTES SOMMÉ(E) DE COMPARAÎTRE DEVANT LA COUR DE JUSTICE DE L'ONTARIO

AT / *À* ______________________________

On the / *Le* ________ day of ________

yr / *an* ______ at / *à* ______ M

Courtroom / *salle d'audience* ________

and to appear thereafter as required by the court in order to be dealt with according to law.

et de comparaître par la suite chaque fois que le tribunal l'exigera de façon à ce que vous soyez jugé(e) selon la Loi.

Issued - *Émis* this *ce* day of ______________ yr / *an* ______

____
SIGNATURE OF PROVINCIAL OFFENCES OFFICER
SIGNATURE DE L'AGENT D'INFRACTIONS PROVINCIALES

Summons confirmed / *Sommation confirmée* ☐ Summons cancelled / *Sommation annulée* ☐

this / *le* ______ day of ______ yr / *an* ____ by / *par* ______________________________
A judge or justice of the peace in and for the Province of Ontario
Juge ou juge de paix dans et pour la province de l'Ontario

DRIVER'S LICENSE NO. *PERMIS DE CONDUIRE NUMÉRO*			CLASS *CATÉGORIE*	COND *RESTRICTION*

SEX *SEXE*	BIRTHDATE *DATE DE NAISSANCE* DAY *JOUR* MO *MOIS* YEAR *ANNÉE*	REGISTRATION NO. *NUMÉRO D'ENREGISTREMENT*	YEAR *ANNÉE*	PROVINCE	MAKE *MARQUE*

OFFICER NO. *AGENT DE POLICE NO*	UNIT *GROUPE*

Defendant's Copy
Copie du défendeur

NOTE This summons is issued under Part III of the Provincial Offences Act.
Cette sommation est émise aux termes de la partie III de la Loi sur les infractions provinciales.

AFFIDAVIT OF SERVICE OF SUMMONS UNDER SECTION
26(6) OF THE PROVINCIAL OFFENCES ACT
R.R.O. 1990, REG. 200

ONTARIO COURT
OF JUSTICE

I, ______________________, of ______________________,
a provincial offences officer make oath and say as follows, that on the ________ day of ______________, yr ________. I did serve the summons in the manner indicated below:

(Check one)

(a) ☐ by delivering it personally on the defendant

(b) ☐ I could not conveniently find the defendant and left the summons for him/her at his/her last known or usual place of abode with ______________________________ ______________________________, an inmate thereof who appeared to be at least sixteen years of age.

Sworn before me at ______________________
____
this ______ day of ______________, yr ____

____
A Justice of the Peace in and for the Province of Ontario

____
Signature

No. ________ Div. ________

____

Summons to Defendant

Form 104 Courts of Justice Act R.R.O. 1990 Reg. 200
Formule 104 Loi sur les tribunaux judiciaires L.R.O. 1990, Règl. 200

SUMMONS TO DEFENDANT
SOMMATION ADRESSÉE AU DÉFENDEUR
Under Section 22 of the Provincial Offences Act
Aux termes de l'article 22 de la Loi sur les infractions provinciales

ONTARIO COURT OF JUSTICE PROVINCE OF ONTARIO
COUR DE JUSTICE DE L'ONTARIO PROVINCE DE L'ONTARIO

CD 756516

YOU ARE CHARGED WITH THE FOLLOWING OFFENCE
VOUS ÊTES ACCUSÉ(E) DE L'INFRACTION SUIVANTE

On the / *Le* ______ day of / *de* ______ yr / *an* ______ at / *à* ______ M

NAME / *NOM* ______
LAST/*NOM DE FAMILLE* FIRST/*PRÉNOM* MIDDLE/*INITIALE*

ADDRESS / *ADRESSE* ______
NUMBER AND STREET/*N° ET RUE*

______
MUNICIPALITY/*MUNICIPALITÉ* P.O./*C.P.* PROVINCE POSTAL CODE/*CODE POSTAL*

AT / *À* ______

______
MUNICIPALITY/*MUNICIPALITÉ*

DID COMMIT THE OFFENCE OF
VOUS AVEZ COMMIS L'INFRACTION SUIVANTE ______

______

______

______

CONTRARY TO
PAR DÉROGATION À ______

______ SECTION / *ARTICLE* ______

THEREFORE YOU ARE COMMANDED IN HER MAJESTY'S NAME TO APPEAR BEFORE THE ONTARIO COURT OF JUSTICE

À CES CAUSES, AU NOM DE SA MAJESTÉ, VOUS ÊTES SOMMÉ(E) DE COMPARAÎTRE DEVANT LA COUR DE JUSTICE DE L'ONTARIO

AT / *À* ______

______

On the / *Le* ______ day of ______

yr / *an* ______ at / *à* ______ M

Courtroom / *salle d'audience* ______

and to appear thereafter as required by the court in order to be dealt with according to law.

et de comparaître par la suite chaque fois que le tribunal l'exigera de façon à ce que vous soyez jugé(e) selon la Loi.

Issued - *Émis*
this *ce*
day of ______ yr / *an* ______

______
SIGNATURE OF PROVINCIAL OFFENCES OFFICER
SIGNATURE DE L'AGENT D'INFRACTIONS PROVINCIALES

Summons confirmed / *Sommation confirmée* ☐
Summons cancelled / *Sommation annulée* ☐

this / *le* ______ day of ______ yr / *an* ______ by / *par* ______
A judge or justice of the peace in and for the Province of Ontario
Juge ou juge de paix dans et pour la province de l'Ontario

DRIVER'S LICENSE NO. *PERMIS DE CONDUIRE NUMÉRO* CLASS / *CATÉGORIE* COND / *RESTRICTION*

SEX / *SEXE* BIRTHDATE / *DATE DE NAISSANCE* DAY / *JOUR* MO / *MOIS* YEAR / *ANNÉE* REGISTRATION NO. / *NUMÉRO D'ENREGISTREMENT* YEAR / *ANNÉE* PROVINCE MAKE / *MARQUE*

OFFICER NO. / *AGENT DE POLICE NO* UNIT / *GROUPE*

Defendant's Copy
Copie du défendeur

NOTE This summons is issued under Part III of the Provincial Offences Act.
Cette sommation est émise aux termes de la partie III de la Loi sur les infractions provinciales.

AFFIDAVIT OF SERVICE OF SUMMONS UNDER SECTION
26(6) OF THE PROVINCIAL OFFENCES ACT
R.R.O. 1990, REG. 200

ONTARIO COURT
OF JUSTICE

I, ______ ,of ______,
a provincial offences officer make oath and say as follows, that on the ______ day of ______, yr ______, I did serve the summons in the manner indicated below:
(Check one)

(a) ☐ by delivering it personally on the defendant

(b) ☐ I could not conveniently find the defendant and left the summons for him/her at his/her last known or usual place of abode with ______ ______, an inmate thereof who appeared to be at least sixteen years of age.

Sworn before me at ______ ______ *Signature*

this ______ day of ______, yr ______ No. ______ Div. ______

______
A Justice of the Peace
in and for the Province of Ontario

APPENDIX B

Provincial Offences Forms

Certificate of Parking Infraction

CERTIFICATE OF PARKING INFRACTION

THE CORPORATION OF THE CITY OF BARRIE

PROVINCIAL OFFENCES ACT

883752

I ______________________ believe from my personal knowledge and certify that

ON YR. | MO. | DAY | AT HRS.

PLATE NUMBER | PROV. ☐ ONT | RENEWAL MONTH | MAKE OF VEHICLE

LOCATION OF INFRACTION | METER NO.

BARRIE, ONTARIO

did commit the parking infraction of:

PARKING INFRACTION	X	BY-LAW SECTION	EARLY PAYMENT *	SET FINE
1. PARK AT EXPIRED METER		80-138 5(9)	$ 6.00	$ 9.00
2. PARK ON STREET PROHIBITED BY SIGN		80-138 4(2)(d)	$20.00	$30.00
3. STOP DURING HOURS (OR DAYS) PROHIBITED BY SIGN		80-138 4(8)	$20.00	$30.00
4. PARK ON STREET EXCEEDING TIME LIMIT POSTED BY SIGN		80-138 4(4)	$20.00	$30.00
5. FAIL TO PARK ENTIRELY IN SINGLE PARKING SPACE		80-138 5(6)	$20.00	$30.00
6. PARK DURING HOURS (OR DAYS) PROHIBITED BY POSTED SIGN		80-138 4(3)	$20.00	$30.00
7. PARK ON (OR OVER) SIDEWALK		80-138 4(1)(a)	$20.00	$30.00
8. PARK IN PHYSICALLY DISABLED ZONE (SPACE)		87-290 (5)(i)	$50.00	$75.00
9. PERMIT VEHICLE TO REMAIN PARKED BEYOND MAXIMUM TIME INDICATED BY METER		80-138 5(16)	$20.00	$30.00
10. PARK ON STREET BETWEEN 3:00 A.M. AND 6:00 A.M.		2251 11(a)	$20.00	$30.00
11. PARK WHERE TEMPORARY SIGNS DISPLAYED FOR SNOW REMOVAL		2251 11(b)	$20.00	$30.00
12. PARK IN FIRE ROUTE		89-86 2	$50.00	$75.00
13. PARK ON PRIVATE PROPERTY (MUNICIPAL PROPERTY) (LOCAL BOARD PROPERTY) WITHOUT PERMISSION		87-290 1	$20.00	$30.00
14. PARK ON BOULEVARD		80-138 4(1)(b)	$20.00	$30.00
15.		80-138	$20.00	$30.00

I further certify that I:

A. ☐ served a parking infraction notice on the owner of the vehicle identified therein by affixing it to the vehicle in a conspicuous place at the time of the alleged infraction.

B. ☐ served a parking infraction notice on the owner (or operator) of the vehicle identified therein by delivering it personally to the person having care and control (or operator) of the vehicle at the time of the alleged infraction.

______________________ Signature of Issuing Provincial Offences Officer ________ Number

IF A TRIAL IS REQUESTED IT WILL BE HELD AT
ONTARIO COURT OF JUSTICE
56 MULCASTER STREET
BARRIE, ONTARIO

COMPLETE ONLY IF OPERATOR IS CHARGED

NAME OF OPERATOR ______________________

ADDRESS ______________________

____

DRIVER'S LICENCE NO. ______________________

BIRTH DATE ______________________ SEX ________

Certificate of Parking Infraction CONTINUED

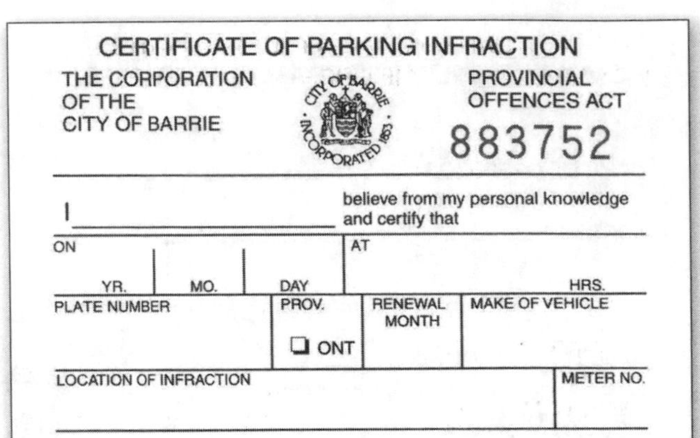

CERTIFICATE OF PARKING INFRACTION

THE CORPORATION OF THE CITY OF BARRIE

PROVINCIAL OFFENCES ACT

883752

I ________________ believe from my personal knowledge and certify that

ON YR. | MO. | DAY AT HRS.

PLATE NUMBER | PROV. ❑ ONT | RENEWAL MONTH | MAKE OF VEHICLE

LOCATION OF INFRACTION | METER NO.

BARRIE, ONTARIO

did commit the parking infraction of:

PARKING INFRACTION	X	BY-LAW SECTION	EARLY PAYMENT *	SET FINE
1. PARK AT EXPIRED METER		80-138 5(9)	$ 6.00	$ 9.00
2. PARK ON STREET PROHIBITED BY SIGN		80-138 4(2)(d)	$20.00	$30.00
3. STOP DURING HOURS (OR DAYS) PROHIBITED BY SIGN		80-138 4(8)	$20.00	$30.00
4. PARK ON STREET EXCEEDING TIME LIMIT POSTED BY SIGN		80-138 4(4)	$20.00	$30.00
5. FAIL TO PARK ENTIRELY IN SINGLE PARKING SPACE		80-138 5(6)	$20.00	$30.00
6. PARK DURING HOURS (OR DAYS) PROHIBITED BY POSTED SIGN		80-138 4(3)	$20.00	$30.00
7. PARK ON (OR OVER) SIDEWALK		80-138 4(1)(a)	$20.00	$30.00
8. PARK IN PHYSICALLY DISABLED ZONE (SPACE)		87-290 (5)(i)	$50.00	$75.00
9. PERMIT VEHICLE TO REMAIN PARKED BEYOND MAXIMUM TIME INDICATED BY METER		80-138 5(16)	$20.00	$30.00
10. PARK ON STREET BETWEEN 3:00 A.M. AND 6:00 A.M.		2251 11(a)	$20.00	$30.00
11. PARK WHERE TEMPORARY SIGNS DISPLAYED FOR SNOW REMOVAL		2251 11(b)	$20.00	$30.00
12. PARK IN FIRE ROUTE		89-86 2	$50.00	$75.00
13. PARK ON PRIVATE PROPERTY (MUNICIPAL PROPERTY) (LOCAL BOARD PROPERTY) WITHOUT PERMISSION		87-290 1	$20.00	$30.00
14. PARK ON BOULEVARD		80-138 4(1)(b)	$20.00	$30.00
15.		80-138	$20.00	$30.00

I further certify that I:

A. ❑ served a parking infraction notice on the owner of the vehicle identified therein by affixing it to the vehicle in a conspicuous place at the time of the alleged infraction.

B. ❑ served a parking infraction notice on the owner (or operator) of the vehicle identified therein by delivering it personally to the person having care and control (or operator) of the vehicle at the time of the alleged infraction.

Signature of Issuing Provincial Offences Officer | Number

IF A TRIAL IS REQUESTED IT WILL BE HELD AT
ONTARIO COURT OF JUSTICE
56 MULCASTER STREET
BARRIE, ONTARIO

Parking Infraction Notice

PARKING INFRACTION NOTICE

THE CORPORATION OF THE CITY OF BARRIE

PROVINCIAL OFFENCES ACT

883752

I ______________ believe from my personal knowledge and certify that

ON YR. MO. DAY AT HRS.

PLATE NUMBER | PROV. ❑ ONT | RENEWAL MONTH | MAKE OF VEHICLE

LOCATION OF INFRACTION | METER NO.

BARRIE, ONTARIO

did commit the parking infraction of:

PARKING INFRACTION	X	BY-LAW SECTION	EARLY PAYMENT *	SET FINE
1. PARK AT EXPIRED METER		80-138 5(9)	$ 6.00	$ 9.00
2. PARK ON STREET PROHIBITED BY SIGN		80-138 4(2)(d)	$20.00	$30.00
3. STOP DURING HOURS (OR DAYS) PROHIBITED BY SIGN		80-138 4(8)	$20.00	$30.00
4. PARK ON STREET EXCEEDING TIME LIMIT POSTED BY SIGN		80-138 4(4)	$20.00	$30.00
5. FAIL TO PARK ENTIRELY IN SINGLE PARKING SPACE		80-138 5(6)	$20.00	$30.00
6. PARK DURING HOURS (OR DAYS) PROHIBITED BY POSTED SIGN		80-138 4(3)	$20.00	$30.00
7. PARK ON (OR OVER) SIDEWALK		80-138 4(1)(a)	$20.00	$30.00
8. PARK IN PHYSICALLY DISABLED ZONE (SPACE)		87-290 (5)(i)	$50.00	$75.00
9. PERMIT VEHICLE TO REMAIN PARKED BEYOND MAXIMUM TIME INDICATED BY METER		80-138 5(16)	$20.00	$30.00
10. PARK ON STREET BETWEEN 3:00 A.M. AND 6:00 A.M.		2251 11(a)	$20.00	$30.00
11. PARK WHERE TEMPORARY SIGNS DISPLAYED FOR SNOW REMOVAL		2251 11(b)	$20.00	$30.00
12. PARK IN FIRE ROUTE		89-86 2	$50.00	$75.00
13. PARK ON PRIVATE PROPERTY (MUNICIPAL PROPERTY) (LOCAL BOARD PROPERTY) WITHOUT PERMISSION		87-290 1	$20.00	$30.00
14. PARK ON BOULEVARD		80-138 4(1)(b)	$20.00	$30.00
15.		80-138	$20.00	$30.00

NOTICE

Within 15 working days of the date noted above, choose one of the options on the back of this notice. If you do not pay the set fine shown above or if you do not deliver a Notice of Intention to Appear in court, or if you do not appear for trial, you will be deemed not to dispute this charge and a conviction may be entered against you. Upon conviction you will be required to pay the set fine plus court costs. An administration fee is payable if the fine goes into default and the information may be provided to a credit bureau.

* EARLY PAYMENT ONLY ACCEPTED WITHIN 7 WORKING DAYS OF THE DATE OF INFRACTION

Signature of Issuing Provincial Offences Officer   Number

IF A TRIAL IS REQUESTED IT WILL BE HELD AT
ONTARIO COURT OF JUSTICE
56 MULCASTER STREET
BARRIE, ONTARIO

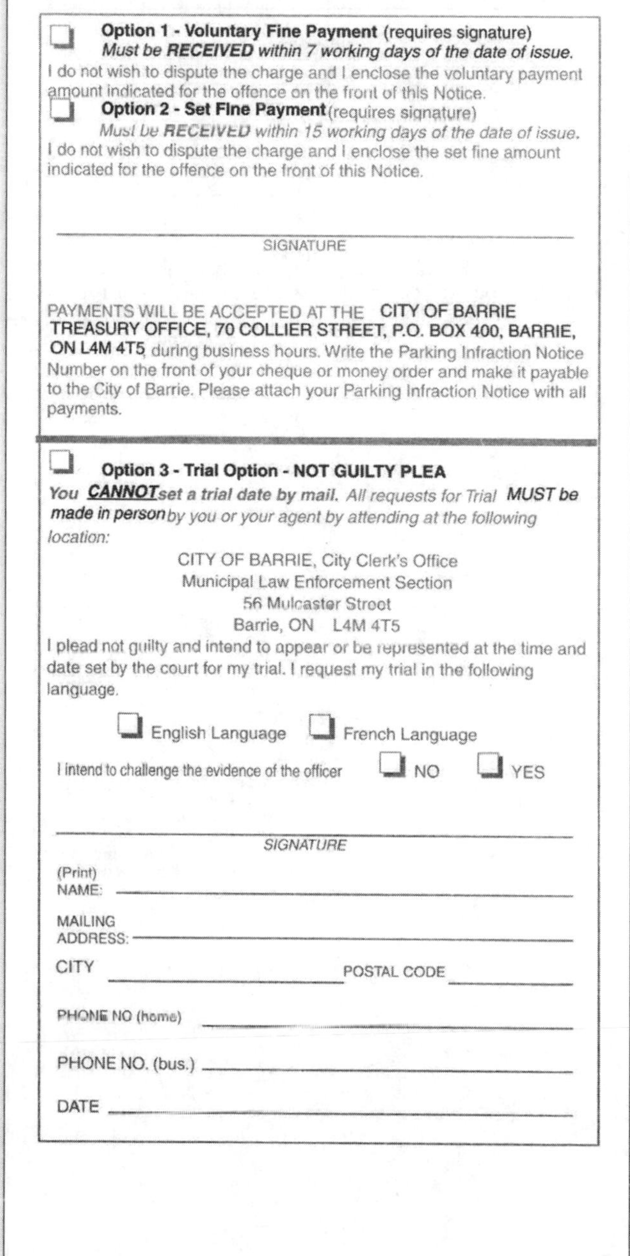

IMPORTANT - READ CAREFULLY

WITHIN 15 WORKING DAYS of the alleged Parking Infraction, you may choose one of the following options. Complete the selected option and sign where indicated. Deliver this Parking Infraction Notice (and payment where applicable) to the place indicated under the option which you have selected. All inquiries concerning this alleged infraction should be made to ***CITY OF BARRIE, CLERK'S OFFICE, MUNICIPAL LAW ENFORCEMENT SECTION, 56 MULCASTER STREET, P.O. Box 400, BARRIE, ONTARIO (705)-739-4241)*** *during business hours.*

NOTICE TO ONTARIO MOTORISTS

Failure to pay the fine imposed upon conviction will result in an order that your Ontario Vehicle Permit not be renewed and no new permit being issued to you until the fine and all court costs and fees have been paid.

❑ **Option 1 - Voluntary Fine Payment** (requires signature)
*Must be **RECEIVED** within 7 working days of the date of issue.*
I do not wish to dispute the charge and I enclose the voluntary payment amount indicated for the offence on the front of this Notice.

❑ **Option 2 - Set Fine Payment** (requires signature)
*Must be **RECEIVED** within 15 working days of the date of issue.*
I do not wish to dispute the charge and I enclose the set fine amount indicated for the offence on the front of this Notice.

SIGNATURE

PAYMENTS WILL BE ACCEPTED AT THE **CITY OF BARRIE TREASURY OFFICE, 70 COLLIER STREET, P.O. BOX 400, BARRIE, ON L4M 4T5** during business hours. Write the Parking Infraction Notice Number on the front of your cheque or money order and make it payable to the City of Barrie. Please attach your Parking Infraction Notice with all payments.

❑ **Option 3 - Trial Option - NOT GUILTY PLEA**
You CANNOT set a trial date by mail. *All requests for Trial* ***MUST be made in person*** *by you or your agent by attending at the following location:*

CITY OF BARRIE, City Clerk's Office
Municipal Law Enforcement Section
56 Mulcaster Street
Barrie, ON L4M 4T5

I plead not guilty and intend to appear or be represented at the time and date set by the court for my trial. I request my trial in the following language.

❑ English Language ❑ French Language

I intend to challenge the evidence of the officer ❑ NO ❑ YES

SIGNATURE

(Print) NAME:

MAILING ADDRESS:

CITY   POSTAL CODE

PHONE NO (home)

PHONE NO. (bus.)

DATE

Summons to Defendant

Form 104 Courts of Justice Act R.R.O. 1990 Reg. 200
Formule 104 Loi sur les tribunaux judiciaires L.R.O. 1990, Règl. 200

SUMMONS TO DEFENDANT
SOMMATION ADRESSÉE AU DÉFENDEUR
Under Section 22 of the Provincial Offences Act
Aux termes de l'article 22 de la Loi sur les infractions provinciales

ONTARIO COURT OF JUSTICE PROVINCE OF ONTARIO
COUR DE JUSTICE DE L'ONTARIO PROVINCE DE L'ONTARIO

CD 756516

YOU ARE CHARGED WITH THE FOLLOWING OFFENCE
VOUS ÊTES ACCUSÉ(E) DE L'INFRATION SUIVANTE

On the / *Le* ______ day of ______ yr / *an* ______ at / *à* ______ **M**

NAME / *NOM* ______
LAST/*NOM DE FAMILLE* FIRST/*PRÉNOM* MIDDLE/*INITIALE*

ADDRESS / *ADRESSE* ______
NUMBER AND STREET/*N° ET RUE*

______
MUNICIPALITY/*MUNICIPALITÉ* P.O./*C.P.* PROVINCE POSTAL CODE/*CODE POSTAL*

AT / *À* ______

______
MUNICIPALITY/*MUNICIPALITÉ*

DID COMMIT THE OFFENCE OF
VOUS AVEZ COMMIS L'INFRACTION SUIVANTE ______

______

______

______

CONTRARY TO
PAR DÉROGATION À ______

______ SECTION / *ARTICLE* ______

THEREFORE YOU ARE COMMANDED IN HER MAJESTY'S NAME TO APPEAR BEFORE THE ONTARIO COURT OF JUSTICE

À CES CAUSES, AU NOM DE SA MAJESTÉ, VOUS ÊTES SOMMÉ(E) DE COMPARAÎTRE DEVANT LA COUR DE JUSTICE DE L'ONTARIO

AT / *À* ______

______ On the / *Le* ______ day of ______

yr / *an* ______ at / *à* ______ **M** Courtroom / *salle d'audience* ______

and to appear thereafter as required by the court in order to be dealt with according to law.

et de comparaître par la suite chaque fois que le tribunal l'exigera de façon à ce que vous soyez jugé(e) selon la Loi.

Issued - *Émis* this *ce* day of ______ yr / *an* ______

______
SIGNATURE OF PROVINCIAL OFFENCES OFFICER
SIGNATURE DE L'AGENT D'INFRACTIONS PROVINCIALES

Summons confirmed / *Sommation confirmée* ☐ Summons cancelled / *Sommation annulée* ☐

this / *le* ______ day of ______ yr / *an* ______ by / *par* ______
A judge or justice of the peace in and for the Province of Ontario
Juge ou juge de paix dans et pour la province de l'Ontario

DRIVER'S LICENSE NO. *PERMIS DE CONDUIRE NUMÉRO* | CLASS *CATÉGORIE* | COND *RESTRICTION*

SEX *SEXE* | BIRTHDATE *DATE DE NAISSANCE* DAY *JOUR* MO *MOIS* YEAR *ANNÉE* | REGISTRATION NO. *NUMÉRO D'ENREGISTREMENT* | YEAR *ANNÉE* | PROVINCE | MAKE *MARQUE*

OFFICER NO. *AGENT DE POLICE NO* | UNIT *GROUPE*

Defendant's Copy
Copie du défendeur

NOTE This summons is issued under Part III of the Provincial Offences Act.
Cette sommation est émise aux termes de la partie III de la Loi sur les infractions provinciales.

AFFIDAVIT OF SERVICE OF SUMMONS UNDER SECTION
26(6) OF THE PROVINCIAL OFFENCES ACT
R.R.O. 1990, REG. 200

ONTARIO COURT
OF JUSTICE

I, ______, of ______, a provincial offences officer make oath and say as follows, that on the ______ day of ______, **yr** ______, I did serve the summons in the manner indicated below:

(Check one)

(a) ☐ by delivering it personally on the defendant

(b) ☐ I could not conveniently find the defendant and left the summons for him/her at his/her last known or usual place of abode with ______ ______, an inmate thereof who appeared to be at least sixteen years of age.

Sworn before me at ______ ______ this ______ day of ______, yr ______

______
Signature

No. ______ Div. ______

______
A Justice of the Peace in and for the Province of Ontario

Summons to Defendant CONTINUED

Form 104 Courts of Justice Act R.R.O. 1990 Reg. 200
Formule 104 *Loi sur les tribunaux judiciaires L.R.O. 1990, Règl. 200*

SUMMONS TO DEFENDANT
SOMMATION ADRESSÉE AU DÉFENDEUR
Under Section 22 of the Provincial Offences Act
Aux termes de l'article 22 de la Loi sur les infractions provinciales

ONTARIO COURT OF JUSTICE PROVINCE OF ONTARIO
COUR DE JUSTICE DE L'ONTARIO PROVINCE DE L'ONTARIO

CD 756516

YOU ARE CHARGED WITH THE FOLLOWING OFFENCE
VOUS ÊTES ACCUSÉ(E) DE L'INFRATION SUIVANTE

On the / *Le* ________ day of ____________________ yr / *an* ______ at / *à* __________ M

NAME / *NOM* ____
LAST/*NOM DE FAMILLE* FIRST/*PRÉNOM* MIDDLE/*INITIALE*

ADDRESS / *ADRESSE* ____
NUMBER AND STREET/*N° ET RUE*

____
MUNICIPALITY/*MUNICIPALITÉ* P.O./*C.P.* PROVINCE POSTAL CODE/*CODE POSTAL*

AT / *À* ____

____
MUNICIPALITY/*MUNICIPALITÉ*

DID COMMIT THE OFFENCE OF
VOUS AVEZ COMMIS L'INFRACTION SUIVANTE ____

____

____

____

CONTRARY TO
PAR DÉROGATION À ____

______________________ SECTION / *ARTICLE* ______________________

THEREFORE YOU ARE COMMANDED IN HER MAJESTY'S NAME TO APPEAR BEFORE THE ONTARIO COURT OF JUSTICE

À CES CAUSES, AU NOM DE SA MAJESTÉ, VOUS ÊTES SOMMÉ(E) DE COMPARAÎTRE DEVANT LA COUR DE JUSTICE DE L'ONTARIO

AT / *À* ____

______________________ On the / *Le* __________ day of __________

yr / *an* ________ at / *à* ________ M   Courtroom / *salle d'audience* __________

and to appear thereafter as required by the court in order to be dealt with according to law.

et de comparaître par la suite chaque fois que le tribunal l'exigera de façon à ce que vous soyez jugé(e) selon la Loi.

Issued - *Émis*
this *ce*
day of ______________________ yr / *an* ________

____
SIGNATURE OF PROVINCIAL OFFENCES OFFICER
SIGNATURE DE L'AGENT D'INFRACTIONS PROVINCIALES

Summons confirmed / *Sommation confirmée* ☐   Summons cancelled / *Sommation annulée* ☐

this / *le* ________ day of ________ yr / *an* ______ by / *par* ______________________
A judge or justice of the peace in and for the Province of Ontario
Juge ou juge de paix dans et pour la province de l'Ontario

DRIVER'S LICENSE NO. *PERMIS DE CONDUIRE NUMÉRO*   CLASS / *CATÉGORIE*   COND / *RESTRICTION*

SEX / *SEXE*   BIRTHDATE / *DATE DE NAISSANCE* DAY / *JOUR* MO / *MOIS* YEAR / *ANNÉE*   REGISTRATION NO. / *NUMÉRO D'ENREGISTREMENT*   YEAR / *ANNÉE*   PROVINCE   MAKE / *MARQUE*

OFFICER NO. / *AGENT DE POLICE NO*   UNIT / *GROUPE*

Defendant's Copy
Copie du défendeur

NOTE This summons is issued under Part III of the Provincial Offences Act.
Cette sommation est émise aux termes de la partie III de la Loi sur les infractions provinciales.

Note to Defendant
You may appear personally, by agent or by counsel.

If you do not appear:

a) the court may issue a warrant for your arrest or,
b) the trial may proceed, and the evidence may be taken in your absence.

If you do appear:

a) the trial may proceed; or
b) you, or the prosecutor, may ask the court to adjourn your case to another date. The court may grant or refuse such a request.

Remarque à l'adresse du prévenu
Vous pouvez comparaître personnellement, par mandataire, ou par un avocat.

Si vous ne comparaissez pas:

a) le tribunal peut émettre un mandat d'arrêt contre vous; ou
b) le procès peut être tenu sans que vous y soyez et la preuve être recueillie en votre absence.

Si vous comparaissez:

a) le procès peut être tenu; ou
b) vous pouvez, vous ou le poursuivant, demander au tribunal un ajournement. Le tribunal peut accorder ou refuser cette demande.

FOR INFORMATION ON ACCESS TO ONTARIO COURTS FOR PERSONS WITH DISABILITIES, CALL **1-800-387-4456** TORONTO AREA **326-0111**

POUR PLUS DE RENSEIGNEMENTS SUR L'ACCÈS DES PERSONNES HANDICAPÉES AUX TRIBUNAUX DE L'ONTARIO, COMPOSEZ LE **1-800-387-4456** RÉGION DE TORONTO **326-0111**

Summons to Defendant CONTINUED

Form 104 Courts of Justice Act R.R.O. 1990 Reg. 200
Formule 104 Loi sur les tribunaux judiciaires L.R.O. 1990, Règl. 200

SUMMONS TO DEFENDANT
SOMMATION ADRESSÉE AU DÉFENDEUR
Under Section 22 of the Provincial Offences Act
Aux termes de l'article 22 de la Loi sur les infractions provinciales

ONTARIO COURT OF JUSTICE PROVINCE OF ONTARIO
COUR DE JUSTICE DE L'ONTARIO PROVINCE DE L'ONTARIO

CD 756516

YOU ARE CHARGED WITH THE FOLLOWING OFFENCE
VOUS ÊTES ACCUSÉ(E) DE L'INFRACTION SUIVANTE

On the / *Le* ______ day of / *de* ______ yr / *an* ______ at / *à* ______ M

NAME / *NOM* ______
LAST/*NOM DE FAMILLE* FIRST/*PRÉNOM* MIDDLE/*INITIALE*

ADDRESS / *ADRESSE* ______
NUMBER AND STREET/*N° ET RUE*

______
MUNICIPALITY/*MUNICIPALITÉ* P.O./*C.P.* PROVINCE POSTAL CODE/*CODE POSTAL*

AT / *À* ______
MUNICIPALITY/*MUNICIPALITÉ*

DID COMMIT THE OFFENCE OF
VOUS AVEZ COMMIS L'INFRACTION SUIVANTE ______

CONTRARY TO
PAR DÉROGATION À ______

SECTION / *ARTICLE* ______

THEREFORE YOU ARE COMMANDED IN HER MAJESTY'S NAME TO APPEAR BEFORE THE ONTARIO COURT OF JUSTICE

À CES CAUSES, AU NOM DE SA MAJESTÉ, VOUS ÊTES SOMMÉ(E) DE COMPARAÎTRE DEVANT LA COUR DE JUSTICE DE L'ONTARIO

AT / *À* ______

On the / *Le* ______ day of ______

yr / *an* ______ at / *à* ______ M

Courtroom / *salle d'audience* ______

and to appear thereafter as required by the court in order to be dealt with according to law.

et de comparaître par la suite chaque fois que le tribunal l'exigera de façon à ce que vous soyez jugé(e) selon la Loi.

Issued - *Émis* this *ce* day of ______ yr *an* ______

______
SIGNATURE OF PROVINCIAL OFFENCES OFFICER
SIGNATURE DE L'AGENT D'INFRACTIONS PROVINCIALES

Summons confirmed / *Sommation confirmée* ☐ Summons cancelled / *Sommation annulée* ☐

this / *le* ______ day of ______ yr / *an* ______ by / *par* ______
A judge or justice of the peace in and for the Province of Ontario
Juge ou juge de paix dans et pour la province de l'Ontario

DRIVER'S LICENSE NO. *PERMIS DE CONDUIRE NUMÉRO*			CLASS *CATÉGORIE*	COND *RESTRICTION*

SEX *SEXE*	BIRTHDATE *DATE DE NAISSANCE* DAY *JOUR*	MO *MOIS*	YEAR *ANNÉE*	REGISTRATION NO. *NUMÉRO D'ENREGISTREMENT*	YEAR *ANNÉE*	PROVINCE	MAKE *MARQUE*

OFFICER NO. *AGENT DE POLICE NO*	UNIT *GROUPE*

Defendant's Copy
Copie du défendeur

NOTE This summons is issued under Part III of the Provincial Offences Act.
Cette sommation est émise aux termes de la partie III de la Loi sur les infractions provinciales.

Summons to Defendant CONTINUED

Form 104 Courts of Justice Act R.R.O. 1990 Reg. 200
Formule 104 Loi sur les tribunaux judiciaires L.R.O. 1990, Régl. 200

SUMMONS TO DEFENDANT
SOMMATION ADRESSÉE AU DÉFENDEUR
Under Section 22 of the Provincial Offences Act
Aux termes de l'article 22 de la Loi sur les infractions provinciales

ONTARIO COURT OF JUSTICE PROVINCE OF ONTARIO
COUR DE JUSTICE DE L'ONTARIO PROVINCE DE L'ONTARIO

CD 756516

YOU ARE CHARGED WITH THE FOLLOWING OFFENCE
VOUS ÊTES ACCUSÉ(E) DE L'INFRATION SUIVANTE

On the / *Le* ______ day of ______________ yr / *an* ______ at / *à* ______ **M**

NAME / *NOM* ________________________________
LAST/*NOM DE FAMILLE* FIRST/*PRÉNOM* MIDDLE/*INITIALE*

ADDRESS / *ADRESSE* ________________________________
NUMBER AND STREET/*N° ET RUE*

____
MUNICIPALITY/*MUNICIPALITÉ* P.O./C.P. PROVINCE POSTAL CODE/*CODE POSTAL*

AT / *À* ________________________________

____
MUNICIPALITY/*MUNICIPALITÉ*

DID COMMIT THE OFFENCE OF
VOUS AVEZ COMMIS L'INFRACTION SUIVANTE ________________________________

CONTRARY TO
PAR DÉROGATION À ________________________________

SECTION / *ARTICLE* ______________

THEREFORE YOU ARE COMMANDED IN HER MAJESTY'S NAME TO APPEAR BEFORE THE ONTARIO COURT OF JUSTICE

À CES CAUSES, AU NOM DE SA MAJESTÉ, VOUS ÊTES SOMMÉ(E) DE COMPARAÎTRE DEVANT LA COUR DE JUSTICE DE L'ONTARIO

AT / *À* ________________________________

On the / *Le* ______ day of ______

yr / *an* ______ at / *à* ______ **M**

Courtroom / *salle d'audience* ______

and to appear thereafter as required by the court in order to be dealt with according to law.

et de comparaître par la suite chaque fois que le tribunal l'exigera de façon à ce que vous soyez jugé(e) selon la Loi.

Issued - *Émis* this *ce* day of ______________ yr / *an* ______

____
SIGNATURE OF PROVINCIAL OFFENCES OFFICER
SIGNATURE DE L'AGENT D'INFRACTIONS PROVINCIALES

Summons confirmed / *Sommation confirmée* ☐ Summons cancelled / *Sommation annulée* ☐

this / *le* ______ day of ______ yr / *an* ______ by / *par* ______________
A judge or justice of the peace in and for the Province of Ontario
Juge ou juge de paix dans et pour la province de l'Ontario

DRIVER'S LICENSE NO. *PERMIS DE CONDUIRE NUMÉRO*	CLASS *CATÉGORIE*	COND *RESTRICTION*

SEX *SEXE*	BIRTHDATE *DATE DE NAISSANCE* DAY *JOUR* MO *MOIS* YEAR *ANNÉE*	REGISTRATION NO. *NUMÉRO D'ENREGISTREMENT*	YEAR *ANNÉE*	PROVINCE	MAKE *MARQUE*

OFFICER NO. *AGENT DE POLICE NO*	UNIT *GROUPE*

Defendant's Copy
Copie du défendeur

NOTE This summons is issued under Part III of the Provincial Offences Act.
Cette sommation est émise aux termes de la partie III de la Loi sur les infractions provinciales.

POLICE RECORD - COURT DISPOSITION

Date ______________ ☐ GUILTY ☐ WITHDRAWN ☐ DISMISSED

SENTENCE

____

Information to Obtain Search Warrant

ONTARIO COURT
OF JUSTICE
PROVINCE OF ONTARIO
COUR DE JUSTICE
DE L'ONTARIO
PROVINCE DE L'ONTARIO

INFORMATION TO OBTAIN SEARCH WARRANT
DÉNONCIATION EN VUE D'OBTENIR UN MANDAT DE PERQUISITION
Under Section 158 of the Provincial Offences Act
aux termes de l'article 158 de la Loi sur les infractions provinciales

Form 140
Formule 140
Courts of Justice Act
Loi sur les tribunaux judiciaires
R.R.O. 1990, Reg. 200
L.R.O. 1990, Règl. 200

This is the information of
Les présentes constituent la dénonciation de
(name / *nom*)

of / *de*
(address / *adresse*) (occupation / *profession*)

I have reasonable grounds to believe and do believe that in a certain building, receptacle, or place, namely
J'ai des motifs raisonnables de croire que, dans un bâtiment, contenant ou lieu, à savoir

(building, receptacle or place / *bâtiment, contenant ou lieu*)

of / *de*
(owner / *propriétaire*)

at / *à*
(address / *adresse*)

there are the following thing(s) / *se trouvent les objets suivants :*

(check appropriate box / *cochez la case appropriée*)

- ☐ upon or in respect of which an offence has been or is suspected to have been committed / *une chose sur laquelle ou concernant laquelle une infraction a été commise ou est soupçonnée avoir été commise.*
- ☐ that there are reasonable grounds to believe will afford evidence as to the commission of an offence. / *il existe des motifs raisonnables de croire qu'elle fournira une preuve concernant la perpétration d'une infraction.*

And further say that my grounds for so believing are: / *Et je le crois pour les motifs suivants :*

Therefore I request that a search warrant be issued to search the said
Je demande donc qu'un mandat de perquisition soit décerné pour fouiller ledit . . . .
(building, receptacle, or place / *bâtiment, contenant ou lieu*)

for the said thing(s)
dans le but d'y trouver la(les) dite(s) chose(s)

(signature of informant / *signature du dénonciateur*)

Sworn before me at /
Assermenté devant moi à

this day of
le jour de

yr
an

Judge or Justice of the Peace in and for the Province of Ontario
Juge ou juge de paix dans et pour la province de l'Ontario

CD 0140 (rev. 05/99)

Information (One Accused/Charge)

ONTARIO COURT OF JUSTICE
PROVINCE OF ONTARIO
COUR DE JUSTICE DE L'ONTARIO
PROVINCE DE L'ONTARIO

INFORMATION/*DÉNONCIATION*
Under Section 23 of the Provincial Offences Act
En application de l'article 23 de la Loi sur les infractions provinciales

Form/Formule 105
Courts of Justice Act
Loi sur les tribunaux judiciaires
R.R.O. 1990, Reg. 200
R.R.O. 1990, Règl. 200

This is the information of ....
Dénonciation déposée par

.... of/*de* ....,

.... I have reasonable and probable grounds to believe and do believe that,
(occupation/*profession*) *j'ai des motifs raisonnables de croire et je crois effectivement que*

(name
nom)

on or about the/*le ou vers le*

...... day of / *jour de* ...., yr/*an* ...... at / *à* ....
(location /*lieu*)

.... did commit the offence of
a commis l'infraction de

contrary to/*en contravention à* ....
section/*l'article* ....

(Signature of informant/*signature du dénonciateur*)

SUMMONS RETURNABLE/*SOMMATION À RAPPORTER*

Sworn before me
Déclaré sous serment devant moi
at / *à* ....

this/*le* ...... day of/*jour de* ...... yr/*an* ......

Judge or Justice of the Peace in and for the Province of Ontario
Juge ou juge de paix dans et pour la province de l'Ontario

at / *à* ....

on the/*le* ...... day of/*jour de* ...... yr/*an* ...... at/*à* ...... M, at/*h, dans la* ......
(courtroom)
(salle d'audience)

(Sec./*Art.* 24) ☐ Summons for/*Sommation pour* .... yr/*an* ...... Confirmed on/*Confirmée le* ...... yr/*an* ....
Justice of the Peace
Juge de Paix

Date

Pleads/*Plaidoyer* ☐ Guilty/*Coupable* ☐ Not Guilty/*Non coupable* ☐ Withdrawn/*Accusation(s) retirée(s)*

Found/*Décision* ☐ Guilty/*Coupable* ☐ Not Guilty/*Non coupable* ☐ In Absentia/*Défaut de comparution*

☐ Sentence Suspended
Condamnation avec sursis

Fined $ .... & $ .... costs. Time to pay ....
Amende de $ et $ pour les frais. Délai de paiement

.... Date of Birth ....
Date de naissance Day/*jour* Mo./*mois* Yr./*année*

Probation for ....
Période de probation de

Sentenced to imprisonment for ....
Peine d'emprisonnement de

Exhibits Filed
Pièces déposées
☐ Yes/*Oui* ☐ No/*Non*

Judge or Justice of the Peace in and for the Province of Ontario
Juge ou juge de paix dans et pour la province de l'Ontario

CD 0001 (rev.05/99)

FOR INFORMATION ON ACCESS TO ONTARIO COURTS FOR PERSONS WITH DISABILITIES, CALL 1-800-387-4456 TORONTO AREA 326-0111

POUR PLUS DE RENSEIGNEMENTS SUR L'ACCÈS DES PERSONNES HANDICAPÉES AUX TRIBUNAUX DE L'ONTARIO, COMPOSEZ LE 1-800-387-4456 RÉGION DE TORONTO 326-0111

Information (One Accused/Charge) CONTINUED

ONTARIO COURT
OF JUSTICE
PROVINCE OF ONTARIO
COUR DE JUSTICE
DE L'ONTARIO
PROVINCE DE L'ONTARIO

INFORMATION/*DÉNONCIATION*
Under Section 23 of the Provincial Offences Act
En application de l'article 23 de la Loi sur les infractions provinciales

Form/Formule 105
Courts of Justice Act
Loi sur les tribunaux judiciaires
R.R.O. 1990, Reg. 200
R.R.O. 1990, Règl. 200

This is the information of ......
Dénonciation déposée par
...... of/*de* ......,
...... I have reasonable and probable grounds to believe and do believe that,
(occupation/*profession*) *j'ai des motifs raisonnables de croire et je crois effectivement que*

(name
nom)

on or about the/*le ou vers le*
...... day of/*jour de* ......, yr/an ...... at/*à* ......
(location/*lieu*)
...... did commit the offence of
a commis l'infraction de

contrary to/*en contravention à* ......
section/*l'article* ......

(Signature of informant/*signature du dénonciateur*)

SUMMONS RETURNABLE/*SOMMATION À RAPPORTER*

Sworn before me
Déclaré sous serment devant moi
at/*à* ......
this/*le* ...... day of/*jour de* ...... yr/*an* ......

Judge or Justice of the Peace in and for the Province of Ontario
Juge ou juge de paix dans et pour la province de l'Ontario

at/*à* ......
on the/*le* ...... day of/*jour de* ...... yr/*an* ...... at/*à* ...... M, at/*h, dans la* ......
(courtroom)
(salle d'audience)

(Sec./*Art.* 24) ☐ Summons for/*Sommation pour* ...... yr/*an* ...... Confirmed on/*Confirmée le* ...... yr/*an* ......
Justice of the Peace
Juge de Paix

Date

Pleads/*Plaidoyer* ☐ Guilty/*Coupable* ☐ Not Guilty/*Non coupable* ☐ Withdrawn/*Accusation(s) retirée(s)*

Found/*Décision* ☐ Guilty/*Coupable* ☐ Not Guilty/*Non coupable* ☐ In Absentia/*Défaut de comparution*

☐ Sentence Suspended
Condamnation avec sursis

Fined $ ...... & $ ...... costs. Time to pay ......
Amende de *$ et* *$* *pour les frais.* *Délai de paiement*

...... Date of Birth/*Date de naissance* ...... Day/*jour* Mo./*mois* Yr./*année*

Probation for ......
Période de probation de

Sentenced to imprisonment for ......
Peine d'emprisonnement de

Exhibits Filed
Pièces déposées
☐ Yes/*Oui* ☐ No/*Non*

Judge or Justice of the Peace in and for the Province of Ontario
Juge ou juge de paix dans et pour la province de l'Ontario

CD 0001 (rev.05/99)

FOR INFORMATION ON ACCESS TO ONTARIO COURTS FOR PERSONS WITH DISABILITIES, CALL 1-800-387-4456 TORONTO AREA 326-0111

POUR PLUS DE RENSEIGNEMENTS SUR L'ACCÈS DES PERSONNES HANDICAPÉES AUX TRIBUNAUX DE L'ONTARIO, COMPOSEZ LE 1-800-387-4456 RÉGION DE TORONTO 326-0111

Information (Multiple Accused/Charges)

INFORMATION/*DÉNONCIATION*

Under Section 23 of the Provincial Offences Act
En application de l'article 23 de la Loi sur les infractions provinciales

Form 105 / Courts of Justice Act
Formule 105 Loi sur les tribunaux judiciaires
R.R.O. 1990, Reg. 200 / *L.R.O. 1990, Règl. 200*

ONTARIO COURT
OF JUSTICE
PROVINCE OF ONTARIO
COUR DE JUSTICE
DE L'ONTARIO
PROVINCE DE L'ONTARIO

This is the information of ....
Dénonciation déposée par

of/de ....

....
(occupation/*profession*)

I have reasonable and probable grounds to believe and do believe that
J'ai des motifs raisonnables de croire et je crois effectivement que

on or about the ....day of ....yr. ...., at the ....
le ou vers le *jour de* *an* , *à*

..........did commit the offence of
a commis l'infraction de

LONG FORM – TWO OR MORE CHANGES
FORMULE COMPLÈTE – DEUX ACCUSATIONS OU PLUS

FOR INFORMATION ON ACCESS TO ONTARIO COURTS FOR PERSONS WITH DISABILITIES, CALL
1-800-387-4456
TORONTO AREA 326-0111

POUR PLUS DE RENSEIGNEMENTS SUR L'ACCÈS DES PERSONNES HANDICAPÉES AUX TRIBUNAUX DE L'ONTARIO, COMPOSEZ LE
1-800-387-4456
RÉGION DE TORONTO 326-0111

CD 0002 (rev.10/99)

Information (Multiple Accused/Charges) CONTINUED

Date *Date*	Defendant Appears Adjournment *Défendeur Comparaît Ajournement*	Parties Consent *Consentement des parties*	Bail and/or other action *Cautionnement et/ou autre mesure*	Fails to Appear *Omet de comparaître*	Bench Warrant *Mandat du tribunal*	Certificat of Default *Certificat de défaut*

Date *Date*	Clerk *Greffier*	Reporter *Sténographe*	Prosecutor *Poursuivant*	For Defendant *Pour le défendeur*	Justice's initials *Initiales du juge de paix*

CD 0002 (rev.10/99)

Information (Multiple Accused/Charges) CONTINUED

Sworn before me at the ....
Assermenté devant moi au

this ....day of ....yr. ....
le *jour de* *an*

Judge or Justice of the Peace in and for the Province of Ontario
Juge ou juge de paix dans et pour la province de l'Ontario

Informant
Dénonciateur

Sec. 24/art. 24

☐ Summons for ....yr. ....
Sommation pour *an*

☐ Confirmed on ....yr. ....
Confirmée le *an* Justice of the Peace/*Juge de paix*

Date *Date*	Defendant *Défendeur*	Pleads/*Plaide* Guilty to Counts *Coupable sous les chefs*	Pleads/*Plaide* Not Guilty to Counts *Non coupable sous les chefs*	Found Guilty on Counts *Déclaré coupable sous les chefs*	Not Guilty on Counts *Déclaré non coupable sous les chefs*

Date

☐ In Absentia
Défaut de comparution

☐ counts/*chefs d'accusation*

Fined $.......... & $ .... costs. Time to pay ....
amende de *$ et* *$ de frais. Délai de paiement*

..........Date of Birth..........
date ne naissance D/J M Y/A

Probation ....
Période de probation de

Sentenced to Imprisonment for ....
Peine d'emprisonnement de

☐ withdrawn *accusations(s) retirée(s)* ☐ sentence suspended *condamnation avec sursis*

☐ counts/*chefs d'accusation*

Fined $.......... & $ .... costs. Time to pay ....
amende de *$ et* *$ de frais. Délai de paiement*

..........Date of Birth..........
date ne naissance D/J M Y/A

Probation ....
Période de probation de

Sentenced to Imprisonment for ....
Peine d'emprisonnement de

☐ withdrawn *accusations(s) retirée(s)* ☐ sentence suspended *condamnation avec sursis*

☐ counts/*chefs d'accusation*

Fined $.......... & $ .... costs. Time to pay ....
amende de *$ et* *$ de frais. Délai de paiement*

..........Date of Birth..........
date ne naissance D/J M Y/A

Probation ....
Période de probation de

Sentenced to Imprisonment for ....
Peine d'emprisonnement de

☐ withdrawn *accusations(s) retirée(s)* ☐ sentence suspended *condamnation avec sursis*

☐ counts/*chefs d'accusation*

Fined $.......... & $ .... costs. Time to pay ....
amende de *$ et* *$ de frais. Délai de paiement*

..........Date of Birth..........
date ne naissance D/J M Y/A

Probation ....
Période de probation de

Sentenced to Imprisonment for ....
Peine d'emprisonnement de

☐ withdrawn *accusations(s) retirée(s)* ☐ sentence suspended *condamnation avec sursis*

☐ counts/*chefs d'accusation*

Fined $.......... & $ .... costs. Time to pay ....
amende de *$ et* *$ de frais. Délai de paiement*

..........Date of Birth..........
date ne naissance D/J M Y/A

Probation ....
Période de probation de

Sentenced to Imprisonment for ....
Peine d'emprisonnement de

☐ withdrawn *accusations(s) retirée(s)* ☐ sentence suspended *condamnation avec sursis*

☐ counts/*chefs d'accusation*

Fined $.......... & $ .... costs. Time to pay ....
amende de *$ et* *$ de frais. Délai de paiement*

..........Date of Birth..........
date ne naissance D/J M Y/A

Probation ....
Période de probation de

Sentenced to Imprisonment for ....
Peine d'emprisonnement de

☐ withdrawn *accusations(s) retirée(s)* ☐ sentence suspended *condamnation avec sursis*

☐ counts/*chefs d'accusation*

Fined $.......... & $ .... costs. Time to pay ....
amende de *$ et* *$ de frais. Délai de paiement*

..........Date of Birth..........
date ne naissance D/J M Y/A

Probation ....
Période de probation de

Sentenced to Imprisonment for ....
Peine d'emprisonnement de

☐ withdrawn *accusations(s) retirée(s)* ☐ sentence suspended *condamnation avec sursis*

Judge or Justice of the Peace in and for the Province of Ontario
Juge ou juge de paix dans et pour la province de l'Ontario

CD 0002 (rev.10/99)

Information (Multiple Accused/Charges) CONTINUED

No. of Information/*N° de la dénonciation*
Return Date of summons/*Sommation rapportée le* yr./*an*

INFORMATION Against/*DÉNONCIATION* visant

Address/*Adresse*

CHARGE/*ACCUSATION*

☐ Summons *Sommation*	☐ Warrant *Mandat*	☐ Arrest *Arrestation*	
☐ Reportable M.V. Offence (H.T.A. 210) *Rapport V.M. (Code de la route 210)*	C.V.O.R. No. (Commercial Vehicles Only) *Numéro I.C.V.U. (véhicules utilitaires seulement)*		
Sex *Sexe*	Birth Date/*Date de naissance*: Day/*Jour* · Month/*Mois* · Year/*Année*	Was defendant owner? *Le défendeur était-il propriétaire?* ☐ Yes/*Oui* ☐ No/*Non*	
Driver's License Number/*Numéro du permis de conduire*			
Plate No./*Numéro de plaque*	☐ Involves an Accident *Infraction reliée à un accident*		
Informant *Dénonciateur*			
Date Sworn *Date d'assermentation*			
Officier *Agent de police*	No. *N°*		
Div. *Div.*	Dist. *Dist.*		
Courtroom/*Salle d'audience*			
At/*À*			

CD 0002 (rev.10/99)

Information/Summons (Snap Set)

ONTARIO COURT OF JUSTICE
PROVINCE OF ONTARIO
COUR DE JUSTICE DE L'ONTARIO
PROVINCE DE L'ONTARIO

INFORMATION/*DÉNONCIATION*

Under Section 23 of the Provincial Offences Act.
En vertu de l'article 23 de la Loi sur les infractions provinciales

Form/*Formule* 105
Courts of Justice Act
Loi sur les tribunaux judiciaires
R.R.O. 1990, Reg. 200
L.R.O. 1990, Règl. 200

This is the information of .... of ....
Dénonciation déposée par ... *de*

.... I have reasonable and probable grounds to believe and do believe that
occupation/*profession* ... *j'ai des motifs raisonnables de croire et je crois effectivement que*

on or about the
a, le ou vers le

...... day of .... yr .... at ....
jour de ... *an* ... *à* ... location/*lieu*

.... did commit the offence of
commis l'infraction suivante

contrary to ....
en violation de

section ....
article

Sworn before me at ....
Assermenté devant moi à

this .... day of ...., yr ....
ce ... *jour de* ... *an*

A Judge or Justice of the Peace in and for the Province of Ontario
Juge ou juge de paix dans et pour la province de l'Ontario

Signature of Informant/*Signature du dénonciateur*

SUMMONS RETURNABLE/
SOMMATION À RAPPORTER

At ....
À

On the .... day of .... yr at .... M,
Le ... *jour de* ... *an* ... *à* ... *h*

At/*À* ....
Courtroom/*salle d'audience*

(Sec./*Art.* 24)

☐ Summons for .... yr ...... Confirmed on .... yr ....
Sommation pour le ... *an* ... *Confirmée le* ... *an* ... Justice of the Peace / *Juge de paix*

Date

Pleads / *Plaidoyer* ☐ Guilty / *Coupable* ☐ Not Guilty / *Non coupable* ☐ Withdrawn / *Accusation retirée*

Found / *Décision* ☐ Guilty / *Coupable* ☐ Not Guilty / *Non coupable* ☐ In Absentia / *Défaut de comparution* ☐ Sentence Suspended / *Sursis*

Fined $ .... & $ .... costs. Time to pay ....
Amende ... *$ dépens $* ... *Délai de paiement*

.... Date of Birth ....
Date de naissance D/J M Y/A

Probation for ....
Durée de la probation

Sentenced to Imprisonment for ....
Peine d'emprisonnement de

Exhibits Filed
Pièces déposées
☐ Yes/*Oui* ☐ No/*Non*

A Judge or Justice of the Peace in and for the Province of Ontario
Juge ou juge de paix dans et pour la province de l'Ontario

CD 0003 (rev. 05/99)

FOR INFORMATION ON ACCESS TO ONTARIO COURTS FOR PERSONS WITH DISABILITIES, CALL 1-800-387-4456 TORONTO AREA 326-0111

POUR PLUS DE RENSEIGNEMENTS SUR L'ACCÈS DES PERSONNES HANDICAPÉES AUX TRIBUNAUX DE L'ONTARIO, COMPOSEZ LE 1-800-387-4456 RÉGION DE TORONTO 326-0111

Information/Summons (Snap Set) CONTINUED

Date *Date*	Defendant Appears Adjournment *Défendeur Comparaît Ajournement*	Parties Consent *Consentement des parties*	Bail and/or other action *Cautionnement et/ou autre mesure*	Fails to Appear *Omet de comparaître*	Bench Warrant *Mandat du tribunal*	Certificat of Default *Certificat de défaut*

No. of Information/N°. de la dénonciation

Return Date of summons/Sommation rapportée le

yr/an

INFORMATION Against/DÉNONCIATION visant

Address/Adresse

CHARGE/ACCUSATION

☐ Summons *Sommation* ☐ Warrant *Mandat* ☐ Arrest *Arrestation*

☐ Reportable MV Offence (H.T.A. 210) *Rapport V.M. (Code de la route 210)*

C.V.O.R. No. (Commercial Vehicles Only) *Numéro I.C.V.U. (véhicules utilitaires seulement)*

Sex *Sexe*

Birth Date/*Date de naissance* Day/*Jour* Month/*Mois* Year/*Année*

Was defendant owner? *Le défendeur était-il propriétaire?* ☐ Yes/*Oui* ☐ No/*Non*

Driver's Licence Number/*Numéro du permis de conduire*

Plate No./*Numéro de plaque*

☐ Involves an Accident *Infraction reliée à un accident*

Informant *Dénonciateur*

Date Sworn *Date d'assermentation*

Officer *Agent de police* No. *N°.*

Div. *Div.* Dist. *Dist.*

Courtroom/*Salle d'audience*

At/*À*

CD 0003 (rev. 05/99)

Date *Date*	Clerk *Greffier*	Reporter *Sténographe*	Prosecutor *Poursuivant*	For Defendant *Pour le défendeur*	Justice's Initials *Initiales du juge de paix*

Information/Summons (Snap Set) CONTINUED

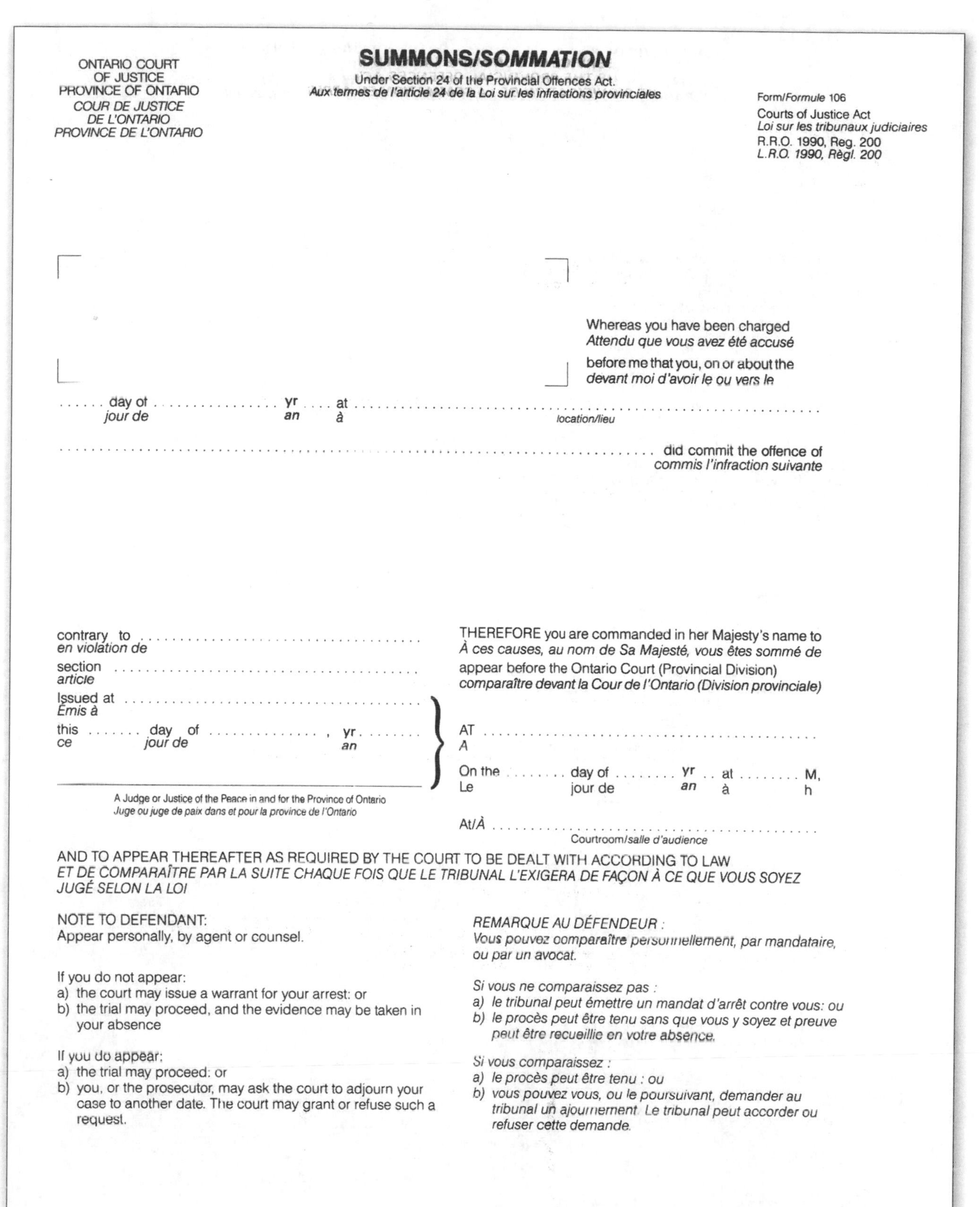

ONTARIO COURT
OF JUSTICE
PROVINCE OF ONTARIO
COUR DE JUSTICE
DE L'ONTARIO
PROVINCE DE L'ONTARIO

SUMMONS/*SOMMATION*
Under Section 24 of the Provincial Offences Act.
Aux termes de l'article 24 de la Loi sur les infractions provinciales

Form/*Formule* 106
Courts of Justice Act
Loi sur les tribunaux judiciaires
R.R.O. 1990, Reg. 200
L.R.O. 1990, Règl. 200

Whereas you have been charged
Attendu que vous avez été accusé
before me that you, on or about the
devant moi d'avoir le ou vers le

...... day of / *jour de* .... yr / *an* .... at / *à* .... location/*lieu*

.... did commit the offence of
commis l'infraction suivante

contrary to / *en violation de* ....
section / *article* ....
Issued at / *Émis à* ....
this / *ce* .... day of / *jour de* ...., yr / *an* ....

A Judge or Justice of the Peace in and for the Province of Ontario
Juge ou juge de paix dans et pour la province de l'Ontario

THEREFORE you are commanded in her Majesty's name to
À ces causes, au nom de Sa Majesté, vous êtes sommé de
appear before the Ontario Court (Provincial Division)
comparaître devant la Cour de l'Ontario (Division provinciale)

AT / *A* ....
On the / *Le* .... day of / *jour de* .... yr / *an* .. at / *à* .... M, / *h*
At/*À* .... Courtroom/*salle d'audience*

AND TO APPEAR THEREAFTER AS REQUIRED BY THE COURT TO BE DEALT WITH ACCORDING TO LAW
ET DE COMPARAÎTRE PAR LA SUITE CHAQUE FOIS QUE LE TRIBUNAL L'EXIGERA DE FAÇON À CE QUE VOUS SOYEZ JUGÉ SELON LA LOI

NOTE TO DEFENDANT:
Appear personally, by agent or counsel.

If you do not appear:
a) the court may issue a warrant for your arrest: or
b) the trial may proceed, and the evidence may be taken in your absence

If you do appear:
a) the trial may proceed: or
b) you, or the prosecutor, may ask the court to adjourn your case to another date. The court may grant or refuse such a request.

REMARQUE AU DÉFENDEUR :
Vous pouvez comparaître personnellement, par mandataire, ou par un avocat.

Si vous ne comparaissez pas :
a) le tribunal peut émettre un mandat d'arrêt contre vous: ou
b) le procès peut être tenu sans que vous y soyez et preuve peut être recueillie en votre absence.

Si vous comparaissez :
a) le procès peut être tenu : ou
b) vous pouvez vous, ou le poursuivant, demander au tribunal un ajournement. Le tribunal peut accorder ou refuser cette demande.

CD 0003 (rev. 05/99)

Information/Summons (Snap Set) CONTINUED

AFFIDAVIT OF SERVICE OF SUMMONS UNDER SUBSECTION 26(6) OF THE PROVINCIAL OFFENCES ACT
AFFIDAVIT DE SIGNIFICATION DE LA SOMMATION EN APPLICATION DU PARAGRAPHE 26(6) DE LA LOI SUR LES INFRACTIONS PROVINCIALES

ONTARIO COURT
OF JUSTICE
PROVINCE OF ONTARIO

COUR DE JUSTICE
DE L'ONTARIO
PROVINCE DE L'ONTARIO

I, ... , of ....,
Je soussigné(e) *demeurant à*

a provincial offences officer make oath and say as follows, that on the .... day of .... yr ....,
agent des infractions provinciales, déclare sous serment par les présentes que le *an*

I did serve the summons in the manner indicated below:
j'ai signifié la sommation de la manière suivante:

(Check one/*cocher la case applicable)*

(a) ☐ by delivering it personally to the defendant;
en la remettant en main propre au défendeur

(b) ☐ I could not conveniently find the defendant and left the summons for him/her at his/her last known or usual place of abode
le défendeur ne pouvant être commodément trouvé, en laissant la sommation à son intention,

with .... ,
à son adresse habituelle ou sa dernière adresse connue en la remettant à

an inmate thereof who appeared at least sixteen years of age;
occupant des lieux qui a manifestement 16 ans révolus

(c) ☐ service on a municipal corporation: by leaving it personally with ....
signification à une municipalité: en la remettant en main propre à name/*nom*

the .... (the mayor, reeve, warden, or other chief officer, or the Clerk of the Corporation)
le postition/*titre* *(maire, préfet, président du conseil de comté, ou autre dirigeant ou secrétaire de la municipalité)*

☐ at the address shown on the summons
à l'adresse figurant sur la sommation

☐ at ....
à

(d) ☐ service on a corporation other that a municipal corporation: by leaving it personally with
signification à toute autre personne morale: en la remettant en main propre à

.... the ....
name/*nom* *le(la)* postion/*titre*

(manager, secretary, or other executive officer of the corporation, or person apparently in charge of the branch office thereof/*directeur, secrétaire ou autre dirigeant, ou personne ayant manifestement la responsabilité de la succursale)*

☐ at the address shown on the summons
à l'adresse figurant sur la sommation

☐ at ....
à

(e) ☐ by mailing it by registered mail to the corporation at ....
en l'envoyant par courrier recommandé à la personne morale à

.... an address held out by the corporation to be its address
l'adresse indiquée par la personne morale comme la sienne

(f) ☐ by mailing it by registered mail to the defendant, who is not resident in Ontario,
en l'envoyant par courrier recommandé au défendeur, qui ne réside pas en Ontario

at ....
à

his/her last known or usual place of abode.
sa dernière adresse connue ou sa résidence habituelle

Sworn before me at ....
Assermenté devant moi à

....

this .... day of .... yr ....
ce *an*

....
A Justice of the Peace in and for the Province of Ontario/
Commissioner for Taking Affidavits
Juge de paix dans et pour la province de l'Ontario
Commissaire à l'assermentation

____
Signature

No. .... Div. ....

....

CD 0003 (rev. 05/99)

Information/Summons (Snap Set) CONTINUED

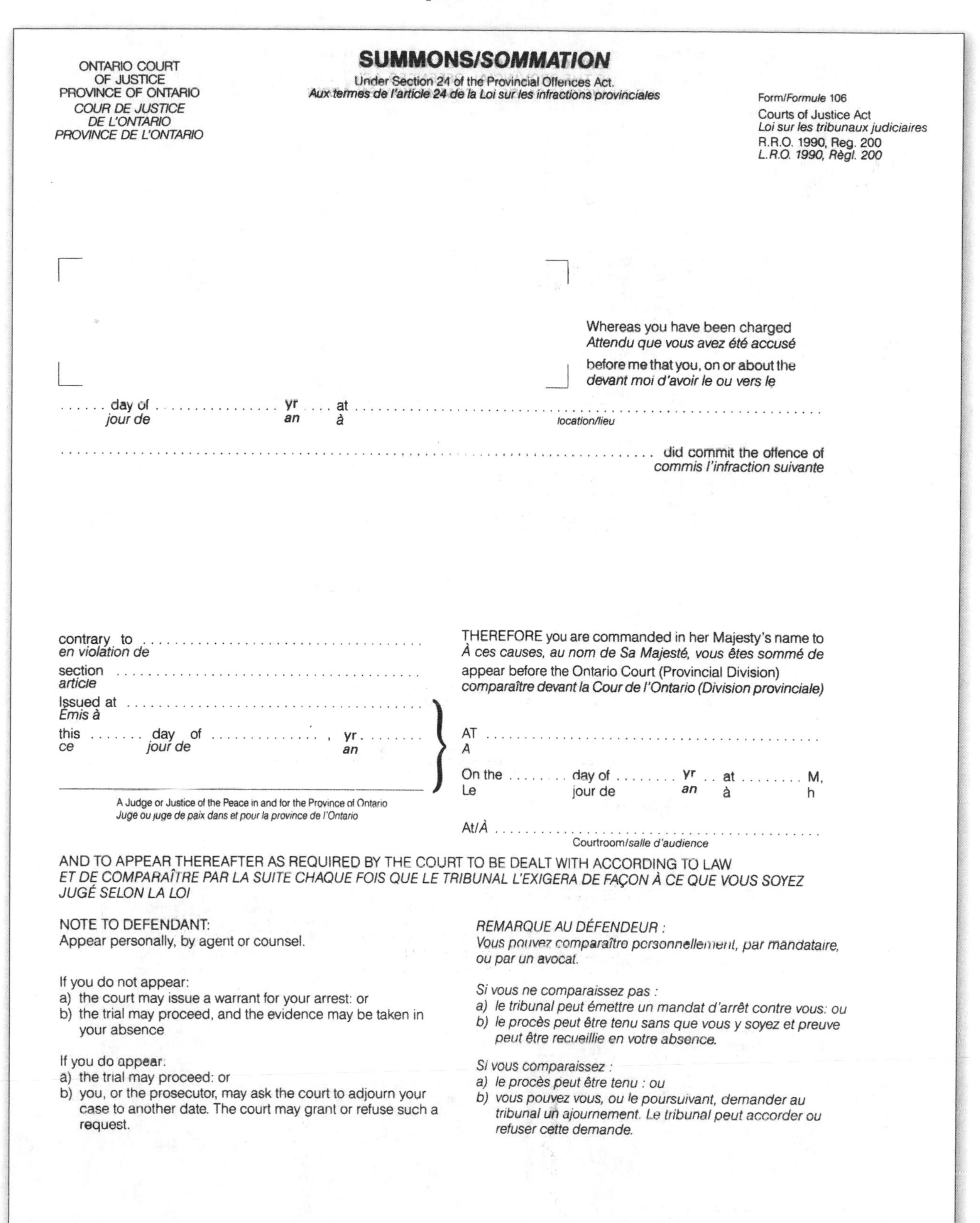

ONTARIO COURT
OF JUSTICE
PROVINCE OF ONTARIO
COUR DE JUSTICE
DE L'ONTARIO
PROVINCE DE L'ONTARIO

SUMMONS/*SOMMATION*

Under Section 24 of the Provincial Offences Act.
Aux termes de l'article 24 de la Loi sur les infractions provinciales

Form/*Formule* 106
Courts of Justice Act
Loi sur les tribunaux judiciaires
R.R.O. 1990, Reg. 200
L.R.O. 1990, Règl. 200

Whereas you have been charged
Attendu que vous avez été accusé
before me that you, on or about the
devant moi d'avoir le ou vers le

...... day of .... yr .... at ....
jour de *an* *à* *location/lieu*

.... did commit the offence of
commis l'infraction suivante

contrary to ....
en violation de
section ....
article
Issued at ....
Émis à
this .... day of ...., yr. ....
ce *jour de* *an*

A Judge or Justice of the Peace in and for the Province of Ontario
Juge ou juge de paix dans et pour la province de l'Ontario

THEREFORE you are commanded in her Majesty's name to
À ces causes, au nom de Sa Majesté, vous êtes sommé de
appear before the Ontario Court (Provincial Division)
comparaître devant la Cour de l'Ontario (Division provinciale)

AT ....
A

On the .... day of .... yr .. at .... M,
Le *jour de* *an* *à* *h*

At/*À* ....
Courtroom/*salle d'audience*

AND TO APPEAR THEREAFTER AS REQUIRED BY THE COURT TO BE DEALT WITH ACCORDING TO LAW
ET DE COMPARAÎTRE PAR LA SUITE CHAQUE FOIS QUE LE TRIBUNAL L'EXIGERA DE FAÇON À CE QUE VOUS SOYEZ JUGÉ SELON LA LOI

NOTE TO DEFENDANT:
Appear personally, by agent or counsel.

If you do not appear:
a) the court may issue a warrant for your arrest: or
b) the trial may proceed, and the evidence may be taken in your absence

If you do appear:
a) the trial may proceed: or
b) you, or the prosecutor, may ask the court to adjourn your case to another date. The court may grant or refuse such a request.

REMARQUE AU DÉFENDEUR :
Vous pouvez comparaître personnellement, par mandataire, ou par un avocat.

Si vous ne comparaissez pas :
a) le tribunal peut émettre un mandat d'arrêt contre vous: ou
b) le procès peut être tenu sans que vous y soyez et preuve peut être recueillie en votre absence.

Si vous comparaissez :
a) le procès peut être tenu : ou
b) vous pouvez vous, ou le poursuivant, demander au tribunal un ajournement. Le tribunal peut accorder ou refuser cette demande.

CD 0003 (rev. 05/99)

Information/Summons (Snap Set) CONTINUED

AFFIDAVIT OF SERVICE OF SUMMONS UNDER SUBSECTION 26(6) OF THE PROVINCIAL OFFENCES ACT
AFFIDAVIT DE SIGNIFICATION DE LA SOMMATION EN APPLICATION DU PARAGRAPHE 26(6) DE LA LOI SUR LES INFRACTIONS PROVINCIALES

ONTARIO COURT
OF JUSTICE
PROVINCE OF ONTARIO

COUR DE JUSTICE
DE L'ONTARIO
PROVINCE DE L'ONTARIO

I, ... , of ....,
Je soussigné(e) *demeurant à*

a provincial offences officer make oath and say as follows, that on the .... day of .... yr ....,
agent des infractions provinciales, déclare sous serment par les présentes que le *an*

I did serve the summons in the manner indicated below:
j'ai signifié la sommation de la manière suivante:

(Check one/*cocher la case applicable)*

(a) ☐ by delivering it personally to the defendant;
en la remettant en main propre au défendeur

(b) ☐ I could not conveniently find the defendant and left the summons for him/her at his/her last known or usual place of abode
le défendeur ne pouvant être commodément trouvé, en laissant la sommation à son intention,

with ....,
à son adresse habituelle ou sa dernière adresse connue en la remettant à

an inmate thereof who appeared at least sixteen years of age;
occupant des lieux qui a manifestement 16 ans révolus

(c) ☐ service on a municipal corporation: by leaving it personally with ....
signification à une municipalité: en la remettant en main propre à name/*nom*

the .... (the mayor, reeve, warden, or other chief officer, or the Clerk of the Corporation)
le postition/*titre* *(maire, préfet, président du conseil de comté, ou autre dirigeant ou secrétaire de la municipalité)*

☐ at the address shown on the summons
à l'adresse figurant sur la sommation

☐ at ....
à

(d) ☐ service on a corporation other that a municipal corporation: by leaving it personally with
signification à toute autre personne morale: en la remettant en main propre à

.... the ....
name/*nom* *le(la)* postion/*titre*

(manager, secretary, or other executive officer of the corporation, or person apparently in charge of the branch office thereof/*directeur, secrétaire ou autre dirigeant, ou personne ayant manifestement la responsabilité de la succursale)*

☐ at the address shown on the summons
à l'adresse figurant sur la sommation

☐ at ....
à

(e) ☐ by mailing it by registered mail to the corporation at ....
en l'envoyant par courrier recommandé à la personne morale à

.... an address held out by the corporation to be its address
l'adresse indiquée par la personne morale comme la sienne

(f) ☐ by mailing it by registered mail to the defendant, who is not resident in Ontario,
en l'envoyant par courrier recommandé au défendeur, qui ne réside pas en Ontario

at ....
à

his/her last known or usual place of abode.
sa dernière adresse connue ou sa résidence habituelle

Sworn before me at ....
Assermenté devant moi à

....

this .... day of .... yr ....
ce *an*

....
A Justice of the Peace in and for the Province of Ontario/
Commissioner for Taking Affidavits
Juge de paix dans et pour la province de l'Ontario
Commissaire à l'assermentation

____
Signature

No. .... Div. ....

....

CD 0003 (rev. 05/99)

Search Warrant

ONTARIO COURT
OF JUSTICE
PROVINCE OF ONTARIO
COUR DE JUSTICE
DE L'ONTARIO
PROVINCE DE L'ONTARIO

SEARCH WARRANT
MANDAT DE PERQUISITION
Under Section 158 of the Provincial Offences Act
aux termes de l'article 158 de la Loi sur les infractions provinciales

Form 141
Formule 141
Courts of Justice Act
Loi sur tribunaux judiciaires
R.R.O. 1990, Reg. 200
R.R.O. 1990, Règl. 200

To / *À*
and to the police officers of Ontario / *et aux agents de police de l'Ontario*

Whereas, on the information upon oath of / *Attendu que, à la suite de la dénonciation faite sous serment par*

I am satisfied that there are reasonable grounds to believe that
je me suis assuré qu'il existe des motifs raisonnables de croire que
(describe things to be searched for / *décrire ce qui fait l'objet de la perquisition*)

(check appropriate box / *cocher ce qui s'applique ici*)

☐ upon or in respect of which the offence / *sur lequel ou au sujet duquel l'infraction*
of / *de*

contrary to / *par dérogation à* section / *article*
is suspected to have been committed, or / *est soupçonnée avoir été commise, ou*

☐ that there is reasonable ground to believe will afford evidence as the commission of the
offre un motif raisonnable de croire qu'il fournira une preuve de la perpétration de
offence of / *l'infraction*

contrary to / *par dérogation à* section / *article*

may be found at / *peut être trouvé dans*
(building, place, receptacle / *bâtiment, lieu, contenant*)

of / *de*
at / *à*
(address / *adresse*)

hereinafter called the premises / *ci-après appelé les lieux.*

This is therefore to authorize you to enter such / *À ces causes, vous êtes autorisés par les présentes à entrer dans*

(name of building, receptacle or place / *nom du bâtiment, contenant ou lieu*)

between the hours of 6:00 a.m. and 9:00 p.m. standard time, or / *entre 6 h 00 et 21 h 00, heure normale, ou* . . . .
(time warrant to be executed / *heure à laquelle le mandat doit être exécuté*)

and to search there for the said things and to seize them and carry them before me or another justice so that they may be dealt with according to the law.
et à y faire une perquisition pour y trouver ce que vous recherchez et pour vous en saisir et pour me l'apporter ou pour l'apporter à un autre juge qui siège, afin qu'il en soit fait usage selon la loi.
This warrant expires on the / *Ce mandat expire en date du* day of / *jour de* , yr / *an*
a day not later than the fifteenth day after its issue / *une date qui n'est pas postérieure au 15e jour qui suit l'émission du mandat.*

Issued at / *Décerné*
this / *ce* day of / *jour de* , yr / *an*

Judge or Justice of the Peace in and for the Province of Ontario
Juge ou juge de paix dans et pour la province de l'Ontario

CD 0141 (rev. 05/99)

Warrant for Arrest of Defendant

ONTARIO COURT
OF JUSTICE
PROVINCE OF ONTARIO
COUR DE JUSTICE
DE L'ONTARIO
PROVINCE DE L'ONTARIO

WARRANT FOR ARREST OF DEFENDANT
MANDAT D'ARRESTATION DÉCERNÉ CONTRE LE DÉFENDEUR
Under Section 24 of the Provincial Offences Act
aux termes de l'article 24 de la Loi sur les infractions provinciales

Form 107
Formule 107
Courts of Justice Act
Loi sur les tribunaux judiciaires
R.R.O. 1990, Reg. 200
R.R.O. 1990, Règl. 200

To all police officers in the Province of Ontario:
À tous les agents de police de la province de l'Ontario :
of / *de*

This warrant is for the arrest of
Le présent mandat est décerné en vue de l'arrestation de
of / *de* *(address / adresse)* *(occupation / profession)*

hereinafter called the defendant.
ci-après appelé le défendeur.

Whereas the defendant has been charged that the defendant, on or about the day of
Attendu que le défendeur a été inculpé d'avoir, le ou vers le jour de

, Yr. / *an* , at / *à*

did commit the offence of
commis l'infraction suivante

contrary to
par dérogation à

section / *article*

And whereas
(a) the arrest of the defendant is authorized by statute; and
(b) I am satisfied on reasonable and probable grounds that it is necessary in the public interest to issue this warrant for the arrest of the defendant.

Et attendue que,
(a) l'arrestation du défendeur est autorisée par la loi, et que
(b) je me suis assuré que, pour des motifs raisonnables et probables, il est nécessaire dans l'intérêt public de décerner ce mandat pour procéder à l'arrestation du défendeur.

Therefore, you are commanded in Her Majesty's name to arrest the defendant and bring the defendant forthwith before a justice to be dealt with according to law.

À ces causes, ordre vous est donné, au nom de Sa Majesté, de procéder à l'arrestation du défendeur et de le conduire sans délai devant un juge ou un juge de paix pour être traité selon la loi.

Issued at / *Décerné à* this / *ce* day of / *jour de* , Yr. / *an*

Judge or Justice of the Peace in and for the Province of Ontario
Juge ou juge de paix dans et pour la provincee de l'Ontario

NOTE: Subsection 27(2) of the **Provincial Offences Act,** is as follows: A warrant issued under section 24 remains in force until it is executed and need not be made returnable at any particular time.

REMARQUE : *Le paragraphe 27(2) de la **Loi sur les infractions provinciales** se lit comme suit : Un mandat décerné aux termes de l'article 24 demeure en vigueur jusqu'à ce qu'il soit exécuté, et il n'est pas nécessaire d'en fixer le rapport à une date particulière.*

CD 0107 (rev. 05/99)

FOR INFORMATION ON ACCESS TO ONTARIO COURTS FOR PERSONS WITH DISABILITIES, CALL **1-800-387-4456** TORONTO AREA **326-0111**

POUR PLUS DE RENSEIGNEMENTS SUR L'ACCÈS DES PERSONNES HANDICAPÉES AUX TRIBUNAUX DE L'ONTARIO, COMPOSEZ LE **1-800-387-4456** RÉGION DE TORONTO **326-0111**

APPENDIX C

Provincial Offences Grid

Provincial Offences Grid

Statute	Common Offences and/or Provisions	Arrest Powers	Search Powers	Use of Force	Limitation Period	Non-Police Agencies Involved
Provincial Offences Act						
Liquor Licence Act						
Trespass to Property Act						
Residential Tenancies Act, 2006						
Blind Persons' Rights Act						
Mental Health Act						

Provincial Offences Grid CONTINUED

Statute	Common Offences and/or Provisions	Arrest Powers	Search Powers	Use of Force	Limitation Period	Non-Police Agencies Involved
Coroners Act						
Child and Family Services Act						
Family Law Act						
Children's Law Reform Act						
Motorized Snow Vehicles Act						
Off-Road Vehicles Act						

Index